Security at Sea
Naval Forces and Arms Control

sipri

Stockholm International Peace Research Institute

SIPRI is an independent international institute for research into problems of peace and conflict, especially those of arms control and disarmament. It was established in 1966 to commemorate Sweden's 150 years of unbroken peace.

The Institute is financed mainly by the Swedish Parliament. The staff, the Governing Board and the Scientific Council are international.

The Governing Board and the Scientific Council are not responsible for the views expressed in the publications of the Institute.

Governing Board

Ambassador Dr Inga Thorsson, Chairman (Sweden)
Egon Bahr (Federal Republic of Germany)
Professor Francesco Calogero (Italy)
Dr Max Jakobson (Finland)
Professor Dr Karlheinz Lohs (German Democratic Republic)
Professor Emma Rothschild (United Kingdom)
Sir Brian Urquhart (United Kingdom)
The Director

Director

Dr Walther Stützle (Federal Republic of Germany)

sipri

Stockholm International Peace Research Institute
Pipers väg 28, S-171 73 Solna, Sweden
Cable: PEACERESEARCH STOCKHOLM
Telephone: 46 8/55 97 00

Security at Sea
Naval Forces and Arms Control

Edited by
Richard Fieldhouse

sipri
Stockholm International Peace Research Institute

OXFORD UNIVERSITY PRESS
1990

Oxford University Press, Walton Street, Oxford OX2 6DP
Oxford New York Toronto
Delhi Bombay Calcutta Madras Karachi
Petaling Jaya Singapore Hong Kong Tokyo
Nairobi Dar es Salaam Cape Town
Melbourne Auckland
and associated companies in
Berlin Ibadan

Oxford is a trade mark of Oxford University Press

Published in the United States
by Oxford University Press, New York

© SIPRI 1990

British Library Cataloguing in Publication Data
Security at sea: naval forces and arms control.
1. Naval Weapon Systems. Arms control
I. Fieldhouse, Richard
327.1'74
ISBN 01-9-829130-2

Library of Congress Cataloging in Publication Data
Security at sea: naval forces and arms control / edited by Richard Fieldhouse.
Includes bibliographical references
1. Nuclear arms control—Congresses. 2. Sea-power—United States—Congresses.
3. Sea-power—Soviet Union—Congresses. 4. Security, International—Congresses.
I. Fieldhouse, Richard
JX1974.7.S432   1989   327.1'74-dc20   89-36984
ISBN 0-19-829130-2

Typeset and originated by Stockholm International Peace Research Institute
Printed and bound in Great Britain by
Biddles Ltd., Guildford and King's Lynn

Contents

Part I. Introduction and conclusions

Part II. The case for naval arms control

Paper 3. Maritime change in developing countries: the implications for naval arms control

Derek Boothby

Part III. Challenges of naval arms control

Paper 4. Navies of the superpowers: the strategic background

Hervé Coutau-Bégarie

Paper 5. Verification of nuclear weapons at sea

Herbert Lin

Part IV. Approaches to naval arms control

Part V. Confidence-building measures

Annexes

Preface

This book is the second publication of the SIPRI Research Project on Naval Forces and Arms Control, which began in the autumn of 1986. In October 1986 Shunji Taoka, Senior Staff Correspondent on Military Affairs for the *Asahi Shimbun* newspaper (Tokyo), joined SIPRI as a Visiting Fellow for one year to work on the project and to prepare a study comparing the major navies of East and West. In December of that year the Swedish Government generously gave SIPRI a substantial grant to carry out the project and to cover the costs of holding an international conference on the subject of the project.

In October 1987 SIPRI held a three-day Conference on Naval Forces and Arms Control. Sixteen international experts from nine nations participated in the conference to present papers on and to discuss questions concerning the prospects and possibilities for naval arms control. Many of the papers presented at the conference appear in this book. The participants presented excellent material for the conference, and the discussion provided many insights on the issue of navies and arms control. They are all to be commended for their hard work, lively comments and solid contributions to the conference.

The conference participants were: Admiral Nikolai Amelko, Ret. (USSR), William M. Arkin (USA), Derek Boothby (UK), Admiral Eugene J. Carroll, Jr, Ret. (USA), Hervé Coutau-Bégarie (France), Jens Evensen (Norway), Richard Fieldhouse (SIPRI), Jozef Goldblat (SIPRI), Dale Herspring (USA), Admiral Richard Hill, Ret. (UK), Commander Patrick Howard (Denmark), Herbert Lin (USA), Sean M. Lynn-Jones (USA), Jan Prawitz (Sweden), Shunji Taoka (SIPRI) and Walther Stützle (SIPRI). Ove Bring (Sweden) did not attend the conference but contributed one of the papers in this volume. Lars-Hjalmar Wide of the Swedish Ministry for Foreign Affairs and Commander Björn Eklind of the Swedish Naval Staff were invited to observe the conference.

Two companion books resulted from the project. The first volume, *Superpowers at Sea: An Assessment of the Naval Arms Race,* by Richard Fieldhouse and Shunji Taoka, is a study of the US–Soviet naval competition. It presents the facts and analyses necessary for a consideration of naval forces in the arms control process—to chart the waters for the present volume. It is hoped that these books will be a useful contribution to an emerging and important debate on arms control and security.

Acknowledgements

The preparation of this book required many individual efforts which I would like to acknowledge. Several people assisted with the SIPRI Conference on Naval Forces and Arms Control. Jozef Goldblat graciously agreed to chair half of the conference and provided many good suggestions for the project, in addition to his fine paper. Cynthia Loo provided fine secretarial assistance. Ian Anthony and Eric Arnett kindly served as rapporteurs. Ian Thomas and Matthew Yeo assisted with research and bibliographic tasks. Åsa Pihlstrand and Ricardo Vargas-Fuentes patiently typed the manuscripts for the volume.

This book has benefited from the dedicated work of two of SIPRI's skilled editors. Barbara Adams guided the editing process during 1987–88 (until leaving SIPRI). Connie Wall devoted great energy and talent to completing the editing and setting the entire book in its final camera-ready format. I extend my gratitude to them all.

Richard Fieldhouse
SIPRI Research Fellow and Project Leader
1 August 1989

Foreword

Naval arms control is one of the most complicated subjects of our time. From whichever angle you approach it, it does not become easier to manage. History, past or recent, holds no comfort in this respect, nor does experience with the arms control negotiations of our time.

Reviewing the 1922 Washington Treaty, Jozef Goldblat concluded that, as a consequence of an omission in the treaty, 'the signatories began extensive programmes of warship construction in the categories which were not restricted'.[1] He referred to the fact that there was no agreement on the total tonnage of cruisers, destroyers and submarines. Although the 1930 London Treaty marked a major improvement over the 1922 agreement—in that for the first time the three major sea powers (the USA, the UK and Japan) accepted quantitative and qualitative limitations on all categories of warship—the treaty ultimately did not do what it was meant to do, namely, to help prevent states from resorting to war in order to secure political gains.

With the advent of the nuclear age, the situation changed profoundly. Not that the earth has become a war-free planet; unfortunately, the opposite is true. However, the major powers of today have come to understand that resort to the use of force has become an obsolete instrument, at least in their mutual relations, for the simple reason that the risks far outweigh the possible gains. It did not require the 1986 Reykjavik summit meeting between President Reagan and General Secretary Gorbachev to establish this principle, and yet it signalled great progress in terms of political psychology that the two most powerful political leaders firmly embraced it.

The question, however, remains: Where do we move from here?

From the excellent papers presented in this book we know the following:

1. The history of the non-nuclear age provides us with no blueprint for how to solve the problems of arms control in general and of naval arms control in particular.

2. There is no shortage of international treaties and charters that rule out the use of force or the threat thereof. From the 1945 United Nations Charter, a document of the pre-nuclear age, right through to the reaffirmation of the principle of the renunciation of force in the 1986 Stockholm Document, there is sufficient language to that effect.

3. Armed forces are for the most part not created for arms control purposes. Their existence results from the perception an individual country entertains of its security needs, and this in itself is a notion that is composed of a number of requirements, each of which is of a very different nature: military, political,

[1] Goldblat, J., SIPRI, *Agreements for Arms Control: A Critical Survey* (Taylor & Francis: London, 1982), p. 2.

economic, psychological and international status. When it comes to the naval arm of military forces, this is even more obvious—with all the complicating consequences for arms control and arms reduction. Given the trade-mark of navies—the right to operate world-wide—one could argue that navies and arms control are mutually exclusive propositions.

The question is thus: What is needed to include naval forces in the arms control process? Assuming that there is no short-cut to disarmament and assuming that disarmament will never be realized if it is not approached via arms control and controlled arms reductions, a few observations may help to promote consideration of this subject.

1. The main step to take here is to broaden the problem beyond that of navies. Like other parts of the armed forces, navies are specially designed to serve within an overall framework of given conditions. The proposition is consequently that, without taking into account the particular role navies must fulfil in the overall strategic context of the respective country, it will be virtually impossible to design arms control arrangements that satisfy the notion of equal security.

2. Assuming that deterrence as a major prerequisite for maintaining a non-war situation will not simply disappear and that nuclear weapons form its hard core, arms control designs can hardly be arrived at without properly understanding what the role of nuclear weapons is and what it is not. With the advent of strategic nuclear parity, this role has undergone a major change. As opposed to the belief of the 1950s and 1960s, nuclear weapons can no longer serve the function of a cheap gap-filler for negligence in the field of conventional defence.

This observation leads to two immediate conclusions. First, there are far more nuclear weapons available than are needed to fulfil the only function they can fulfil, which is to deter war, first and foremost between the nuclear powers, and if war should break out to ensure that nuclear weapons deter the use of nuclear weapons. Second, nuclear weapons need to be placed under much tighter control and thus removed from areas where they could accidentally become involved in war-fighting.

If one follows the logic of the nuclear age, nuclear weapons for so-called defensive tactical use can hardly be justified any longer and should therefore be considered as a prime candidate for arms reduction agreements. This in itself would lead to an appreciable denuclearization of navies and land forces alike. At the same time, strict observance of the changed role of nuclear weapons would open up the possibility to cut the strategic nuclear inventories considerably. In fact, there would be no reason to cut them by only 50 per cent, as currently envisaged by both the United States and the Soviet Union.

3. Assuming that for some time to come deterrence remains an essential part of defence and that defence is meant to serve what the term implies, namely,

defence, then arms control positions will be strongly influenced by the definition applied to the term by each individual country.

No doubt, in raising this subject we touch on a very complicated issue, composed of both objective and a great number of subjective considerations. Objectively speaking—and this is in line with Article 51 of the UN Charter, which deals with the right of self-defence—defence postures should not provide for more than the military capability of the nation-state to maintain its territorial and social integrity in case of an attack. Applying this standard to the question of naval arms control is complicated by the fact that perceptions of deterrence and defence have to operate under the widely differing strategic conditions that apply to nation-states or alliances.

The question then is what to do in order to de-block conceptually the road to arms control and controlled arms reductions. First, the vicious circle of defensive intentions and offensive capabilities must be broken. Thus NATO–WTO consultations about security concepts, military doctrine and military strategy are very relevant. Second, arms control must deal with strategic military missions rather than take a symmetrical approach in looking at individual branches of the armed forces, such as the navy.

Both requirements call for a co-operative approach, at the beginning of which there must be a thorough understanding of the factors that constitute the security concerns of either side. It is only after this understanding has been achieved that both sides will find it possible to understand each other's definition of defence and associated procurement policies.

This observation leads to the subject that has come to be known as confidence-building measures (CBMs). Given the intricacy of arms control in general and naval arms control in particular, we will probably see little progress without CBMs preparing the ground for more substantial agreements. Of course, co-operation and dialogue are in themselves CBMs of an important nature.

We know from the world of medicine that the more complex the problem, the greater the need for careful preparation before conducting major surgery. Not only does the patient need to be prepared carefully, but it must also be certain that the person who is to survive can function again as a sound body. Or—to put it differently—without the guarantee that arms control will not diminish security, this very important goal of international politics does not stand a chance of being realized.

Dr Walther Stützle
Director, SIPRI
1 August 1989

Abbreviations and acronyms

AAW	Anti-air warfare
ABM	Anti-ballistic missile
ALCM	Air-launched cruise missile
ANZUS	Australia–New Zealand–United States (alliance)
ASBM	Air-to-surface ballistic missile
ASCM	Anti-ship cruise missile
ASEAN	Association of South-East Asian Nations
ASM	Air-to-surface missile
ASMP	Air-sol moyenne portée (missile) (France)
ASROC	Anti-*s*ubmarine *ro*cket
ASTOR	Anti-*s*ubmarine *tor*pedo
ASUW	Anti-*su*rface *w*arfare
ASW	Anti-submarine warfare
BMD	Ballistic missile defence
C^3I	Command, control, communications and intelligence
CAPTOR	En*cap*sulated *tor*pedo
CBM	Confidence-building measure
CCD	Conference of the Committee on Disarmament
CD	Conference on Disarmament
CDE	Conference on Confidence- and Security-building and Disarmament in Europe (Stockholm Conference)
CFE	(Negotiation on) Conventional (Armed) Forces in Europe
CIC	Combat information centre
CM	Cruise missile
CNO	Chief of Naval Operations (US)
CO	Commanding officer
CSBM	Confidence- and security-building measure
CSCE	Conference on Security and Co-operation in Europe
CVBG	Aircraft-*c*arrier (a*vi*ation*) b*attle *g*roup
DC	Disarmament Commission (UN)
DDA	Designated deployment area
DOD	Department of Defense (US)
EEZ	Exclusive economic zone
ENDC	Eighteen-Nation Disarmament Committee
FAO	Food and Agriculture Organization (UN)
FEBA	Forward edge of the battle area
FOST	*Force Océanique Stratégique*
FRAS	Free rocket anti-submarine
FROD	Functionally related observable difference
GIUK	Greenland–Iceland–United Kingdom (Gap)

GLCM	Ground-launched cruise missile
ICBM	Intercontinental ballistic missile
ICRC	International Committee of the Red Cross
INC	Insertable nuclear component
INF	Intermediate-range nuclear forces
JCS	Joint Chiefs of Staff (US)
MIRV	Multiple independently targetable re-entry vehicle
Mod.	Modification
NATO	North Atlantic Treaty Organization
NCA	National Command Authority
NCND	Neither confirm nor deny
NG	Nouvelle génération [new generation]
NNA	Neutral and non-aligned (state)
NSNW	Non-strategic nuclear weapon
NST	Nuclear and Space Talks
PAL	Permissive action link
PDMA	Prevention of Dangerous Military Activities (Agreement)
PTBT	Partial Test Ban Treaty
R&D	Research and development
RDF	Rapid Deployment Force
SALT	Strategic Arms Limitation Talks
SAM	Surface-to-air missile
SDI	Strategic Defense Initiative
SIOP	Single Integrated Operational Plan
SLBM	Submarine-launched ballistic missile
SLCM	Sea-launched cruise missile
SLOC	Sea line(s) of communication
SNA	Soviet Naval Aviation
SOSUS	*Sound Surveillance System* (US)
SOSS	Soviet Ocean Surveillance System
SSBN	*Nuclear-powered ballistic missile (strategic) submarine*
SSM	Surface-to-surface missile
SSN	Nuclear-powered attack submarine
START	Strategic Arms Reduction Talks
SUBROC	*Submarine rocket*
TNF	Theatre nuclear forces
UNCLOS	United Nations Convention on the Law of the Sea
URG	Underway replenishment group
USN	US Navy
VLA	Vertical launch ASROC
VLS	Vertical launch system
V/STOL	Vertical/short take-off and landing
WTO	Warsaw Treaty Organization

Part I
Introduction and conclusions

Naval forces and arms control

Richard Fieldhouse
SIPRI

I. Introduction

Twenty years ago SIPRI published its first book, a monograph entitled *Towards a Better Use of the Ocean*, which surveyed the 'contemporary legal problems of ocean development'.[1] It is appropriate that SIPRI again focuses on the ocean, in this book to examine the issue of naval arms control. Much has changed since 1969, and today there are new possibilities for improving East–West security in ways that were impossible during the cold war. One of the possibilities is to include naval forces in the arms control process. That is the point of departure for this book.

This book focuses on the relationship between naval forces and arms control, including the risks inherent in the East–West naval competition, and problems of and possibilities for designing arms control for these naval forces and activities. It concentrates primarily on the two major naval powers—the USA and the USSR. Their naval activities and forces, especially naval nuclear weapons, pose the greatest potential danger to peace and security and are of primary concern in the overall concept of security at sea. None the less, given the international nature of the seas and the global nature of naval activity, the issues addressed affect all nations.

Although the two superpower navies dominate current naval arms control concerns, it is possible that smaller navies will also be involved in disputes in the future, perhaps involving their new responsibilities for patrolling and protecting the exclusive economic zones (EEZs) established by the 1982 United Nations Convention on the Law of the Sea (UNCLOS).[2] In paper 3 of this book Derek Boothby points out that growing naval forces and activities will lead to 'greater opportunities for misunderstanding and greater risk of untoward incidents at sea potentially involving a large number of states'. The focus in this volume on superpower and East–West naval arms control does not preclude consideration of other maritime security problems. If the US–Soviet and NATO–WTO naval situations are first addressed (and hopefully improved), other dimensions of security at sea can then also be addressed.

The book is organized in five parts. This part surveys the subject of naval forces and arms control and offers recommendations for arms control measures. Part 2 presents three views in favour of pursuing naval arms control. Part 3 examines some of the considerable difficulties involved in controlling naval forces and activities. Part 4 discusses several specific approaches towards naval arms control. Part 5 focuses on naval confidence-building measures, which hold promise for improving security at sea. Two annexes present reference material: annexe A documents official Soviet and US views concerning naval arms control; and annexe B presents the texts or excerpts of international agreements relevant to naval forces, with lists of states parties in 1989.

II. Why focus on naval arms control?

Since World War II, navies have not been a major focus of arms control efforts. They have generally been considered less dangerous than nuclear forces and conventional land forces. Today the improving relationship between the USA and the USSR, and between the North Atlantic Treaty Organization (NATO) and the Warsaw Treaty Organization (WTO), calls for a reappraisal of the role of naval forces in the East–West security order and of the possibilities for addressing naval issues in arms control forums. If relations between East and West continue to improve and current arms control negotiations succeed in substantially reducing US and Soviet nuclear forces and NATO and WTO conventional forces in Europe, this will create an interesting situation in which: (a) naval forces will be the only military forces not included in the East–West process of arms control; (b) the changed situation for ground and air forces in Europe will provide opportunities for naval arms control; and (c) naval arms control agreements—at least between the USA and the USSR—may be a prerequisite for achieving a desirable level of security and stability in Europe, as elsewhere. Thus, the time is right for turning the arms control focus also to naval forces and activities.

It is important to include naval forces and activities in the East–West arms control process for several related reasons. The first is a simple principle: *if* the USA and the USSR want to improve their mutual security and minimize the risks of armed conflict, superpower naval forces and activities *should* be subject to constraints, as should all their military forces. In this regard navies are no different from ground or air forces. This principle is important because numerous important security objectives can be achieved only through arms control, confidence-building and other co-operative efforts. Confrontation and arms competition do not lead to mutual security, as four decades of the cold war have demonstrated.

Second, superpower naval forces and activities present risks and potential threats that should be reduced or minimized. Two agreements concluded by the United States and the Soviet Union—the Incidents at Sea Agreement of 1972 and the Prevention of Dangerous Military Activities (PDMA) Agreement of 1989—demonstrate that the two nations recognize some of these risks and wish to reduce them. But US and Soviet naval forces have other capabilities and characteristics that are also of considerable concern to each other—for example, the Soviet capacity to interrupt US and allied shipping in a crisis or war, or the US capacity to attack the USSR with nuclear weapons from naval platforms.

There are many existing and potential dangers that need to be addressed in arms control measures (see papers 2, 8 and 9). In other words, if naval issues continue to be excluded from arms control and co-operative security endeavours, a number of insecurities and instabilities will remain. Furthermore, both nations undoubtedly harbour misperceptions that exacerbate their real insecurities. Arms control, in the broadest sense of the term, is the only available means of eliminating unwarranted fears and misunderstandings.

Third, there is the question of timing. It can be argued that there has never been a better time than the present to pursue US–Soviet (and, generally, East–West) measures of naval arms control in the context of general arms control efforts. Political relations between the superpowers have dramatically improved since the early 1980s, and there has been an extraordinary degree of co-operation and progress on security matters, including several recent and pending arms control agreements and confidence-building measures, summit meetings between the leaders of the two nations, increased contact and improved working relations between their political and military officials, exchanges of information concerning military forces and activities, exchanges of naval port visits and personnel, and general trends that augur well for improved security.[3] These manifestations of improved US–Soviet relations demonstrate new possibilities for naval arms control and may even require a certain amount of progress in the field. Existing negotiations—particularly the Strategic Arms Reduction Talks (START) in Geneva, and the Negotiation on Conventional Armed Forces in Europe (CFE) and the Conference on Security and Co-operation in Europe (CSCE) Negotiations on Confidence- and Security-Building Measures (CSBMs) in Vienna[4]—may affect naval forces, activities and behaviour. In the case of the CFE negotiations, if NATO and the WTO are able to greatly reduce the level and offensive capabilities of their military forces in Europe, this might change the basic naval force planning requirements of NATO, thus providing more opportunity for naval arms control measures.

Finally, both the USSR and the USA are experiencing economic constraints that are forcing them to reconsider or cut back their military programmes in general, including their naval programmes. This presages major changes and reductions in the world's two largest fleets by the year 2000 that could be managed in a predictable and acceptable manner through arms control. Since 1986, the USSR has reduced its shipbuilding rate and its naval operating tempo for several consecutive years. Based on the age of many of its ships and submarines, the Soviet Navy can be expected to retire a large fraction of its forces by the turn of the century and will probably replace only a portion of these vessels.[5] This process of retirement began in earnest in 1988. The USA, too, has had to reduce its military budget to fit within national budget limits. In fiscal year 1989 this resulted in a reduction of more than $30 billion in the US Navy budget request (as part of an overall reduction in the Department of Defense budget) and in a scaling back of the much-publicized plan to build a 600-ship navy. While economic problems are far more acute in the USSR, neither nation is likely to be able to increase naval or any other military spending for the foreseeable future. Given the inevitability of changes in force structure—and possibly in the perceived need for certain naval missions—the USA and the USSR could benefit from a co-operative approach to reductions that would also establish confidence and predictability.

All these factors could create propitious conditions for bringing naval arms control on to the official international agenda and debating it fully.

III. What is naval arms control?

In answering this question it is useful to think of the concept as 'including naval forces in the arms control process', because this phrase suggests the most realistic, likely and feasible possibility. In other words, the term 'naval arms control' can be misleading because it suggests that there could be arms control of naval forces by themselves, independent or exclusive of other forces and activities. While it is possible to have such agreements (e.g., agreements on preventing incidents at sea) it is conceptually more appropriate to think in terms of including naval forces and activities in the broader existing arms control process, because the other forces and overall security situation must be considered in the calculation of which controls are desirable, acceptable and possible for naval forces and activities. There is no independent naval balance at sea. Naval forces are not independent of land forces and activities; ultimately, they exist entirely in relation to events on land. Thus, seeing naval forces in the larger context of their overall security circumstances will facilitate the search for security at sea.

For the purposes of this book and for the general debate on naval arms control issues, it is also useful to have a broad conception of the term 'arms control' to encompass the whole range of possible approaches, measures and agreements. Arms control should be seen as a co-operative *process* to reduce the risk of military conflict and improve mutual security; this will permit viewing it as a whole instead of as many separate parts. Indeed, all arms control measures have the same objective: to bring military activities and forces under control, by various means (including limitation, reduction or elimination, risk reduction or confidence-building, information exchange and other forms of co-operation), in order to reduce the dangers, risks and possibilities of military confrontation and to improve mutual security. The long-term goal of arms control is to help realize the principles set forth in the United Nations Charter: to prevent the threat or use of military force as a political instrument, to solve political problems peacefully and to limit military forces to a level adequate for no more than self-defence.

Thus, naval arms control could be construed broadly as comprising those measures and activities that seek to prevent or avert military confrontation (war) by eliminating or reducing the sources of danger that stem from the naval forces or activities of nations. This is a more comprehensive construction than the traditional but narrow concept of arms control (i.e., negotiated agreements to limit or reduce arms) and could include everything from formal, negotiated bilateral and multilateral agreements to various forms of joint co-operation—ranging from exchanges of information and personnel to structured dialogue—to unilateral or non-negotiated measures, with or without reciprocity. The objectives could be to restrain military capabilities and activities that are excessive, destabilizing or threatening to other nations; to replace suspicion, secrecy and fear with openness, predictability and mutual understanding; and to create a security regime in which legitimate concerns and interests can be accommodated in a straightforward and co-operative manner.

Categories of arms control measures

There are two levels of arms control measures: (*a*) formal and negotiated measures embodied in agreements, and (*b*) informal measures of co-operation or self-restraint that may or may not produce agreement but that are important for promoting mutual security and arms control. On the first level of arms control there are three categories of possible measures: structural measures, operational measures and confidence-building measures.

Naval arms control efforts in the first category include the more traditional efforts to limit or reduce naval equipment or capabilities (for example, the number, type, size or armament of naval forces, including ships, submarines, aircraft, personnel and support infrastructure, such as bases and ports). These can be considered to be measures of *structural* arms control since they aim to create structural limitations on naval forces. The Washington and London naval treaties of 1922 and 1930, respectively, are perhaps the most well-known examples of structural naval arms control (see paper 1). Nuclear arms control agreements—such as the USA–USSR SALT (Strategic Arms Limitation Talks) agreements, the Treaty on the Elimination of Their Intermediate-Range and Shorter-Range Missiles (INF Treaty) and the prospective START agreement—are other examples of structural arms control.

Controls on the activities of naval forces—their operations, exercises, behaviour, formations, movements, deployment areas, and so on—can be considered *operational* arms control measures since they aim to regulate naval operations.[6] Operational measures have been negotiated in such agreements as the bilateral Incidents at Sea agreements which provide agreed rules of behaviour for naval forces and establish procedures for direct communication, thereby reducing certain risks associated with naval operations (see paper 11 and annexe B). Broader agreements have also been concluded, such as the 1989 USA–USSR PDMA Agreement that applies the incidents at sea principle to all military forces of the superpowers in special circumstances (see annexe B). On a multilateral basis, naval operational controls could be negotiated which are similar to those measures adopted by the CSCE that regulate military activities in Europe.

Operational measures often merge with the third category of possible control: *confidence-building measures* (CBMs). Generally, CBMs are designed to reduce the risks of armed conflict and foster openness, understanding and assurance of the defensive and non-threatening nature of other nations' military forces and activities. The most well-known recent CBMs are those of the Conference on Confidence- and Security-Building Measures and Disarmament in Europe (also known as the Conference on Disarmament in Europe [CDE], or the Stockholm Conference), namely, those in the 1986 Document of the Stockholm Conference.[7] However, virtually any measure that results in increased confidence, openness or understanding, or that reduces the likelihood of dangerous incidents or armed conflict resulting from miscalculation or misperception, can be considered a CBM. Although all arms control agreements contain some confidence-building elements, there are CBMs that have no structural or operational effects. As they apply to naval forces, such CBMs could presumably include prior notification of naval activities (including manoeuvres, amphibious activities and large-scale movements) and exchanges of information about naval force levels, structures, construction plans, and so on.

In addition to the three categories of formal, negotiated and agreed arms control, there are possibilities for measures of co-operation and less formal, non-negotiated or unilateral measures of self-restraint that either achieve similar ends—although with less force than negotiated agreements provide—or that lay the foundation for further measures.

It is conceivable that some forms of co-operation between nations or navies in peacetime could lead to understandings or agreements that would reduce the likelihood of miscalculation or dangerous or provocative behaviour. The meeting between US Secretary of Defense Frank Carlucci and Soviet Defence Minister Dmitri Yazov in March 1988 and the subsequent meeting between the Chairman of the US Joint Chiefs of Staff Admiral William J. Crowe and the Soviet Chief of the General Staff Marshal Sergey Akhromeyev in July 1988 led to the 1989 PDMA Agreement. Planned meetings between the leaders of the US and Soviet navies and reciprocal port visits are two other examples of ways in which the two navies could gain a better understanding of each other and promote security-building efforts. Expanded contacts between political and military officials of East and West also have a confidence-building effect, such as the July 1989 appearance of Soviet Marshal Sergey Akhromeyev as a witness before the US Congress, and information exchanges at these levels. These contacts are CBMs of a tacit or routine nature although their cumulative effect could be very significant, and they could pave the way for more far-reaching agreements.[8]

In the field of unilateral measures the possibilities include national (or alliance) decisions or policies to take or not to take certain action in order to improve the military or political situation with respect to naval forces and international security. These decisions could be communicated or publicized in the hope of encouraging a similar or reciprocal action or self-restraint from another nation or to facilitate arms control. One can imagine a wide variety of options in the naval area, from national decisions on procurement, force structure or choice of armament, to naval strategies, deployment patterns and policies concerning 'naval diplomacy'.

There are recent examples of nations taking unilateral decisions to reduce or eliminate weapon systems or armaments (in the same manner as they decide to develop and deploy them), although usually for management, economic or domestic political reasons rather than for arms control purposes. The difficulty lies in designing and implementing unilateral measures in such a way as to promote confidence and reciprocal self-restraint on the part of other nations. In April 1989 it was revealed that the US Navy had decided to retire three of its tactical nuclear weapon systems for sea warfare, ahead of schedule and without planned replacements (see paper 9). The USSR and its WTO allies have begun to implement their announced unilateral reductions in military forces, including naval forces. Given the asymmetrical nature of NATO and WTO maritime requirements and consequent naval forces, as well as the inherent complexity of formal naval arms control agreements, unilateral measures may be a necessary supplement and lubricant to bilateral or multilateral arms control. Clearly, the options and possibilities for unilateral action or restraint have not been exhausted and may play an increasingly important role in naval and other arms control efforts.

General considerations

Ideally, it would be desirable for the superpowers and their allies to approach naval arms control from the so-called mission approach, that is, to define and agree on the missions of their naval forces that are considered essential and try to control the other's countering capabilities.[9] Obviously, this naval calculation must be integrated within the overall security equation and include other military forces as well. For example, the USA deems it absolutely essential to be able to keep open the shipping lanes across the seas to its allies and trading partners, primarily in the Atlantic (to NATO Europe) and the Pacific Oceans. Consequently, the USA sees the large number of Soviet submarines as a potentially grave threat to these shipping lanes or so-called sea lines of communication (SLOCs). Conversely, the USSR appears to consider the survivability of its ballistic missile submarine (SSBN) force to be of paramount importance. It therefore sees the strong US and NATO anti-submarine warfare (ASW) capability as a serious threat to its own submarines. This insecurity is compounded by US Navy declarations that under its current Maritime Strategy it would actively seek to destroy Soviet SSBNs early in a conventional US–Soviet or NATO–WTO war.[10]

Logically, each nation should have an interest in limiting or controlling those capabilities of the other side that most threaten its own essential military missions. However, this approach would require a degree of understanding and co-operation that does not yet exist between the superpowers, a degree strong enough to overcome the numerous difficulties inherent in naval arms control. Would it be possible for the USA and the USSR to come to an explicit understanding of each other's perceived minimum security requirements, accept the forces and capabilities deployed for those requirements and agree not to achieve a capability to threaten those forces? Although it may seem to be an impossible task, this is essentially what the SALT I Agreement and the Anti-Ballistic Missile (ABM) Treaty, both signed in 1972, accomplished in the area of strategic offensive and defensive forces. It remains to be seen whether the superpowers can apply the same standard to current arms control negotiations or future efforts, but it may be a good avenue to explore, given the potential security benefit and the possibility for addressing problems of otherwise uncontrollable or future military technology.

With regard to naval forces, it would be necessary to start with an understanding of the role they play in the overall security situation of the two major alliances and then find some means of agreeing to preserve that which is considered essential and limit that which is deemed undesirable. This approach would doubtless require great openness and co-operation, not to mention much effort and good faith. While the prospects may not seem good for such an approach today, it is certainly worth pursuing—especially given the complexity of achieving arms control that includes naval forces and activities.

One last general comment about naval arms control is that if two or more nations can agree on an arms control objective and if they have sufficient political will to make their domestic political processes work in a co-ordinated fashion, there should be room for progress. However, arms control measures negotiated between nations require all parties involved to co-operate in good faith; otherwise there will be no possibility for agreements. It is safe to assume that nations will continue to act on the side of caution and prudence when it comes to safeguarding their national security and will not enter into negotiations or agreements that they believe to be neither in their interest nor feasible. Arms control restraints cannot be *imposed* on nations against their will. In other words, there is no need for concern that nations will sign agreements that are dangerous or that will diminish their security. The objective is to improve mutual security by moving countries away from their excessive and destabilizing military capabilities and activities, away from their over-emphasis on military force and away from unwarranted fears of potential adversaries, and towards co-operative, stable patterns of behaviour and force structures.

IV. Challenges

Naval arms control is a difficult enterprise for many reasons, some fundamental and some practical. This section outlines the most important challenges to naval arms control: (*a*) differences in US and Soviet security circumstances, and the consequent superpower views of naval arms control; (*b*) practical difficulties in designing acceptable naval arms control measures; and (*c*) verification difficulties.

Strategic security differences between the superpowers

Unquestionably the most important and fundamental obstacle to the inclusion of naval forces and activities in the arms control process is the great difference in security circumstances and perspectives of the two major maritime powers—the USA and the USSR. These differences, which Hervé Coutau-Bégarie describes in paper 4 of this volume, comprise political, military, economic and geographic factors that determine the strategic outlook of these two alliance leaders. Stated simply, the USA sees itself as a maritime island nation—with numerous alliance security commitments and responsibilities around the world—whose fortunes and security depend on its unrestricted use of the seas. Its economic and alliance relationships are trans-oceanic, and it has built the world's most powerful navy to help secure and protect its interests. The USSR, by contrast, is fundamentally a land power that does not depend on the seas for its economic or military security, but rather on land territory and forces. Its major allies are all neighbouring states. Nevertheless, the Soviet Union has a large navy built for different missions and purposes than its US counterpart.[11]

Consequently, the two superpowers have widely differing views of their own and each other's reliance on the seas. These views shape their perceived security requirements, strategies and military force structures, as well as their interest or lack of interest in naval arms control. Thus the perspectives of these two nations have a decisive influence on the prospects and possibilities for measures of naval arms control. If both nations see it in their interest to pursue such measures, then there is opportunity for progress. However, if either nation does not perceive naval arms control to be in its interest then this fact alone will prevent progress. It is therefore important to examine the perspectives of the USA and the USSR on the question of naval arms control.

US and Soviet perspectives

This discussion of US and Soviet views of naval arms control is supplemented by a selection of official texts presented in annexe A. Generally speaking, the USA is extremely wary of naval arms control because it appears to be inimical to US security interests. Its reliance on the oceans and its navy is such that the US Government has been hesitant even to discuss naval arms control publicly.[12] In 1989, under increasing pressure, this hesitation gave way to a greater willingness to explain US concerns about arms control at sea. By comparison, the USSR has expressed an interest in naval arms control for many years and since the mid-1980s has steadily intensified its advocacy. The Soviet Union argues that US naval forces are threatening and destabilizing, and has made numerous public proposals for various types of control or limitation—both on a regional and a global level.

US perspectives

Given its strong maritime orientation, the USA has traditionally exhibited little interest in naval arms control. With a few notable exceptions, it has generally perceived no need to place arms control restraints on its naval forces and activities and no appreciable security improvement to be achieved by such controls.[13] In October 1988 General William Burns, Director of the US Arms Control and Disarmament Agency (ACDA), stated the US position on naval arms control to the UN General Assembly First Committee:

We understand that this committee may be presented with arms [control] proposals for limits or constraints on naval activities. This makes it necessary to state the firm position of the United States regarding such proposals. Requirements for naval armaments and activities of various nations are inherently asymmetrical and are based on broader geographic, political, strategic and other military factors. Located between and separated from allies by two oceans, the United States relies on maritime activities and freedom of navigation under international law to protect its security and trade interests. Therefore, the United States cannot agree to any arms limitations or additional constraints on its naval activities.[14]

In light of the 1987 joint US–Soviet commitment to seek limits on nuclear sea-launched cruise missiles (SLCMs) in a START agreement (see paper 9), and in light of the 1989 USA–USSR PDMA Agreement, this statement may sound somewhat extreme. But it succinctly summarizes the general US view, especially if the measures are perceived to constrain or limit naval capabilities that are considered essential to US national security. The USA is naturally inclined to prize and jealously guard the flexibility and mobility afforded by its naval forces.

To the most sceptical observer it might appear to be the case that the USA has nothing to gain and everything to lose from any naval arms control measures. In describing Soviet naval arms control proposals in his testimony to Congress, Rear Admiral Thomas Brooks, US Director of Naval Intelligence, stated that 'Soviet public proposals would require significant US naval concessions for minimal tradeoffs in Soviet naval operations. The Soviets stand to gain militarily and the United States to lose, were these initiatives successful'.[15]

The combination of progress at the Vienna CFE and CSCE negotiations on CSBMs in 1989 and Soviet calls for starting naval arms control talks have put pressure on the USA to defend its position. US officials are quick to draw a broad line between reducing conventional forces in Europe *on land*—which is a high priority for the USA and NATO—and seeking controls on naval forces, which all the NATO and WTO nations agreed explicitly to exclude from the CFE negotiations.[16] Admiral Carlisle Trost, the US Chief of Naval Operations

(CNO), stressed this notion in 1989: 'In particular, [US] naval forces must not become a bargaining chip. Our unrestricted use of the seas is more important than any agreement. If the Soviets are sincere, they will agree first to asymmetrical reductions in their own offensive forces, and then after a time of settling out, it will become apparent to both sides that Western sea power doesn't threaten them.'[17] The USSR would not agree with Admiral Trost's assessment, as is evident from official Soviet statements. It will be interesting to observe the interrelationship of the CFE negotiations with the maritime concerns of the USSR, especially as the May 1989 NATO proposal announced by President George Bush includes all combat aircraft based on land in Europe—presumably including Soviet naval aircraft while excluding US naval aircraft.

The US view appears to be overwhelmingly opposed to any naval arms control, in which case no such measures would even be negotiated. But it must be pointed out that the view may be more flexible than it appears to be and that it may change over time. The USA has recently signed a number of arms control agreements with the USSR that—although not considered measures of naval arms control—contain provisions which affect their navies (see annexe B). For example, the 1988 Ballistic Missile Launch Notification Agreement provides for at least 24 hours' prior notification of submarine-launched ballistic missile (SLBM) launches. The 1989 Prevention of Dangerous Military Activities Agreement applies to naval forces as well as to ground and air forces, an important CBM precedent. Both nations have agreed to find a way of limiting nuclear SLCMs in the START negotiations. If the START and CFE negotiations produce agreements—both of which would affect naval forces either directly or indirectly—and if US–Soviet relations continue to improve then the USA may have some interest in further arms control measures that apply to naval forces and activities. In April 1989 this possibility was acknowledged by Admiral Larson in his testimony to Congress on naval arms control (see annexe A): 'Once a mutually agreed upon arms control regime for land forces has been established that enhances stability in Europe, then the Western allies can examine the possibility of limitations on naval forces as they would affect the European balance of power'. He goes on to say that 'the United States and its allies may consider a naval arms control dialogue with the Eastern Bloc to be advantageous'.[18] For the time being, many other arms control priorities and activities are absorbing US attention and energy. Presumably there will be increasing debate on the topic as it moves closer to the centre of the security and arms control spotlight.

Soviet perspectives

The USSR is clearly interested in naval arms control. This has been evident in numerous speeches and proposals made by senior Soviet officials, notably President Mikhail Gorbachev and Marshal Sergey Akhromeyev, the former Chief of the General Staff (see annexe A).[19] These official statements have repeatedly stressed Soviet concern about the dangers of the superpower naval competition and called for various forms of control, limitation and reduction. In several major foreign policy speeches, President Gorbachev has discussed Soviet concerns of regional naval activities and called for arms control solutions.[20]

In his unprecedented testimony to the House Armed Services Committee in July 1989, Marshal Akhromeyev emphasized Soviet interest in naval arms control, stating:

We in the USSR are greatly concerned over the reluctance of the US administration to open negotiations with the USSR on bilateral reductions of our naval forces. We are regarding this as the US desire first to reach agreement with us on cutting the ground forces in Europe . . . and then build up its naval forces without any constraints, especially its carrier battle groups, thus gaining military superiority in order to dictate its will to the USSR from the position of strength. . . . We regard reaching agreement on starting the talks to reduce our naval forces and limit military activities at sea to be a major prerequisite for further improvement of Soviet–American relations and switching them onto really peaceful rail tracks.[21]

Describing Soviet willingness to accommodate the concerns of West European nations, Akhromeyev stated that the USSR will work to radically reduce and restructure its ground and air forces to a minimum level in Europe and elsewhere. He went on to say:

But the Soviet Union and its allies expect that the US will also accommodate our concerns with regard to naval forces. We believe that the situation when all the armed services of the two sides are being negotiated and cut down, with the naval forces remaining intact, should be discontinued. The Soviet Union is deeply concerned about such an attitude of the US side. . . . If you follow this line, no drastic reductions of the armed forces and armaments in the world will be possible. Talks on the reduction of the naval forces should be started first between the USSR and the US and later between the NATO and the WTO. Conditions should be created for the whole range of armed services and armaments of the sides to become the subject of the talks and subsequent cuts.[22]

Soviet views of naval arms control are shaped by several interrelated factors—military, political and economic. Two maritime facts weigh heavily on the minds of Soviet security planners: the combat capabilities of the US Navy and its potential capacity to influence or decide the course of a conventional East–West war. Two scenarios serve to illustrate the point.

One of the worst fears of a Soviet military planner must be that a war between East and West could result in nuclear weapons being used against Soviet targets, possibly leading to the nuclear devastation of the USSR. It is clearly a high Soviet priority to do everything possible in peacetime and in wartime to prevent nuclear weapons from striking its national territory, including efforts to denuclearize Europe and to reduce as many foreign nuclear weapons as possible.[23] Naval non-strategic nuclear weapons—especially nuclear SLCMs and nuclear bombs aboard aircraft-carriers—are among the only US nuclear weapons capable of being used against Soviet territory but not currently subject to limitations in arms reduction negotiations. This may account for the many public Soviet proposals for constraints on superpower naval nuclear forces.

A second Soviet security nightmare is that, in the event of a major war with NATO, the great strength of the US and allied navies would enable NATO to reinforce its European-based forces and mobilize its vast industrial capacity to win a long conventional war of attrition. If NATO cannot sustain its war effort for more than a few weeks then the WTO numerical advantage in certain categories of highly mobile ground forces equipment might be able to prevail in combat, or at least prevent the defeat of the USSR. Thus, although NATO strongly claims the defensive nature of its naval forces (while relying on offensive tactics—see paper 4) these forces appear to the USSR and the WTO to be offensive and threatening. It is understandable that the Soviet Union wishes to alleviate some of its security concerns about NATO naval forces through arms control measures.

The USSR has legitimate security concerns about US naval forces. The US Navy has more than 7000 nuclear warheads available for attacks against Soviet targets, at which most of them are normally aimed—more than 5500 strategic SLBM warheads and about 1700 'non-strategic' nuclear SLCMs and gravity bombs.[24] The US Navy non-strategic nuclear arsenal is comparable in size and firepower to the US nuclear stockpile dedicated to NATO. Additionally, the US Marine Corps has a capability to land about 200 000 Marines on foreign shores. US aircraft-carriers deploy more than 1000 attack aircraft capable of bombing the USSR. Furthermore, the posture, operations and declared strategy of the US Navy (and its NATO counterparts) serve to exacerbate Soviet insecurities (see paper 8).

Even if one dismisses such war scenarios as wildly improbable—which does not absolve war planners from the duty of planning for them—US naval forces and capabilities prompt the Soviet military to take expensive countermeasures, such as air defences against cruise missiles or naval aircraft, anti-submarine defences (which also have offensive capabilities), land-based naval attack aircraft, and so on. The USSR would prefer not to spend so much of its limited economic resources on the military sector if it can be avoided. Given the current Soviet reform programme, this economic imperative may be one of the major impetuses for arms control efforts.

Thus there is compelling evidence that naval arms control is truly in the Soviet security interest, especially as the USA has the preponderant naval forces and capabilities. These forces would appear even more important and threatening to the USSR if a CFE agreement reduces the preponderance of Soviet ground and air forces in Europe. This is why the USSR is trying to make a conceptual link between the forces on land and those at sea as inseparable components of overall military forces, all of which should be subject to arms control. Reducing the former while ignoring the latter does not offer the USSR the security enhancement it desires. Thus it might be perceived by some that the Soviet Union has everything to gain and nothing to lose from naval arms control.

The USSR has made many public proposals for measures of naval arms control. These measures can be divided into the following categories: (a) disengagement or withdrawal of US and Soviet naval forces from certain ocean areas, such as the Indian Ocean and the Mediterranean Sea; (b) ASW-free zones in certain areas, such as the Baltic, Norwegian, Okhotsk and Japan Seas; (c) zones or areas where naval 'activity' or manoeuvres are prohibited, such as international straits or shipping lanes; (d) CBMs for naval operations and movements, including prior exchange of information on such activities, invitation of observers and limits on the overall size, duration and number of naval activities; and (e) restrictions on naval vessels carrying nuclear arms.

Some of these proposals are not acceptable to the USA and NATO because they would impinge on their use of the seas and their maritime flexibility in a way that is perceived as weakening NATO security. Other ideas proposed, however, are not objectionable in principle and might be acceptable in a form modified so as to be balanced and desirable by both sides.

At the CFE negotiations in Vienna, the USSR has agreed to the concept of huge and asymmetrical reductions in its ground forces. The Soviet Union argues that it would be appropriate for the USA and NATO to include their navies in the European arms control process (see the article by Marshal Akhromeyev in annexe A). Besides, the USSR has already decided to reduce its obsolescent navy, so it is logical for the USSR to try to include NATO naval forces in a reduction process. Soviet officials want to build public pressure in the West in favour of naval arms control, hoping that this will help pressure foreign governments to accept the idea.

Practical difficulties

Even if both superpowers can find some mutual interest in pursuing naval arms control there are a number of practical difficulties involved in designing desirable, equitable and feasible measures. Some of these considerations are described by Richard Hill in paper 6 of this volume. Other difficulties concern the unique characteristics of the maritime environment and naval forces. The three most important among these characteristics are: (a) the asymmetry of the navies of East and West, including requirements, missions, force structures, capabilities and operations; (b) the legal regime of the seas; and (c) the inherently mobile and global nature of naval forces.[25] If arms control measures are to include naval forces they must take these practical difficulties into account and accommodate them.

Maritime asymmetry

Given the major differences in security perspectives described above, it is natural that the US and Soviet navies are markedly different in nature, structure and operation.[26] This fact complicates arms control efforts because equitable agreements would have to be asymmetrical to be acceptable to Western nations. Numerical measures applied equally to NATO and WTO naval forces—such as equal force structures or numbers of ships—would be ridiculously imbalanced in their negative effect on the USA. Naval arms control measures cannot, therefore, aim to achieve some abstract notion of parity or equality at sea; they must satisfy the special security requirements of each nation involved. Some concrete examples illustrate this point.

The US Navy operates its vessels throughout the world in a pattern of 'forward deployment', that is, near its allies and adversaries and thus often far from home waters. The Soviet Navy operates predominantly in or near its home waters. This reflects the different missions of the two navies. The USA and its allies depend on unhindered use of shipping lanes across the seas, whereas the USSR depends on defending its territory and naval forces from Western attack. Whereas the US Navy has a force of 14 aircraft-carriers and more than 1000 carrier-based attack aircraft, Soviet naval aircraft operate primarily from land bases. These facts show that arms control measures will not be acceptable to the USA or its allies if they do not permit the continued forward deployment of allied naval forces, or if they restrict sea-based aircraft but not land-based ones. Soviet suggestions for ASW-free zones are not welcomed by NATO because they would have little effect on Soviet operations and capabilities but would restrict NATO to a much greater degree. These are but a few examples of the many differences between the US and Soviet navies. Unless they are carefully crafted, most proposals for limitations on naval forces or activities will encounter such problems of asymmetry. It is important to note, however, that the principle of asymmetric force reductions has been accepted by both superpowers and their allies.

In order to design equitable measures of naval arms control it will be necessary to determine areas of common interest and principles of operation required by or acceptable to both sides and to build from that point. This can only be done in the context of the overall security situation and other military forces of the nations involved. This will require much effort and much greater understanding between East and West. Direct communication and open dialogue are prerequisites to progress.

Legal regime of the seas

The high seas are not subject to national jurisdiction. This means that they are free for all nations to use, and navies are free to sail basically wherever their governments send them. The long-standing principle of the freedom of the seas is fundamental to maritime nations and will be fiercely preserved, guarded and defended by the major maritime powers as well as by smaller nations with important maritime interests. No arms control measure is likely to be accepted if it contradicts this principle, but consideration must also be given to the principle of balancing the rights and obligations of flag (shipping) states and coastal states. The 1982 United Nations Convention on the Law of the Sea provides an international regime for peaceful uses of the ocean and a framework for future ocean regulation, including arms control. As Ove Bring points out in paper 7, the principle of the freedom of the seas does not give navies absolute freedom to do as they wish; it is in fact compatible with multilateral restrictions on military activities at sea.

The special legal regime of the seas complicates naval arms control because naval forces are not under the same restrictions as land forces on or over sovereign territory. Since ships are free to sail the high seas they cannot be excluded from any region, and maritime nations are generally inclined to demonstrate their right to operate globally as a matter of principle (see paper 8). Naval arms control agreements must work within the framework of the special conditions that apply at sea, including the UNCLOS, to be acceptable and workable.

Mobile and global navies

The final maritime characteristic which merits consideration here is the inherent mobility of naval forces and the global nature of their missions. Although naval forces may be assigned to a fleet or a region (e.g., the US Atlantic Command or Sixth Fleet, or the Soviet Northern Fleet or Pacific Fleet) they are not limited to operations in one theatre because they can sail to different ocean areas as required. The Soviet Mediterranean Squadron is comprised mainly of units from the Northern Fleet based on the Kola Peninsula. From June 1983 until May 1984 the newly recommissioned US battleship *USS New Jersey* sailed 76 000 miles (122 300 km) on what was intended to be its initial (or 'shakedown') cruise, and operated in the western Pacific, off Central America and in the Mediterranean Sea near Lebanon.[27] This global role of navies means that—unlike ground and air forces—they are fundamentally not limited to theatre roles. Consequently, this must be taken into account in naval arms control measures, which should not necessarily be limited to a single region—such as Europe.

Despite the fact that the US Navy is primarily concerned with the Soviet Navy as a potential adversary, it is by no means exclusively oriented towards the USSR. It can be argued that the US Navy is most likely to be involved in crises and conflicts that do not directly involve the USSR but that take place in other regions, such as the Middle East, the Caribbean and the Persian Gulf. This has certainly been the case during the 1980s, when the US Navy has been involved in crises in the Persian Gulf, Libya, Lebanon and Grenada. This is one reason why the USA resists including naval forces in a European arms reduction process. Much of the discussion of naval arms control possibilities focuses on Europe, particularly given the CFE and the CSCE negotiations on CSBMs in Vienna and the evolving security regime on the continent. While the naval forces of East and West play an important role in European security, they cannot be considered only in a European context.

These practical difficulties (and those described in paper 6) are not necessarily insuperable, but they complicate naval arms control efforts and foreclose certain approaches that apply to land forces. They are among the fundamental challenges to arms control at sea.

Verification

The final challenge which merits discussion is the issue of verification. This is often seen to be a major impediment to naval arms control agreements, partly because of the practical difficulties mentioned above and, where it concerns nuclear weapons, because of the difficulty of designing satisfactory verification regimes to reliably account for or distinguish nuclear warheads from conventional ones on dual-capable weapon systems. In paper 5 Herbert Lin examines the issue of verification of nuclear weapons at sea. This discussion will focus on more general considerations of the topic, as well as its nuclear aspect.

Verification must be considered in the context of the objectives of a particular agreement or negotiation and the commitment made by participating nations to conclude a given agreement. The essential requirement of a verification regime is that a nation must feel satisfied that it will be able to monitor, with an acceptable degree of certainty, whether other nations are complying with the terms of an agreement. Certain arms control limitations may be technically or politically impractical or unfeasible, at least for the present time. These difficulties will circumscribe the boundaries of negotiation. That which cannot be adequately verified will not be subject to limitation. Successful arms control verification does not require national omniscience or the surrender of national sovereignty. Nor can verification be absolute; adequacy is a sufficient standard. If nations wish to co-operate towards concluding an agreement they should be able to design mutually satisfactory verification measures. Political will and technology both play critical roles.

Many of the actual or predicted verification problems regarding naval forces concern the operational characteristics of the vessels involved. For example, verifying certain limits on submarine forces or activities could be extremely difficult because submarines are designed to operate covertly. This fact has led nations to exclude submarines from some arms control agreements, as in the bilateral Incidents at Sea agreements. However, as with other types of arms control, some limits are easier to verify than others. It is relatively easy for the superpowers to count each other's submarines; it is more difficult to know what weapons they carry and where they are operating. The more difficult tasks require co-operative measures and a willingness to facilitate verification. If nations refuse to permit observers or inspectors aboard their naval vessels this will undoubtedly make certain verification tasks very difficult if not impossible. Presumably if nations want to conclude an agreement they will be willing and able to take the steps required to make it work, including allowing verification provisions.

Given the complexity and requirements of verifying current and pending arms control agreements, there has been and must still be great progress in the field of verification. The USA and the USSR have come a long way from the days of the SALT negotiations, and the 35 CSCE nations have also made great progress in the arms control field. The verification provisions of the Stockholm Document and the INF Treaty were both unprecedented. The amount of information all sides have exchanged is massive by comparison with previous agreements. Future agreements will require much more extensive exchanges of information and much greater openness and co-operation than would have been imaginable in the early 1980s. If nations want arms control they must permit verification.

It appears that naval nuclear arms control is the most difficult of the naval verification tasks. Nuclear SLCMs are the most difficult obstacle at the START negotiations, and verification is the proximate cause of the difficulties. Two observations on recent developments in verification deserve mention.

First, the USA and the USSR seem to be taking a new approach to verification, at least at the START negotiations. It appears that both sides have agreed in principle to try a system proposed by the USA in which verification ideas and methods are tested during the course of the negotiations, prior to signing an agreement.[28] This approach grew out of the INF Treaty experience, which left many verification details unresolved even after the Treaty was in force. If this new venture proves to be successful it may set a precedent that could help solve some of the verification problems that will surely accompany future arms control agreements. It appears, however, that the initial US 'advance verification' effort at START did not include the issue of SLCM verification.[29]

Despite their joint commitment in December 1987 to 'seek mutually acceptable and effective methods of verification of [SLCM] limitations, which could include the employment of national technical means, cooperative measures and onsite inspection',[30] the USA and the USSR have not (as of August 1989) made progress on fulfilling this commitment. And, although both nations agreed to co-operate on experiments that would test the feasibility of SLCM verification, no joint intergovernmental experiments have been conducted to date. Instead, there has been an experiment between scientific organizations from the two nations.

On 5 July 1989 an SLCM verification experiment took place aboard the Soviet cruiser *Slava*, anchored in the Black Sea near Yalta and equipped with one nuclear-armed SS-N-12 anti-ship cruise missile. The experiment was co-sponsored by the Soviet Academy of Sciences (with the co-operation of the Soviet Government and Navy) and the Natural Resources Defense Council

(NRDC), a private environmental organization in the USA. Scientists from the two nations measured radiation emitted by the nuclear warhead using a variety of passive gamma-ray and neutron detectors placed at varying distances from the warhead—from directly on top of the launcher and from a nearby ship and helicopter.[31] This unprecedented experiment was admittedly only an initial step (further co-operation is planned) but one which has gone much further than the US Government has been willing to go, official statements about the difficulty of SLCM verification notwithstanding.[32] This type of semi-private experiment could play an important role in arms control efforts, as it did in the case of nuclear test monitoring, whether or not it proves possible to verify SLCMs.[33] It is a useful start to a process that should be conducted jointly by the US and Soviet governments, as was agreed.

Verification, while essential to arms control, should not assume the dominant position in the naval arms control debate. It is one element among many and may depend as much on political commitment as on questions of technical feasibility. If nations want an arms control outcome they should be able to make use of existing technologies and design appropriate and mutually satisfactory agreements. If a particular weapon technology or measure is deemed to be too difficult to verify, nations could try to agree on alternative measures, perhaps in the operational or confidence-building categories.

V. Possible approaches

What approaches could nations take to pursue naval arms control? This section considers a number of possible ways to include naval forces and activities in arms control efforts, including structural and operational measures introduced in section III above. In addition to these measures, it discusses the possibility of expanding existing agreements as well as unilateral measures. It does not include confidence-building measures, which are discussed separately in section VI.

Structural measures

Structural measures are those which limit military equipment and force structure—the traditional idea of arms limitation. By limiting armaments one limits capabilities (and thus possibilities) for their use. This could have the effect of preventing nations from gaining a dangerous preponderance of military force or of stabilizing an arms competition. It could also possibly lead to economic savings, although this is by no means assured.

In the naval area structural controls would probably apply to naval platforms and their weapons or equipment, and would set quantitative or qualitative limits on them. Current examples include the USA–USSR SALT I and SALT II agreements (see annexe B), which set limits on the numbers of ballistic missile submarines and the numbers of SLBM launchers. In the START negotiations in

Geneva the USA and the USSR are seeking to reduce their strategic offensive forces by 30–50 per cent, including limits on their SSBNs, SLBMs and their warheads. Nuclear-armed SLCMs are being discussed in START, but it remains unclear whether or how they will be included in an agreement. Thus, current efforts at structural arms control measures that include naval forces are limited to strategic nuclear forces. Naval non-strategic nuclear weapons appear to be the most likely area for future structural naval arms control efforts since they are of greatest concern and possibly the least utility (see papers 6 and 9).

Given the great security disparities between the USA and the USSR, it seems most unlikely that they would agree to limits or reductions of their general naval force structures—their ships, submarines and aircraft. However, it is conceivable that they might be able to increase their mutual security (as well as that of other nations) if they could work on a mission approach to find a formula for limits of certain categories of vessel, namely, attack submarines, aircraft-carriers and vessels armed with long-range nuclear-capable cruise missiles. In theory this would require a trade-off in Soviet submarines that could interdict shipping for US vessels capable of attacking Soviet territory, particularly with nuclear weapons. In practice this would require a careful balance of interests and consideration of many other factors. Complexity alone might doom such an effort—if it were ever launched.

However, the evolving security situation in Europe and elsewhere, especially concerning Soviet military forces, will probably require a reassessment of superpower security circumstances, including military doctrine, strategy, missions, requirements and force structure. Such a reassessment might lead to unforeseen opportunities and possibilities for positive change. But it must be said that the degree of change and stability possible in the international security structure is dependent on the actions of many countries. Although the USSR is experiencing important changes that may offer new possibilities for improved international security, this will depend to a large extent on the USA. If the USA acts positively and co-operates with the USSR, it can bring about greater and more substantial improvements than if it takes a 'wait and see' attitude.

Both nations are going to make changes in naval force structure. Might they be able to do so in a co-operative, predictable and stable manner that minimizes risks, misperceptions and costs and improves their overall security? It seems possible that the two nations might agree to provide each other with detailed information about their existing and planned naval force structures—construction, retirement and deployment figures—although this falls in the category of CBMs. Such information exchanges, however, might help the navies make more rational choices about force structure than would otherwise be possible.

Structural measures of naval arms control may be the least likely and most difficult to pursue, with the exception of non-strategic naval nuclear weapons (see paper 9). Many other fundamental improvements in the general East–West security relationship would be necessary, including other naval measures, before negotiated general reductions of superpower naval forces would be acceptable or of interest to the USA.

Operational measures

Military activities are a major source of concern to many nations. Naval operations and activities, particularly those of the superpowers, have caused dangerous incidents and are one possible area for arms control efforts. Operational measures of naval arms control are intended to bring the activities of naval forces under control and to reduce the risks involved when naval forces of different nations operate in close proximity to each other or near each other's territory. The general idea is that by controlling the behaviour of naval forces nations can prevent dangerous or provocative activities that in peacetime might endanger naval personnel or equipment, or cause a military incident or crisis.

Contemporary efforts to control naval operations are fairly well established in one respect: preventing incidents and accidents at sea. In 1972 the USA and the USSR signed the first bilateral Incidents at Sea Agreement regulating naval operations and behaviour at sea. In paper 11 of this volume Sean Lynn-Jones examines this agreement and analyses its impact for subsequent agreements. In 1986 the USSR and the UK signed a similar agreement to prevent incidents at sea, and in 1988 the Federal Republic of Germany and the USSR signed a nearly identical agreement. The texts of these agreements are reproduced in annexe B. While the three existing Incidents at Sea agreements are considered to be successful in helping to prevent dangerous naval encounters between the four signatory states, they do not apply to other nations. There is therefore an international effort in the UN, led by Sweden, to design a multilateral agreement for preventing incidents at sea, similar to and in harmony with the three existing bilateral agreements.[34] Jan Prawitz presents the basic ideas and components of such a multilateral agreement in paper 12. It has been reported that several additional bilateral agreements are being discussed by the USSR and several other nations, notably France, Norway, China and Canada.[35] It is possible that these discussions will lead to more bilateral agreements.

While the issue of collisions, accidents and incidents has been and continues to be addressed, several other aspects of naval operations have received far less attention. In paper 8 William Arkin describes a pattern of provocative superpower naval operations and exercises that peaked during the mid-1980s for which there had been no corresponding bilateral effort at restraint until the late 1980s, and even then only to a limited degree. Because of the special legal regime at sea, navies are basically free to do many things which either are not, or would not be, permitted on land. US and Soviet naval forces have practised mock attacks against each other and conducted other measures of harassment and intimidation as part of their 'routine' peacetime training and operations, causing concern that dangerous behaviour might lead to incidents or even crises. Whereas the CSCE efforts have introduced limited constraints and considerable confidence-building measures concerning military activities and exercises on land in Europe (through the Stockholm Document), there has been no similar effort at sea, largely because the USA and its NATO allies do not wish to begin such a process.

Preventing dangerous activities

In June 1989 the USA and the USSR concluded the Agreement on Preventing Dangerous Military Activities, which includes naval forces and activities (see annexe B). This is the first agreement on operational measures to go beyond those covering incidents at sea; it basically applies the principle of the Incidents at Sea agreements to all US and Soviet military forces in certain conditions, and goes a certain way towards supplementing the 1972 USA–USSR agreement. The PDMA Agreement is a mixture of operational measure, risk reduction measure, CBM, institutionalized communication channel and military-to-military contact—a modern hybrid of co-operative arms control.

The PDMA Agreement provides a set of rules of behaviour for US and Soviet military forces operating in proximity to one another in peacetime in four cases that are considered to have inherent risks: entering into the national territory of the other state, using lasers in a dangerous manner, interfering with command and control networks and equipment of the other state, and interfering with the military forces of the other state in areas agreed to be 'Special Caution Areas'. Each of these four activities applies to naval forces (including naval air forces)—perhaps uniquely so. The agreement establishes basic procedures to prevent dangerous forms of these activities that could cause harm to the personnel or damage the equipment of the armed forces of the other side. Should an incident occur, both sides pledge to resolve it peacefully without the threat or use of force (i.e., they would not open fire). Communication channels, procedures and special signals are established, and a Joint Military Commission is created to consider the implementation of the agreement and possible ways to improve it.

Although this agreement focuses on the safety of the personnel and equipment of the two nations' armed forces, it should be seen essentially as a risk reduction measure, one that will force both sides to talk to each other and seek peaceful resolution to potentially dangerous activities and incidents. The fact that it applies to all military forces of the two nations is of interest because it demonstrates the utility of including naval forces in arms control efforts. Its essentially co-operative nature reflects the marked improvement in US–Soviet relations and demonstrates the value of military-to-military contacts. The PDMA Agreement covers a fairly narrow area of military operations but leaves room for future agreement on other activities, as stressed by the officials who negotiated and signed it. It is a useful model for other nations to follow and provides general principles that could become a standard for other nations to uphold.

Operational measures could also be designed to limit other activities that are determined to be dangerous or unwarranted. In paper 13 Patrick Howard describes one type of superpower naval 'strategic behaviour' that creates suspicion and concern about the intentions of the other side. It includes naval exercises or operations that instil fear of aggressive or offensive intentions. For example, sudden deployments of large numbers of attack or ballistic missile submarines from their home ports to sea—known as 'surging'—has been practised by both the USA and the USSR, with predictably disquieting effects. This is the sort of movement that might occur if a nation were intending to attack, or it might be a sign of an imminent crisis. Both nations could agree to regulate, curtail or cease such provocative activities.

Although this book does not treat the question of naval strategic arms reduction at length, something should be said about the operational considerations of the prospective START reduction of numbers of SSBNs to 20–30 for the USSR and 15–20 for the USA. This raises concern about ASW operations and crisis stability in a world with fewer SSBNs. In this regard US declarations that it will try to destroy Soviet SSBNs quickly in a conventional war are most disturbing.[36] The US view of military stability in a crisis relies on the invulnerability of its SSBNs, as Richard Wagner, the chief US official responsible for US nuclear weapon programmes, told Congress in 1986:

After completing 2393 strategic deterrent patrols since 1960, everything we know at every level of security classification convinces me that the Soviets cannot find our missile submarines now and will not be able to find them for the foreseeable future. . . . This survivability of our strategic submarines equates to stability in a crisis. Since our SSBNs cannot be attacked successfully, no enemy is likely to initiate aggression when his attack cannot deny our capability to retaliate effectively.[37]

This view should suggest to the USA the stabilizing value in not threatening the survivability of Soviet SSBNs, which is not served by publicly proclaiming the intent to destroy them early in a conventional war. Given US and Soviet interest in preserving the survivability of their strategic nuclear forces—one of the Bush Administration's highest priorities at the START negotiations[38]—the USA should recognize Soviet concerns on this topic and try to make it clear that the US Navy would not automatically try to sink Soviet SSBNs early in a war. It is difficult to imagine a workable operational measure that would achieve this, but perhaps a US declaration would be appreciated. US ASW exercises could also, on a unilateral basis, reflect a commitment to not practise pre-emptive operations against Soviet SSBNs.

Expanding existing agreements

Another possible approach to naval arms control would be to work within the framework of existing multilateral or bilateral agreements and international law—especially the UN Convention on the Law of the Sea (see paper 7)—to build upon successful regimes that can be updated or expanded to include current maritime concerns. Here the idea is that it may be possible for nations to go beyond previous commitments and improve certain regimes as applicable.

There are a number of arms control agreements relevant to naval forces which fit into this category; prominent among them are the 1972 Seabed Treaty and the 1959 Antarctic Treaty. In paper 10, Jozef Goldblat reviews the Seabed Treaty and examines some possibilities for further action within the framework of the treaty. In paper 1, Jan Prawitz outlines several other possibilities for enhancing certain existing agreements, such as including the sea areas south of latitude 60° South in the Antarctic Treaty and modernizing the laws of naval warfare, particularly the 1907 Hague Convention VIII relative to the Laying of Automatic Submarine Contact Mines.[39] Modernizing the laws of sea warfare was one of the recommendations of the UN study on the naval arms race prepared in 1985.[40] As explained by Ove Bring in paper 7, it would be important not to attach arms control efforts to the UNCLOS but to keep them in harmony with it. The most probable method for expanding existing agreements would be in the form of amendments, additional protocols, and so on.

Unilateral measures

Arms control is fundamentally a co-operative international venture, requiring at least two nations to work together. But unilateral measures can also play a significant role in the arms control process. Unilateral measures can encompass all categories of arms control—structural, operational and CBMs—as well as less formal measures. Although unilateral initiatives have sometimes been disparaged in the past, they are already an important component of security considerations and arms control and may be important to the success of future arms control efforts. The difficulty lies in designing and implementing such measures in a way that increases security, builds confidence and promotes reciprocal (or other) measures of self-restraint.

It should be remembered that nations make their decisions on foreign policy, strategy, doctrine and military force structure primarily on a unilateral basis (based on national interest, although sometimes in an alliance context). These decisions result in the military forces, capabilities and activities which are the subjects of arms control concern and effort. A unilateral decision not to develop or procure a certain weapon system or military capability, or to refrain from certain kinds of activity, may be simpler and more effective than relying on arms control efforts to redress the insecurities that would otherwise be produced. In other words, unilateral self-restraint is itself a kind of tacit arms control. So too are decisions to retire or remove military equipment or forces without replacing them.

Unilateral measures could be important in the naval arms control field for several reasons. The challenges to naval arms control described above make it complex and difficult to agree on structural and operational measures. Given these challenges, unilateral measures may be able and necessary to build confidence, reduce suspicion or demonstrate interest in or the feasibility of a certain measure. Where two nations have considerable asymmetries—in force structure or requirements—and cannot agree on the same arms control objective or procedure, unilateral measures may be able to facilitate the process. For example, the July 1989 SLCM verification experiment in the Black Sea was intended to examine the feasibility of verifying naval nuclear weapon limits, as well as to demonstrate Soviet interest in such limits and willingness to permit ship-board inspections.

Numerous unilateral measures have already been taken or are under consideration, notably in the East–West context. Since 1986 the USSR has proclaimed a major change in its foreign policy and military doctrine, and has produced considerable evidence to support this claim. In the naval sphere it has reduced its shipbuilding rate, reduced the tempo of its naval operations and scaled back the scope and number of its naval exercises. For economic reasons both the USSR and the USA have reduced their naval budgets and reduced the inventory of active warships, either by placing them in reserve or by retiring or scrapping them. In October 1988, for the first time, the USSR presented data to the UN General Assembly on the number and composition of its naval forces.[41] In December 1988 Soviet General Secretary Mikhail Gorbachev announced to the UN a unilateral reduction of Soviet military forces, including naval forces. Those reductions are being implemented, as are unilateral reductions in the forces of other WTO member states. In April 1989 it was revealed that the US Navy had decided to retire three non-strategic nuclear weapon systems ahead of schedule and without replacement (see paper 9). These are only some of the more prominent unilateral measures relevant to naval forces taken since 1985. They, along with other measures, have helped to demonstrate the seriousness of changes in the USSR, pointed to the economic constraints on both the USA and the USSR and highlighted opportunities for new measures of arms control.

Unilateral measures also play a notable role in several current arms control negotiations or discussions. At the US–Soviet START negotiations, the USA has proposed—as a way to deal with the difficult question of SLCM limits—that each side make a unilateral declaration of its planned inventory of long-range nuclear-armed SLCMs and declare that it will not exceed these plans. In May 1989, after the NATO internal compromise on the question of short-range nuclear force (SNF) modernization and negotiations on SNF missiles with the WTO, NATO challenged the USSR to reduce unilaterally its inventory of SNF missiles to the NATO level of Lance missiles.

Many unilateral measures are possible, although it is difficult to predict or suggest which ones might be most useful. They may make a considerable difference to calculations of the evolving security situation and should not be dismissed out of hand. It is also possible that unilateral measures may be developed in a bilateral context, as a new approach for seemingly intractable arms control problems. As suggested in paper 9, it might prove possible for nations to take complementary unilateral measures with a mutually acceptable CBM component to satisfy the other's concerns—an invited and negotiated assurance element to make such measures more effective and binding. The

SLCM issue at the START negotiations might be steered in this direction if verification problems prove unsolvable. In that case, both sides could not only declare their plans but also agree on measures to demonstrate their compliance with the declaration, possibly by permitting monitoring, inviting observers to relevant facilities, or other CBMs. This would represent a significant development of unilateral measures and arms control alike.

VI. Confidence-building measures

All arms control is a form of confidence-building measure and all arms control agreements contain confidence-building components, such as verification, mechanisms for resolving disputes, direct communication provisions, information exchange, and so on. Some agreements containing operational measures are particularly oriented towards building confidence in the behaviour of other nations' military forces—such as the Incidents at Sea agreements, the Stockholm Document and the PDMA Agreement—while other agreements are intended exclusively to be CBMs, with no structural or operational elements. Thus, CBMs are the broadest category of arms control.

This section focuses on confidence-building measures (also known as confidence- and security-building measures, or CSBMs) as a special category of arms control because they appear to be the most likely and promising type of measure in the field of naval arms control, at least in the near term. They may have the greatest potential for helping to improve political relations, enhance security and prepare the way for further and more difficult measures of arms control. When other arms control measures (structural or operational) are not feasible, nations that wish to improve their security through co-operative arms control efforts may be able to design CBMs that move them closer to a stable and reliable security regime. CBMs can be designed bilaterally or multilaterally, or can be implemented unilaterally as appropriate.

Both political and military factors contribute to the desire for confidence-building measures. When nations experience situations of insecurity, misunderstanding or misperception that are created by the military forces, capabilities—perceived or actual—or activities of another nation (or alliance), or because of insufficient information or knowledge about those forces and activities, there is a need for CBMs. In the extreme case it is important to prevent situations which, because of these doubts, miscalculations, misperceptions or misunderstandings, might lead to a crisis or even an armed conflict. CBMs can contribute to this process.

Various goals have been ascribed to confidence-building measures, ranging from reducing the possibility of surprise attack, to reducing the risk of war or crisis caused by accident, misperception or a failure of communication, to dissuading the threat or use of force in international politics, to fostering understanding of the forces, activities and intentions of nations. As stated in the CSCE Madrid mandate of September 1983, the Stockholm Conference was intended to adopt CSBMs designed to 'reduce the risk of military confrontation in Europe'.[42] The effect of these measures has been to increase openness, predictability and understanding, decrease suspicion and miscalculation, and overcome unwarranted mistrust caused by the secrecy and military capabilities of other nations. It is often noted that because nations cannot measure the intentions of their potential adversaries, they estimate military capabilities instead and assume the worst corresponding intentions—a process that has led the USA and the USSR, and many other nations, to exaggerated fears and over-armament. Thus, CBMs are intended to permit greater confidence in the non-aggressive nature of other nations' intentions and capabilities. The 1986 Stockholm Document states that its CSBMs are intended to 'give effect and expression to the duty of states to refrain from the threat or use of force in their mutual relations'.[43]

Types of CBM

Confidence-building measures can be distinguished on two levels: (a) agreed and explicit measures that are intended to build confidence through binding and formal arrangements, and (b) tacit or implicit measures that have a CBM effect, whether intended or not. Although this distinction is not absolute, it points to a type of CBM that is frequently overlooked or unappreciated. This means that CBMs are much more pervasive than is often recognized, and that there are many possibilities for creating new ones.

Examples of explicit CBMs include a wide variety of bilateral and multilateral arms control agreements, such as: the four bilateral agreements establishing direct communication links (DCLs) between the national leaders of the USSR and those of the USA (1963), France (1966), the UK (1967) and the Federal Republic of Germany (1989); the 1971 USA–USSR Agreement to Reduce the Risk of Outbreak of Nuclear War; the three bilateral Incidents at Sea agreements; the 1975 Helsinki Final Act; the 1986 Stockholm Document of the CDE; the 1987 USA–USSR Nuclear Risk Reduction Center Agreement; the 1988 USA–USSR Ballistic Missile Launch Notification Agreement; the 1989 USA–USSR PDMA Agreement, and so on, just to mention some prominent cases.

Tacit CBMs are of a more routine and informal nature than explicit ones and can take many forms. Virtually any co-operative international mechanism that produces increased understanding of, or confidence in, another nation—including direct communication and dialogue—can be a CBM, whether acknowledged or not. This conception of tacit CBMs broadens the scope of the term considerably, but it is meant to help focus on their potential for improving international relations and security in ways that are important to arms control and security at sea. Recent examples of such tacit East–West CBMs include summit meetings between national leaders; ministerial meetings concerning security issues; the current US–Soviet programme of military-to-military contacts, including reciprocal tours of previously inaccessible facilities;

exchanges of personnel and port visits; discussions of strategy, doctrine, force structure, planning and decision making; information and data exchanges, and so on. Obviously, some of these (and other) measures can be included in formal CBM agreements, but it is now common that they take place in the course of routine relations between the nations of East and West, sometimes in an informal manner.

In a press conference before his June 1989 visit to the USSR, Chairman of the Joint Chiefs of Staff Admiral Crowe told reporters that the purpose of the trip was to 'improve mutual understanding' and said that one theme he would discuss with his Soviet hosts is that 'secrecy does not work in the best interests of large powers'.[44] According to Crowe, 'openness really better suits and fits their purposes. That's one of the inspirations or incentives I have—that we are fully straightforward with each other as to what we want to do and what we can achieve and what we are all about'. In describing his first meeting with Akhromeyev in July 1988, Crowe reported that they 'clarified things . . . and attempted to brush away any misunderstandings. There is a built-in and a natural tendency which we both are subject to . . . to overestimate the strengths of our opponents'.[45] Establishing such a dialogue between military officials is a practical way of building confidence, an institutionalized tacit CBM.

As communication is vital to understanding, many forms of direct communication between government officials—military and civilian—can have a valuable confidence-building effect, both on an explicit and a tacit level. Bilateral agreements establishing direct communication links (or 'hot lines') provide the *possibility* for direct communication between national leaders. Incidents at Sea agreements assure the *regularity* of communication between naval leaders.

Direct communication can also be important as a CBM on the tacit level. In 1975 an international Maritime Symposium was convened in Stockholm, Sweden, bringing together for the first time the senior naval leaders of 16 nations from East and West.[46] As the programme intended, the participants were able to 'examine and discuss various forms of peaceful international cooperation and strengthen their relationships'. The first symposium was considered such a success that the Second Maritime Symposium was held in Helsinki, Finland, in 1978, with naval participants from the same 16 nations.[47] These symposia permitted the participants to explore areas of possible co-operation and, more importantly, an opportunity to meet each other informally. These were excellent examples of tacit CBMs. Participants of both symposia concluded that such gatherings were very useful and should be continued. It should be possible to re-establish such meetings on a regular basis.

Possible CBMs

In the area of agreed and explicit CBMs, considerable attention has been given to the idea of including naval forces in a CSBM regime of the CSCE process.

So far, naval forces and activities have been largely excluded from the CSCE, and it remains a devisive and unsolved issue—although of growing interest. In paper 13 Patrick Howard discusses naval CBMs from a CSCE perspective and considers the problems and possibilities involved in applying the Stockholm Document model of CSBM to naval forces. He explains that simply transferring the land-oriented Stockholm CSBMs to naval forces and activities is not appropriate because of the different nature of land and sea activities. Several related points are useful here.

It is clear that more thought needs to be given to the relationship between naval activities and security in Europe. The Madrid mandate that set the terms for negotiation at the Stockholm Conference effectively excluded 'independent' naval and air activities from the regime of CSBMs adopted in the Stockholm Document by its definition of the zone of application for the CSBMs. The relevant portions of this definition are as follows:

On the basis of equality of rights, balance and reciprocity, equal respect for the security interests of all CSCE participating States, and of their respective obligations concerning confidence- and security-building measures and disarmament in Europe, these confidence- and security-building measures will cover the whole of Europe as well as the adjoining sea area* and air space. They will be of military significance and politically binding and will be provided with adequate forms of verification which correspond to their content.

As far as the adjoining sea area* and air space is concerned, the measures will be applicable to the military activities of all the participating States taking place there whenever these activities affect security in Europe as well as constitute a part of activities taking place within the whole of Europe as referred to above, which they will agree to notify. Necessary specifications will be made through the negotiations on the confidence- and security-building measures at the Conference.

    * In this context, the notion of adjoining sea area is understood to refer also to ocean areas adjoining Europe.[48]

This definition has been interpreted differently by the NATO states and the WTO states. Importantly, it concedes that the essential details—'necessary specifications'—were left for later elaboration. It does not specifically exclude naval activities but includes them only under the stated conditions, including the functional link to 'activities taking place within the whole of Europe'. NATO holds that this approach, called the 'functional approach', serves to exclude all naval activities that do not meet the functional test. Nevertheless, the 'necessary specifications' remain to be negotiated. The Madrid mandate still serves as the mandate for the second stage of CSBM negotiations that commenced in Vienna in March 1989, and the CFE mandate specifically excludes naval forces and concentrates on forces *on land* in Europe.

These facts require several observations. First, naval activities in the adjoining sea area may not be functionally related to a particular land activity, but they are not independent of the security situation on land, which includes ground forces and activities. Naval forces basically exist to influence events on land—in a nation—to assist and complement or support land forces in war. NATO's entire maritime orientation is predicated on the need for reinforcement of military forces and equipment on land in Europe, thus requiring sealift and protection of shipping lanes. Ultimately, virtually all naval activity is focused on land activity—supporting the land campaign. Navies have no purpose which is unrelated to land objectives and are never truly independent of it. This must be remembered in the coming debate about naval CBMs. If a new security regime in Europe includes drastic reductions in the size, structure and capabilities of armed forces—as the CFE negotiations intend—the need for naval forces in the European context (and elsewhere) may also change considerably. This is why naval forces and activities must be included in the process of European security developments.

Second, given the current importance of naval forces to NATO and their potential impact on a war in Europe, naval forces cannot logically be excluded forever from the CSBM process. The reluctance to address navies comes from the NATO nations, particularly the USA. Naturally, there has been long-standing interest from WTO countries in naval CBMs—often expressed in proposals that are patently unacceptable to NATO. If future CSBMs are indeed designed on the basis of 'equal respect for the security interests of all CSCE participating States', then naval activities must be included in the overall picture. In the late 1980s some recognition of this idea has emerged from parliamentary members of NATO nations, as reflected in North Atlantic Assembly activities.[49]

Finally, it should be obvious that one cannot simply transfer the CDE model of CSBMs directly to sea; the Stockholm Document was designed for land forces and activities. But most of the principles could apply to naval activities if amended to suit the particular conditions at sea, or—as Jan Prawitz puts it in paper 1—'sailor-made' to fit the maritime environment. Several efforts have begun the hard work of defining and applying the Stockholm standard to naval activities, including such measures as: exchange of calendars of planned major naval activities, prior notification of such activities, invitation of observers to manoeuvres, possible limits on the number, size and duration of activities, and so on.[50] In March 1989 four WTO nations submitted a proposal on CSBMs, including some of these naval measures, to the Vienna CSBM negotiations convened under the CSCE.[51] It is possible to imagine a number of other measures that could appeal to both East and West, given the right conditions and balanced proposals. Much more work will be necessary in order to find a mutually satisfactory way of addressing naval forces and activities in a future CSBM regime, but logically it appears to be only a matter of time before a solution can be found.

It should be stressed that the foregoing ideas on CBMs are quite well established and accepted for land forces and activities, especially in the CSCE context. Information exchange is considered an essential element of both the CFE and the CSCE negotiations on CSBMs in Vienna. The 1989 CFE mandate states that the verification regime for an agreement 'will include on-site inspections as a matter of right and exchanges of information. Information shall be exchanged in sufficient detail so as to allow a meaningful comparison of the capabilities of the forces involved. Information shall also be exchanged in sufficient detail so as to provide a basis for the verification of compliance.'[52] Such a standard will require a great quantity of information to be exchanged and confirmed.

Furthermore, the 35-nation CSBM negotiations of the CSCE in Vienna are considering a wide variety of measures concerning information exchange, structured dialogue, and generally to 'build upon and expand the results already achieved at the Stockholm Conference'.[53] At the opening of the Vienna CSCE negotiations on CSBMs, the NATO states tabled a proposal containing 12 measures and the idea of a structured dialogue about:

military doctrine in relation to the posture and structure of conventional forces in the CDE zone, including *inter alia*: exchanging information of their annual military spending; exchanging information on the the training of their armed forces, including references to military manuals; [and] seeking clarification of developments giving rise to uncertainty, such as changes in the number and pattern of notified military activities.[54]

The NATO proposal seeks to establish a regular, detailed and confirmed exchange of information on forces and equipment 'on land in the zone', including: command organization, unit designations, personnel strengths and deployment locations, weapon systems and equipment assigned to units, aircraft units and strengths, and prior information on major weapon systems and equipment intended to be introduced into service within an agreed period. In short, the NATO proposal would make a vast array of CBMs a permanent part of the co-operative security regime in Europe, with one major exception—naval forces. These proposed measures could be applied in a modified form to naval forces without damaging NATO security and with a beneficial increase in understanding about the Soviet Navy. This is likely to be suggested at the negotiations.

One other possible tacit CBM involves increased direct contact between military personnel, such as the reciprocal visits of the US and Soviet Defence Ministers and Chiefs of Staff, naval port calls and future exchanges of personnel. Since 1988 the USSR has conducted or planned reciprocal port calls with the USA, the UK and the FRG. During his July 1988 visit to the USA Marshal Akhromeyev and Admiral Crowe initiated a three-year programme of military-to-military contacts and exchange visits, including naval personnel.[55] The US and Soviet armies agreed in 1988 to exchange cadets at their military academies.[56] Such exchanges would also be possible for naval cadets.

The potential contribution of military-to-military contacts as CBMs (explicit or tacit) was summarized by Admiral Crowe in his speech to a Soviet military academy during his visit to the USSR in June 1989:

If the political relationship between Moscow and Washington continues to improve, I see vast potential for more extensive military contacts than those of the past. They would be governed by a mutual intent to ensure crisis stability and confidence in each other's desires to avoid conflict. Through open and fundamental discussion about the nature of military strategy, the sharing of information on such issues as budgets and procurement schedules, the expanded exchanges of our personnel, the further development of regimes for verification of arms reductions, and the evolution of confidence- and security-building measures, we will be able to help our governments construct a more sustainable relationship overall, and enhance the prospects for avoiding conflict.[57]

Confidence-building measures clearly are the most likely form of naval arms control for the near term and thus potentially most significant. Although the USA and NATO have so far refused to negotiate explicit naval CBMs in any of the CSCE negotiations, they have already instituted a number of important tacit CBMs with the USSR, of which more are planned. The possibilities for naval CBMs have not been fully explored, although it is in the interests of all parties to do so.

VII. Conclusions and recommendations

As the above discussion suggests and papers 1–13 demonstrate, there are numerous possibilities for measures of arms control (including confidence-building) that include naval forces and activities. The challenge is to determine which possibilities are worth pursuing and how to pursue them. Ideally, this will require a full and open debate on naval forces and arms control.

To achieve significant and lasting security in East–West relations—particularly in Europe—requires moving from the politics of confrontation and military competition to a regime of co-operation and mutual confidence. Such a situation should accommodate the security concerns of all sides. Logically, this means that naval forces and activities should be included in the general East–West security and arms control framework.

Some Western concerns about the possible negative effects of certain naval arms control measures are understandable, reasonable and legitimate. Their blanket refusal to consider any naval arms control measure, however, is none of these. If NATO wishes to improve security and stability in Europe it must, at a minimum, be willing to listen to and try to accommodate the real security concerns of the WTO, including those about NATO naval forces.

For its part, WTO nations need to build confidence in the minds of the NATO leaders that its maritime concerns are legitimate and that its political intentions are acceptable. This will require the WTO to understand NATO concerns and accommodate them in its proposals for naval arms control and confidence-building. Proposals that would undermine the security of other nations only serve to reduce the security of all, and minimize the chances for constructive dialogue and understanding—let alone agreed arms control measures.

It should be recognized that a considerable amount of activity and momentum already exists in the field of arms control concerning naval forces and activities. Perhaps this activity will lead to a form of tacit arms control by default, resulting from increased confidence and self-restraint imposed by economic limitations. It is not clear whether the NATO allies of the USA can sustain political support for excluding naval forces from arms control indefinitely. In time, such circumstances could improve the environment for naval arms control.

The SIPRI Conference on Naval Forces and Arms Control reached four areas of general agreement, although this was not the intention of the conference.

1. There is a need to pursue naval non-strategic nuclear arms control that seeks reductions and maybe the elimination of stockpiles.

2. 'Neither confirm nor deny' policies concerning the presence of nuclear weapons aboard naval vessels are not necessary or helpful for international security. They cause unwanted political problems and obstruct naval arms control efforts. They should be changed or dropped.

3. Incidents at Sea agreements are important and useful. Additional bilateral agreements, and possibly also a multilateral regime, are worth pursuing.

4. Confidence-building measures appear to be the most likely and most useful arms control measures for naval forces and activities at present. They can help to create the proper climate for other arms control measures.

Thus it would seem appropriate to embark upon naval arms control first by exploring and pursuing CBMs that are of mutual interest. This would include both explicit and tacit measures such as those discussed above. Information exchange and dialogue about military doctrine appear to be two areas with great potential for building confidence and understanding. International meetings such as the 1975 and 1978 Maritime Symposia could provide similar benefits deriving from direct contact between the senior naval leaders of East and West. The 1990s are likely to provide many opportunities for CBMs

The following measures are recommended for consideration in the debate about naval forces and arms control. They are organized by type, without priority.

Structural measures: (*a*) include SLCMs in the START negotiations and either limit or eliminate them; (*b*) begin negotiations on non-strategic nuclear weapons, related to SLCMs, with global elimination as the objective;

Operational measures: (*c*) place permissive action links (PALs) on all naval nuclear weapons; (*d*) agree not to conduct sudden and unnotified surge exercises of submarines; (*e*) negotiate a multilateral incidents at sea regime; (*f*) give prior notification of naval activities above a certain agreed size and permit observers at exercises; (*g*) try to develop stabilizing rules of engagement;

Confidence-building measures: (*h*) resume regular (bi-annual) multinational East–West maritime symposia among senior naval leaders; (*i*) institute regular contacts among naval and defence officials to talk about doctrine, security and arms control; (*j*) institute detailed exchanges of information on naval force structure and activities, future procurement and retirement plans for naval vessels, major weapon systems and equipment; (*k*) alter or abandon 'neither confirm nor deny' policies;

Expand existing agreements: (*l*) extend the Seabed Treaty to cover all sea floor areas; (*m*) extend the zone of application of the Antarctic Treaty to include sea areas south of latitude 60° South; (*n*) modernize the laws of naval warfare, particularly the 1907 Hague Convention VIII.

This list is not exhaustive, but it provides enough recommended measures and ideas to serve as a basis for serious consideration of arms control and security at sea.

Notes and references

[1] *Towards a Better Use of the Ocean*, a SIPRI Monograph (Almqvist & Wiksell: Stockholm, 1969).

[2] The issues of expanding navies and naval responsibility for EEZs are discussed in Anthony, I., SIPRI, *The Naval Arms Trade*, a Strategic Issue Papers monograph (Oxford University Press: Oxford, 1989).

[3] These measures include the 1986 Stockholm Document on Confidence- and Security-Building Measures of the CSCE; the 1987 USA–USSR INF Treaty; the 1988 USA–USSR Ballistic Missile Launch Notification Agreement; the 1989 USA–USSR Agreement on the Prevention of Dangerous Military Activities; the progress and principle agreements in the START negotiations; the 35-nation CSCE Vienna follow-up meeting of 1986–89, including the negotiating mandate for the CFE; progress in the CFE negotiations since Mar. 1989; numerous summit meetings between Soviet President Gorbachev and the respective leaders of the USA, the UK, the Federal Republic of Germany and France; and an expanded programme of direct US–Soviet and British–Soviet military-to-military contacts. For texts of or relevant excerpts from the agreements, see annexe B.

[4] It may be useful to clarify the terminology surrounding CSCE activities. The 1983 Concluding Document of the Second CSCE follow-up meeting in Madrid—containing the so-called Madrid mandate—established the Conference on Confidence- and Security-Building Measures and Disarmament in Europe, the CDE. It was agreed that the first stage of the CDE was to be held in Stockholm from Jan. 1984, and it was commonly called the Stockholm Conference. The Stockholm Conference concluded in Sep. 1986 and adopted a Final Document containing CSBMs, commonly known as the Stockholm Document. The second stage of negotiations on CSBMs, which began in Vienna in Mar. 1989, does not use the same formal name as the CDE but is called the CSCE Negotiations on Confidence- and Security-Building Measures, also called the Vienna CSBMs negotiations. All these activities take place with all 35 participating CSCE states. The CFE negotiations, which also began in Vienna in Mar. 1989, are held between the 16 NATO nations and the 7 WTO nations, although still 'within the framework of the CSCE process'.

[5] For an explanation of this approaching obsolesence, see the companion book to this volume: Fieldhouse, R. and Taoka, S., SIPRI, *Superpowers at Sea: An Assessment of the Naval Arms Race*, a Strategic Issue Papers monograph (Oxford University Press: Oxford, 1989).

[6] The terms 'structural' and 'operational' are borrowed from R. E. Darilek's analysis of conventional arms control in Europe. See SIPRI, *SIPRI Yearbook 1987: World Armaments and Disarmament* (Oxford University Press: Oxford, 1987), pp. 339–54.

[7] The term 'confidence- and security-building measure' (CSBM) was used in the CDE and is the term generally used in the CSCE process. CBM and CSBM are used interchangeably in this book. For an analysis and the text of the Document of the Stockholm Conference, see *SIPRI Yearbook 1987* (note 6), pp. 339–69.

[8] In July 1988 the USA and the USSR agreed to a three-year programme of military-to-military contacts and exchanges. In July 1989, during the first visit of a Soviet Defence Minister (Yazov) to Britain, the UK and the USSR began to plan a similar programme.

[9] See Bertram, C., *The Future of Arms Control, Part II: Arms Control and Technological Change: Elements of a New Approach,* Adelphi Papers no. 146 (International Institute for Strategic Studies: London, 1978).

[10] See Watkins, J., 'The Maritime Strategy', US Naval Institute *Proceedings*, supplement, Jan. 1986, pp. 2–17, esp. pp. 11, 13.

[11] The missions, structures and capabilities of the US and Soviet navies are explained in Fieldhouse and Taoka (note 5).

[12] For example, despite considerable encouragement by SIPRI, the US Navy did not find it possible to send a representative to the Oct. 1987 SIPRI Conference on Naval Forces and Arms Control nor to contribute an official explanation of the US position on the subject. Additionally, before 1988 there were almost no official US statements available about naval arms control, because the Government chose not to address the issue publicly.

[13] The 1972 USA–USSR Incidents at Sea Agreement is an obvious exception but was not considered to be an arms control agreement by the USA at the time of its signing (see papers 11 and 12). Restrictions in the SALT I and SALT II agreements on strategic submarines and their ballistic missiles are also exceptions, but these are considered to be measures of strategic nuclear arms control and, again, not naval arms control. This argument depends somewhat on one's conceptual framework. If one accepts the broad conception of naval arms control introduced in section III, then clearly naval forces have been included in a number of important arms control efforts and agreements (see annexe B).

[14] Speech of William Burns, Director of the US Arms Control and Disarmament Agency (ACDA), to the First Committee of the UN General Assembly, 18 Oct. 1988, reprinted in 'US will continue hard bargaining for START', *Wireless File*, US Information Service, US Embassy, Stockholm, Sweden, 18 Oct. 1988, p. 8.

[15] Brooks, T. (Rear Admiral), Director of Naval Intelligence, testimony to House Armed Services Committee, 22 Feb. 1989, excerpted in 'Soviet Navy smaller, but more capable', *Wireless File*, US Information Service, US Embassy, Stockholm, Sweden, 27 Feb. 1989, p. 13.

[16] The agreed CFE negotiating mandate states *inter alia*: 'The subject of the negotiation shall be the conventional armed forces, which include conventional armaments and equipment, of the participants based on land within the territory of the participants in Europe from the Atlantic to the Urals. . . . Naval forces and chemical weapons will not be addressed.' See SIPRI, *SIPRI Yearbook 1989: World Armaments and Disarmament* (Oxford University Press: Oxford, 1989), pp. 420–26.

[17] Trost, C. A. H. (Admiral), 'The morning of the empty trenches: Soviet politics of maneuver and the US response', US Naval Institute *Proceedings*, Aug. 1988, p. 16.

[18] The House Armed Services Committee held a hearing on 27 Apr. 1989 with witnesses from the State Department, Defense Department and US Navy. The Navy testimony is reproduced in annexe A.

[19] See also the comments of Fleet Admiral Vladimir Chernavin, Commander-in-Chief of the Soviet Navy, in 'Chernavin responds', US Naval Institute *Proceedings*, Feb. 1989, pp. 75–79.

[20] These include his speeches in Vladivostok (July 1986), New Delhi (Nov. 1986), Murmansk (Oct. 1987), Belgrade (Mar. 1988) and Krasnoyarsk (Sep. 1988), as well as his interview with the Indonesian newspaper *Merdeka* (July 1987).

[21] Statement of Marshal Sergey Akhromeyev to the House Armed Services Committee, 21 July 1989, reprinted in *Wireless File*, US Information Service, US Embassy, Stockholm, Sweden, 22 July 1989, pp. 26–27.

22 Statement of Marshal Sergey Akhromeyev (note 21), p. 34.

23 For an excellent discussion of Soviet military objectives relating to nuclear weapons see MccGwire, M., *Military Objectives in Soviet Foreign Policy* (Brookings Institution: Washington, DC, 1987).

24 See Fieldhouse and Taoka (note 5), p. 109.

25 These problems are also discussed in Fieldhouse and Taoka (note 5), esp. pp. 5–13.

26 For a description of the different structures, missions and capabilities of the US and Soviet navies, see Fieldhouse and Taoka (note 5), esp. chapter 2.

27 US Congress, House Armed Services Committee, *The 600-Ship Navy and the Maritime Strategy*, Hearings, HASC No. 99-33 (US Government Printing Office: Washington, DC, 1986), p. 23.

28 For details of the so-called Verification and Stability Initiative, see the speech of Ambassador Richard Burt, chief US START negotiator, to the Conference on Disarmament in Geneva, 3 Aug. 1989, reprinted in 'US details verification measures for START treaty', *Wireless File*, US Information Service, US Embassy, Stockholm, Sweden, 4 Aug. 1989, pp. 5–10. See also the transcript of a news conference with Burt in Geneva, 20 June 1989, reprinted in 'More open approach seen on key START issue', *Wireless File*, US Information Service, US Embassy, Stockholm, Sweden, 21 June 1989, pp. 1–6.

29 See interview with Capt. Linton Brooks, deputy head of the US START Delegation, in Newman, R., 'US views START round as "businesslike", "productive"', *Wireless File*, US Information Service, US Embassy, Stockholm, Sweden, 31 July 1989, pp. 11–13.

30 'Joint Summit Statement, 10 December 1987', *Department of State Bulletin*, Feb. 1988, p. 13.

31 See Smith, R. J., 'Glasnost at sea: US visitors get to look at a Soviet missile cruiser', *International Herald Tribune*, 7 July 1989, p. 1; Smith, R. J., 'Americans examine a Soviet warhead', *Washington Post*, 6 July 1989, p. A19; Smith, R. J., 'Arms control advance cited in US, Soviet test', *Washington Post*, 7 July 1989, p. A22; Natural Resources Defense Council, 'News Release', 12 July 1989, with fact sheets on 'The Black Sea experiment' and 'The cruiser *Slava*'; and 'Soviet–American sea experiment on verification of sea-based nuclear weapons', joint statement on test results, Moscow, 8 July 1989, mimeo.

32 Interview with Brooks in Newman (note 29), p. 13. Concerning SLCMs, Capt. Brooks stated that, 'the United States believes that there is no way to verify such missiles' and that the USA opposes proposals that 'would disrupt the operation of navy ships on which our security and the security of NATO depends, and that would violate our long-standing policy of neither confirming nor denying the presence or absence of nuclear weapons' aboard ships.

33 In 1986 the Soviet Academy of Sciences and the NRDC sponsored a nuclear test monitoring and verification experiment, first in the USSR and then in the USA. Scientists from the USA were permitted to place seismometers at locations around the Soviet nuclear weapon test site near Semipalatinsk. Later, Soviet and US scientists installed similar equipment at locations around the US Nevada Test Site. The experiment eventually led to a joint seismic information exchange and helped establish the precedent of on-site monitoring, which has become central to the US–Soviet Joint Verification Experiment and negotiations on nuclear test limitation. See *SIPRI Yearbook 1989* (note 16), pp. 52–55.

34 Sweden submitted a working paper to the UN Disarmament Commission in May 1989 on a multilateral agreement for preventing incidents at sea. UN Document A/CN.10/121, 10 May 1989.

35 As this book was going to press, it was learned that France signed an Incidents at Sea Agreement with the USSR in Moscow on 4 July 1989. The text of the agreement was not available for publication in this book.

36 Admiral James Watkins, then Chief of Naval Operations, wrote in his public statement of the US Maritime Strategy that 'we will wage an aggressive campaign against all Soviet submarines, including ballistic missile submarines' and that during a conventional war allied 'antisubmarine warfare forces would continue to destroy Soviet submarines, including ballistic missile submarines'. Watkins, J. D., 'The Maritime Strategy', US Naval Institute *Proceedings*, supplement, Jan. 1986, pp. 11, 13.

[37] US Congress, HASC, *Hearings on Department of Energy National Security Programs Authorization Act for Fiscal Years 1987 and 1988*, HASC No. 99-55 (US Government Printing Office: Washington, DC, 1987), p. 21.

[38] See speech of Ambassador Richard Burt, 3 Aug. 1989 (note 28).

[39] In 1989 Sweden submitted a working paper to the UN General Assembly proposing a new draft protocol to Hague Convention VIII. UN Document A/CN.10/129, 16 May 1989.

[40] United Nations, *The Naval Arms Race*, Report of the Secretary-General, UN Study series no. 16, UN document A/40/535 (United Nations: New York, 1986), para. 322.

[41] On 18 Oct. Deputy Foreign Minister Vladimir Petrovsky told the First Committee that, as of 1 July 1988, the Soviet Navy had 4 aircraft-carriers, 376 submarines, 96 missile-equipped cruisers, destroyers and frigates, 174 escort frigates and minor surface combatants, 613 mine warfare vessels and 107 amphibious warfare vessels. These comprise a total of 1380 combat vessels. Additionally, the Soviet Navy had a total of 1142 combat aircraft and helicopters and 12 600 naval infantry troops (Marines). 'Moscou publie inventaire de ses forces navale', *Le Monde*, 20 Oct. 1988, p. 6. See also: Soviet Mission to the United Nations, Press Release no. 172, 18 Oct. 1988, pp. 9–10.

[42] The concluding document of the Second CSCE follow-up meeting in Madrid, 6 Sep. 1983, is commonly referred to as the 'Madrid mandate' because it contains the negotiating mandate of the Conference on Confidence- and Security-Building Measures and Disarmament in Europe. For relevant portions of the Madrid mandate, see SIPRI, *World Armaments and Disarmament: SIPRI Yearbook 1984* (Taylor & Francis: London, 1984), pp. 570–71.

[43] Stockholm Document, article 6. For the text of the Stockholm Document, see *SIPRI Yearbook 1987* (note 6), pp. 355–69.

[44] These remarks are paraphrased from Crowe's comments, and not reported as direct quotations. 'Crowe to visit USSR to build mutual understanding', *Wireless File*, US Information Service, US Embassy, Stockholm, Sweden, 6 June 1989, pp. 31–32.

[45] See note 44.

[46] Representatives were from Belgium, Canada, Denmark, the FRG, Finland, France, the GDR, Iceland, Ireland, the Netherlands, Norway, Poland, Sweden, the USSR, the UK and the USA. See the 'Report of the Maritime Symposium: Stockholm, 9–13 June 1975', with enclosures, prepared by the Royal Swedish Navy, mimeo, Stockholm, Sep. 1975.

[47] See 'Report of the Second Maritime Symposium: Helsinki, 16–19 May 1978', prepared by the Finnish Navy, Helsinki, Nov. 1978.

[48] The Madrid mandate text is reprinted verbatim as the definition of the zone of application for CSBMs in the Stockholm Document, Annex I. See *SIPRI Yearbook 1987* (note 6), pp. 367–68.

[49] For example, North Atlantic Assembly Resolution 200 on Confidence-Building Measures of 13 Dec. 1988, AF 261, SA (88)15, recommends several naval CBMs, including point 14, which 'urges the North Atlantic Alliance to explore naval confidence-building measures'. See also North Atlantic Assembly, Defence and Security Committee, *General Report on Alliance Security: Towards Conventional Stability in Europe; and The US Maritime Strategy and Crisis Stability at Sea*, AF 216, MC (88)6 (North Atlantic Assembly: Brussels, Nov. 1988), esp. pp. 41–46. Karsten Voigt (FRG), the rapporteur who prepared the report, concludes that 'arms control at sea needs to be treated with much more seriousness by NATO authorities than is currently the case'; see p. 46.

[50] See, for example, Foundation for International Security, 'Moscow conversations on the limitations of naval activities and confidence building measures at sea', Draft Report, Mar. 1989, unpublished mimeo, esp. appendix I. The Foundation for International Security, a private group in the UK, has worked with an international group of naval experts from the UK, the USA and the USSR in an informal search for common ground on questions of co-operative measures of security and arms control at sea. See also, Grove, E., 'Conventional arms control in Europe: the naval dimension', paper presented to the International Institute for Strategic Studies Conference on Arms Control, Barnett Hill, UK, 4 May 1989.

[51] The proposal, submitted on 9 Mar. 1989 by Bulgaria, Czechoslovakia, the GDR and Hungary at the opening of the negotiations, includes 11 naval CSBMs; see CSCE Document CSCE/WV.2. Romania later endorsed the proposal.

[52] Mandate for Negotiation on Conventional Armed Forces in Europe, 10 Jan. 1989, reprinted in *SIPRI Yearbook 1989* (note 16), p. 421.

[53] Concluding Document of the 1986–89 Vienna CSCE follow-up meeting, 10 Jan. 1989, excerpted in *SIPRI Yearbook 1989* (note 16), p. 419.

[54] US Department of State, 'Strengthening stability through openness,' May 1989, excerpted in 'Optimism, realism, prudence to guide CSBM approach', *Wireless File*, US Information Service, US Embassy, Stockholm, Sweden, 9 May 1899, p. 6.

[55] See Almond, P., 'Soviet ends tour, provides no answers', *Washington Times*, 12 July 1988, p. 5.

[56] 'Swap planned for US and Soviet cadets', *International Herald Tribune*, 4–5 Feb. 1989, p. 2.

[57] Speech of Admiral William Crowe to the Voroshilov General Staff Military Academy, Moscow, 14 June 1989, reprinted in 'Crowe says USSR still has powerful military', *Wireless File*, US Information Service, US Embassy, Stockholm, Sweden, 14 June 1989, p. 11.

Part II
The case for naval arms control

Paper 1. Naval arms control: history and observations

Jan Prawitz

Swedish Ministry of Defence, Stockholm, Sweden

I. Introduction

While disarmament negotiations held since World War II have not managed to halt the arms race between the two major military alliances, nearly all branches of military activity, with one important exception, have in one way or another been addressed at such negotiations. Naval activities and forces have attracted little attention since 1945 compared to their role in world military affairs.

In the mid-1980s a new interest was expressed in the United Nations in the possibility of including naval arms and forces in the discussion of possible measures of confidence-building, arms control and disarmament. The adoption in December 1982 of the new Convention on the Law of the Sea provided both the political and the legal basis for such a discussion. Naval forces are part of military forces in general and should therefore be considered in that general context. Special legal consideration of measures to be applied at sea may also be necessitated by the different legal status of sea areas as compared to land areas.

In this paper a brief account is given of some of the naval arms control measures agreed before World War II and the few agreements concluded after 1945, as a background to consideration of basic principles for naval applications of the disarmament process.[1]

A number of arms control agreements relating to naval forces were concluded before World War II. Among them were the 1922 Washington Treaties and the 1930 and the 1936 London Treaties, all agreed between the five major naval powers at that time (the United States of America, the British Empire, France, Italy and Japan). These were the 'Strategic Arms Limitation Talks' of that time. Numerous regional restrictions in the maritime domain have also been agreed during the past 150 years.

Twenty-seven pre-1945 agreements on demilitarization and other arms control and confidence-building measures applying to the maritime domain were listed in a 1986 expert report prepared for the Secretary-General of the United Nations.[2] Some of them are referred to here, and an expanded list is reproduced in appendix 1A. The formal texts of the pre-1945 treaties and agreements referred to in this paper can, if not otherwise indicated, be found in the source-books also listed in this appendix.

Among these old laws and treaties, some are still in force and play an important role today; others went out of force or have been made obsolete by events. Some never entered into force but nevertheless played a role in the formation of international law.

II. The pre-World War I period

The classical example of an old treaty which is still in force but truly obsolete in a political sense is the Rush–Bagot Agreement of 1817 between the United States and Great Britain (relating to Canada) on the limitation of naval forces on the North American Great Lakes. The agreement limited the naval forces on each side to a few vessels of limited size and with limited arms. It prescribed that 'all other armed Vessels on these Lakes shall be forthwith dismantled, and that no other Vessels of War shall be there built or armed'. The Rush–Bagot Agreement is thus an early example of both disarmament and quantitative and qualitative arms control.[3]

The Treaty of Paris of 1856 marked the end of the Crimean War. It provided for two elements relevant to naval forces.

One was the neutralization of the Black Sea and demilitarization of its shores. Naval ships of both the Black Sea coastal states and other states were banned from the waters and ports of the Black Sea. However, according to a special protocol between Russia and Turkey, a few ships of limited size could be maintained 'for the service of their coasts'. Russia and Turkey were also obliged 'not to establish or to maintain upon that coast any Military-Maritime Arsenal'. This part of the treaty remained in force until 1871, when it was replaced by a new regime resulting from the Franco-Prussian War of 1870–71.

The other naval element was a provision that the Åland Islands in the Baltic Sea 'will not be fortified and that no military or naval establishment will be maintained or set up in them'. This part of the treaty was respected until World War I.

One month later, the signatories of the Treaty of Paris adopted the 1856 Declaration of Paris respecting Maritime Law, which replaced the *Consolato del Mare* that had, for the most part, been generally recognized since the Middle Ages. The Declaration of Paris abolished privateering and required that blockades had to be effective—not merely declared—to be considered binding.[4]

In Latin America, border disputes between Argentina and Chile were frozen by arms control agreements between the two states. As early as 1881 they agreed on demilitarization of the Magellan Straits.

In the Pactos de Mayo of 1902, the two countries agreed not to receive warships under construction for them, to reduce existing fleets over a period of one year and not to acquire new vessels for five years unless notified 18 months in advance. Argentina withdrew from the agreement in 1972.

Among the 13 Hague Conventions of 1907, 8 referred to rules of sea warfare: Convention VI relative to the Status of Enemy Merchant Ships at the Outbreak of Hostilities; Convention VII relative to the Conversion of Merchant Ships into Warships; Convention VIII relative to the Laying of Automatic Submarine Contact Mines; Convention IX respecting Bombardment by Naval Forces in Time of War; Convention X for the Adaptation to Maritime Warfare of the Principles of the Geneva Convention of 22 August 1864 on Wounded, Sick and Shipwrecked in War; Convention XI relative to certain Restrictions with regard to the Exercise of the Right of Capture in Naval War; Convention XII relative to the Creation of an International Prize Court (never entered into force); and Convention XIII concerning the Rights and Duties of Neutral Powers in Naval War.

The Hague Conventions were an important step in the development of the laws of sea warfare, based on the humanitarian principles developed in the second half of the nineteenth century.

A further step was taken by the 1909 London Declaration concerning the Laws of Naval War, which codified rules on blockades, contraband and prizes. While the Declaration never entered into force, it did, however, play an important role in developing customary international law.

The Hague Conventions, while in many instances technically obsolete, are still in force and have essentially not been replaced by more modern rules. One exception is that, among the four Geneva Conventions of 12 August 1949, the second—on the Amelioration of the Condition of Wounded, Sick and Shipwrecked Members of Armed Forces at Sea—modernizes Hague Convention X. When the humanitarian laws of war were again modernized in 1977, the Additional Protocols to the 1949 Geneva Conventions did not fully address the issues of sea warfare.

Thus, the 1907 Hague Conventions would be the essential point of departure for a possible modernization of the laws of sea warfare.

III. The inter-war period

During the 21 years between the two world wars, a number of international arms control agreements included naval applications. The most important agreements were those concluded in Washington in 1922 and in London in 1930 and 1936.

The 1922 Washington Treaty Limiting Naval Armament prescribed in detail the number and size of capital ships that could be retained by each party and the kind of arms those ships could carry. These rules essentially entailed a freeze, although provisions were made for replacements of ships. The treaty also prescribed a freeze on the parties' fortifications and naval bases in their Pacific Ocean possessions.

A second treaty was simultaneously agreed in Washington on the Use of Submarines and Noxious Gases in Warfare, providing protection to 'the lives of neutrals and non-combatants at sea in time of war'. However, this treaty never entered into force because France failed to ratify it.

The parties to the 1922 Washington Treaties agreed in 1930 to further limitations and reductions of their naval arms, resulting in the 1930 London Treaty, which also included a confirmation of the rules of submarine warfare established in the second 1922 Washington Treaty. It was agreed that the London Treaty would remain in force until the end of 1936.

At the end of that period a third treaty—the 1936 London Treaty on Limitation and Reduction of Naval Armaments—was negotiated. However, considerable difficulties emerged among the parties, and the treaty remained in force for only two years, at which point the international order collapsed into World War II.

Several other agreements were reached in connection with the Washington and London Treaties. A Greek–Turkish Naval Protocol of 1930 provided for six months' prior notification of the acquisition of naval armaments. A similar Naval Protocol to be applied in the Black Sea was agreed one year later between the Soviet Union and Turkey. For the purpose of extending the 1936 London Treaty to additional countries, Great Britain entered into agreements on limitation and exchange of information with Germany and the Soviet Union in 1937, and with Poland and the Nordic countries in 1938. This treaty structure collapsed when World War II broke out in 1939.

A few agreements from this period, with subregional geographical applications, are still in force. One is the 1920 Paris Treaty concerning the Archipelago of Spitzbergen in the Arctic Ocean prohibiting 'the establishment of any naval base in the territories specified' and prescribing that the archipelago, which belongs to Norway, 'may never be used for warlike purposes'. This treaty applies to an area which was considered icy and remote at the time but which today is located in the centre of strategic confrontation, thus being more important now than then.

Another treaty, agreed within the League of Nations in 1921, is the Convention relating to the Non-fortification and Neutralization of the Åland Islands in the Baltic Sea, based on the 1856 Treaty of Paris mentioned above. The treaty provides for a regime of demilitarization and limited access for naval vessels into the waters of the treaty zone.

The 1936 Montreux Convention is a most important agreement which regulates the transit of ships in and out of the Black Sea through the Turkish Straits. The treaty prescribes limitations on the number, size and kind of warships transiting the Straits. The Black Sea states enjoy somewhat more generous rules than other states: they can send capital ships other than aircraft-carriers of any size through the straits, while other states can transit only ships not exceeding 10 000 tons each. Except for forces of Black Sea states, the peacetime maximum aggregate tonnage of foreign naval ships in transit may not exceed 15 000 tons. The convention is still in force, and its provisions are observed by all parties.[5]

IV. The post-World War II period

The relative lack of interest after World War II in arms control related to naval forces is not due to a lack of appreciation of their importance but rather to the fact that the legal regime at sea was until recently not clearly defined. There was an attempt during the Third United Nations Law of the Sea Conference (1973–82) to raise the question of limiting the military use of the vast high sea areas of the world, considered to be the common heritage of mankind. However, the issue was considered to fall under the general mandate of the Geneva Disarmament Conference, but the conference considered it difficult to deal with naval issues before the Third United Nations Conference on the Law of the Sea had defined the legal regime of the sea. Without such a legal clarification it would be unclear who would be entitled to agree on what.

Despite this difficulty, a few agreements regarding naval forces and armaments were reached after 1945—bilaterally between the two superpowers, multilaterally and regionally.

Bilateral agreements

In 1972, the USA and the USSR concluded two treaties—the Anti-Ballistic Missile (ABM) Treaty and the SALT I Agreement—which include some provisions with maritime relevance.

According to the ABM Treaty (Article V.1), 'each party undertakes not to develop, test or deploy ABM systems or components which are sea-based'. According to the SALT I Agreement (Article III), the parties 'undertake to limit submarine-launched ballistic missile (SLBM) launchers and modern ballistic missile submarines to the numbers operational and under construction on the date of signature'. It was understood in a separate protocol that the USA would have no more than 710 SLBM launchers and 44 SSBNs, and that the USSR would be permitted to have slightly more, or 950 SLBM launchers and 62 SSBNs (see annexe B).

In anticipation of a second, more limiting SALT treaty, the SALT I Agreement was to expire after five years, that is, in 1977. Its provisions have nevertheless been observed.

In 1979 the USA and the USSR concluded the SALT II Treaty, limiting the aggregate number of intercontinental ballistic missiles (ICBMs), SLBMs, heavy bombers and air-to-surface ballistic missiles (ASBMs) to 2400 on each side on the date of entry into force and to 2250 from 1 January 1981. The aggregate number of MIRVed ICBMs, SLBM launchers and ASBMs was limited to 1200 on each side. SLBMs would not carry more re-entry vehicles than the maximum number flight-tested before the agreement. In a separate protocol the parties undertook not to deploy cruise missiles capable of a range in excess of 600 km on sea-based launchers. The protocol was agreed to remain in force until the end of 1980.

The SALT II Treaty was intended to remain in force until the end of 1985, but was never ratified and thus did not enter into force. However, the relevant parts of its central provisions were observed for a long time, and many of them are still observed today (see annexe B).[6]

In 1972 a confidence-building measure was also agreed bilaterally—the Agreement on the Prevention of Incidents on and over the High Seas (see annexe B). The agreement includes rules of behaviour at sea complementing the International Regulations for Preventing Collisions at Sea (Rules of the Road). One year later an additional protocol was adopted prohibiting simulated attacks on non-military ships. The implementation of this agreement is considered a great success (see paper 11).

In 1986 Britain and the USSR concluded a similar bilateral prevention of incidents at sea agreement, as did the Federal Republic of Germany and the USSR in 1988 (see annexe B), and France and the USSR in 1989.[7]

In 1988 the USA and the USSR agreed on another confidence-building measure—the Ballistic Missile Launch Notification Agreement—which provides for at least 24 hours' pre-notification of launches of intercontinental ballistic missiles and submarine-launched ballistic missiles (see annexe B).[8] The agreement is an addition to earlier treaties aimed at reducing the risk of outbreak of nuclear war by misinterpretation, miscalculation or accident, and to the 1972 USA–USSR Incidents at Sea Agreement.

In June 1989, the USA and the USSR signed an Agreement on the Prevention of Dangerous Military Activities. This confidence-building agreement extends the principle of the incidents at sea agreements to cover all US and Soviet military forces, including navies and in their territorial waters. Both sides agreed to try to prevent incidents from occurring and to resolve them peacefully should they occur. The agreement provides for direct communications between the ranking officers on the scene (see annexe B).

Multilateral agreements

Two multilateral treaties relevant to the maritime domain were agreed after 1945. One is the 1963 Partial Test Ban Treaty prohibiting nuclear weapon test explosions or any other nuclear explosions, *inter alia,* under water, including territorial waters or high seas, at any place under the jurisdiction or control of the parties (see annexe B).[9]

The other is the 1971 Seabed Treaty (see paper 10) in which the parties undertake not to emplant or emplace any nuclear weapons or any other types of weapon of mass destruction on the seabed and the ocean floor and in the subsoil thereof beyond 12 nautical miles off their coast (see annexe B).[10]

Regional agreements

A relevant regional agreement is the 1959 Antarctic Treaty providing for the demilitarization of 'the area south of 60° South Latitude, including all ice shelves' (see annexe B). There is no restriction, however, of rights under international law on the high seas within the area (Article VI). The treaty outlines a unique system of verification prescribing, *inter alia,* that *all ships* 'at points of discharging or embarking cargoes or personnel in Antarctica, shall be open at all times to inspection' (Article VII.3).

Another relevant regional agreement is the 1967 Treaty for the Prohibition of Nuclear Weapons in Latin America, also known as the Tlatelolco Treaty.[11] Once the treaty fully enters into force, the area of its application will include large portions of the Atlantic and the eastern Pacific Oceans (see annexe B).

The area of application of the Tlatelolco Treaty encompasses the territories of the parties, including their territorial waters, over which they exercise sovereignty in accordance with their own legislation (Article 3).When the treaty has entered into force for all states and territories in Latin America and the Caribbean, the zone of application will be the entire area that is situated roughly between the latitudes 35°N and 60°S and the line stretching between longitudes 115° to 150°W in the Pacific and 50° to 20°W in the Atlantic.

According to Additional Protocol II of the Treaty, the nuclear weapon states will respect the status of the nuclear weapon-free zone and not deploy nuclear weapons within it, including its sea areas. However, all nuclear weapon powers, when acceding to the treaty, filed reservations with slightly differing formulations regarding the extension of arms control measures into sea areas beyond the 12-nautical mile territorial water limit, referring to 'recognized international law'. Some Latin American states claim territorial waters of up to 200 nautical miles' breadth.

In 1985 the states members of the South Pacific Forum agreed to establish a nuclear-free zone in the South Pacific, known as the Treaty of Rarotonga (see annexe B).[12] The zone is the second in a densely inhabited area[13] and extends from the border of the Latin American zone in the east to the west coast of Australia and from the Antarctic area in the south to the equator (and even above it for some areas of Kiribati) in the north (Article I and Annex I). The zonal perimeter encompasses vast sea and ocean areas, but the treaty does not limit any existing 'freedom of the seas', including innocent and transit passage through territorial and archipelagic waters of zonal states (Article 2). Its provisions apply to the 'territories' of its parties and leave out the sea areas beyond territorial limits. Two provisions apply 'anywhere' in the zone, however. Dumping of radioactive waste (Article 7) and testing of nuclear explosive devices (Protocol 3, Article 1) are prohibited throughout the entire zonal area. Nuclear weapon powers are invited to subscribe to three protocols concerning inclusion of dependencies, guarantees and testing. Among them, China and the USSR have acceded to the guarantee and testing protocols. The three Western nuclear weapon powers (France, the USA and the UK) have chosen not to accede to the protocols for the time being.

The Conference on Security and Co-operation in Europe

The negotiations on confidence- and security-building measures (CSBMs) at the Conference on Security and Co-operation in Europe (CSCE) have clearly focused on military issues on land. The Final Act of the CSCE, signed in Helsinki in 1975, contains a provision for prior notification, 21 days in advance, of 'major military manoeuvres exceeding a total of 25 000 troops, independently or combined with any possible air or naval components (in this context the term "troops" includes amphibious and airborne troops)'. There was no provision for prior notification of independent naval exercises.

At the second CSCE follow-up meeting in Madrid (1980–83), agreement was reached in 1983 on the mandate (the so-called Madrid mandate[14]) for the following Stockholm Conference on Confidence- and Security-building Measures and Disarmament in Europe (CDE), stipulating that agreed measures would 'cover the whole of Europe as well as the adjoining sea area and air space'. The extension of the adjoining sea area was defined in functional rather than geographic terms. Agreed measures would apply to military activities in the adjoining sea area 'whenever these activities affect the security in Europe as well as constitute a part of activities taking place within the whole of Europe'. Again, independent naval exercises were not covered.

At the Stockholm Conference (1984–86), negotiations on the issue of CSBMs applying to independent naval activities were postponed to a later stage. However, special provisions were worked out for amphibious landings. While the agreement reached, the Stockholm Document,[15] generally provides for prior notification of military activities exceeding 13 000 troops and invitation of observers to such activities exceeding 17 000 troops, special, strict provisions apply in the case of amphibious landings with corresponding limits of 3000 and 5000 troops, respectively.

The functional definition of the concept 'adjoining sea areas' implies, for example, that prior notification of military activities on land in Europe would also include related naval activities. Depending on the circumstances, activities in rather distant waters might then be involved. However, this formula would not require notification of independent naval activities that do not involve amphibious landings, however large they are or however close to European land areas they operate.

V. The Law of the Sea Convention

While the prime objective of the current Law of the Sea Convention is to provide an agreed legal order for the peaceful use of the world's seas and oceans, many of the rules related to navigation, if properly implemented, would also promote confidence- and security-building between states. This is so despite the fact that the concept of 'freedom of the high seas',[16] presented as early as in 1609 in Hugo Grotius' work *Mare Liberum,*[17] was introduced in order to provide for the opposite of arms control: its aim was arms non-control at sea.

After long negotiations, the United Nations Convention on the Law of the Sea (UNCLOS) was signed at Montego Bay, Jamaica, on 10 December 1982 (see annexe B for relevant articles of the UNCLOS). From that date, there has been a firm legal base for discussing arms control and disarmament at sea. From that date, there should be no excuse for not addressing arms control and disarmament issues in the maritime domain.

A few major Western powers did not sign the UNCLOS, but their reason for not doing so was not disagreement over security-related provisions in the convention but was linked to the regime for exploitation of economic resources on the ocean floor.[18] There should thus be general agreement on security-related provisions, especially because the majority of those provisions are customary law as much as treaty law, and thus apply to all states of the world.

According to the UNCLOS, a coastal state exercises full and exclusive jurisdiction in its *internal waters* only, that is, inside a coast-line perimeter, the so-called baseline. A coastal state further exercises full jurisdiction in its *territorial sea* extending up to 12 nautical miles from the baseline, except over 'innocent passage' by ships of other states. 'Innocent' is defined in some detail in Article 19 of the UNCLOS. A coastal state has jurisdiction over the exploitation of natural resources in its *exclusive economic zone* extending up to 200 nautical miles from the baseline. A coastal state has no jurisdiction in *the high seas*, that is, the area beyond territorial waters and economic zones. An archipelagic state may establish *archipelagic waters* within baselines surrounding all islands of the state, in which a jurisdiction similar to that in territorial seas applies.

All states have the right of *innocent passage* for their ships in the territorial sea of other states and in archipelagic waters, and of *transit passage* in international straits[19] and are subject to virtually no military restraints in economic zones and on the high seas.

Thus, because of the different legal regimes, there is a significant difference between applying arms control to sea areas as compared to land areas. Almost all land is subject to the jurisdiction of one state, a well-known exception being the demilitarized area of Antarctica. As a consequence, adversary military forces on land are geographically separated from each other in peacetime. Naval forces of different states, however, may mix all over the sea, on the surface, in the water, on the seabed and sometimes under the ice. Indeed, they frequently do so.

The UNCLOS flatly declares that 'the high seas shall be reserved for peaceful purposes' (Article 88), that the international seabed area 'shall be open to use exclusively for peaceful purposes' (Article 141) and that 'marine scientific research shall be conducted exclusively for peaceful purposes' (Article 240.a). This strong wording is considerably conditioned in Article 301, which stipulates that states 'shall refrain from any threat or use of force against the territorial integrity or political independence of any State, or in any other manner inconsistent with the principles of international law embodied in the Charter of the United Nations'. Therefore, military activities consistent with the Charter, including the 'inherent right of individual or collective self-defence' (UN Charter, Article 51), would not be prohibited under the UNCLOS.

VI. The UN expert study

The adoption of the UNCLOS in 1982 apparently lifted the long-time taboo on discussion of naval arms control. One year later, in December 1983, the United Nations General Assembly initiated an expert study on the naval arms race in order to 'facilitate the identification of possible areas for disarmament and confidence-building'.[20] After considering the experts' report, in 1985 the General Assembly initiated a new process of deliberations which began in the UN Disarmament Commission in May 1986 and which continues to this day.

The UN report summarizes in five categories the proposals for naval arms control and confidence-building that had been put forward by 1985: (*a*) quantitative restraints; (*b*) qualitative and technological restraints; (*c*) geographical and/or mission restraints; (*d*) confidence-building measures; and (*e*) modernization of the laws of sea warfare.

As a matter of principle, the UN report assigned no priorities among the listed measures, but it stressed the general importance of nuclear weapon-related issues. It recommended four measures for early consideration:[21] (*a*) multilateralization of the 1972 USA–USSR Agreement on the Prevention of Incidents on and over the High Seas; (*b*) continuation of negotiations to widen the scope of the Seabed Treaty in accordance with its Article V; (*c*) extending the nuclear weapon-free regime of the Antarctic Treaty to sea areas within its area of application (south of 60° South); and (*d*) modernization of the laws of sea warfare.

It is obvious that drafting policies for maritime arms control for the future cannot appreciably draw on historical experience. There are several new factors that make the problems of today fundamentally different from those that existed before 1945, including nuclear weapons and propulsion; command, control and communications; electronics; the increasing independence of naval forces from weather conditions; submarine and offshore technology; and the Law of the Sea. This general observation has one important exception, however: modernization of the laws of sea warfare will have to be based also on international law adopted long ago.

The report of the UN experts concluded that there would be two basic objectives for action. The first would be the achievement by negotiation of effective measures of nuclear and conventional arms control. The other, no less important objective would be for naval forces and capabilities to contribute to effective ocean-management policies or peaceful uses of the seas.

As to the arms control aspect, the report stated, however, that because of the special problems arising from treating naval armaments separately from land forces—which could be required because of the very different legal regimes of land and sea areas—negotiating arms control and disarmament in the maritime domain should be governed by four 'axioms':

First, disarmament measures should be balanced and should not diminish the security of any state. But as naval forces are not independent of other military forces, they should be considered in their general military context. There is no such thing as an independent naval balance or parity. Disarmament measures in the maritime field should thus be balanced in that general sense.

Second, this fact combined with the very differing geographical situations of states could require multilateral measures of restriction for naval forces and weapons to be numerically asymmetrical in order to maintain an overall military situation in balance.

Third, because of the universal nature of the Convention on the Law of the Sea, such measures should not take the legal form of amendments to the Convention. They should be embodied in separate legal instruments in harmony with the Convention.

Fourth, as in all arms control and disarmament, appropriate verification and complaints procedures are essential for the proper implementation of agreed measures.[22]

The axioms have later been confirmed politically in the discussions of the UN Disarmament Commission.[23] These axioms were formulated in response to concerns that the military effect of naval arms control measures could be unbalanced because one of the two major military alliances—NATO—is by far more dependent on sea lanes of communication than is the other—the WTO—and that such measures could infringe generally on the freedom of navigation. The axioms could be said to accommodate naval arms control issues to other issues of arms control elaborated after 1945.

VII. Categories of possible objectives and measures

As there are a variety of naval forces deployed for a variety of purposes, there should also be a variety of objectives to be pursued by arms control and disarmament measures in the maritime domain.

An attempt is made below to organize different arms control objectives into broad categories of possible measures, based on how various issues have previously been referred to in existing negotiating forums (e.g., in the CSCE and the CD).

1. *Limitation and reduction of sea-based strategic nuclear weapons.* Bilateral negotiations between the USA and the USSR regarding strategic nuclear weapons—first SALT and then the Strategic Arms Reduction Talks (START)—have been held since the Non-Proliferation Treaty was concluded in

1968 and have included consideration of sea-based weapons as well. The purpose has been to establish a more stable central balance at a lower level of forces. There were few special naval problems in the past. When sea-based cruise missiles and verification related to naval forces are taken into account, such problems as distinguishing between nuclear and conventionally armed missiles and of immunities of naval vessels will have to be addressed.

2. *General prohibition of carrying nuclear weapons on board naval vessels except on board specifically recognized units*. The purpose would be to avoid actual or suspected nuclearization of routine patrols and the nuclearization of possible incidents at sea. Such a measure would require that vessels with nuclear weapons on board could be distinguished from those without nuclear weapons on board and that the nuclear weapon powers abandon their present policy of neither confirming nor denying the presence or absence of any nuclear weapons on board any specific ship at any specific time.

3. *Limitations of blue-water forces of the major maritime power blocs, their amphibious forces and special military transportation vessels*. The purpose would be to provide a maritime contribution to an attempt to achieve a general balance between the major military alliances at a lower level and to limit the overall capabilities for gunboat diplomacy and overseas power projection. It is dubious whether such limitations will have much value for the international situation at large. It is also true that even dramatic measures of this kind would not significantly help the small and medium-sized coastal states, because naval forces of major powers, even if substantially reduced, could during a limited period of time easily be concentrated for 'gunboat diplomacy', power projection and aggression directed against an overseas neighbour. For smaller coastal states, confidence- and security-building measures would be of more interest.

4. *Confidence- and security-building measures*. These could include, for example, exchange of information on naval forces and activities; limitation of the cruising of warships and of naval and amphibious activities, in terms of numbers, mode of operation, areas and time; special codes of conduct for ships with nuclear weapons on board; special codes of conduct for submarines and other submerged activities; and limited or full demilitarization on a regional or subregional basis. Ships with nuclear weapons on board—possibly distinguished by means of a special flag or other mark, while being subject to possible CSBM restrictions—could also be granted special navigational and immunity privileges in addition to those other warships currently enjoy. The purpose of CSBMs would be to relax tension, build confidence, decrease the presence of military force regionally and provide 'seaboard security' to coastal states. The latter term was introduced in the UN expert study to summarize the interest of coastal states. The relevant paragraph reads:

The principle of freedom of navigation on the world's oceans makes a coastal state the neighbour across the sea of every other coastal state, including all significant naval Powers. While naval forces have the recognized legal right to cruise and operate off the coasts of foreign states, coastal states, particularly those which are small or medium in size, have on the other hand a legitimate claim for a reasonable 'seaboard security' and should not be subjected to power projection possibly originating from such activities. It should be noted in this regard that the Convention on the Law of the Sea includes balanced provisions which would meet security needs of both flag states and coastal states provided they are strictly implemented. It should also be noted that the security of both categories of states could be further enhanced by means of agreed confidence- and security-building measures in harmony with the Convention and customary international law.[24]

5. *Provisions for guaranteeing safe access to the seas and oceans for ships and aircraft of states, neutral or otherwise, not involved in ongoing conflicts.* The purpose would be to distinguish vessels of states involved in military conflict from those of states not thus involved and to give a general priority to shipping, fishing, offshore industry or other peaceful activities at sea.

6. *Modernization of the laws of war to be applied at sea,* an issue which was overlooked when the Additional Protocols of 1977 to the 1949 Geneva Conventions were negotiated. Much of the relevant current law was agreed at the beginning of the century. Technological and other developments have created problems in relation to various kinds of warfare, blockade, total exclusion and other zones at sea, to the use of long-range weapons (fire-and-forget missiles), sea mines and torpedoes and to possible environmental consequences of armed activities.

VIII. Current negotiations

Since the adoption of the UN Convention on the Law of the Sea in 1982, and particularly since the presentation of the UN expert report in 1985,[25] arms control applied in the maritime domain has been considered more legitimate than before. There has also been some negotiated progress since then, but no major achievements have been made. Confidence-building measures seems to be the category of measures which attracts the greatest political interest. A survey of recent negotiations on CBMs has been published by Borawski.[26]

Bilateral negotiations

Earlier strategic arms agreements have taken into account the maritime sector of the nuclear arsenals. Most of them required no special maritime provisions. Only the agreements on the prevention of incidents at sea are purely naval.

This trend will probably prevail. It must be noted, however, that the December 1987 INF Treaty does not cover any sea-based missiles. However, the May 1988 Ballistic Missile Launch Notification Agreement (see annexe B) does include naval systems—SLBMs.

At the continuing US–Soviet START negotiations, sea-based nuclear weapons—SLBMs and sea-launched cruise missiles—are at least being discussed. Further confidence-building measures regarding sea-based nuclear weapons are also being dealt with.[27]

Multilateral negotiations

The political development of the issue of naval arms control after the publication in 1986 of the UN Secretary-General's expert report has been slow. Deliberations on the issue have taken place in the UN Disarmament Commission.

At its 1986 meeting, the Commission produced a document giving political endorsement to the aforementioned 'axioms' as guiding principles for future negotiations. It recommended pursuing the possibility of negotiating a multilateral agreement on the prevention of incidents at sea. The need for updating the laws of sea warfare was also acknowledged. These statements were agreed by consensus 'among those participating', that is, all states but the USA. The US Delegation tried unsuccessfully to prevent the issue of 'naval armaments and disarmament' from appearing on the agenda of the meeting and did not take part in consultations on the issue.[28]

At the Disarmament Commission's 1987 meeting, the issue was developed a little further. Confidence-building measures were emphasized as important 'at this stage'. Prior notification of naval activities, exchange of observers at such activities, and extended general information on naval forces of states were measures mentioned as desirable subjects for future negotiations. The need for updating Hague Convention VIII of 1907 on the Laying of Automatic Submarine Contact Mines was explicitly mentioned. It was also stressed that maintenance of the freedom of navigation and other uses of the sea were an important objective for all states neutral to or otherwise not involved in ongoing armed conflicts.[29]

At its 1988 and 1989 meetings, the Disarmament Commission developed the issue of naval armaments and disarmament somewhat further with some more specific conclusions on confidence-building measures and laws of sea warfare.[30] The US attitude remained negative during the 1987 and 1988 meetings.

The CSCE

The terms for the continued negotiations after the Stockholm Conference were adopted at the conclusion of the CSCE follow-up meeting in Vienna in January 1989. According to its Concluding Document, there will be two separate forums for considering further arms control in Europe.

One will be the Negotiations on Confidence- and Security-Building Measures that will 'build upon and expand the results already achieved at the Stockholm Conference'. These negotiations will be based on the original Madrid mandate of 1983 and will therefore deal only with such naval activities as are part of relevant activities on land. They could not be expected to lead to measures applying to independent naval activities or to special provisions regarding nuclear weapons.

The CSCE process has also established a second forum, for a Negotiation on Conventional Armed Forces in Europe (CFE) between the 23 states members of the two military alliances—NATO and the WTO—on more substantial measures of arms control and disarmament regarding conventional forces in Europe. Naval forces will not be addressed, however. These talks will cover conventional armed forces, including armament and equipment, on the territory of the participating states in Europe from the Atlantic to the Urals, including all their European island territories.[31]

Laws of sea warfare

Modernization of the laws of sea warfare has been recommended as a priority issue by the UN Disarmament Commission. This issue is different from most other naval arms control applications in that new proposals have to be prepared against the background of a legal tradition from the nineteenth century.

At the Commission's meeting in 1989, the Government of Sweden submitted a draft Protocol on Prohibitions or Restrictions on the Use of Naval Mines, intended to replace the obsolete 1907 Hague Convention VIII.[32] It is also important to note that the academic world has recently focused considerable interest in the laws of sea warfare. The well-known San Remo Institute for International Humanitarian Law has organized several conferences for scholars in the field.

IX. Concluding remarks

Is there a future for naval arms control? The difficulties are obvious. Such issues are in many respects militarily and legally different and new as compared to other arms control issues. The most important maritime power, the USA, maintains a negative attitude to multilateral solutions. Tabled proposals have not passed the stage of declarations and general principles.

However, a great majority of the states of the world have expressed a positive interest in these issues. There is agreement that the 'four axioms' should be guidelines for future negotiations. The Convention on the Law of the Sea and its norms for freedoms on the high seas would not be infringed upon by an effort to achieve naval arms control based on these axioms. A process of deliberation and negotiation within the United Nations has started and could probably not be stopped.

The answer should thus be yes: naval arms control does exist and does have a future.

In the bilateral sector, results might be expected as a matter of course, but it will be some time before multilateral efforts begin to produce new agreements;

this probably also applies to the CSCE process. The main interest would then probably focus on various kinds of confidence- and security-building measures.

It is natural and understandable that when new naval CSBMs are proposed they are based upon the CSBMs already agreed upon for land forces. It has been proposed that the Stockholm Document CSBMs—designed for land activities—should be extended to the sea as well (see paper 13). However, if a lesson can be drawn from the experiences of the past 25 years of arms control talks, it is that armies on land should be treated differently from navies at sea. Measures of naval CSBMs and arms control should be 'sailor-made' to fit the general maritime environment.

The considerable confidence-building effect of the many provisions of the UNCLOS should be appreciated. One example is the provision that submarines and other underwater vehicles, exercising their right of innocent passage in the territorial sea, 'are required to navigate on the surface and to show their flag' (Article 20). The UNCLOS could in many instances be the point of departure for a general development of CSBMs in the maritime domain.

A further conclusion is that globally applicable measures are generally preferable to regional approaches. Regional arms control mainly centres on a land region with an adjoining sea area that is defined more or less precisely. A system of regional arms control regimes spread over the world could then give rise to ambiguous and complex legal situations where such regimes meet or overlap. However, this observation does not exclude special regimes for very special regions, for example, the ice-covered Arctic.

Notes and references

[1] This author has touched upon the subject in earlier papers and seminar contributions. See, for example, 'The naval arms race and arms control', in eds J. Rotblat and S. Hellman, Pugwash, *Nuclear Strategy and World Security* (Macmillan: London, 1985), pp. 76–80; and 'Naval arms and naval arms control', in eds J. P. Maas and R. A. C. Stewart, *Towards a World of Peace* (University of the South Pacific: Suva, Fiji, 1986), pp. 49–58.

[2] United Nations, *The Naval Arms Race,* Report of the Secretary-General, UN Study series no. 16, UN document A/40/535 (United Nations: New York, 1986), annex I.

[3] For a description of the agreement and its implementation up to 1963, see Eayrs, J. 'Arms control and the Great Lakes', *Disarmament and Arms Control*, vol. 2, no. 4 (1964), pp. 372–404.

[4] See Ronzitti, N. (ed.), *The Law of Naval Warfare: A Collection of Agreements and Documents with Commentaries* (Martinus Nijhoff: Dordrecht, Netherlands, 1988), pp. 61–69.

[5] On 18 July 1976, the Soviet 37 000-ton aircraft-carrier *Kiev,* constructed at a Black Sea shipyard, passed the Turkish Straits on its way to the ocean, pre-notified as a submarine-hunting cruiser. A debate arose about the status of the ship, but the Turkish authorities chose to let it pass as a 'cruiser'. See Froman, D., 'Kiev and the Montreux Convention: the aircraft carrier that became a cruiser to squeeze through the Turkish Straits', *San Diego Law Review*, vol. 14 (1977), p. 681. Later three more ships of the same class (*Minsk, Novorossisk* and *Baku*) passed the Straits, the most recent on 8 June 1988. In 1989, the convention will probably be put to a new test when the USSR is expected to notify Turkey of the transit of a much larger aircraft-carrier, the 70 000-ton *Tbilisi.* For a discussion of this case, see Maehcling, C., Jr., 'Crisis at the Turkish Straits', US Naval Institute *Proceedings*, vol. 114, no. 8 (Aug. 1988), pp. 63–71.

[6] In accordance with the Vienna Convention on the Law of Treaties, Art. 18.

[7] The text of the France–USSR Incidents at Sea Agreement was not available for publication in this book.

[8] Conference on Disarmament Document CD/847. The full title of the agreement is 'Agreement between the United States of America and the Union of Soviet Socialist Republics on Notifications of Launches of Intercontinental Ballistic Missiles and Submarine-Launched Ballistic Missiles' (see annexe B).

[9] The Partial Test Ban Treaty entered into force in 1963 and had 118 parties as of 1 June 1989 (see annexe B for the list of parties).

[10] The Seabed Treaty entered into force in 1972 and had 82 parties as of 1 June 1989 (see annexe B for the list of parties).

[11] The Tlatelolco Treaty was agreed in 1967, and 23 states of Latin America and the Caribbean were parties as of 1 June 1989 (see annexe B for the list of parties). Another 10 potential zonal states are not yet parties. All dependencies but the French are subject to the zonal regime in accordance with Protocol I. Protocol II (the guarantee protocol) is in force for all nuclear weapon states.

[12] The Treaty of Rarotonga was agreed in 1985 and is open for signature to all states of the South Pacific Forum. Its three protocols are open to relevant nuclear weapon powers. It had entered into force for 9 parties as of 1 June 1989 (see annexe B for the list of parties). For the full text, see SIPRI, *World Armaments and Disarmament: SIPRI Yearbook 1986* (Taylor & Francis: London, 1986), p. 509.

[13] The vast ocean areas of the South Pacific are not densely populated, but the term is regularly used in order to distinguish the Latin American and the South Pacific zones from the 'almost' uninhabited Antarctica.

[14] For extracts from the Concluding Document of the Madrid follow-up meeting, see SIPRI, *World Armaments and Disarmament: SIPRI Yearbook 1984* (Taylor & Francis: London, 1984), appendix 15A, pp. 570–71.

[15] For the text of the Stockholm Document, see SIPRI, *SIPRI Yearbook 1987: World Armaments and Disarmament* (Oxford University Press: Oxford, 1987), p. 355.

[16] The modern definition of the 'freedom of the high seas' is specified in UNCLOS Art. 87, as the freedom of navigation, overflight, laying submarine cables and pipelines, constructing artificial islands and other installations, fishing, and scientific research. Some of these freedoms are subject to various provisions of the UNCLOS.

[17] de Groot (Grotius), H., '*Mare Liberum*', a chapter in his book *De Jure Praedae* (1609).

[18] The United Nations Convention on the Law of the Sea was opened for signature in Dec. 1982. Three important states have not yet signed, i.e., the Federal Republic of Germany, the United States and the United Kingdom. The convention had not entered into force as of 1 Sep. 1989.

[19] The rules of transit passage are included in the UNCLOS, Part III, and apply to territorial-water straits between one part of the high seas or an exclusive economic zone and another part of the high seas or an exclusive economic zone. See annexe B.

[20] UN Resolution 38/188 G.

[21] UN Document A/40/535, para. 322.

[22] UN Document A/40/535, para. 285.

[23] See UN Document A/CN.10/83, which was issued by the Chairman of the Disarmament Commission, a body composed of all UN member states. The document was adopted by all participating members (i.e., excluding the USA).

[24] UN Document A/40/535, para. 264.

[25] The UN report was presented in 1985 and made available as UN Document A/40/535. It was published in 1986 (see note 2).

[26] Borawski, J., 'Risk reduction at sea: confidence-building measures', *Naval Forces*, vol. 8, no. 1 (1987), p. 18.

[27] CBMs for strategic nuclear weapons are discussed in Mobbs, M. H., 'CBMs for stabilizing the strategic nuclear competition', in ed. J. Borawski, *Avoiding War in the Nuclear Age* (Westview: London, 1986), pp. 152–65.

[28] See note 23.

[29] UN Document A/CN.10/102.

[30] UN Documents A/CN.10/113 and A/CN.10/134.

[31] See the mandate for the Negotiation on Conventional Armed Forces in Europe of 10 Jan. 1989, especially Annex 2. Excerpts from the Vienna Concluding Document can be found in *SIPRI Yearbook 1989* (note 8), pp. 416–26 (Annex 2, Modalities for Meetings to Exchange Views and Information Concerning the Course of the Negotiation on Conventional Armed Forces in Europe, on pp. 425–26).

[32] UN Document A/CN.10/129.

Appendix 1A

Pre-World War II naval arms limitation measures

Demilitarization agreements

1817   *Rush–Bagot Agreement* between Great Britain (Canada) and the United States. Limitation of naval forces on the Great Lakes

1856   *Treaty of Paris*. Peace treaty concluding the Crimean War. Provided for the neutralization of the Black Sea and demilitarization of its shores, and for the demilitarization of the Åland Islands in the Baltic Sea

1881   *Treaty of Buenos Aires* between Argentina and Chile. Demilitarization of the Magellan Straits

1905   *Treaty of Portsmouth*. Non-fortification of Sakhalin and the adjacent islands

1920   *Paris Treaty concerning the Archipelago of Spitzbergen*. Norway undertook not to establish any naval bases or other fortifications on the islands

1920   *Peace Treaty of Dorpat*. Demilitarization of Finnish territorial waters in the Finnish Gulf, Lake Ladoga and the Arctic Ocean

1921   *Convention relating to the Non-fortification and Neutralisation of the Åland Islands*. Confirmation and extension of the demilitarization effected by the 1856 Treaty of Paris

1923   *Peace Treaty of Lausanne*. Resulting in two naval demilitarization regimes:
> *(a)* Demilitarization zones along the shores of the Straits of Dardanelles and Bosphorus. Demilitarized islands in the Sea of Marmara;
> *(b)* Demilitarization of two groups of islands in the Aegean Sea, one group west of the Dardanelles (Samothraki, Imbros, Lemnos, Tenedos and Rabbit Islands) and one flanking the approaches to the Gulf of Smyrna (Mytilene, Chios, Samosa and Nikaria)

1936   *Montreux Convention on the Turkish Straits*. Rescission of the Lausanne Peace Treaty demilitarization of the shores of the straits. New provisions on passage of warships in time of peace and in time of war

---

Source: This list was compiled from the source-books listed in the last section of this appendix, and from the list published in annex I of: United Nations, *The Naval Arms Race*, Report of the Secretary-General, UN Study series no. 16, UN document A/40/535 (United Nations: New York, 1986).

Other arms control agreements

1856   *Declaration of Paris respecting Maritime Law.* Agreement not to seize enemy goods on neutral vessels or neutral goods on enemy vessels with the exception of contraband of war. Blockades, in order to be binding, must be effective.

1902   *Pactos de Mayo.* Limitation of naval armaments between Argentina and Chile

1907   *Hague Conventions* on:
    VI. Status of Enemy Merchant Ships at the Outbreak of Hostilities;
    VII. Conversion of Merchant Ships into Warships;
    VIII. Laying of Automatic Submarine Contact Mines;
    IX. Bombardment by Naval Forces in Time of War;
    X. Adaptation to Maritime Warfare of the Principles of the Geneva Convention of 22 August 1864 on Wounded, Sick and Shipwrecked in war;
    XI. Certain Restrictions with regard to the Exercise of the Right of Capture in Naval War;
    XII. Creation of an International Prize Court (never entered into force);
    XIII. Rights and Duties of Neutral Powers in Naval War

1909   *London Declaration concerning the Laws of Naval War.* Rules on blockade, contraband and prizes (never entered into force)

1922   *Washington Treaty Limiting Naval Armament.* Qualitative and numerical restrictions on warships

1922   *Washington Treaty relating to the Use of Submarines and Noxious Gases in Warfare* (never entered into force)

1930   *London Treaty on Limitation and Reduction of Naval Armament:*
    (a) further restrictions (quantitative and qualitative) on warships;
    (b) reaffirmation of the 1922 restrictions on the use of submarines

1936   *London Protocol* on the use of submarines in war (never fully applied in practice)

1936   London Treaty on Limitation and Reduction of Naval Armament. Qualitative restrictions on warships

Confidence-building measures

1902   *Pactos de Mayo.* Notification between Argentina and Chile of new naval construction

1922   *Washington Treaty.* Notification of replacement construction

1930   *Greek–Turkish Naval Protocol.* Exchange of information on prospective changes in naval inventories

1931   *Soviet–Turkish Naval Protocol.* Exchange of information on prospective changes in naval inventories

1936   *Montreux Convention.* Notification to Turkey of the passage of warships through the Turkish Straits

Sources of texts of pre-World War II naval agreements

Dupuy, T. N. and Hammerman, A., *A Documentary History of Arms Control and Disarmament* (Bowker Co.: New York, 1973).

Goldblat, J., SIPRI, *Agreements for Arms Control: A Critical Survey* (Taylor & Francis: London, 1982).

Roberts, A. and Guelff, R. (eds), *Documents on the Laws of War* (Oxford University Press: Oxford, 1982).

Ronzitti, N. (ed.), *The Law of Naval Warfare: A Collection of Agreements and Documents with Commentaries* (Martinus Nijhoff: Dordrecht, Netherlands, 1988).

Schindler, D. and Toman, J., *The Laws of Armed Conflicts, A Collection of Conventions, Resolutions and Other Documents* (Henri Dunant Institute: Geneva, 1981).

Paper 2. US–Soviet naval competition: dangers and risks

Eugene J. Carroll, Jr

Center for Defense Information, Washington, DC, USA

I. Introduction

Since the end of World War II, the United States and the Soviet Union have been engaged in a costly naval competition. Beginning in the early 1960s, the Soviet Navy grew from a largely coastal force to the world's second most powerful navy. The US Navy remains the world's most powerful navy and has undergone a rapid expansion since 1980. While to date these two navies have avoided a shooting war at sea, the US–Soviet naval competition has contributed to the general political ill-will existing between the two countries. More importantly, that competition has the potential to provoke serious military crises leading to nuclear war in the future.

The extent to which the 'general-purpose' navies of both countries have been nuclearized and the relative 'suitability' of tactical nuclear weapons for naval warfare, combined with the difficulty of maintaining central control of naval forces in wartime, make it likely that a US–Soviet war at sea would rapidly escalate to the nuclear level. Execution of the US Navy's current 'forward' strategy would virtually guarantee that such escalation would occur. Although generally less provocative, elements of the Soviet Navy's wartime strategy would also encourage escalation. Once nuclear weapons are used at sea, escalation to global nuclear war appears inevitable.

The other path to nuclear escalation at sea is through the use of SLBMs. In 1989 the United States plans to deploy the Trident II (D-5) SLBM, the first SLBM accurate enough to destroy hardened ICBM silos. By increasing the vulnerability of the Soviet ICBM force, the Trident II's deployment will inevitably increase the likelihood that the Soviet Union will feel compelled to strike first in times of crisis, thus increasing the probability of early nuclear escalation. Undoubtedly, within a few years of the Trident II deployment, the Soviet Union will deploy a highly accurate SLBM of its own, increasing escalatory pressures still further.

Although a US–Soviet conflict at sea could be triggered by any number of incidents at sea or on land, it is increasingly likely that such an incident will involve naval confrontations in Third World areas. The likelihood of such confrontation has grown dramatically over the past 20 years as the Soviet Navy has acquired some capability to intervene in the Third World. The United States and its allies retain a massive superiority in naval intervention capability, but they no longer enjoy a monopoly. Increasingly, US naval forces sent to the world's 'hot spots' find Soviet forces present, raising the potential for conflict.

These increasing dangers of US–Soviet naval competition could and should be reduced through both unilateral changes in strategy and force structure and negotiated arms control agreements. Without such constraints, the threat of superpower confrontation and nuclear escalation at sea will only increase.

II. US–Soviet naval competition in peacetime

At least two aspects of naval competition have contributed to political ill-will between the United States and the Soviet Union in peacetime: 'incidents at sea', such as collisions between US and Soviet warships; and naval exercises and operations conducted near the home waters of or in other waters deemed important by the adversary. Incidents at sea and provocative naval operations lead to growing concerns about each side's naval capabilities and intentions and help perpetuate the naval arms race.

The US and Soviet navies often respond to the exercises and operations of the other by sending in naval and air forces of their own. Occasionally this interference gets out of hand, resulting in collisions and other incidents. In March 1984, for example, a Soviet submarine and the US carrier *Kitty Hawk* collided during exercises in the Sea of Japan. In the 1960s the number of US–Soviet incidents at sea reached over 100 a year. After the Incidents at Sea Agreement was signed in 1972 (see annexe B), the number of incidents declined significantly. Nevertheless, the risk of collisions or other incidents has not disappeared (see papers 8 and 11). According to Navy Secretary John F. Lehman, in 1983 there were some 40 incidents between US and Soviet naval forces that were considered 'serious . . . where there was a potential for danger'.[1] The probability of incidents occurring may increase further in the future if both countries continue to conduct operations in sensitive waters, particularly in or near the home waters of the other nation.

Partly as a reflection of changing wartime strategies and partly as a reflection of political brinkmanship, the US and Soviet navies have conducted increasingly provocative naval operations in recent years. The US Navy routinely conducts exercises near Soviet waters in the Baltic and Black Seas. In 1983 the US Navy held its first exercise in the Sea of Japan in 13 years. In 1984 it conducted the largest Pacific Fleet exercise ever, which involved five aircraft-carriers and included sending two carriers to within 50 miles (80 km) of the Soviet Navy's main Pacific base at Vladivostok. More recently, in September 1986 the US Navy sent a task force headed by the battleship *New Jersey* into the Sea of Okhotsk, adjacent to the Soviet Union.[2] Each of these operations has elicited angry denunciations from Soviet officials and overflights by Soviet Naval Aviation or nearby manoeuvres by Soviet warships.

In February 1988 two US warships, the cruiser *USS Yorktown* and the destroyer *USS Caron*, entered into Soviet territorial waters south of the Crimean Peninsula in the Black Sea. After issuing a warning to the US ships to leave the territorial waters, two Soviet warships bumped into the two US vessels.[3] Although this incident caused no injuries and little damage to the ships, it did raise serious questions about such dangerous exercises. At their meeting in July 1988, US Admiral William Crowe, Chairman of the Joint Chiefs of Staff, and Soviet Marshal Sergey Akhromeyev, Chief of the General Staff, agreed to pursue joint efforts to prevent dangerous military incidents such as the ship collisions in February.[4]

For its part, the Soviet Union has expanded its exercises in the North Atlantic and elsewhere, raising concerns in the West. In 1984 the Soviet Navy held its largest exercise ever in the North Atlantic. Over 200 surface combatants and 70 submarines, as well as Soviet Navy and Air Force bombers, took part in the operation. In 1985 the Soviet Navy conducted a North Atlantic exercise which included sorties by over 200 aircraft, making it the largest such effort in a decade. The Soviet Navy conducted large exercises in the Pacific as well in both 1985 and 1986.[5]

III. General-purpose naval forces and strategies: the nuclear dimension

Both the US and Soviet general-purpose navies are heavily nuclearized. Over 80 per cent of US warships[6] and virtually all Soviet warships are equipped with nuclear-capable systems. These include nuclear-capable surface-to-air missiles (SAMs), anti-submarine rockets and depth bombs, anti-ship and ground-attack surface-to-surface missiles (SSMs), gravity bombs delivered from carrier- and land-based naval aircraft and, in the Soviet Navy, nuclear torpedoes and perhaps nuclear naval mines. Altogether the US Navy has about 3600 tactical nuclear weapons[7] carried aboard some 264 surface warships and attack submarines.[8] The Soviet Navy has a similar number of such weapons carried aboard about 550 surface warships and attack submarines.[9] The extent to which the general-purpose forces of both the US and Soviet navies are nuclearized greatly increases the likelihood that any US–Soviet war at sea will quickly escalate to the nuclear level. Neither nation is likely to accept a major naval defeat without resorting to its most destructive weapons.

It is impossible to say with certainty at what stage in a war at sea US or Soviet naval forces would initiate the use of tactical nuclear weapons. In theory, even a full-scale NATO–WTO war at sea could be waged indefinitely without resort to these weapons. In practice, however, it is very likely that naval nuclear weapons would be used by one side or the other relatively early in a crisis and almost certainly at the outset of any 'shooting war' between the two superpowers.

The pressures for nuclear escalation at sea arise from a variety of sources including: (*a*) the degree to which both sides' navies have been nuclearized; (*b*) the apparent suitability of nuclear weapons for certain naval missions; (*c*) the relatively low cost—in terms of collateral damage—of using nuclear weapons at sea; (*d*) the difficulty of maintaining control of naval forces and thus the nuclear weapons they carry in wartime; and (*e*) the provocative nature of the current US (and to a lesser extent Soviet) wartime naval strategies.

Naval commanders on both sides might see substantial benefits in using nuclear weapons at sea.[10] Nuclear weapons are much more efficient killers of enemy surface ships and submarines than are conventional weapons. Nuclear weapons are particularly well suited for destroying surface ships. Over 100 conventional anti-ship missiles might be required to defeat an aircraft-carrier battle group, for example. On the other hand, just one nuclear near-miss on a carrier might well be sufficient for the task.

Submarines are less vulnerable to nuclear attack than are surface ships because their ability to operate while submerged makes them much more difficult to find and target. This is of course why both the United States and the Soviet Union elected to put the sea-based leg of their strategic nuclear forces on submarines rather than on surface ships. Moreover, nuclear detonations under water can interfere with sonar operation, making it more difficult to detect and track other submarines after the first explosion. Once a submarine has been detected, however, the surest way to destroy it is to use nuclear weapons

With respect to their availability and destructive efficiency, the military logic for using tactical nuclear weapons at sea is roughly similar to the logic for using such weapons on land. The US and Soviet armies and tactical air forces are no less well equipped with tactical nuclear weapons—ranging from nuclear artillery shells to gravity bombs—and these weapons are as efficient at destroying infantry and armour as naval nuclear weapons are at destroying warships. What makes using tactical nuclear weapons at sea more attractive is the fact that, in stark contrast to the situation on land where any use of nuclear weapons would result in civilian casualties and the destruction of homes and factories as well as enemy forces, the detonation of even large numbers of nuclear weapons at sea would cause relatively little 'collateral damage'.

Notwithstanding the fact that the military incentives for using tactical nuclear weapons at sea may be greater than they are for using them on land, it is clearly not a step which national military and political leaders in either country would take lightly. Among other things, the fact that a nuclear attack at sea would cause relatively limited collateral damage would hardly guarantee that the victim of such an attack would not respond with nuclear attacks on land targets. In fact, official US statements have suggested that nuclear attacks on US ships would result in nuclear retaliation against shore bases.[11] Where the danger lies and what makes the potential for nuclear escalation at sea especially acute is the fact that whether tactical nuclear weapons are used by naval forces may not be up to national authorities.

Unlike US ground-based tactical and strategic nuclear weapons, which have electro-mechanical devices (called permissive action links, or PALs) requiring the insertion of presidential codes before the weapons can be used, US Navy nuclear weapons have no physical controls to prevent their unauthorized use. The primary justification for not employing PALs in US Navy nuclear weapons concerns the fact that communication links between national authorities and ships at sea might be rapidly cut in wartime. Therefore, unless the capability to use these weapons resides with the local commanders, the nuclear capability of the entire US Fleet could be negated by a 'decapitating' Soviet nuclear attack which destroyed a handful of command and communications facilities. It is not clear whether Soviet naval commanders have a comparable capability to use nuclear weapons in the absence of formal authorization.

Naval strategies

Taken together, the above factors create an environment in which nuclear escalation at sea would be difficult to prevent in times of US–Soviet tension and nearly impossible in a high-intensity war at sea. If the provocative wartime strategies of the US and to a lesser extent the Soviet navies are brought into this environment, all the ingredients needed to create a disaster are present. Execution of the US Navy's current wartime strategy would increase the incentives on both sides to use nuclear weapons at sea early in a shooting war.

The maritime strategy embraced by the Reagan Administration—often referred to as the Lehman Doctrine, after its most forceful advocate, former Navy Secretary John Lehman—calls for the US Navy to 'take the fight to the enemy', to attack and destroy the main strength of the Soviet Navy in its home waters. Early in the offensive phase, US nuclear-attack submarines (SSNs) would be sent in against the Soviet Northern and Pacific Fleets to destroy their nuclear ballistic missile submarines (SSBNs) and attack submarines. With the Soviet submarines neutralized, US carrier battle groups would be used to attack Soviet naval and air bases and surface warships operating in those waters.

In response to such an attack, the Soviet Navy might well be expected to use nuclear weapons. Because of the unique ability of SSBNs to ride out a nuclear surprise attack, both the United States and the Soviet Union rely on SLBMs to provide a secure retaliatory capability. The importance the USSR attaches to its SSBN fleet is acknowledged by the Pentagon, which concedes that 'most Soviet general purpose surface, submarine and naval air forces would likely be assigned initial wartime tasks [in waters adjacent to the Soviet Union] where they could provide both protection for SSBNs and defense against sea-based land-attack platforms'.[12] Fearing the loss of its SSBNs and hoping to avoid the 'use 'em or lose 'em' dilemma, the USSR might decide to use tactical nuclear weapons at sea to destroy US SSNs and aircraft-carriers in order to protect its SSBNs.

The Soviet Union's willingness to resort to tactical nuclear weapons in order to protect its SSBNs might also be strengthened by a belief that the Soviet Navy would, on net, have more to gain from first use of those weapons than would the US Navy. As mentioned above, tactical nuclear weapons are best suited for sinking surface ships, and in general the United States is more dependent on surface warships than is the Soviet Union. It might also see an advantage in using nuclear anti-submarine warfare (ASW) weapons, since the US Navy (which has far more sensitive and effective sonar equipment) might be expected to suffer more from the interference with sonar operation caused by underwater nuclear detonations. In particular, underwater nuclear detonations might be expected to degrade seriously the effectiveness of the US Sound Surveillance System (SOSUS) used for long-range detection of Soviet submarines.

The incentive for the Soviet Union to use nuclear weapons will also inevitably be increased by the wide-scale deployment of long-range nuclear sea-launched cruise missiles (SLCMs). The US Tomahawk SLCM entered service in 1984. As of January 1989 about 200 nuclear-armed SLCMs had been deployed aboard approximately 65 US warships and submarines.[13] Pentagon plans call for some 4000 SLCMs, including 758 nuclear versions,[14] to be put aboard up to 198 US surface ships and submarines by the mid-1990s.[15] The Soviet Union has begun deploying its own long-range SLCM, dubbed the SS-N-21 'Sampson' by NATO. According to the Pentagon, the SS-N-21 will be deployed aboard Soviet Akula, Sierra and Victor III Class submarines and on specially configured Yankee Class submarines.[16] In fact, there is good reason to believe that the SS-N-21 could also be deployed aboard Soviet surface warships and many submarines, since it can be fired from the standard 533-millimetre torpedo tube present on most of those ships.

The long-range SLCM adds a new dimension to the threat posed by naval tactical nuclear weapons. In the past, the only naval forces capable of launching long-range nuclear attacks against ground targets were SSBNs and aircraft-carriers. The SLCM, with a range of more than 2500 km, will give this capability to virtually all warships and many submarines. Clearly, this capability will make these general-purpose warships higher-value targets.

While tactical nuclear weapons might be better suited to Soviet requirements, the United States might also be tempted to use tactical nuclear weapons. In particular it is easy to see how a US task force commander might want to use nuclear ASW weapons to protect his carriers. While using nuclear ASW weapons might seem extreme, in some cases one could argue that they are appropriate for protecting carriers because carriers represent most of the offensive striking power of the US Navy. In terms of both dollars and personnel, carrier battle groups represent a greater investment on the part of the US military than any other battle forces. The temptation to resort to nuclear weapons rather than risk the loss of a carrier with 6000 men and 85 aircraft would be particularly great as the carrier approached Soviet waters, since those waters are likely to be 'infested' with Soviet attack submarines.

The US Navy might also be tempted to employ nuclear weapons at the outbreak of hostilities against any Soviet SSBNs it happened to be trailing, since tactical nuclear weapons would be the surest and fastest way to destroy the submarine. The pressures to use nuclear ASW weapons would be especially great because, once hostilities began, time would be at a premium. Any delay in destroying the submarine might mean losing its trail. And, of course, any submarine not destroyed can fight later. This problem would be further aggravated by the knowledge that the Soviet Union could at any time degrade the performance of the US SOSUS system by detonating nuclear weapons, thus making it more difficult to relocate Soviet submarines.

Finally, the US strategy might provide the United States with an incentive to use nuclear weapons to launch a pre-emptive attack against Soviet submarine bases. A pre-emptive strike would serve to catch the Soviet Union off-guard while most of its SSBNs are still in port. On a day-to-day basis, only about 15 per cent of Soviet SSBNs are on station at sea.[17] In periods of tension, this rate could be increased substantially. Once this were done, the destruction of the Soviet SSBNs would obviously become much more difficult. The Lehman Doctrine does not require that the USA launch a first strike against Soviet SSBN bases, but such a strike would certainly be consistent with the doctrine.

The Soviet Union's wartime naval strategy is generally less provocative than the US Navy's strategy, but elements of it could foster nuclear escalation. As noted above, that strategy basically involves keeping most of its submarines and surface warships in or close to Soviet waters and using them to protect Soviet SSBNs and the Soviet coast. Soviet planning does, however, contain some potentially escalatory elements. In particular the Soviet emphasis on 'winning the battle of the first salvo' could lead to nuclear escalation.

The Soviet Navy very often trails US carrier battle groups and other forces in peacetime with small units of surface ships and submarines. These forces would not last long in a shooting war. They might, on the other hand, be able to launch a single salvo of missiles before being destroyed themselves if the missiles were fired the moment hostilities broke out. Alternatively, they could provide targeting information to Soviet forces located some distance from the task force. In either case, the Soviet forces would have to act quickly and might well use nuclear weapons to be effective.

IV. Sea-based strategic nuclear forces

The preceding sections of this paper considered only the possibility of nuclear escalation occurring through the actions of US and Soviet general-purpose naval forces. Nuclear escalation could also occur through the action of US and Soviet strategic ballistic missile submarines. This danger will grow as both countries deploy more accurate SLBMs in the coming years. Although the existence of these weapons will not make such a course imperative nor guarantee a successful first strike, their existence will inevitably increase the incentive to attack first in times of crisis. The mechanisms that could lead to escalation through the use of SLBMs are more straightforward than they are in the case of tactical nuclear weapons.

According to the Pentagon, the Soviet force of 308 SS-18 ICBMs 'has the capability to destroy 65–85 per cent of US ICBM silos using two warheads against each'.[18] This vulnerability has raised a great deal of concern in the United States that the country could be 'disarmed' by a Soviet nuclear surprise attack. The concern is so great that the United States is currently planning to deploy a mobile ICBM in the 1990s at a cost of tens of billions of dollars to ensure the continued survivability of the ICBM leg of the US strategic nuclear triad. Even if along with 85 per cent of US ICBMs the Soviet Union were able to destroy all non-alert US bombers and in-port SSBNs in a surprise attack, the United States would still possess some 5000 surviving strategic nuclear weapons (including those aboard SSBNs at sea, alert strategic bombers and some 150 remaining ICBMs) with which to retaliate. Thus, in fact, US fears of a disarming first strike appear to be unjustified in military terms. The perception of vulnerability, however, continues to be a powerful political issue in the United States.

The reality of the situation has not prevented many US military and political leaders from expressing concern over the vulnerability of the ICBM leg of the US nuclear arsenal. These expressions of concern should alert the United States to how the Soviet Union is likely to view the deployment of the Trident II SLBM currently under development by the US Navy and scheduled for deployment aboard US Trident SSBNs beginning in December 1989.

The Trident II (D-5) will be the first SLBM with the combination of explosive power and accuracy required for effective use against hard targets such as ICBM silos. The Trident II is potentially far more threatening to the Soviet Union than the SS-18 is to the United States because the USSR depends on its ICBMs more than the USA does. Only about 20 per cent of US strategic nuclear weapons are carried on ICBMs, while ICBMs account for over 60 per cent of the Soviet Union's total arsenal. The prospect of losing a major part of its ICBMs in a surprise first strike will be all the more alarming to the Soviet Union if, as a result of a US naval offensive, the USSR is also faced with the prospect of losing the sea-based leg of its nuclear forces. The combination of the Trident II and the Lehman Doctrine could lead to a very unstable situation—one in which the Soviet Union might genuinely perceive, on the basis of worst-case analysis, greatly increased vulnerability to a disarming first strike. Whether or not the Soviet perception of vulnerability were accurate would be largely irrelevant if it would lead to a fear-driven decision to launch its own first strike.

To say that the introduction of the Trident II will increase Soviet concerns about the vulnerability of its nuclear forces and thus increase its incentive to launch first in times of crisis is of course not to say that introduction of the Trident II will make nuclear war inevitable. In military reality, the Trident II may be less threatening to Soviet ICBMs than it could be in political theory. While the Soviet Union may be more vulnerable to a first strike than is the United States, even in the worst case the USSR would have hundreds of nuclear weapons in surviving silos, on mobile SS-24s and SS-25s and in SSBNs at sea with which it could respond to a US attack. The reality of mutual assured destruction is thus likely to survive the introduction of the Trident II, just as it survived the introduction of the SS-18.

V. Naval competition in the Third World

It is becoming increasingly likely that the US and Soviet naval forces operating in Third World areas could become involved in a shooting war with each other. The potential for such escalation has grown as the Soviet Union has increased its capability to intervene with naval forces in the Third World.

US and allied navies are much better suited for operations in distant waters of the world than is the Soviet Navy. The Soviet Union, however, is itself developing significant capabilities for such operations. When the USSR deploys its first large-deck aircraft-carrier in the 1990s, it will be taking another step towards a navy that can establish a strong naval presence in distant waters. The Soviet Union cannot soon match the superior US force projection capability, but in the future the United States may not be the only power sending naval forces—and carrier battle groups in particular—to trouble spots in the Third World.

It seems unlikely that the USSR would intentionally escalate a naval confrontation far from the Soviet Union while the USA maintains a massive advantage in carriers and other ocean-going warships. But the existence of opposing US and Soviet carrier battle groups in close proximity could create a very unstable situation. Each side might believe that it could survive in a confrontation only if it were the one to deliver the opening attack.

Alternatively, the opposing carrier battle groups might avoid confrontation at sea but inadvertently engage in combat ashore. For example, if both sides used carrier-based aircraft to conduct air strikes in support of forces on land, these aircraft might cross paths, resulting in air-to-air combat. At best, such fighting would have severe political consequences; at worst, it could lead to attacks on the carriers or to nuclear escalation.

The potential for such inadvertent escalation would be increased by the fact that confrontations in the Third World occur far from national authorities and are thus difficult to control.

Finally, as events in the Persian Gulf have demonstrated, the US–Soviet naval competition can also be exploited by third countries. The US decision to escort Kuwaiti tankers stemmed primarily from a fear that if the USA did not do it the USSR would—in which case the USA would lose prestige in the eyes of the world and of Persian Gulf states in particular. Thus, a US–Soviet naval confrontation might come about as the result of manipulation by third countries.

VI. Unilateral and negotiated solutions

In light of the growing potential for the US–Soviet naval competition to exacerbate tensions in peacetime and to create situations likely to lead to nuclear escalation in wartime, it is imperative that, through both unilateral actions and negotiations, the two countries take steps to constrain that competition. The 1972 Incidents At Sea Agreement has worked well to lessen the likelihood of serious US–Soviet naval incidents in peacetime. It should, however, be strengthened. The goal of these improved 'rules of the road' should be to maintain the physical separation of US and Soviet naval forces in peacetime to the greatest extent possible. Obviously, as long as such separation is maintained, collisions between warships of the two countries cannot occur.

One way to reduce the likelihood of collisions and other incidents at sea would be for the two countries to agree to disengagement zones in various waters of the world. Such zones would also serve the larger and perhaps more important purpose of limiting the size and nature of naval operations conducted by the superpowers in politically sensitive waters. This, in turn, would both limit the amount of ill-will generated by naval operations and reduce the probability of naval confrontations leading to open hostilities.

In the past, suggestions for naval disengagement have centred on the Mediterranean Sea and the Indian Ocean. Given the relatively large size of US and Soviet naval deployments in these waters and the level of conflict and political instability in the adjacent land areas, these remain logical areas for negotiations. Agreements to limit naval activities in waters within several hundred miles of the adversary's coast could also prove beneficial.

Whether or not the two sides are able to negotiate serious limitations on overseas deployments, they would do well to institute changes in naval strategies and force structure. These changes should be designed to lessen the probability that a crisis would lead to open conflict and that a conflict would rapidly escalate to the nuclear level. Although agreements to regulate the size and structure of opposing navies have been reached in the past, there is slight opportunity for successful negotiations on this complex subject today.

The USA and the USSR have very different navies with very different peacetime and wartime missions. Given the existence of these asymmetries, there is every reason to believe that negotiations on naval arms could be even more problematic than negotiations on strategic nuclear arms. Thus, the best hope for these changes may be in unilateral actions. In fact, this should not prove to be a stumbling-block because the following recommended actions would make sense even if they were taken by one side alone.

Both the United States and the Soviet Union should denuclearize their general-purpose naval forces—leaving only their SSBNs with nuclear weapons. Once tactical nuclear weapons are used, escalation to global nuclear war appears inevitable. Tactical nuclear weapons, such as SLCMs in particular, blur the distinction between tactical and strategic nuclear weapons because they can be used for attacks on the homelands of both nations.

The US and Soviet navies should alter their wartime strategies and the forces intended to carry out those strategies. A much more feasible and non-provocative US maritime strategy would focus on bottling up the Soviet Navy in wartime, rather than an offensive plan to carry the war into Soviet home waters and mount attacks against Soviet territory from sea bases. The US Navy's wartime strategy should be to achieve the following goals: (a) first and foremost, to control the sea lines of communication (SLOCs) connecting the USA and its European and Pacific allies with each other and with the Third World; (b) to support allied ground operations around the NATO periphery, particularly in southern Norway and the Mediterranean littoral states; and (c) to cut the Soviet Union's SLOCs. While the Soviet Union is much less dependent on transoceanic trade than are the USA and its allies, in a long war allied interdiction of Soviet SLOCs would help attrite its industrial base.

The best way to bottle up the Soviet Navy would be through the use of a combination of naval mines, land-based ASW patrol aircraft and attack submarines. Wartime anti-submarine barriers would be set up across various geographic chokepoints, including the Greenland–Iceland–United Kingdom (GIUK) Gap, through which Soviet attack submarines must pass to reach allied Atlantic SLOCs. US and other NATO attack submarines and mines could be used to form barriers across these chokepoints. Ground-based ASW patrol aircraft would also be used to patrol the chokepoints as well as other waters. Finally, merchant and other shipping crossing the Atlantic and Pacific Oceans would be escorted by frigates equipped with first-rate ASW capabilities, including ASW helicopters.

The ability to carry out this strategy would not require a navy organized around 15 large aircraft-carriers and their escorts, plus 100 SSNs. A limited power projection capability would still be useful to help ensure that NATO's flanks, particularly Norway, could be reinforced in the event of a Warsaw Pact attack. Reinforcing Norway does not require that the USA operate carrier battle groups in the northern portion of the Norwegian Sea or send US SSNs into the Soviet Union's SSBN sanctuaries. US carriers operating from the southern Norwegian Sea, in conjunction with land-based aircraft and US and allied attack submarines operating near Norwegian coastal waters, should be able to prevent large-scale Soviet amphibious landings along the coast of northern Norway.

This alternative strategy would be much less likely to escalate a crisis to open conflict and nuclear war because: it would not threaten Soviet SSBNs; it would not require the movement of US naval forces into Soviet waters; and it would not put a premium on pre-emption.

For its part, the Soviet Navy should abandon its plans for winning the battle of the first salvo. The Soviet Navy should concentrate on defending SSBN sanctuaries near its home waters. In addition, the expansion of Soviet naval bases to such remote locations as Cam Ranh Bay in Viet Nam should be curtailed since it is seen in the United States as clear evidence of plans for Soviet aggression.

In order to lessen the probability of nuclear escalation stemming from the actions of SSBNs, controls on the development and deployment of SLBMs can and should be negotiated. A depressed-trajectory flight-test ban would prevent the United States and the Soviet Union from developing confidence that their SLBMs could be launched in surprise attacks against coastal targets within a very few minutes. Ideally, it would be desirable to preclude the two nations from developing SLBMs with the accuracy required to destroy hardened targets such as ICBM silos. However, since the USA has conducted more than half the planned tests of its Trident II (D-5) missile and plans to begin deployment of the missile in late 1989, it may be too late to implement a general US–Soviet ban on SLBM flight-tests.

Along with controls on the development of SLBMs, restrictions on the deployment of SSBNs could also reduce the danger of nuclear escalation. Restrictions on SSBN deployments could be of two types.

1. The superpowers might agree to prohibit the deployment of SSBNs in waters within perhaps 1000 miles (1600 km) of the adversary's coast. Such restrictions would limit the ability of either country to threaten time-urgent targets such as bomber bases and command and communications facilities by taking full advantage of the short flight-times possible with SLBMs. Restrictions of this sort could be made either separately or as part of a broader agreement to limit naval operations off the adversary's coast.

2. The superpowers could agree to set aside sanctuaries for SSBNs—ocean areas where neither country would attempt to locate or trail the other side's SSBNs.

While in either case the restrictions would probably not be observed once war broke out, they would nevertheless serve a useful purpose by reducing fears of a first strike in periods of tension short of open hostilities.

The prospects for successfully negotiating a US–Soviet agreement on naval weapons or deployment patterns would depend greatly on the nature of the agreement sought. An agreement simply to improve the rules of the road for US and Soviet forces operating near each other in order to protect against collisions and other incidents would be relatively straightforward. On the other hand, an agreement to restrict deployment patterns or ban the development and deployment of new SLBMs would be highly contentious and thus difficult to negotiate.

The likelihood of the USA and the USSR unilaterally initiating changes in force structure and strategy is difficult to assess. The departure of Navy Secretary Lehman and the effect of tighter budgets in the coming years may reduce the US Navy's commitment to the current offensive maritime strategy and provide an opening for the Bush Administration to begin reshaping the Navy's structure and strategy. At the same time the prospects for such changes in the Soviet Navy may benefit from President Gorbachev's apparent willingness to challenge military interests and his drive for an improved Soviet economy.

In any event, it is imperative that measures to reduce naval competition receive careful consideration in parallel with measures, such as the 1987 INF Treaty, to regulate nuclear competition. In reality, it will accomplish little to concentrate on only one form of co-operation and accommodation while intensifying competition and confrontation in other spheres. Naval restraint on both sides would be an important contribution to the reduction of military tensions and an improved US–Soviet relationship.

Notes and references

[1] Atkinson, R., 'Superpowers maneuvering for supremacy on high seas', *Washington Post*, 4 Apr. 1984, p. 2.

[2] *Nuclear Free Seas* (Greenpeace Campaign for Nuclear Free Seas: July 1987), brochure, pp. 4–5.

[3] See Carroll, E. J., 'Black day on the Black Sea', *Arms Control Today*, May 1988, pp. 14–17.

[4] 'Marshal Akhromeyev about the visit to the USA', *Krasnaya Zvezda*, 17 July 1988, official English translation from *Daily Review*, Novosti Press Agency (APN), 18 July 1988.

[5] Arkin, W. M., *The Nuclear Arms Race at Sea*, Neptune Papers no. 1 (Greenpeace and the Institute for Policy Studies: Washington, DC, Oct. 1987).

[6] O'Rourke, R., *Nuclear-Powered and Nuclear-Weapon-Capable Ships in the U.S. Navy: An Aid to Identification*, Library of Congress, Congressional Research Service (US Government Printing Office: Washington, DC, 16 Apr. 1987), p. 1.

[7] Handler, J. and Arkin, W. M., *Nuclear Warships and Naval Nuclear Weapons: A Complete Inventory*, Neptune Papers no. 2 (Greenpeace and the Institute for Policy Studies: Washington, DC, May 1988), p. 2.

[8] See O'Rourke (note 6), pp. 8–9; and *US Naval Ship Battle Forces, 30 April 1987* (Office of the Chief of Naval Operations: Washington, DC, 30 Apr. 1987).

[9] Arkin (note 5), p. 6.

[10] For a good discussion of these benefits, see Donald, C. F. D., 'The Soviet Navy and tactical nuclear war at sea', *Survival*, July/Aug. 1987, pp. 318–35.

[11] Wilson, G. C., 'Pentagon guidance document seeks tougher sea defenses', *Washington Post*, 25 May 1982, p. 1.

[12] US Department of Defense (DOD), *Soviet Military Power 1985* (US Government Printing Office: Washington, DC, 1985), p. 92.

[13] SIPRI, *SIPRI Yearbook 1989: World Armaments and Disarmament* (Oxford University Press: Oxford, 1989), pp. 8, 11.

[14] *Authorization for Military Procurement, Fiscal Year 1985*, Hearing on H. R. 5167 before the Committee on Armed Services, US House of Representatives, 98th Congress (US Government Printing Office: Washington, DC, 1984), Part 2, p. 362.

[15] See Fieldhouse, R. and Taoka, S., SIPRI, *Superpowers at Sea: An Assessment of the Naval Arms Race*, a Strategic Issue Papers monograph (Oxford University Press: Oxford, 1989), pp. 122–25.

[16] US DOD, *Soviet Military Power 1988* (US Government Printing Office: Washington, DC, 1988), p. 53.

[17] Arkin, W. M. and Fieldhouse, R. W., *Nuclear Battlefields: Global Links in the Arms Race* (Ballinger: Cambridge, Mass., 1985), p. 46.

[18] US DOD, *Soviet Military Power 1987* (US Government Printing Office: Washington, DC, 1987), p. 29.

Paper 3. Maritime change in developing countries: the implications for naval arms control

Derek Boothby

Department for Disarmament Affairs, United Nations, New York, USA

I. The management of change

The most consuming political activity of the past 40 years or so has been, and will continue to be, the management of change. Whether initiating or reacting, supervising or suppressing, governments have been challenged by dynamic change of extraordinary dimensions—extraordinary in the sense that such rapid and often unpredictable change was not experienced by previous generations. Three centuries ago most people could confidently expect that their standards of living and surroundings would not be much different at the end of their lives from the days of their childhood.

However, with the development of science and learning, the expansion of trading and territorial interests by the maritime powers of the age, and the Industrial Revolution, the pace of change increased. By the end of the nineteenth century, so much had changed that it was already felt in some quarters that science and technology had probably achieved all that could be achieved. The Director of the US Patents Office even suggested that his office should be closed down, as everything had been invented and there would probably be no more patents.

Since the start of the twentieth century, the pace of change has continued to quicken. Encouraged by constant advances of science and technology, energized by ever-rising human expectations, and spurred by two world wars and, more recently, ideological conflicts, rapid change is no longer extraordinary. It is now a regular feature of modern life.

All too often, however, governments are so busy dealing with yesterday's change that they are unable to address effectively the new problems of today. In such circumstances, and surrounded by all manner of prophecies, it is perhaps not surprising that they frequently fail to identify correctly the challenges of the future.

The subject of maritime change in the developing countries falls into this category. As yet, the effects do not represent a major challenge to the navies and maritime policies of the superpowers, but their significance is growing, and the issues therefore deserve more serious attention than they have been awarded hitherto.

II. Developing navies and new weapons

From the original 51 member states of the United Nations in 1945, the membership has risen to its present 159; only a handful of countries or entities remain outside the organization. Other than 30 or so developed states (mostly either Western, socialist or neutral), the remainder are developing countries—approximately 130. The index of the reference book *Jane's Fighting Ships*,[1] an internationally recognized and respected source of naval information, listed 67 navies in the edition of 1958–59, 91 in 1966–67, 135 in 1976–77 and 150 in 1986–87. Most of this increase reflects the emergence of newly independent states.

Before their independence, many of these countries were colonies. Such maritime interests as they had were looked after by their respective parent states. Although there were differences of interest from time to time, in the 1950s and early 1960s there were very few that led to high tension or incidents of conflict. For the most part, the established maritime powers of the day were able to proceed with their naval developments, exercises and operations without having to take account of many extraneous considerations. For instance, British and French operations in connection with the Suez Canal in 1956 were scarcely hindered by Egyptian naval forces.

With independence came new and heavy responsibilities for national security. Not surprisingly, military emphasis was usually placed on armies and subsequently air forces rather than on navies. New states felt it necessary to protect land borders which might be arbitrary inheritances from colonial days and also—and often more important—to buttress insecure governments against the prospect of internal threats. In the late 1960s and the early 1970s, most developing countries had neither the incentive nor the resources to develop even modest naval forces.

In so far as it is possible to identify the early indications of new developments, perhaps the first sign might be traced to the sinking in 1967 of the Israeli destroyer *Eilat* by a Styx missile from a Soviet-supplied Egyptian patrol boat. As many commentators have pointed out, that first occasion of successful naval use of a surface-to-surface missile gave countries with established navies much cause to think. It also caused many smaller countries to realize that the acquisition of some level of effective naval force did not necessarily mean major expenditure on large or even medium-sized ships.

Development of comparable missile systems accelerated, and by the mid-1970s there were six basic types of anti-ship missile system available for export outside the Soviet Union: the Exocet (France), Otomat (France/Italy), Sea Killer (Italy), Penguin (Norway), Gabriel (Israel) and Harpoon (USA). Most of these weapons were compact enough to be fitted on patrol boats, thereby providing coastal navies with fast attack craft armed with highly potent weapons at comparatively small cost.

Numbers

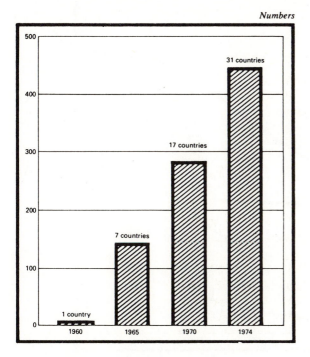

Figure 3.1. Missile-armed patrol boats, 1960–74

Source: SIPRI, *World Armaments and Disarmament: SIPRI Yearbook 1975* (Almqvist & Wiksell: Stockholm, 1975), chart 10.15, p. 280.

The *SIPRI Yearbook 1975* noted these developments with the comment that 'in 1960 only the Soviet Union possessed missile-armed patrol boats, but by 1974 there were nearly 450 of these vessels in 31 countries',[2] and accompanied this remark with a chart (see figure 3.1). Demonstrating that patrol boats in general were growing in popularity in developing countries rather than in the navies of NATO and the Warsaw Treaty Organization, SIPRI also illustrated the increases with another chart (see figure 3.2).

In the years since the assessment in figure 3.1, the number of vessels has continued to grow. By 1986, 60 countries possessed missile-armed patrol boats or patrol hydrofoils, amounting to almost 1100 craft.[3] Of that total, approximately 270 were in the navies of developed countries; the remainder were in service with China (approximately 235) and other developing countries (approximately 590).

While the numbers available for full operational service would, of course, be less, it should also be noted that these statistics do not include other missile-armed naval forces such as destroyers, frigates and corvettes, many of which

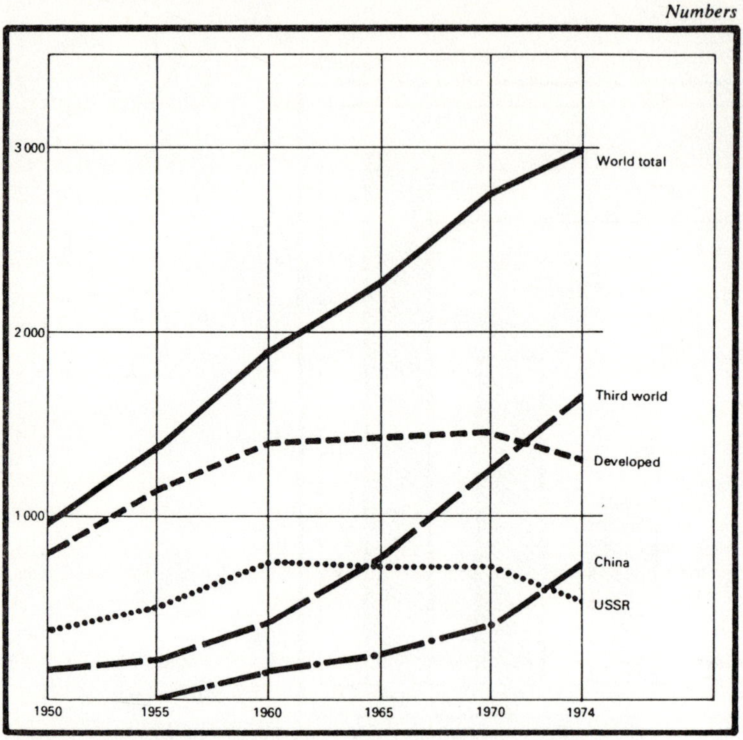

Numbers

Figure 3.2. Patrol boats, torpedo boats and gunboats, 1950–74

Source: SIPRI, *World Armaments and Disarmament: SIPRI Yearbook 1975* (Almqvist & Wiksell: Stockholm, 1975), chart 10.14, p. 279.

are in service in the navies of developing countries. Nor are patrol craft armed only with guns and/or torpedo tubes included.

It is also relevant to note that from 6 basic types of conventional ship-borne surface-to-surface missile available for export in the mid-1970s, there are in 1989 more than 12, excluding systems developed by the USSR and the USA for their own use.

In the area of air-to-surface missiles, 12 countries now produce or are developing a large range of various forms of missile system, including several for anti-ship use. With ranges of up to 100 kilometres, these weapons are highly attractive to those countries with aircraft able to carry them. The sinking in 1982 of the British ship *Sheffield* by the Argentine Air Force and in May 1987 the damage to the *USS Stark* by the Iraqi Air Force—both caused by Exocet missiles—brought dramatically to the fore the ship-stopping capability of much smaller forces. It is true that in both instances the warships were caught off-guard, and that defence systems exist that are designed to deal with the sub-sonic missile threat. But development of faster and more effective missiles continues; and, with the evidence of anti-shipping attacks of the Iran–Iraq War, the fact that more than 60 countries have either a ship-borne or an airborne anti-ship missile capability introduces a factor of major significance into naval consideration.

Such forces do not represent a major threat to the navies of the superpowers, or even as yet to the navies of other significant maritime powers, which will continue to be able to achieve local supremacy if they choose to deploy enough strength. However, there is no doubt that the stakes of the betting will be at a higher level, and therefore decision-making will be politically more complex. No longer will the navies of maritime powers be able to do what they want, almost whenever they want. Indeed, the gunboat—in its original sense of a small armed vessel capable of exerting military and political pressure—is reborn. With an ironic twist, the boot of 'gunboat diplomacy' is now shifting to the other foot.

Of as much, or perhaps even more, concern to the developing countries themselves is the recognition that military, particularly naval, capabilities now exist where before they did not. Local tensions that might spill over into local conflicts present opportunities for naval engagements between the navies of developing countries that were not previously possible, thereby extending the reach and the scope of conflict.

III. Political change

So much for capabilities—but will conditions arise in which they might be used? What aspects of political change affect the maritime scene in developing countries?

The principal change is, of course, the existence of so many sovereign states, each feeling it necessary to assert statehood and demonstrate independence. In such circumstances, states will not necessarily look kindly on naval activities in their regional areas by extra-regional navies. Naval deployments may be viewed by some as important means of protecting vital economic, political or security interests, or encouraging friendly relations with other states, but the same deployments may be seen by others as sources of potential intervention, pressure or interference in the internal affairs of states.

Nearer to home, individual states will watch local developments closely, particularly if political relations with neighbours are strained. For several developing countries, in the absence of military alliance arrangements, naval construction or purchases by neighbouring states can quickly arouse suspicions and mistrust, especially if there exist long-standing political differences.

These aspects are not unique, but they do tend to be overlooked by commentators in established maritime countries, conditioned as they are to focusing on the competitive struggle between the Soviet Union and the United States, and between NATO and the WTO.

Law of the Sea

Perhaps the most significant maritime development in the next few years, in the political sense, will be the entry into force of the United Nations Convention on the Law of the Sea (UNCLOS). Adopted on 30 April 1982 by the Third UN Conference on the Law of the Sea (and opened for signature on 10 December 1982), as of 1 May 1989, 41 states and entities had ratified the Convention which will enter into force 12 months after the receipt of 60 ratifications or accessions.[4] Although there are some important absentees among the signatories (e.g., the United States, the United Kingdom and the Federal Republic of Germany), their objections largely, but not solely, concern provisions relating to the exploitation of the resources of the seabed rather than the other aspects of the new constitution for the oceans. Despite their reluctance to subscribe to the Convention, as the Law of the Sea becomes an established feature of international maritime law, non-signatory states will not be able to ignore its effects. Indeed, they are already bound by those provisions which codify or elaborate existing measures of international law.

In efforts to establish a legal maritime order which could embrace the needs of developing countries and the maritime interests of developed countries, a very difficult balancing act was achieved by the Third United Nations Conference on the Law of the Sea. As subsequently described in a UN study:

There were three important interests, among others, which had to be reconciled by the Conference: on the one hand, the security interests of coastal States and the need to protect the mainly resource-oriented interests of the developing coastal States and on the other hand, the necessity of preserving the freedom of navigation of ships and aircraft. In this the Conference was successful as the Convention on the Law of the Sea has managed to balance these interests.[5]

In pursuit of this balance and among many other provisions, the UNCLOS adopted a 12-nautical mile territorial sea, specific conditions concerning archipelagic waters, and the concept of the exclusive economic zone (EEZ).

The EEZ introduces a change of truly historic proportions into maritime affairs. In a zone which may extend up to 200 nautical miles from the baseline from which the territorial sea is measured, a coastal state will have sovereign rights for the purpose of exploring and exploiting, conserving and managing with respect to the natural resources, whether living or non-living, of the waters superjacent to the seabed and of the seabed and its sub-soil. The coastal state will also have sovereign rights with regard to other activities for the economic exploitation and exploration of the zones, such as the production of energy from the water, currents and winds.

Furthermore, a coastal state will have jurisdiction in accordance with the relevant provisions of the UNCLOS with regard to the establishment and use of artificial islands, installations and structures; marine scientific research; and the protection and preservation of the marine environment. The extent of jurisdiction is broad: for instance, the coastal state will be responsible for determining the allowable catch of the living resources in its EEZ; for regulating seasons and areas of fishing; for regulating the types, sizes and numbers of fishing vessels that may be used; for appropriate conservation and management laws and regulations; and for enforcement procedures.

These developments will bring major new responsibilities for coastal states over significant sea areas: for example, a state with an 800-kilometre coastline will find itself faced with the task of policing more than 290 000 square kilometres of EEZ. The duties will include such activities as fishery protection, anti-smuggling of drugs and other contraband, maritime safety, search and rescue, and pollution control. In some areas there may also be additional duties such as anti-piracy, maritime traffic control and river surveillance.

For some developing countries, fishery protection duties will be of great importance. According to the United Nations Food and Agriculture Organization (FAO), at present more than 95 per cent of the world's annual fish catch is caught within 200 nautical miles of shore. Protein from fish is a major ingredient of the human diet and, if countries are ranked by reliance on animal protein derived from fish, 39 of the first 40 places are occupied by developing countries.[6] With the world population continually increasing, particularly in the developing countries, there will be a rising demand for—and rising competition over—ocean fisheries. Developing countries will not only seek to exploit the marine resources of the EEZ but will also be faced with problems of how to protect their interests and enforce compliance by other states fishing in their respective zones. On the other side of the coin will be efforts by states seeking to maintain access to traditional fishing grounds but which in the future will fall under the EEZ jurisdiction of the coastal state.

By Article 73 of the Convention, the coastal state is empowered to take a wide range of enforcement measures in order to protect its rights over the living resources of its EEZ. In order to carry out permitted activities such as boarding, inspection and arrest, the coastal state will need appropriate vessels and personnel. For most developing countries, such duties will probably have to be discharged by naval forces. Instances in which powers of detention or hot pursuit may have to be exercised—for example, occurrences of pollution in the EEZ—will require the vessels of enforcement to be capable of high speed and reasonable endurance, and of carrying ship-borne weapons.

The Convention reaffirms the principle of freedom of navigation, but there are different levels of freedom according to the different parts of the sea. While all ships may enjoy the right of innocent passage through the territorial sea, certain military or quasi-military activities are identified in Article 19 of the UNCLOS as being not innocent (e.g., any threat or use of force against the coastal state, any act of wilful and serious pollution, and any fishing activities—see annexe B). Furthermore, arising from the adoption of the 12-nautical mile territorial sea, the legal status of several straits used for international navigation will be altered by such straits falling within the sovereignty of the bordering states. Accordingly, instead of freedom of navigation as previously applied, the regime of innocent passage will obtain, and certain rights and obligations concerning transit passage will be applicable.[7]

Another very significant change that will be introduced when the UNCLOS enters into force will be the new concept of archipelagic waters. Under certain conditions, an archipelagic state may draw straight baselines joining the outermost islands and drying reefs of the archipelago. Within such lines the archipelagic state will exercise sovereignty over the waters and their seabed, subsoil and superjacent airspace. While ships and aircraft may proceed on passage through such areas, the archipelagic state may designate sea lanes and air routes from which vessels and aircraft may not deviate by more than 25 nautical miles either side of the axis lines.

From this very brief and selective description of only a few of the effects of the Convention on the Law of the Sea, it will be appreciated that it will have major implications for the conduct of international maritime affairs. To quote again from the United Nations study:

New resources, new developments, new activities, new responsibilities—all will demand more co-ordinated maritime policies, administrative machinery and policing capabilities. There are likely to be more, not fewer, disputes over fishing rights and laws and the activities of trawlers. There will probably be increased competition between various parties endeavouring to exploit the same area for different resources. More sea traffic and greater industrialization will create a greater need for more effective pollution controls and improved protection of the marine environment.[8]

IV. Implications for naval arms control

What does all this have to do with naval arms control?

In the process of drawing all these threads together, a maritime scenario of great complexity begins to form. In the place of non-existent naval forces a few years ago, there is now a growing number of developing countries with naval capabilities that cannot be easily ignored. Among these naval capabilities the numbers and distribution of missile-armed fast attack craft, supplemented by aircraft with anti-ship missiles and perhaps shore-based anti-ship missiles, introduce a significant new factor into the naval equation.

Such vessels will be ideally suited to discharge the vastly greater responsibilities that will devolve from the entry into force of the Convention on the Law of the Sea. There is therefore every reason to expect that their numbers will continue to increase significantly in the years ahead.

The expansion of naval forces for the entirely valid and legitimate reasons described above will nevertheless have a number of unsettling effects. In terms of local effects, they will be factors in local tensions and conflicts. In circumstances involving extra-regional forces, they may provide new options to governments which object to exercises or other activities that they regard as interference or potential intervention on the part of forces from outside the region.

There will therefore be greater opportunities for misunderstanding and greater risk of untoward incidents at sea potentially involving a large number of states.

These developments are occurring just as the general climate for measures of naval arms control seems to be unfavourable. As happens so often, all eyes are turned to the situation between the two superpowers and the principal navies of the NATO and WTO member states. In recent years a number of proposals have been made by the USSR, but the general Western view—particularly strongly held by the United States—is that conditions in the 1980s are far different from conditions in 1922 and 1930 when quantitative and qualitative restrictions were internationally agreed at the Washington and London naval conferences. It is widely held that in these modern times there is no such commodity as an independent naval balance or parity, and that measures of naval arms control are of very doubtful value and can be considered only in the context of arms control in general.

It is probably also true to say that, as a maritime (as opposed to a continental) country, the United States perceives little to be gained and much to be lost by agreeing to controls and constraints on its own naval forces that will limit its freedom of maritime action. In such a frame of mind, not only are present circumstances unlikely to lead to agreement between the United States and the Soviet Union on naval arms control *per se*, but there have also been other repercussions. For instance, following the action of the New Zealand Government in 1985 to prohibit nuclear ship visits, in April 1986 the United States declared that it would end its ANZUS (Australia–New Zealand–United States) defence commitments to New Zealand if visits of US nuclear-armed or nuclear-powered ships continued to be forbidden. Despite this stance by the United States, in June 1987 the New Zealand Parliament adopted the anti-nuclear legislation.[9] The firm action by the United States is intended to convey a message not only to New Zealand but also to any other state that might be contemplating measures which would limit the maritime policies of the United States.

In early 1987, the USA and the UK joined France in declining to sign the protocols to the 1985 South Pacific Nuclear Free Zone Treaty (Treaty of Rarotonga) agreed by the members of the South Pacific Forum. Charles E. Redman, speaking on behalf of the US State Department, declared that US practices and activities in the South Pacific region were not inconsistent with the treaty and its protocols but that the United States was not, under current circumstances, in a position to sign the protocols. It was reported that US officials had said that a principal concern was that other nations would catch the 'non-nuclear fever'.[10]

Furthermore, the United States has expressed strong opposition to proposals by the Association of South-East Asian Nations (ASEAN) to institute a South-

East Asian nuclear weapon-free zone on the grounds that the United States needs to keep the sea lanes of South-East Asia open as a key link between the Pacific and Indian Oceans.

Partly because of long lead times in ship design and construction, and partly because of the nature of naval activities, naval issues tend to move slowly and usually away from the glare of publicity. However, after a period of quiescence in the late 1970s, the 1980s have seen a number of events, developments and changes which although often separate in themselves are indicators of unsettling trends: the South Atlantic War of 1982 between Argentina and the United Kingdom; incidents of mining in the Red Sea, the Persian Gulf and off Nicaragua; over 350 attacks on shipping over the nearly 10 years of the war between Iran and Iraq; battleship guns used against shore targets near Beirut; significant building programmes by the Soviet and US navies; US naval operations off Grenada and Libya; increased Soviet and US use of bases at Cam Ranh Bay and Diego Garcia, respectively; major expansion of the Indian Navy; unidentified submarine operations and territorial intrusions in the Baltic Sea; and ever-widening deployments of tactical naval nuclear weapons and sea-launched cruise missiles with nuclear warheads.

Many of these events have created questions of confidence among developing and developed countries alike, but in addition there are the significant changes under way in the naval strengths and responsibilities of developing countries that are discussed in this paper.

Thus, the naval situation as a whole is a complex one, composed of shifting winds and changing currents. In the circumstances prevailing between the major maritime powers, bold and effective measures of naval arms control will be difficult to achieve. However, a continued absence of efforts, and failure to recognize the implications of many of the changes that are taking place, will lead to greater problems later on. Such problems may be localized disputes over fishing rights or other economic activities, but they may also be political disagreements of a much more serious nature. They may either involve the navies of established maritime powers from the beginning or escalate, as in the naval situation in the Persian Gulf, to the level of major politico-naval confrontation. Looking ahead, one cannot help wondering how much longer non-nuclear weapon countries will accept the existing policies of nuclear weapon states refusing either to confirm or to deny the existence of nuclear weapons aboard visiting warships.

Together, these elements add up to the challenges posed by the management of significant change. For some observers at least, they would seem to establish a clear political need for measures of confidence-building at sea.

V. Possible measures

What sort of measures are needed? The most feasible measures are primarily those of a *regional* nature. It is easier to find agreement among 10 or 15 countries in a region or sub-region than it is to find measures that can be agreed and applied world-wide. These include measures such as limits on certain deployments in specific geographical areas; limits on exercises and manoeuvres; prior notification of such activities; provisions for inspections; perhaps agreements not to acquire certain naval weapons or technologies; and measures of declared restraint on the part of nuclear powers, including a careful review of the 'neither confirm nor deny' policy (see paper 9 and, for a document on the US policy, annexe A).

Such measures would need not only recognition by established maritime powers but also their participation. Reassessment and cautious compromise would be required from all states, whether large or small, in the interests of establishing a framework within which these maritime developments can be accommodated. Similarly, it would be in the interests of the superpowers and other major maritime states to take steps and contribute to agreements that limit the chances of naval tensions and conflicts, wherever they might occur.

VI. Conclusion

The modern world is a world of change—political, economic, technological and social change. The combination of political developments and advances in naval weapon technology will increasingly present new circumstances and risks which will demand new attitudes and policies on the part of states. There will inevitably be encroachment on the traditional, absolute freedoms of the high seas, but as we approach the millenium it is apparent that we no longer live in the world of Hugo Grotius of almost 400 years ago. Perhaps the maritime change taking place in the developing countries will act as a spur. If the evolving situation can be recognized for what it is, then its effects might be dealt with while they are still manageable.

No sailor enjoys being caught on a lee shore, but it is the prudent sailor who avoids being caught in that predicament in the first place.

Notes and references

The views expressed in this paper are entirely the author's; in no way whatsoever do they necessarily represent the views of the Secretary-General of the United Nations.

[1] *Jane's Fighting Ships* (Jane's: London, annual).
[2] SIPRI, *World Armaments and Disarmament: SIPRI Yearbook 1975* (Almqvist & Wiksell: Stockholm, 1975), p. 280.
[3] *Jane's Weapon Systems 1986-87* (Jane's: London, 1986), pp. 1027–45.
[4] *The Law of the Sea: United Nations Convention on the Law of the Sea* (United Nations: New York, 1983). The implications of the Convention for navies are discussed in a UN disarmament study, *The Naval Arms Race* (see note 5).
[5] United Nations, *The Naval Arms Race*, Report of the Secretary-General, UN Study series no. 16, UN document A/40/535 (United Nations: New York, 1986), p. 46.
[6] *The Economist*, 23 June 1984.

[7] In Article 38 of the Convention on the Law of the Sea, transit passage is defined as 'the exercise . . . of the freedom of navigation and overflight solely for the purpose of continuous and expeditious transit of the strait between one part of the high seas or an exclusive economic zone and another part of the high seas or an exclusive economic zone'.

[8] See note 5, p. 69.

[9] *The Arms Control Reporter—1987* (Institute for Defense and Disarmament Studies: Brookline, Mass., 1987), p. 456.B.68.

[10] *New York Times,* 5 Feb. 1987; *Washington Post,* 6 Feb. 1987.

Part III
Challenges of naval arms control

Paper 4. Navies of the superpowers: the strategic background

Hervé Coutau-Bégarie

Ecole Pratique des Hautes Etudes, Paris, France

I. Introduction

Alfred Thayer Mahan has popularized the concept of sea power and Halford Mackinder the concept of land power. Since the time of their writings, it has become common in strategic analysis to present history as a struggle between land powers and sea powers: Great Britain *versus* France in the eighteenth and nineteenth centuries; Great Britain *versus* Germany during the first decades of the twentieth century; and today the United States *versus* the Soviet Union. The opposition between the heirs of Mahan and those of Mackinder are only at the level of the conclusions—the first saying that sea power must win in the end and the second giving the advantage to land power.

Even if this scheme is partly invalid (history cannot be reduced to a fight between land and sea forces), it has the virtue of giving an impressive image of a fundamental fact which must be observed in discussions of naval disarmament: the naval instrument is not a static and isolated one; it must be considered from a global point of view. While very sophisticated and conscientious studies have been made to assess rival fleets, this type of exercise is in fact not useful, for two reasons.

First, sea power is not a matter of naval strength alone. A valid comparison would necessarily have to cover the whole range of means whereby power can be exerted, that is, 'the total force, real and potential, which a country can mobilize to serve its foreign policy'.[1] Such an assessment is very difficult to make. Sea power represents a combination of factors—a fleet, foreign bases, a command and intelligence system, a strategic doctrine, and so on—and the existence of a navy, although essential, is neither the only nor necessarily the most important of these factors. Thus, contrary to common belief, the Soviet Navy was in 1955 numerically stronger than in 1980, with a fall from 800 000 to 433 000 men under arms and from 4000 to 1400 naval aircraft, as well as reductions, although less marked, in major surface combat ships and submarines. Nevertheless, few believed that the Soviet Navy was a threat in 1955. Clearly, then, if Soviet sea power has increased, it is not because Soviet warships are more numerous today but because there was a change in Soviet naval doctrine and in the place of the navy in the military organization and in Soviet foreign policy. During the Gorshkov years, the *Morskoi Flot* (Soviet Navy) ceased to be a fortress fleet which did not travel beyond the coastal

Table 4.1. Comparison of numbers of vessels in the US and Soviet navies, 1969 and 1979

Type of vessel	1969		1979	
	USA	USSR	USA	USSR
Aircraft-carriers	22	0	13	2
Other surface vessels	279	220	165	272
Submarines	156	354	123	355
Command vessels	2	0	0	0
Various patrol ships	9	148	3	129
Amphibious vessels	153	103	65	100
Minesweepers	74	165	3	176
Mobile supply ships	112	56	61	147
Other ancillary craft	119	624	22	596
Total	**926**	**1 670**	**455**	**1 769**

Source: Défense nationale (Paris), June 1979, p. 202.

Table 4.2. Comparison of the tonnage of the US and Soviet navies, 1980

Type of vessel	USA	USSR
Strategic ocean-going forces	240 500	608 600
Combat vessels	2 013 950	2 025 600
Amphibious craft	692 300	141 900
Naval supply ships	880 000	499 700
Total	**3 826 750**	**3 275 800**

Source: Labayle-Couhat, J., *Les flottes de combat* [*Combat Fleets*] (Éditions Maritimes et d'Outre-Mer: Paris, 1982).

Note: These tables show the risks of comparison: comparing the number of ships, the US inferiority grew dramatically in the 1970s; but comparing overall tonnages, the USA retains its superiority.

waters to become a blue-water navy. It showed the Soviet flag on every ocean in the world and challenged US warships during crises, as was publicly demonstrated during the Six-Day War (1967), the Yom Kippur War (1973), and in the Angolan (1975) and Ethiopian (1977) crises.[2]

From a *naval* point of view, this illustrates the first axiom of a truly comparative method: one must consider not only the warships, the dead forces of Clausewitz, but also the material, the men, the logistics and the doctrines—in sum, the combination of dead forces and live forces, in Clausewitzian language. In other words, a technical comparison does not mean a purely physical comparison (see tables 4.1 and 4.2).

However, this is still not sufficient to ensure a valid and useful comparison. To make a 'useful' comparison, one must in fact go beyond the naval element to consider the *maritime* component of the global strategy of the countries considered. And instead of researching similarities between countries—

regardless of its validity—one must first consider the differences in the respective structures of power. Navies are no longer built up for a battle 'in line'; they are integrated in global strategic objectives, and their value must not be assessed by a comparison with a potential adversary but rather in the light of the needs of the country. That is to say, before comparing two countries' navies, one must first evaluate within each country the correlation between the means and the ends. The United States and the Soviet Union provide a very clear example of this process.

II. The maritime dimension

When the strategic equations of the two rivals are examined, one immediately sees the very marked differences between them.

The US strategic equation

The United States is the centre of an alliance which is totally dependent on the sea lanes, from both economic and strategic points of view. Needless to say, the industrialized Western countries are very highly dependent on imported raw materials, primarily on oil. It is well known that their stocks would allow only three months of self-sufficiency, or a little longer if domestic public consumption were severely reduced. Efforts to diminish their dependency since the oil crises of 1973 and 1979 have not fundamentally altered this situation. On the contrary, the dependence of the United States on imported oil will grow over the coming decades. More generally, the modern developed economies would not survive an interruption in the flow of imports and exports.

From a strategic point of view, the NATO alliance is also totally dependent on the sea for supplies and reinforcements for the theatres of operations in time of war. The USA has land boundaries with only two countries—Canada and Mexico. Every other allied country must be reached by a sea route, and it is a widely accepted assumption that NATO in Europe, and Japan or South Korea in the Far East, could not withstand a Soviet offensive without US intervention. The air route would be marginal—perhaps decisive in the first hours but marginal in the long term; 95 per cent by volume of goods transported would be moved by sea.

Sea control is not a luxury or even a commodity for the Western alliance; it is a question of life or death. With control of the sea, the Western alliance is not sure to win; but without control of the sea, it is bound to lose. Hence, the US Navy and its NATO allies, with the forces of Japan and Australia, would have as their primary task to keep open the sea lanes, without which their countries could not survive. Thus, if viewed from the highest level of strategy, the basic use of sea power would be defensive,[3] although recourse to a tactical offensive[4] would not be excluded. These are the ideas behind the US Navy's Maritime Strategy, now several years old and the object of a good deal of debate.[5] The aim would be to deprive the Soviet Union of the initiative by forcing it to give priority to its own defence. Ever since 1982 very large-scale naval exercises have simulated attacks on Soviet bases from the White Sea and the northern Pacific Ocean. But the fact that the offensive is once again in favour does not mean that control of the sea lanes—a defensive function—is no longer vitally important.[6] Perhaps here lies one of the greatest criticisms which can be made of the US Maritime Strategy: the projection of power is possible only if sea control has already been secured (in terms of the tetralogy of Admirals Zumwalt and Turner),[7] and the insistence on the forward battle on the Northern Flank of Europe can be dangerous if it causes an underestimation of the importance of sea control in the North Atlantic. Before considering the *exploitation* of sea control against land, the Western Alliance has to consider the *acquisition* and the *conservation* of sea control.

In this context, whichever doctrine is adopted (compare the current debate on maritime strategy *versus* coalition defence[8]), the place of the navy is not discussed. There were periods, during the late 1940s and more recently during the Carter Administration, when the navy was 'under attack', the Pentagon estimating that large aircraft-carriers were too expensive and no longer suitable for the strategic environment, but the need for an oceanic navy, 'second to none', was never seriously challenged. The US Navy is perfectly integrated in US global strategy; the Chairman of the Joint Chiefs of Staff is (in August 1989) an admiral, and the share of the US Navy in the defence budget is not inferior to the shares of the Army or Air Force (in fact, it was greater in some years). This 'maritime spirit' is so profoundly embedded that history has been rewritten as a result of it: naval analysts developed the theme of the 'manifest destiny' of the USA and recalled the cry of Paul Jones, one of the 'founding fathers' of the navy: 'without a strong navy, alas America!'. This is largely a myth because during the entire nineteenth century the US Navy was a fortress fleet, designed for coastal defence. It became a truly blue-water navy only during the Administration of Teddy Roosevelt,[9] but the success of the myth partly proves the pervasiveness of the maritime mentality.

The Soviet strategic equation

The Soviet Union is in a very different situation. It depends on overseas supplies only for certain raw materials, notably bauxite and phosphates, and could survive on its own for lengthy periods. A blockade would have very little effect on the USSR. From a geopolitical point of view, it is in a central position, and its major allies form a continental block around the country in Eastern Europe and in Asia (Mongolia). The only true exception to this rule is Viet Nam; the other allies, such as Cuba, Ethiopia and the People's Democratic Republic of Yemen, would not be of great value in case of general war. Certainly, sea communications would be essential in time of war between the European USSR and the Far East, since the Trans-Siberian railway, even though recently reinforced along part of the route by the Baikal–Amur line,[10] could not possibly transport adequate supplies to Soviet forces along the Chinese frontier. The geographical difficulty, however, seems insuperable, since the northern route, via the Arctic Ocean, is open for only a few months each year, and even then it is immensely difficult to use this route. The southern route, through the Indian Ocean, is too long, and there are too many Western-held chokepoints. It would be a great vulnerability for the Soviet Union in time of war.

The conclusion is obvious: the Soviet Navy would not be concerned about the protection of sea lanes which are either not vital or impossible to defend. If it goes beyond its coastal waters, its primary concern would be to cut the Western sea lanes. If it achieves this result, the Soviet Union would be in a position to wib a war. This is the classic distinction between *sea control* and *sea denial*: the United States must at all costs retain command of the sea, not only to win a war but also to avoid losing it. The Soviet Union cannot obtain sea control beyond its coastal waters, but it does not need it: it needs only to deprive the United States of such control. The Soviet Navy can have only an offensive posture on the high seas. The objective of the US maritime strategy is precisely to prevent the Soviet Navy from taking the offensive on the high seas by pushing it back into its coastal waters where it can assume only a defensive posture.

The Soviet Union is truly the 'heartland' described by Mackinder, in a central position and not vulnerable to the activities of the maritime power. The USSR can be attacked by land, as was the case during the Middle Ages from Europe by the Teutonic Knights and from Asia by the Golden Horse, during the nineteenth century by the French (1812; the Crimean War was an attack from the sea, but was limited to the periphery) and during this century twice by the Germans. Conversely, the Soviet Union can attack in every direction by land (Central Europe, the Southern Flank of Europe, Central Asia and Manchuria). It is not surprising in this context that the army has a clear pre-eminence in the military establishment and that it has been difficult for the navy to become recognized as an independent force, with a strategy of its own and not considered as an appendix of the army. The efforts of Soviet Fleet Admiral Sergey Gorshkov have tended to raise the status of the navy and to help it gain complete autonomy. With his successor, Fleet Admiral V. N. Chernavin, it seems that the USSR is returning to an 'integrated strategy' dominated by the army.

III. The naval component

It is therefore not surprising that there are considerable structural differences between the US and Soviet navies. At sea, again more than on land, the arms race is not only an action–reaction phenomenon. It is a complex process which is guided first by each navy's self-image by the missions which are assigned according to the global strategy.

The US Navy

The US Navy is a balanced navy, with a mixture of all the components needed to perform the missions of a superpower maritime force: strategic dissuasion (deterrence); protection of the sea lanes; and projection of power on a large scale and on a global scale. It has two elements which are not available to its Soviet rival.

1. A formidable fleet of 15 aircraft-carriers, 5 of them nuclear-powered (2 more being built) each of them carrying 75–90 aircraft (supersonic fighters and attack aircraft, airborne early-warning systems and helicopters), a tremendous mobile strike force unequalled elsewhere in the world. Their value is enormous: it is with this force that the United States can intervene in any ocean, with a formidable capacity to strike against land. They showed their efficiency during the Korean and Viet Nam Wars; these 'floating airports' were totally out of range of Chinese or Vietnamese attacks. During the Viet Nam War, only one ship—the destroyer *Higbee*—was hit by a bomb, but it did not sustain great damage. Beyond their military value and the doubts about their 'survivability' in war, they are symbols of power. They have replaced battleships as 'capital ships' and provide a conventional deterrence at a distance of thousands of kilometres from the United States. The aircraft-carriers of the Sixth Fleet in the Mediterranean and of the Seventh Fleet in the Far East make the United States truly a world power, constantly interacting with its allies.

2. An impressive array of amphibious craft, including the largest assault craft in the world—the 40 000-ton Tarawa Class (5 units; and units of a new type are being built). This amphibious fleet represents 600 000 tons as compared to 150 000 tons for the Soviet Navy (or twice the tonnage of the entire French Fleet). Furthermore, the US Marine Corps can organize landings of forces of the size of one or two divisions. (There are two Marine Amphibious Units, one normally in the Pacific and one in the Atlantic; in addition, material for them is prepositioned in the Indian Ocean at Diego Garcia.) Even if the United States is unable to organize massive landings such as those of World War II, it is able to intervene quickly anywhere in the world with capabilities which are not in any way symbolic but represent a real fighting power.

These aircraft-carriers and amphibious forces illustrate the importance which the United States attaches to the projection of its maritime power against land, whether this takes the form of action by aircraft and naval forces without army support (as would be the case in the event of help to Greece or Turkey by the Sixth Fleet) or of a landing by the US Marines. (The creation of the Rapid Deployment Force [RDF], now integrated into the US Central Command, with heavy supplies on the island of Diego Garcia provides for such an eventuality in the Indian Ocean.) In contrast to the Soviet Navy, the US Navy does not have to worry about coastal defence of its territory or protection of access to the high seas, in view of the vast distances separating the United States from the rest of the world and the absence of chokepoints. However, owing to an excess of confidence and to some disdain for an arm considered (wrongly) as out-of-date, insufficient attention has been paid to the possibility of enemy mine-laying in US ports, and hence to the provision of adequate mine-sweeping or mine-hunting equipment. In this respect, events in the Persian Gulf in the late 1980s revealed some obvious shortcomings. The US Navy is trying to correct this situation, but the new Avenger Class minehunter is facing some problems.

This insistence on projection of power and the corresponding under-estimation of the protection of the sea lanes are reflected in the structure of forces. In the early 1970s, the US Chief of Naval Operations Admiral Zumwalt tried to respond to the dramatic decline of the number of warships with the 'hi–low mix' concept: a small number of very sophisticated (and therefore expensive) warships for projection of power and operations in high-threat environments combined with relatively 'rustic' and cheaper warships for the protection of the sea lanes. The former group included Los Angeles Class nuclear-powered attack submarines, nuclear aircraft-carriers, and nuclear cruisers of the California and Virginia Classes. The latter group was to include the Sea Control Ship—a small carrier with anti-submarine warfare (ASW) helicopters and vertical/short take-off and landing (V/STOL) aircraft—the Spruance Class destroyers and O. H. Perry Class frigates. This programme has not been completely realized: the Sea Control Ship was cancelled after the retirement of Admiral Zumwalt (the design was sold to Spain, which built one unit, the *Principe de Asturias),* and the programme of frigates was continued only with great difficulties and abandoned after the 60th unit. The US Navy is fascinated by the best (and the most expensive) warships, designed in fact for battle against the Soviet Union—the pinnacle of naval strategy—and assigns to its allies the less 'interesting' task of protecting the sea lanes. This international division of labour could be dangerous if the allies, for political or military reasons, were unable or unwilling to co-operate with the United States.

The *Morskoi Flot*

The structure of the Soviet Navy is very different. Instead of being a truly oceanic navy with a complete panoply of means, it is a mixture of coastal and oceanic navy and lacks a really effective power-projection capability.

With narrow seas (the Baltic Sea, Black Sea and Sea of Japan) and thousands of kilometres of coasts to patrol, the Soviet Navy has in its order of battle some hundreds of patrol ships, light amphibious vessels and other ancillary craft. Therefore, the inferiority (claimed by 'hawks' in the 1970s) of the US Navy has always been a myth: it is true that the US Navy has three times fewer units than its rival (580 *versus* 1800 ships), but this impressive number of Soviet ships includes many small ships that are used exclusively for coastal defence and that are of little value in the world-wide balance of power (regionally, of course, the position may be very different).

For operations on the high seas, Admiral Gorshkov has gone on record as saying that surface ships have yielded priority to submarines and naval aircraft.[11] In this century the submarine (equipped with mines) has always been the preferred arm of the Russian Navy. The Soviet Navy has nearly 250 attack submarines, but most of them are diesel-powered and out-of-date. During the next decade, this number will decrease dramatically. The decline will in part be counterbalanced by an increase in long-range naval aircraft: the Backfire and in the 1990s the new Blackjack bombers. The new dimension of the air threat is regarded with great concern by the United States, even if its ship-borne Aegis air defence system greatly increases its capabilities in this field.

In a NATO–WTO war, Soviet submarines used in conjunction with long-range bombers, and possibly using nuclear weapons, would be the chief instruments in a brutal offensive strike to destroy as many warships and trading vessels as possible as soon as hostilities began, thus throwing NATO's shipping into disarray. Forward-deployed surface ships, notably the Soviet Mediterranean squadron, would take part in this first strike, too, but, dangerously isolated and without air cover, would in all probability soon be destroyed. Hence it is likely that the major units of the Northern, Pacific and Black Sea fleets would stay in port rather than emerge to challenge their Western counterparts. During the last Gorshkov years, there was an evolution from this 'first salvo battle' to more complex tactics: the appearance of new classes of sophisticated warship (Kiev carriers, Kirov battle cruisers, Slava surface cruisers, and Udaloy and Sovremenyy destroyers); and new schemes of exercises around task force equivalents suggested that the Soviet Navy was preparing itself to dispute the sea control of Western forces in areas such as the Norwegian Sea, the Sea of Japan and perhaps the eastern Mediterranean Sea. The offensive posture of the US Navy in the late 1980s and the conceptions of Admiral Chernavin indicate in fact that the USSR has abandoned this ambitious goal. Competing with the US Navy for sea supremacy is no longer a goal. Priority is given to the protection of the SSBN bastions in the Barents and Okhotsk Seas, the protection of the Soviet shores and the co-operation with the army along the coast on the northern flank, in the Baltic and Black Seas. In this sense, the US Maritime Strategy has been remarkably successful, by obliging the Soviet Union to change from an offensive position to a defensive one; but the submarine and air threats against shipping have not disappeared.

IV. Implications for naval disarmament

One conclusion clearly emerges from the above analysis, namely, that a purely quantitative comparison does not provide an adequate picture of the complex balance of power at sea; indeed, the very notion of parity at sea is so abstract as to be virtually meaningless. Between the two world wars, as Admiral Herbert

Richmond so clearly showed, equality in tonnage or in numbers of ships between a country dependent on the sea and a self-sufficient (i.e., not dependent on the sea) rival could only shift the balance of power in favour of the latter, who would be able to attack in an element of vital importance to the enemy.[12] Mackinder put forward the same idea (probably without having read Richmond) in his celebrated article of 1943: Great Britain could not possibly have accepted Kaiser Wilhelm's shipbuilding programme, for it would have meant that the country which already had the central position and the strongest army would have been able to challenge British power at its core.[13]

The same holds true, *mutatis mutandis*, today. The Soviet Union already occupies the central position (Mackinder's 'heartland') and is the strongest military power on land. It now has a navy which threatens the maritime alliance led by the United States. Should it deprive the United States of its control of the seas, the USSR would then be in a position to exert its domination virtually unchecked.

Hence it will be readily appreciated that US and Soviet approaches to naval arms limitation negotiations will be different. Over the past few years, the Soviet Union has made various (usually somewhat vague) proposals to this end, while the West has insisted that no one class of armaments can be limited in isolation from the others and that overall negotiations are required. This point has to a great extent been supported by a United Nations working group of experts, which in its report says:

Naval forces do not exist independently of others, and must be considered in an overall military context. Naval parity or balance in itself means nothing. Hence naval disarmament has to be seen in a broader context. Secondly, this fact, and the geographical situation peculiar to individual States might lead a State to take unilateral action as regards limitation of naval forces and armaments so as to preserve an overall military balance, and hence to disregard numerical equality.[14]

This being so, a general agreement for the limitation of naval armaments similar to those entered into between the two world wars at the Washington and London naval conferences, or even a bilateral agreement between the United States and the Soviet Union, would seem to be difficult to achieve. This is an essential observation. For that matter, it is difficult to imagine that the outlook for naval arms limitation negotiations would be any brighter.

However, there is nothing static about the strategic balance. Indeed, there has been, in recent years, a marked turn of the tide. In the 1970s, the Soviet Navy expanded fast, increasing in numbers and improving in quality. Ships of an increasingly formidable kind were launched at a high rate, such as aircraft-carriers of the Kiev Class, the Kresta II, Kara and Slava Class cruisers, the Krivak Class destroyers, and so on. The two world-wide naval exercises 'Okean' (1970) and 'Okean II' (1975) revealed the Soviet Union's new ocean-going capacities and the tactical progress it had made. The US Navy, however, was at the same time experiencing a grave crisis (1000 units in 1968 and fewer than 500 in 1975; naval analyst Norman Polmar even forecasted that there would be fewer than 350 units at the end of the 1980s).[15] But at about that time the Reagan Administration launched a programme for 600 ships by the end of the 1980s. Despite fairly general scepticism, US Secretary of the Navy John Lehman managed to push through huge naval budgets, and US industry was inundated with orders, with the result that the US Navy today has more than 580 ships.

The Soviet Navy still faces grave difficulties. Many of the ships launched in the 1950s and 1960s are becoming obsolete, so that there may well be a serious shrinkage in Soviet naval tonnage by the end of the century. Moreover, the role of the navy in Soviet strategy is, as shown above, under challenge, with the army attempting to reassert its predominance. During the mid-1970s to the mid-1980s, debate revolved mostly around the theories of Admiral Gorshkov, which gave rise to abundant comment; today, it concentrates on the Maritime Strategy associated with John Lehman and Admiral Watkins.[16]

Lastly, although the tide may not turn under the Bush Administration, we may witness developments which would render some agreement possible, if present budgetary deficits force the United States to cut military expenditure. Nevertheless, the technical obstacles described above will remain, and only a bold person would dare to predict that they will fade away. But the saying attributed to William of Orange is especially appropriate today in connection with naval arms control: hope is not a necessary precondition for action, and perseverance is called for even if the prospects for success seem dim. The question in the case of naval disarmament is to determine whether it is a desirable undertaking.

Notes and references

[1] Richmond, H. (Admiral), *Economy and Naval Security* (Ernest Benn: London, 1931), p. 337.

[2] For a survey of the rise of Soviet naval diplomacy, see McConnell, J. M. and Dismukes, B., *Soviet Naval Diplomacy* (Pergamon: New York, 1979), which covers the decade 1967–76.

[3] Mackinder, H. J., 'The round world and the winning of the peace', *Foreign Affairs*, 1943, pp. 595–96.

[4] United Nations, *The Naval Arms Race*, Report of the Secretary-General, UN Study series no. 16, UN document A/40/535 (United Nations: New York, 1986).

[5] See, for example, Watkins, J. (Admiral), 'The Maritime Strategy', US Naval Institute *Proceedings*, Jan. 1986, special supplement, pp. 3–17; Mearsheimer, J. J., 'A strategic misstep: the Maritime Strategy and deterrence in Europe', *International Security*, vol. 11, no. 2 (autumn 1986), pp. 3–57; and Swartz, P. M., 'Contemporary US naval strategy: a bibliography', US Naval Institute *Proceedings*, Jan. 1986, supplement, pp. 41–47.

[6] The alternation of defence and attack has given rise to an abundant literature. See the summary of basic data in Coutau-Bégarie, H., *La puissance maritime* [*Sea Power*] (Fayard: Paris, 1985).

[7] See Turner, S. (Admiral), 'Mission of the U.S. Navy', *Naval War College Review*, Jan.–Feb. 1974.

[8] See Komer, R., *Maritime Strategy or Coalition Defense?* (Abt Books: New York, 1985) for the defence of the 'coalition point of view'; and Hanks, R. and Record, J., *US Strategy at the*

Crossroads (Institute for Foreign Policy Analysis: Washington, DC, 1985) for the maritime point of view.

[9] For a good survey of this history, see Hagan, K. J. (ed.), *In Peace and War: Interpretations of American Naval History* (Greenwood: Westport, Conn., 1978).

[10] The Baikal–Amur line, although officially completed, is not serviceable over its entire length.

[11] Quoted by Labayle-Couhat, J., *Les flottes de combat [Combat Fleets]* (Éditions Maritimes et d'Outre-Mer: Paris, 1982), p. 693.

[12] Richmond (note 1).

[13] Mackinder (note 3).

[14] See note 4.

[15] Quoted by George, J. L., *The U.S. Navy: View from the Mid-1980s* (Westview: Boulder, Colo., 1985), p. 1.

[16] Cf. Swartz, P. M., 'Maritime Strategy in review', US Naval Institute *Proceedings*, Feb. 1987, pp. 113–16.

Paper 5. Verification of nuclear weapons at sea

Herbert Lin

House Armed Services Committee, Washington, DC, USA

I. Introduction

Until 1987, the United States and the Soviet Union negotiated nuclear arms control agreements that limited only strategic weapons, both offensive and defensive. In December 1987 the two superpowers signed the INF Treaty on the mutual elimination of their land-based, intermediate-range and shorter-range nuclear missiles. This agreement is the first to limit non-strategic nuclear weapons.

Neither side has seriously entertained the possibility of agreements covering non-strategic nuclear weapons based at sea. Many such weapons are deployed at sea by one or both sides: gravity bombs and depth charges, nuclear torpedoes, surface-to-air missiles, air-to-surface missiles, anti-ship missiles and nuclear sea-launched cruise missiles (SLCMs). Given this panoply of naval nuclear weapons, a case could be made for agreements regulating the number and/or types of such weapons.

Judgements about the desirability of such agreements depend on one's view of these weapons. There are basically two views. One is that they can provide meaningful military and operational advantages. Proponents of this view might believe, for example, that naval nuclear weapons could be weapons of last resort in the face of impending conventional defeat or of large-scale failures in conventional arsenals. They might also suggest that, by forcing an adversary to take into account the possible use of nuclear weapons (e.g., by dispersal into 'nuclear-scared' formations), the effectiveness of conventional weaponry can be enhanced. Finally, they could argue that the possession of naval nuclear weapons helps to deter attacks (both nuclear and conventional) on the vessels carrying them. Certain advocates of this view would probably not favour naval nuclear arms control under any circumstances. Other advocates might favour naval nuclear arms control but only under certain verification regimes.

The second view is that the deployment of naval nuclear weapons is inherently disadvantageous. Advocates of this view would, for example, argue that naval nuclear weapons reduce the survivability of US naval vessels. In particular, since Soviet military doctrine places a high priority on the destruction of the enemy's nuclear weapons, the deployment of nuclear weapons aboard US ships makes them higher-priority targets for Soviet attack (especially nuclear attack). A second disadvantage of naval nuclear weapons would arise from the fact that political leaders are unlikely to authorize the use of nuclear weapons except under the most dire of circumstances. Thus, nuclear weapons are much less likely to be used than are conventional weapons, and their effect is largely to reduce the conventional war-fighting capability of the ships upon which they are deployed. A third disadvantage could arise from the fact that the nuclear-armed vessels of both sides operate at sea in relatively close proximity even in peacetime. Under such circumstances, the likelihood of an incident involving nuclear weapons is higher at sea than on land.

A natural corollary to the latter view is to consider naval nuclear arms control as a way of eliminating these disadvantages, others of which are discussed in detail in other papers in this volume (see in particular paper 9). Indeed, some analysts believe that these disadvantages are so compelling that even steps towards unilateral denuclearization of naval assets would be useful. Others believe that a bilateral agreement to reduce or eliminate naval nuclear weapons is the only approach that is politically viable.

A middle ground between these two views is that naval nuclear weapons are necessary for one side as long as the other side has them. According to this argument, a bilateral reduction or elimination of naval nuclear weapons could serve many of the same purposes as having the weapons themselves. For example, eliminating the nuclear threat to naval vessels in turn eliminates the need for a nuclear retaliatory capacity. This view is consistent with the view that, while nuclear weapons may have some marginal operational utility, the primary purpose of nuclear weapons should be to deter the use of other nuclear weapons.

The US and Soviet views of the utility of naval nuclear weapons determine to a large degree the standards of verification to which a naval nuclear arms control agreement would be held. Section II is a discussion of monitoring, that is, the technical process through which information about the naval nuclear weapons of one side can be acquired by the other. Section III addresses verification, that is, the political process by which a nation determines whether or not another nation is in compliance with the terms of a given agreement. Section IV assesses the implications for verification of these two views of the utility of nuclear weapons.

II. Monitoring naval nuclear weapons

Naval nuclear weapons are either strategic or non-strategic. For many years, each side has monitored the other side's strategic naval nuclear weapons with a high degree of confidence. By contrast, many analysts in the United States have expressed the concern that no agreement regulating non-strategic naval nuclear weapons could be monitored effectively.

The discussion below addresses first the characteristics of strategic naval nuclear weapons that facilitate monitoring and then the differences between strategic and non-strategic weapons. Finally, it examines ways of monitoring non-strategic weapons.

Monitoring SLBMs

The primary strategic naval nuclear weapon is the submarine-launched ballistic missile (SLBM). The physical characteristic of SLBMs which is most important for monitoring purposes is their size. SLBMs are physically large missiles, since they must carry all of the fuel and oxidizer needed to travel intercontinental distances. This large size has a number of consequences. First, a large missile requires a large launcher. Large launchers are easier to detect than are small launchers. Indeed, these launchers are constructed as integral and visible parts of submarines, which are much larger than the launch tubes themselves. These submarines take a long time to build; as a result, considerable opportunities exist to detect them. These factors result in very high confidence that the number of SLBM launch tubes can be determined accurately.

The number of SLBMs that corresponds to these launch tubes is then inferred from the number of launch tubes on a one-for-one basis. This inference is first based on the large size of the SLBM, which makes it difficult for missile-carrying submarines to carry SLBMs on board other than those carried in their missile launching tubes. Only after a submarine fires its missiles can it be reloaded from a port or an at-sea replenishment vessel. Since it is difficult to imagine circumstances in which SSBN ports would remain intact after one side had fired SLBMs at sea, SLBMs would have to be reloaded at sea. While both the USA and the USSR maintain capabilities to load SLBMs into SSBNs at sea,[1] such reloads would make little strategic sense given the fact that hundreds of SLBMs would already have been fired by the time reloads were necessary.

The counting of warheads carried by SLBMs is somewhat more difficult. Modern SLBMs carry several independently targetable warheads. A missile loaded into a launch tube cannot be seen by reconnaissance satellites. Even if it were carried outside the submarine or on the deck of a surface ship, reconnaissance satellites cannot look underneath the shroud that protects the post-boost vehicle where the warheads are placed. Thus, observation of the missile itself from the outside alone could not determine the number of warheads it carried.

One approach to this problem has been to assign a 'counting rule' that specifies the number of warheads with which a missile of a given type is to be credited. The basic counting rule of the SALT II Treaty was to specify that any missile of a type tested with x warheads is considered to carry x warheads, regardless of its actual warhead loading. Since long-range ballistic missiles are often tested outside national airspace and even travel outside the atmosphere for much of their trajectory, a wide variety of national technical means can be focused on such testing. More detailed data can be provided by intercepts of unencrypted telemetry from the tested missile. Thus, on the *assumption* that neither side would be willing to deploy for operational purposes a missile with more warheads than the number with which the missile had been tested, it is possible to infer an upper limit on the maximum number of warheads carried by SLBMs.

More recently the USA and the USSR have dealt with the issue of warhead numbers in a more co-operative and verifiable manner. At the Washington summit meeting in December 1987, the two nations declared the number of warheads operational on their strategic ballistic missiles and agreed not to deploy more without notifying each other. At the Moscow summit meeting in May–June 1988, they also agreed to develop procedures to verify these modified counting rules, including on-site inspection. These procedures may have a bearing on future nuclear arms control negotiations and agreements.

Monitoring non-strategic nuclear weapons at sea

The term 'non-strategic nuclear weapons' (NSNWs) generally refers to all nuclear weapons other than intercontinental ballistic missiles (ICBMs), SLBMs and heavy bombers.[2] In contrast to SLBMs, NSNWs are generally weapons of relatively small physical size. Their small size is the result of their relatively short range and slow speed, again compared to that of SLBMs. More importantly, NSNWs are often very similar in external appearance to their counterpart conventionally armed weapons; indeed, in certain cases (notably the US Tomahawk SLCM) the conventional weapon is virtually identical to the nuclear weapon, apart from the warhead itself. As a result, many weapon launchers can fire both conventional and nuclear weapons—the so-called dual-capable systems. Finally, these launchers are usually small compared to the size of the ships on which they are carried. Therefore, a ship can potentially carry many NSNWs, limited only by its total weapon-storage magazine capacity.

In the case of dual-capable delivery systems, the nuclear system that is to be limited or prohibited is externally identical to a (permitted) conventional system. Good examples are modern nuclear-armed sea-launched cruise missiles or nuclear-capable carrier-based aircraft. Any launcher capable of launching the conventional version could also launch the nuclear version. Moreover, some launchers can fire different types of weapon. For example, several US Navy missile launchers can fire different missile types.[3] Only when a launcher can be associated with nuclear systems alone (as in the case of SLBMs) is the approach of monitoring launchers equivalent to monitoring the presence of nuclear weapons. In these cases, the monitoring task may be much easier, since national technical means (specifically photographic intelligence) can generally view launchers.

When these conditions are not met, the determination of whether or not a vessel is actually carrying nuclear warheads becomes a matter of knowing what that particular vessel carries inside. In these situations, only intrusive methods of inspection requiring co-operative arrangements have any chance of providing information about the number or presence of nuclear warheads aboard a given ship. Moreover, the validity of such information can decay rapidly with time, depending on the extent to which the ship was 'specially prepared' for the inspection. Some analysts have suggested that co-operative arrangements could also be used to reassure national leaders during peacetime or crisis that the other side is not preparing aggressive actions. For example, the continued willingness of one side to allow inspection teams aboard its ships even during crisis could be taken as evidence of benign intentions. On the other hand, inspections during crisis could provide a channel for directing misinformation to an adversary as well. If one side were indeed preparing to cheat on an agreement, it would have strong incentives to camouflage its actions in a way that would mislead inspectors to make a false report that it was in compliance.[4]

Indicators and signatures of nuclear weapons

Nuclear warheads are smaller than the delivery systems that carry them. However, nuclear warheads have signatures that can signal their presence. All nuclear warheads carry some fissionable material, which emits a characteristic radiation signature. If the warhead is unshielded, this radiation can be detected and identified at short distances (perhaps a few metres). These short distances imply that any scheme based on the detection of this radiation would necessarily involve the co-operation of the side being monitored.

Radiation detectors can be used in two ways. They can be mounted permanently aboard ship at critical locations such as weapon loading hatches and any other openings through which a nuclear weapon might pass.[5] A weapon that passes the detector at sufficiently slow speed will be detected. Alternatively, teams of human inspectors can carry radiation detectors aboard ship. It is possible (although extremely unlikely) that inspectors could be stationed aboard the ships of the other side;[6] it is somewhat more plausible that inspection teams could visit ships in port or during 'challenge' inspections to which both sides have agreed. These teams would move about the ship, and their detectors could identify the presence of unshielded warheads. In addition, if inspecting teams could examine individual missiles or torpedoes at close range (e.g., 10 centimetres) and place equipment on both sides of the missile or torpedo, it would also be possible to infer the presence of a shielded warhead. This is an important consideration because the US Navy practice is to shield all nuclear warheads.

Indicators that suggest the presence of nuclear weapons could also include special equipment, facilities and procedures used in the handling of nuclear warheads. One example is that both sides are likely to make special arrangements for the physical security of nuclear warheads, such as special storage vaults designed to be much more resistant to unauthorized entry and fire than other weapon storage facilities. Such vaults might be identifiable by independent observers. A second example is that the United States (and most likely the Soviet Union as well) exercises a great deal of caution in its handling of nuclear weapons, taking extraordinary care in operational nuclear safety control procedures and practices. Crews that work with nuclear weapons are likely to undergo extensive training and observe with great rigour highly detailed procedures for handling nuclear weapons. Retired US Admiral Eugene Carroll has noted that such procedures even specify the use of a certain type of grease to lubricate elevators that carry nuclear weapons.[7]

Another indicator might be radio traffic to and from the ship that would be characteristic of nuclear weapons on board. For example, such traffic could contain status information that would be relevant to a National Command Authority (NCA) specially concerned about the state of all nuclear weapons under its control. In other cases, the presence of certain radio traffic might suggest the absence of nuclear weapons. Under current US operating procedures, conventional Tomahawk cruise missiles can receive new missions (i.e., a specific route for the Tomahawk's internal guidance system to follow) via radio, while nuclear Tomahawks receive their missions only through physical packages received while their platforms are in port.[8] Thus, by monitoring the communications of that ship, intelligence agencies might be able to infer the presence or absence of nuclear weapons on board.

Use of signatures and indicators to monitor nuclear weapons

An arms control agreement could ban certain types of weapon or it could limit their number. While a ban is just a special case of a limit (i.e., it is a limit of zero), it is generally regarded as easier to verify than any non-zero limit. The reason is that sensors (national technical means, inspection teams, and so on) pick up information only in the general area in which they are directed. Therefore, a global count is not available at a single instant. A weapon that is detected at any instant may or may not be one allowed under a non-zero limit. Resolving this ambiguity can be difficult. However, under a zero limit, that is, a ban, the detection of any weapon unambiguously signals a violation.

The following sections discuss how these indicators and signatures could be used to monitor limits or bans on naval nuclear weapons.

Determining numbers

Of the signatures described above, only radiation detectors could help to verify non-zero limits, because they count nuclear warheads directly. Detectors could identify nuclear warheads as they were loaded aboard ship, either as they passed by permanent detectors mounted near loading ports, or as human inspectors examined each missile, bomb or torpedo as it was loaded aboard ship under some co-operative inspection arrangement. While on-ship inspections are intrusive, former Secretary of the Navy John Lehman has testified that the Navy 'is prepared to accept on-site inspection for all of our ships, negotiated on a reciprocal basis, as part of any arms control agreement [limiting sea-launched cruise missiles]'.[9]

Since ships routinely replenish their supplies at sea, one side's inspectors would have to be permanently stationed with the other side's ships. They would then be able to observe and therefore potentially compromise their adversary's operational practices and tactics. In addition, one individual cannot monitor all activities aboard a large ship at dockside, and even a guided-missile destroyer is a few hundred feet long, carries a crew of a few hundred and weighs several thousand tonnes. Thus, without a number of inspectors to monitor the replenishment process, the host side could load a nuclear weapon without the knowledge of an observer, especially if normal handling procedures were eliminated. These difficulties could be mitigated to a certain extent if inspections were conducted only in port; but under these circumstances, ships could be loaded at sea with weapons in excess of agreed limits.

Permanently mounted radiation detectors to sense the passage of nuclear warheads would have to be located at every portal through which a weapon might pass. Under current operating practices, the actual nuclear warhead is often mated to its delivery system (e.g., a missile) before it is delivered to the ship, and the entire assembly (missile plus warhead) is loaded and handled as a single unit.[10] Therefore, only portals large enough to pass the delivery system would need to be monitored. However, no technical reason exists that renders it impossible to fit a nuclear warhead to a given delivery system aboard ship. A nuclear warhead by itself is relatively small and may fit through any portal large enough to pass a human being. A nuclear warhead could also be stored on the decks of surface ships far from radiation detectors. In addition, the use of so-called insertable nuclear components (INCs) could, if developed, be used to convert a conventional warhead into a nuclear one.[11]

The determination of the number of nuclear warheads aboard a given ship is more complicated than counting the number of nuclear warheads transferred to the ship. Such a determination would be necessary to 'initialize the count' of nuclear warheads aboard, after which determination of the number of nuclear warheads transferred suffices to verify compliance with non-zero limits. In addition, occasional challenge inspections to obtain a complete count of warheads aboard could be useful to detect warheads that might have been transferred to the ship clandestinely. A complete count of weapons aboard ship would have to be made by inspectors sweeping the entire ship.

If the ship in question is designed to carry nuclear warheads that are not integral to their launch platform (as in the case of nuclear-capable aircraft carrying nuclear gravity bombs), then effective on-ship inspections to determine the absence of nuclear warheads aboard such a ship must search every volume larger than a few cubic feet. The volume of a ship is large, and nuclear warheads can be concealed in many places. More importantly, it is easy to shield a warhead from a radiation detector with a few centimetres of lead. Shielding could even be built into the walls separating compartments. Thus, an agreement could not allow compartments to be declared off-limits to inspectors for any reason. Negotiators would face a difficult trade-off between the desire to protect certain sensitive equipment from inspectors' eyes and the desire to eliminate potential cheating opportunities.

Inspectors searching a ship for nuclear warheads could face special problems on ships powered by nuclear reactors. Since naval nuclear reactors also contain fissionable material, a signal indicating the presence of a nuclear weapon might instead result from the presence of a nuclear power reactor aboard. However, it is possible that these ambiguities could be resolved if inspectors were given relatively free rein to inspect all compartments in the ship.

The task of searching a ship for nuclear warheads is greatly simplified if the ship in question is designed to carry only nuclear weapons in which nuclear warheads are integral to their delivery system. Under these circumstances, only weapon-storage magazines need be inspected. This would reduce the search volume considerably. Such an inspection protocol could have utility especially in conjunction with certain launchers. In particular, the USA is gradually moving towards the use of vertical launch systems (VLSs), which are launch tubes flush with the deck of a ship. A typical VLS carries several dozen missiles. One major characteristic of a VLS tube is that it is its own magazine. VLS tubes carry all of the missiles they will fire until replenished in port or at sea, whereas other missile launchers are fed from the ship's internal magazine.

An in-port inspection of the VLS could establish an initial nuclear missile count. A tamper-proof seal installed on the VLS could keep the tubes from being opened without detection; thus, conventional missiles could not be replaced at sea by nuclear missiles without breaking the seal. The seal could be easily breakable so that the missile could be used in wartime, but it could be designed in such a way that it could not be broken without a signature visible to a subsequent in-port inspection.[12] Of course, such a scheme could hamper training and exercises at sea, although careful planning (e.g., specifying in advance the missile tubes to be fired) could minimize disruptions.

Determining presence or absence of nuclear weapons

In the US Navy (and probably in the Soviet Navy), safety considerations require that all equipment associated with nuclear weapons be specially certified for such use. Thus, if inspectors were able to distinguish between peripheral equipment certified for nuclear use and other equipment not so certified, the presence of the former could be associated with the presence of nuclear weapons. Since such equipment would be present if one or many nuclear weapons were present, such an indicator would be useful only in verifying compliance with a ship-by-ship ban on nuclear weapons associated with that type of peripheral equipment. (A ship-by-ship ban is one in which individual ships are designated, by agreement, to carry or not to carry nuclear weapons in any number. A global ban is one which prohibits deployment of all nuclear weapons of a given type aboard any ship.)

Whether or not peripheral equipment is certified for use with nuclear weapons may of course not be clear from an external inspection. In some cases (such as the warhead storage vault described above), it may be obvious. In other cases it may be difficult to determine. For example, what distinguishes a nuclear fire control system from one that is non-nuclear may be as intangible as computer software, different versions of which could operate in the relevant computers at different times.

Assuming that no switch from regular safety practice had occurred, inspections of vessels for peripheral equipment associated with nuclear weapons could ascertain that no nuclear weapons were on board. However, if for some reason either side saw an advantage in deploying nuclear weapons aboard a ship designated by agreement to be non-nuclear, it could change its safety practices so that it would be very difficult for inspectors to distinguish between equipment certified for nuclear use and equipment not so certified.

The use of certain nuclear procedures could also reveal the presence or absence of nuclear weapons aboard individual ships. Over an extended period of time during which operating procedures were observed, inspectors could probably determine whether or not a ship was carrying nuclear weapons. However, these inspectors would have to oversee every action related to major weapon systems aboard. A nation that was willing to agree to such measures would more easily grant inspections of weapons as they were loaded aboard, thereby eliminating the need for inspections of operating practices. Radio communications could be monitored as well, although modern cryptographic systems can in principle indefinitely prevent decoding of messages. It would be difficult if not impossible to use these signatures to determine numbers of nuclear weapons, although they might be used to establish the presence or absence of nuclear weapons aboard a ship.

The use of either of these signatures requires a good understanding of prior practices in order to provide a baseline from which deviations can be measured. Under an agreement to eliminate nuclear weapons from ships, each side could have an incentive to alter its standard operating practices to conceal the presence of weapons on board if it believed it could obtain a significant advantage from doing so.

III. Standards of verification

If a viable arms control agreement regulating naval nuclear weapons is to be reached, each side must be able to verify to its own satisfaction that the other side is abiding by the terms of the agreement. However, the appropriate verification standard for a naval nuclear arms control agreement depends strongly on one's view of its purpose and of the role of nuclear weapons at sea.

At issue is the incentive that one side or another would have to cheat on an agreement. It is important to distinguish between two types of incentive. One type of incentive is political, the other military. The military incentives to cheat on an agreement could be very important in the judgement of military leaders, yet the political leadership might still judge its own deliberate violation of the agreement not to be in its best overall political interest. In the discussion below, the term 'incentive' will refer only to military incentives.

The belief that nuclear weapons at sea can provide military and operational advantages implies that each side would have a very high incentive to cheat on the terms of an agreement. A meaningful agreement would limit the military capabilities of both sides. Capabilities that one side gives up are compensated by the capabilities that the other side gives up. If one side obeys these limitations and the other does not, the unilaterally complying side is inherently at a disadvantage. In this case, a very demanding standard of verification would be necessary—one in which each side must have very high confidence that even a very small violation could be detected in a very short time. Only with such a standard could each side be confident that the other side would not acquire a meaningful advantage through cheating.

Alternatively, the belief that nuclear weapons provide few military advantages suggests a different verification standard. If one holds that naval nuclear weapons serve primarily to deter the use of nuclear weapons, the incentives for cheating are low, and the corresponding verification measures need only provide high confidence that significant violations will be detected in time to respond appropriately. If one holds that naval nuclear weapons are inherently disadvantageous, there are few incentives to cheat.

The implications for verification of each of these beliefs are discussed below.

Premise 1: nuclear weapons serve military purposes

The premise that nuclear weapons serve military purposes provides incentives for each side not to abide by an agreement. In the absence of an agreement to limit nuclear weapons at sea, the intelligence services of one side are able to monitor to a certain extent the nuclear weapons of the other side in various ways. However, if an agreement is reached on limiting these weapons, then by assumption meaningful military capabilities will be reduced.

In one evasion scenario, nuclear warheads could be developed to fit many weapons that currently carry only conventional warheads. While only a few existing delivery systems are designed to carry either nuclear or conventional warheads, only a very comprehensive ban on nuclear testing could prevent the development and deployment of nuclear warheads intended for such retrofits.

A similar problem exists with launchers that are capable of using both nuclear and conventional weapons of different types. A good example is the 21-inch torpedo tube, nominally designed to fire conventional torpedoes but also capable of launching nuclear SLCMs that have been designed specifically for torpedo-tube launch. Every ship with 21-inch torpedo tubes must be considered a potential nuclear SLCM carrier, and a quick perusal through *Jane's Fighting Ships*[13] reveals that hundreds of Soviet ships of many classes carry such torpedo tubes. The same will apply to US surface ships that are now or will in the future be equipped with VLS missile launchers. In both cases, high-confidence verification that not even one ship carried nuclear weapons in excess of some negotiated limit (perhaps zero) would require a very stringent inspection regime. This regime would have to provide for monitoring each and every naval ship equipped with missile or torpedo launchers, since these launchers could potentially launch nuclear weapons. Indeed, even civilian ships might have to be monitored, since they could also be clandestinely outfitted with missile launchers.[14] Moreover, the required monitoring would have to be essentially continuous, or at least conducted repeatedly on a time-scale that is short compared to the time needed to load additional nuclear weapons aboard an inspected ship. (Whether or not continuous monitoring of active duty naval vessels is politically negotiable is another matter. It will be at least as difficult as negotiating verification measures for a ban on chemical weapon production, which requires continuous monitoring of many industrial plants known to produce chemical products in quantity, and assurances regarding an even larger number of industrial facilities that could potentially conceal a production line for chemical weapons.)

Certain weapons (e.g., the Soviet SS-N-3 SLCM) are most likely armed only with nuclear warheads; they are so large and consume so many resources that arming them with conventional warheads would make little sense. Launchers would indicate the presence of such missiles on certain ships, and thus a ban on such weapons is potentially workable. Nevertheless, the ban could be easily circumvented as new generations of smaller and less costly nuclear-capable missiles are deployed. New missiles could be easily designed to be launched from previously conventional launchers.

Some analysts suggest that certain features of particular nuclear delivery systems are observably different from those of their conventional counterparts. However, given the incentive to do so, a state could conceal or remove these differences. An example is the nuclear cruise missile, which tends to have a longer range than its conventional counterpart, since its warhead is lighter. This might suggest the possibility of an agreement to limit the range at which a cruise missile can be tested. However, a cruise missile designed for long range can be tested with all possible combinations of fuel loading over shorter-range flights.[15] Thus, it would be difficult to monitor range limitations on testing with confidence. In such cases, an agreement would have to consider dual-capable weapons and indeed provide a way to demonstrate through inspections that a weapon alleged to be conventional could not be converted to one carrying a nuclear warhead.

A second evasion scenario is based on the fact that nuclear warheads for different purposes cannot be distinguished, nor can they be distinguished by detailed close-up examination of the associated delivery systems. For example, it is essentially impossible to distinguish between a strategic (long-range) and a non-strategic (short-range) nuclear cruise missile. Therefore, without an agreement that includes both strategic and non-strategic systems, meaningful restraints on strategic nuclear cruise missiles alone (or non-strategic systems alone) are difficult to negotiate.

A third evasion scenario arises from the possible alteration of nuclear safety and handling practices. Each side's intelligence agencies attempt to track the nuclear weapons of the other side. However, if each side undertook to conceal the presence of nuclear weapons, it could alter its procedures in such a way that their transparency is drastically reduced. If one side did not follow procedures related to nuclear training and security after an agreement were signed, the other side would not know if the weapons themselves had been removed or if just the practice of these safety and security measures had been ended. It was noted previously that nuclear Tomahawks do not receive mission profiles by radio. However, it is technically possible for a new mission to be transmitted to a nuclear Tomahawk, and if the USA chose to transmit new missions this way, it could easily do so.

A fourth evasion scenario is possible if radio traffic is used as an indicator of the presence of nuclear weapons. Radio traffic to and from all ships could be encrypted, making it impossible to decipher. Dummy encrypted messages transmitted at regular intervals by each vessel could be used to maintain the volume of radio traffic so that traffic analysis could not discern nuclear-armed vessels.

Given time, such evasions of treaty restraints would be discovered. But the given premise—that nuclear weapons serve military purposes—implies that if war were to break out before such evasions were discovered, the side in violation at that time would have an advantage over the side in compliance. In other words, each side would have incentives to violate the agreement in a clandestine manner. Indeed, if one side decided to cease observing an agreement limiting such weapons, it could in a matter of hours load nuclear weapons on to all ships equipped with the appropriate dual-capable launchers if such weapons had been previously stockpiled.

Premise 2: nuclear weapons serve no military purpose

If one accepts that nuclear weapons serve virtually no military purpose, the verification process is greatly simplified. The reason is that, by assumption, small-scale cheating would provide no military advantages and thus would not occur. Thus, any cheating would be large-scale cheating, thereby providing many opportunities for a violation to be detected.

In section I, two views were associated with the belief that nuclear weapons do not serve military purposes. One was that naval nuclear weapons are inherently disadvantageous. If this is the case, no incentives to cheat exist. The more interesting view analytically is the one in which nuclear weapons serve primarily to deter the use of nuclear weapons.

If deterrence is the primary purpose of nuclear weapons, the existence of naval nuclear weapons must be considered in the context of other (non-naval) nuclear weapons. In particular, this point of view suggests that balance in specific weapon categories matters much less than a kind of rough parity; large numbers of nuclear weapons of different types on both sides reduce the significance of disparities in specific categories. Both sides would still, under any conceivable agreement, have large numbers of nuclear weapons in other categories that would render meaningless weapons in excess of those permitted by agreement. One side would still have to respond to violations of the other side (perhaps by itself violating selected aspects of the agreement, but perhaps not), but for reasons that are much more political and perceptual (e.g., demonstrating will) than military. The existence of these other weapons removes a great deal of the incentive for each side to cheat.

With this standard, the necessary verification can be less stringent. For example, the two sides might agree to design NSNWs so that they could not be fired from launchers also capable of firing conventional weapons. Thus, all missile launchers larger than 30 inches (75 cm) in diameter might be assumed to be nuclear, and all conventional missiles might be fired from smaller launchers. A co-operative regime of this nature would depend on functionally related observable differences (FROD) detectable by national technical means or by on-site inspections. Fewer incentives would exist to violate this agreement (i.e., to design nuclear missiles that would fit smaller launchers) because, by assumption, such missiles would be largely irrelevant to the military situation.

Since by assumption small violations would not have military significance, the verification regime could also be much less complex. For example, only spot checks (rather than continuous monitoring) would be necessary. These spot checks would serve more to deter cheating than to detect every possible violation. Deviations from nuclear procedures established prior to an arms control agreement would be unlikely to occur, since the military value of cheating would be small compared to the cost of a complex effort to alter or eliminate these established procedures. This verification regime would not significantly alter the signatures that underlie one side's intelligence assessments of the other's nuclear capabilities at sea.

Given these conclusions, some of the evasion scenarios described above become less plausible. For example, the design and manufacture of nuclear missiles that could be launched by existing, and currently non-nuclear, missile launchers remain possible in principle, but since recognizable nuclear procedures would have to accompany the actual introduction of such missiles into the inventory, such introduction could be identified. Similarly, the sudden alteration of operating procedures and practices is possible, but unlikely, since the potential dangers of such changes would outweigh the marginal military benefits that would result from clandestine deployments.

The view that nuclear weapons provide few military benefits also makes plausible other verification schemes. Prior to their commitment to pursue a complete ban on ground-launched intermediate-range nuclear missiles as the basis for an arms control agreement, the USA and the USSR had settled on a limit of 100 such missiles world-wide. In order to verify compliance with this limit, the USA had proposed the use of designated deployment areas (DDAs). A DDA (or several DDAs) would have been the only area in which the 100 permitted missile warheads would be allowed. Any missiles outside these areas would be a violation.

An analogue to DDAs for naval nuclear weapons might be the designation of individual ships as nuclear or non-nuclear. A ship designated as nuclear might or might not carry nuclear weapons, but a ship designated as non-nuclear would carry nuclear weapons only in violation of an agreement. If ships were designated in this manner, only ships designated as nuclear would have to be subject to continuous monitoring. Ships designated as non-nuclear would still have to be subject to inspections to determine if they were carrying nuclear weapons, but incentives to load nuclear weapons aboard these ships would be minimal by assumption. Since this verification regime would exempt from continuous monitoring a large number of ships that would probably not carry nuclear weapons anyway, it would be far less intrusive than one which required virtually all ships to be continuously monitored.

A further simplification of the verification regime is possible if counting rules based on nominal nuclear load-outs are adopted. Although certain large ships (e.g., aircraft-carriers, or battleships with VLSs) can carry as many as a few hundred nuclear weapons, a ship so loaded could not carry much conventional weaponry. The two sides would agree to a nominal load-out (e.g., 20 per cent of available magazine capability would be regarded as nuclear), and negotiations on appropriate numerical limits would proceed on that basis. Since additional nuclear weapons would provide little military advantage, neither side would have an incentive to go far beyond these agreed limits. If a verification regime based on counting rules is acceptable to both sides, intrusive inspections are unnecessary.

IV. Summary and conclusions

This analysis began by noting that judgements about the verifiability of agreements to limit or ban naval nuclear weapons depend primarily on judgements about the utility of such weapons. If the USA and the USSR believed that naval nuclear weapons do not serve useful military purposes, the verification of a naval nuclear arms control agreement might be possible. However, their apparent belief that nuclear weapons serve real military purposes suggests that the verification of arms control agreements involving NSNWs at sea will pose enormous difficulties. Since the political debate in the USA is conducted on the often unstated premise that more nuclear weapons mean more military capability, it is assumed by many that the Soviet Union will cheat if given an opportunity to do so.

The analysis in this paper suggests two major conclusions. The first is that piecemeal agreements tend to be more difficult to verify than comprehensive ones. For example, an agreement to limit only the *deployment* of naval nuclear cruise missiles is likely to be more difficult to verify than an agreement to ban the testing, production and deployment of such missiles. An agreement to ban only nuclear cruise missiles is probably more difficult to verify than a ban on all naval nuclear weapons, since disputes could ensue over the purpose of individual nuclear missiles. In both cases, the difficulties arise because signatures and indicators suggesting the presence of nuclear weapons must be resolved into forbidden and permitted categories.

The second conclusion is that if naval forces have substantial military incentives to use dual-capable weapon launchers, naval nuclear arms control agreements will be hard to verify. The small physical size of most non-strategic nuclear weapons, the ability to alter established operating procedures for handling nuclear weapons and the capability to retrofit conventional launchers with nuclear-armed delivery systems combine to suggest that efforts to limit these nuclear capabilities would require unprecedented restraints on conventional weaponry as well.

These conclusions lead the author to believe that naval nuclear arms control agreements are not likely to be reached between the superpowers in the near future.

Notes and references

The views, judgements, opinions and conclusions expressed in this paper are those of the author alone and not those of any organization with which he is now or has ever been affiliated. In particular, they do not necessarily represent the views, opinions and conclusions of the House Armed Services Committee or its staff. The support provided to the author by the American Association for the Advancement of Science under its Congressional Science Fellowship Program throughout the period in which this paper was written is appreciated. Comments from Bill Durch, Tom Stefanick, Matt Bunn and Michael Krepon provided a useful check on this work. Errors are those of the author alone.

[1] Polmar notes that 'FBM [Fleet Ballistic Missile] submarine tenders also store ballistic missiles'. See Polmar, N., *The Ships and Aircraft of the U.S. Fleet,* 13th edn (Naval Institute Press: Annapolis, Md., 1984), p. 304. Similarly, the Department of Defense notes that '[Soviet] resupply systems are available to reload SSBNs in protected waters'. See DOD, *Soviet Military Power 1987* (US Government Printing Office: Washington, DC, 1987), p. 28.

[2] In the discussion that follows, a 'nuclear weapon' will refer to a nuclear-armed delivery system, usually a missile. A 'nuclear warhead' will refer only to the nuclear component of the nuclear delivery system.

[3] These launchers include the Mark 10 Mods 7 and 8, the Mark 11 Mod. 0, the Mark 13 Mod. 4, the Mark 26 and the Mark 41 VLS. See Polmar (note 1), p. 458.

[4] A discussion of the benefits and pitfalls of certain types of co-operative measure is contained in Ben-Horin, Y. *et al., Building Confidence and Security in Europe: The Potential Role of Confidence and Security-Building Measures* (RAND Corporation: Santa Monica, Calif., Dec. 1986).

[5] Cf. Lin, H., 'Technology for the cooperative verification of nuclear weapons', *Arms Control Today*, Apr. 1986.

[6] Cf. Wit, J., 'Dealing with sea-launched cruise missiles: a U.S. strategy for the future', unpublished manuscript, undated, circa 1987, p. 18.

[7] Personal communication.

[8] Personal communication, US Navy Commander.

[9] House Appropriations Committee, *Department of Defense Appropriations for Fiscal Year 1986*, Hearings, Part 2, p. 915. A policy that allowed inspections to determine the presence of ship-board nuclear weapons is directly opposed to the US Navy policy to neither confirm nor deny the presence of nuclear weapons aboard individual ships.

[10] This practice has been documented in public sources in the case of the nuclear Tomahawk. See Senate Armed Services Committee, *Department of Defense Authorization for Appropriations for FY 1986*, Part 7, Strategic and Theater Nuclear Forces, p. 3875. It is most likely true in the case of other nuclear missiles as well, since the logistics associated with the care and maintenance of nuclear weapons would be considerably simpler under such a practice. However, to count on this feature of launch platforms—namely, the complete integration of the nuclear warhead with the platform—for verification purposes would be 'safe' only if some technical means could ensure that the ordnance of the missile could not be separated from the missile itself.

[11] All nuclear warheads depend on a high-explosive charge to initiate the fission reaction. Even if the fissionable material is removed from a nuclear warhead, the high explosive can still be detonated. Thus it is possible in principle to design conventional warheads in such a way that the insertion of an appropriate component can convert the conventional warhead to a nuclear one. Such a feature would be especially attractive on naval vessels, where magazine space is at a premium and conventional rounds are displaced by nuclear rounds that are unlikely to be used. The author's search of the public literature reveals that INCs have to date been considered only for naval weapons, specifically the Harpoon cruise missile and the Mark 48 torpedo. See Cochran, T. *et al.*, *Nuclear Weapons Databook, Volume I: U.S. Nuclear Forces and Capabilities* (Ballinger: Cambridge, Mass., 1984), p. 190 (on the Harpoon); Polmar, N. and Kerr, D., 'Nuclear torpedoes', US Naval Institute *Proceedings*, vol. 112, no. 8 (Aug. 1986), p. 67 (on the Mark 48).

[12] Cf. 'Optical seals record nuclear tampering', *Science News*, vol. 129, no. 3 (Jan. 1986), p. 36.

[13] *Jane's Fighting Ships* (Jane's: London, annual).

[14] For example, there have been proposals to equip civilian vessels with VLS missile launchers; see Truver, S., 'Improving Navy surface warfare capabilities: a near-term solution', *Armed Forces Journal International*, Nov. 1987, p. 53. The presence of a VLS on a merchant ship could easily be hidden from national technical means by an adversary determined to do so.

[15] This insight is due to Richard Garwin.

Paper 6. Superpower naval arms control: practical considerations and possibilities

Richard Hill

Editor, The Naval Review, *UK*

I. Introduction and assumptions

This paper is written from the point of view of one accustomed to planning for, and exercising, maritime power in a practical way in support of his country's security and interests, but who at the same time can see the potential for the common good in discussing arms control in the maritime field. The practical considerations, both strategic and tactical, must from this standpoint precede and influence the discussion of arms control measures, for the practical aspects grow from the interests of the participants and the technology of the time. Arms control measures that take no account of them are in a vacuum. Therefore, after a brief look at the objectives of arms control and of maritime power, this paper discusses first the strategic and tactical factors and then possible arms control measures at sea.

One set of terms needs defining: these concern levels of conflict. 'Peace', 'tension' and 'war' have long proved too crude a set of terms to describe the conditions in which post-1945 maritime international transactions occur. The following formulations are used instead.

1. *Normal conditions*: Change occurs in a controlled way through negotiation; no use of force takes place except at an internationally accepted constabulary level; threats of force are confined to normal processes of deterrence.

2. *Low-intensity operations*: These never merit the title of war; are limited in aim, scope and area; and are subject to the international law of self-defence. In practice they may include sporadic acts of violence by both sides.

3. *Higher-level operations*: Active, organized hostilities involving on both sides fleet units and/or aircraft and the use of major weapons.

4. *General war:* Armed conflict between the superpowers and their allies. By definition, general war carries a far greater risk of eventual escalation to the widespread use of nuclear weapons than does any other form of conflict.

Among the premises of this paper, one is the assumption that the world will continue to be made up of sovereign nation-states, that the major alliances will continue to exist, that states will continue to wish to use the sea for a variety of economic and political (and therefore strategic) purposes, and that the 1982 UN

Convention on the Law of the Sea will be accepted as the basis for sea jurisdiction even though its provisions will be disputed in interpretation and detail. Finally, current arms control negotiations are touched upon where relevant, but particular outcomes cannot be assumed.

II. Objectives

Arms control

The objectives of arms control have been very variously described[1] and are therefore not analysed in detail here. The most commonly stated elements are: (a) 'reducing the risk of war' or stability, divided by one commentator[2] into crisis stability and arms race stability; (b) predictability, which can among other things be called the 'military planner's benefit' because it tends to eliminate future options which he would otherwise have to worry about and allocate resources for; (c) confidence, which tends to grow slowly from a variety of nutrients but which may be boosted by specific measures;[3] (d) damage limitation in the event of conflict, often derided as an objective by disarmers in the field of nuclear weapons[4] but still sought by arms controllers in certain areas;[5] and (e) limitation of resource expenditure that could be diverted to more constructive purposes. It is believed that from these five elements can be built one overarching objective of arms control, which may be called 'improved mutual security'.

It has been rightly said[6] that arms control cannot flourish except in a climate of improving international relations. At the same time it can itself contribute to that improvement. Thus is created the notion of a 'virtuous spiral', one of many interacting processes that could make for a better and safer world.

Maritime power

How far can the objectives of maritime power, as practised particularly by the superpowers, be compatible with the objectives of arms control?

First, unrealistic objectives must be discarded, and of these the most important is any notion that maritime hegemony can now be achieved. Such phenomena have been rare in history, with only one (and that no more than arguably) ever maintained world-wide.[7] In the complexity of modern conditions, with all the challenges available from law, economic assets, force of arms and world opinion, an objective of maritime hegemony is simply not sustainable, and it is very doubtful if responsible statesmen in any state even dream of it.

In practice, all states—even the superpowers—view the objectives of maritime power in a more limited way. First, nearly all have interests at sea in the way of trade and exploitation of living and non-living resources, and these may require protection by the deployment of the military elements of maritime power. Second, many have interests that can be protected or furthered by maritime means, such as access to markets, political and diplomatic influence, and the health of alliances. These objectives apply in normal conditions and in time of conflict, whether the state concerned is a participant in the conflict or not.

At the higher levels of conflict in which a state may be involved, however, they may be overtaken by another set of objectives, which may be summed up as the projection of power. This includes the ability to move troops and supplies across sea and ocean spaces, the ability to bombard the enemy's military assets on land territory and, in the last resort, the ability to inflict unacceptable damage on his homeland with nuclear weapons. A converse or complementary objective may be sought in the means to deny the enemy the ability to do these things.

The overall objective is security, although it is fair to say that this is usually more national than collective in nature. One of its prime instruments is deterrence: to convince a potential opponent that military action will be unprofitable for him. It cannot be stressed too much that deterrence, at sea perhaps even more than on land, operates at all levels. A single patrol craft is a direct deterrent to certain low levels of hostile activity but, properly backed by stronger forces (which need not necessarily be at the scene of action), also deters much higher levels of hostility. Alliances, particularly with superpowers, form an essential part of the higher deterrent structure of most states.[8]

All this said, there are distinct asymmetries between the objectives of the United States and those of the Soviet Union when they concern maritime power.

To the USA, elements of trade and access are relatively more important, and these wash over into the support through maritime power of regimes and situations favourable to the USA and to the West generally—in normal conditions and conflict situations. The Soviet objectives in this field can be summed up in their own language as an improvement in the correlation of forces: that is, the advancement and protection of the Soviet Union's international political, strategic and economic situation, probably in that order of priority.

Conflict objectives also differ markedly. The USA—the power base of an oceanic alliance with a continental core and open flanks—sees an absolute need both to project power on those flanks and to support the centre by reinforcement and resupply, much of which must come by sea.[9] The USSR gives high priority to countering the threat by sea to the Soviet homeland itself[10] and also to the preservation of forces needed for war-termination bargaining; it sees the projection of power by amphibious means, for example, as a more limited objective. Finally, both sides see the deployment of intercontinental nuclear missiles at sea as a fundamental underpinning of their strategies, and its preservation as a vital objective.

If this summary of the objectives sought by the superpowers through the means of maritime power is correct, then they are not incompatible with the objectives of arms control *per se*. The extent to which the arms control process can be carried forward will depend, however, on current strategic concepts (and whether they can safely be changed), on force structures and plans, and on political climates and perceptions.

III. Strategies

Consistent with their objectives, in normal conditions the superpower navies adopt markedly different patterns of deployment. US Navy surface force dispositions are centred on aircraft-carrier battle groups (CVBGs), of which some 11 or 12 may be operational at any one time.[11] The inherent mobility of naval forces means that they can be moved to respond to the perceived need to protect national and allied interests as necessary. The Soviet Navy acts generally in a less responsive way, following in its deployments (which are now themselves substantial) a consistent pattern varied only occasionally when a crisis is perceived to be acute.[12] Soviet areas of deployment, usually more static than those of the US Navy, are often directly related to regimes supported by the USSR, whether those regimes are under active threat or not.

Both sides take a considerable interest in each other's activities and spend commensurate resources to watch each other. Such surveillance is to a degree formalized by the bilateral 1972 Incidents at Sea Agreement (see annexe B), which has been described as a 'set of international rules of engagement'.[13] This is covered in papers 11 and 12 in this volume.

Doctrine for the deployment of SSBNs also differs between the superpowers. With smaller total numbers, the USA actually keeps more submarines on station than does the USSR, and seeks to hide them in the remote oceans. By contrast, the main SSBN patrols of the Soviet Union are stationed in the Barents and Okhotsk Seas and are supported by considerable submarine, surface and air forces for their protection. This has been generally called the 'bastion' concept in Western literature.[14]

In a period of tension, or escalation through the levels of conflict described, the US Navy's actions would be guided by the maritime strategy enunciated in early 1986 by Admiral James D. Watkins and Secretary of the Navy John F. Lehman. This is a strategy of forward movement into areas regarded as important by the USSR in order to 'dilute their effort, divert their attention and force them to divide their forces'.[15] Soviet SSBNs are specifically included as targets for an 'aggressive campaign' once armed combat has broken out.

The actions of the Soviet Navy are not subject to such clear published guidelines. In the writings of Admiral Sergey G. Gorshkov,[16] which in the absence of any unequivocal directive from his successor must be taken as still significant, there are two elements that stand out in this context: the need to win 'the battle for the first salvo'—that is, to achieve a position where a pre-emptive strike on the main forces of the enemy is feasible—and to protect the 'fleet against shore' capability of the Soviet Navy, that is, principally the SSBN. This does not look as though Gorshkov put a high priority on attacking reinforcement or resupply shipping on the so-called sea lines of communication (SLOCs) of the West.

The course of actual hostilities, if it came to that, would initially be governed by the deployments and doctrines set out above—with one important caveat. Strategies that are declared in peacetime must always be treated with a certain reserve. Underlying the US Maritime Strategy is the notion that it is to the US advantage to make the Soviet forces believe that they will be threatened in their bastions, because then the Soviet Navy will be preoccupied with their defence. Once the Soviet Navy has been sold this threat, it may be less necessary for the US Navy to move forward so early or in such force. However, if the Soviet Navy did not buy it and itself moved forward or pre-deployed, the US strategy would have lost much of its original purpose. Conversely, it may be to the Soviet advantage to make the Western forces believe that there is no great threat to their reinforcement and resupply shipping; the Soviet Navy has many suitable submarines to pose such a threat, and an unexpected deployment into the Atlantic Ocean in time of tension would be a forceful move. Even the moves in a period short of conflict, therefore, might take an unexpected turn.

The actual course of conflict is even less predictable. One could expect the actions of both sides to be governed by the overall objectives set out above, but within that very broad framework the variations are numerous. It seems likely that the Norwegian Sea and the Sea of Japan would be major theatres, as would the Mediterranean Sea, and that the Atlantic Ocean would be critical to any land battle in Europe. But all this, of course, falls into the trap of the 'single scenario' which naval planners ought to beware of. Events seldom turn out as predicted, which is as good a reason as any for flexible, responsive maritime forces.

No mention was made above of the use, or non-use, of nuclear weapons. Twenty years ago it would have been necessary to include them in a discussion on strategy at sea, because the evidence pointed to a Soviet doctrine envisaging their use at a very early stage, probably in the 'first salvo'. Now that evidence is much less clear, and many authoritative commentators believe that the Soviet Union would prefer to avoid the use of nuclear weapons entirely in the first phase of a major conflict.[17] US naval doctrine clearly does not envisage early use of nuclear weapons at sea.[18] It is therefore possible to place nuclear weapons—apart, of course, from SLBMs and sea-based land-attack weapons to the extent that they are used for that purpose—in the realm of tactics rather than strategy.

IV. Tactical considerations

Underwater warfare[19]

There are two different factors that bear very heavily on underwater warfare. The first is simply a function of physical laws: under water, sound is the principal sensing medium, and the ability to exploit it is a tactical necessity. The second is a function of the way submarine, and anti-submarine, warfare has developed: like fights like even less than it does in other maritime environments.

The use of sound as a sensing medium against any target involves the processes of detection, classification, localization and tracking. The techniques used can be passive (listening for sound made by the target) or active (transmitting sound pulses which are echoed from the target). The entire process, from detection to the achievement of the precise targeting information required to fire a weapon, will probably involve the use of both techniques and often several vehicles. It can break down at any point if equipment is faulty or inadequate or if the tactics are wrong. Therefore, observing that the behaviour of sound in the sea is responsive to an enormous number of variable factors in that complex and still imperfectly understood medium, effective underwater warfare is bound to be a very complicated and expensive process. It is often believed to be easier for the submarine, particularly the nuclear-powered submarine which is virtually independent of the surface, than for the aircraft or surface ship; and certainly the submarine has more chance of autonomous operation, in both anti-submarine and other modes, than other craft. But it is not, as exercises frequently show and doctrine in both superpower navies reflects, by any means the only or in many cases the most suitable underwater warfare asset.

'Asset' is a word commonly used by anti-submarine warfare (ASW) operators, and it reflects the all-arms approach that is necessary in the field. It is therefore a hard task to pry away from any practitioner of underwater warfare any part of his assets, let alone any that he has come to regard as critical. In this context, for example, the fixed underwater detection systems under the general title of SOSUS (Sound Surveillance System) are regarded by the US Navy as of fundamental importance for its ability to make first detections and sometimes classification over a comparatively wide ocean area.

The same may well go for underwater weaponry. Here there is also some diversity. The high-explosive depth bomb is a relatively crude device, although when dropped by aircraft, including helicopters, it may be more effective than planners think. The only other conventional munition available to the West is the locomotive torpedo, although this comes in many forms including lightweight air-dropped versions, types to be released by intelligent mines, wire-guided submarine-launched heavy torpedoes and ship-launched lightweight versions. The worry about the torpedo is its poor record as a ready weapon at the outset of conflict (German, British and US torpedoes all performed appallingly badly at the start of World War II) and, for the West in particular, uncertainty about its ability to rupture the strong hulls of modern Soviet submarines.[20]

It is probably this more than any other factor that makes the US Navy (and the British Royal Navy and Royal Air Force) maintain a stock of nuclear depth bombs. If in conflict allied torpedoes were unable to impose a sufficient attrition rate on Soviet submarines, the situation could quickly become extremely serious. The same concern almost certainly is reflected by the Soviet Navy in its retention of nuclear ASW systems, even though early use of nuclear munitions in this role is probably no longer part of Soviet doctrine.[21]

Above-water warfare

This is an easier task to handle than underwater warfare, as is shown by the fact that about 100 nations have some kind of surface naval force, about 70 have missile-armed surface craft, only about 30 have submarines, and even fewer have a significant capability against sophisticated submarine forces.[22]

Above-water warfare is easier because it takes place on or above the surface, and the atmosphere is a much freer medium for information gathering and exchange than is the water. Radar, visual, laser and infra-red sensors are all available, and communications can be comprehensive.

The advent of air-breathing missiles with automatic homing has made the threat to surface ships longer-range, more sudden and more accurate. Missiles can be launched by ship, aircraft or submarine. However, defensive missile and gun systems of great accuracy and speed of reaction can be deployed, at a price,[23] and electronic and physical means of decoying missiles are also available.

In this kind of warfare some sorts of activity become critical. The first is surveillance and information. It has been pointed out[24] that the US Navy and the Soviet Navy have very different philosophies in this field: the US Navy seeks to provide a 'bubble', say, 300 miles (480 km) around a naval force in which comprehensive information on all above-water activity is available, while the Soviet Ocean Surveillance System (SOSS) aims at less detailed coverage of a much wider area, that is, the whole of the sea approaches to the Soviet Union.

Second, command and control of forces at sea, and their co-ordination when necessary with forces operating from land bases, are most important. Again, US systems tend to be located at sea, while until recently Soviet command authorities stayed ashore.[25] Some shift has occurred, but how far is not certain. After all, much of the Soviet above-water potential rests with the shore-based Soviet Naval Air Force.

Third, effective air defence at sea rests on the provision of many 'layers': in the case of the US Navy, airborne early-warning, carrier-borne fighters, cruisers · equipped with Aegis (a computerized anti-air warfare system), with phased-array radar controlling long-range area-defence missiles, point-defence systems, last-ditch gun systems, electronic jammers and chaff. Only in this way can the necessary attrition be achieved against a numerous enemy aiming at saturating one's defences.

Finally, air defence in particular—but above-water warfare in general—is likely to be prodigal of ammunition. The time for reaction is so short that at least some false alarms are bound to occur and will result in expenditure of ammunition, to say nothing of real attacks.

The tactical need for nuclear weapons in the above-water environment was, 20 or 30 years ago, felt much more strongly by the USSR than by the USA. It was generally held in the West that the primary mode of the longer-range Soviet anti-surface-ship missiles was nuclear, and that it might well be employed as early as the 'first-salvo' stage. Western nuclear above-water weapons were justified mainly as deterrents or counters to such use, although whether this made sense against a one-shot force might have seemed doubtful. If, as now seems to be the general view, the Soviet philosophy is not to use nuclear weapons early at sea, then the rationales become even more confused, and nuclear weapons in above-water warfare begin to look as if they are for use in desperation only.

V. Arms control measures

Strategic systems

It must first be said that no negotiation on the limitation of sea-borne strategic ballistic missile systems could reasonably take place in isolation from negotiation on strategic systems generally. The United States regards its SLBMs as part of a triad; the Soviet Union considers them as part of the Strategic Rocket Forces.

The SSBN's special quality of low vulnerability to a first strike or other form of pre-emption is apparently much valued by both superpowers, as well as by the other three states that operate such vessels. It is viewed in the Western defence establishments as the final underpinning of the deterrent structure and therefore a stabilizing factor.[26] Soviet doctrine is similarly interpreted by Western experts;[27] the SSBN force is viewed as 'insurance' to deter US attack on the homeland during major, perhaps protracted, conflict.

Given the critical place of SSBNs in the strategic arsenals of both superpowers, it is fair to deduce that only the most radical change in relationships would induce them to give up these instruments altogether. Reductions might be more negotiable. A marked asymmetry already exists, the Soviet vessels outnumbering the US vessels by 2:1 with less disparity in missiles, while in warheads the USA still has the edge.[28] Such asymmetries, however, were taken into account in different ways in both SALT negotiations, and there is no reason why they should not be similarly handled in the future.

A sensible approach to the problem might be to seek progressively to strip off the older, noisier, less reliable classes with shorter-range missiles, which could be considered to contribute an element of instability. The US Poseidon submarines and Soviet submarines of the Golf, Hotel and Yankee Classes would be candidates. It must be said that some of these submarines have more theatre than strategic roles, and limitations might properly be considered in follow-on INF talks. In that forum, the sensitivity of European NATO nations to further reductions in US linkage—which in their view might in no way improve mutual security—would have to be taken into account.

Elimination of these classes, if achieved, would leave the United States with the Ohio Class force (still being built), and some C-4 Lafayettes, while the Soviet Union would retain the Delta and Typhoon Classes—some 30 and 40 boats, respectively.[29] It is uncertain how far either superpower would go with further reductions, but reasonable estimates can be made based on the outline of the Strategic Arms Reduction Talks.

The nature and accuracy of MIRVed SLBM systems, and their effect on deterrent stability in general, are considered to be a separate subject and are not addressed in this paper.

Strategic anti-submarine warfare

This heading ought perhaps to have been put within inverted commas. Anti-submarine warfare, as has frequently been pointed out, is a many-layered affair in an uncertain medium. To suggest, on the one hand, that it is readily divisible into tactical and strategic missions, so that SSBNs can be spared by the one and exclusively targeted in the other, is about as silly as trying to class weapons as offensive or defensive. On the other hand, there is no doubt some difference in *emphasis* in ASW operations that include SSBNs among their targets. The SSBN specifically seeks to avoid detection, using all the techniques of quiet operation and optimizing water conditions. Submarines with a tactical mission do not have that luxury, although in pursuing their targets they will of course try to remain undetected.

ASW is therefore a tough and resource-expensive job against SSBNs, and a recent comprehensive analysis by Donald C. Daniel[30] confirms this. He accepts that the ability of any state to 'take out' a high proportion of the SSBN force of an opponent at will would be bad for strategic stability, but concludes that 'American and Soviet ASW capabilities should not be destabilising in the foreseeable future, in the absence of an unpredictable breakthrough'.[31] Analysis of Daniel's work and that of other writers suggests that the 'unpredictable breakthrough', although extremely unlikely in any field, might be most likely to occur in non-acoustic systems—detection of submarine effects such as thermal scarring, vertical and horizontal water displacements, turbulent and Kelvin wakes, and bioluminescence.[32] Deployment of such systems could be a target for useful if entirely pre-emptive arms control, but since the Soviet Union has apparently put more effort into research into this field than has the United States, negotiation might be difficult.

Restriction of acoustic ASW capabilities would, it is suggested, not only be impossible to negotiate given their extreme importance to all types of maritime conflict, but positively destabilizing because it would encourage all submarine-owning navies to fancy their chances of a successful campaign and thereby damage maritime deterrence generally. Giving gratuitous advantages to the tactical submarine, one of the most escalatory instruments of warfare,[33] is not a way to improved mutual security at sea.

There remains, in the 'strategic ASW' field, the frequently suggested arms control notion of SSBN sanctuaries—agreed and designated areas in which SSBNs could patrol with the agreement of all other parties not to molest them.[34] Sanctuary theory implicitly accepts balance-of-terror or mutual assured destruction (MAD) doctrines and indeed seeks to reinforce them by ensuring that the final step in the escalation ladder is fully secure.

Given that the practical and legal snags (How large an area? How many? Is every other form of shipping to be excluded? What about overflight? Are the rights of third parties under international law to be extinguished? What verification measures are possible? Would monitoring of sanctuaries be more expensive than present SSBN protection measures?) could be ironed out, the actual benefits for stability are doubtful. Indeed a sanctuary regime could easily be destabilizing, given the uncertainty of information under water and the inevitable sensitivity to possible violations. A false alarm would be an international incident; a series of alarms could gravely heighten tension. Where would the areas be? If they were close to coasts, objections from inhabitants could be expected; if out at sea, from other sea users.

Finally, the asymmetry of the superpowers' SSBN deployment patterns makes sanctuaries very difficult to negotiate. The USA, if indeed it chose to use the sanctuary system once negotiated, would be deliberately restricting its SSBNs in a way to which it is unaccustomed, untrained and possibly even unsuited; under present circumstances, it would derive no benefit at all. The USSR however, would to a large degree be legitimizing and securing its current deployments. To this must be added the difficulty, perhaps the greatest of all, that the present US Maritime Strategy seeks by threatening the Soviet Navy's 'bastions' to 'pin down other Soviet forces, particularly SSNs, in protection . . . In strategic terms this is, from the NATO viewpoint, protecting the transatlantic sea lines of communication'.[35] A sanctuary system denying this right to the West would in their eyes be a massive plus for the USSR, gravely damaging Atlantic security without any compensating safeguard.

Limitation of numbers or tonnages

Probably the most effective arms control agreement concluded before World War II was the 1922 Washington Treaty.[36] Although there were many other aspects to this complex negotiation,[37] it rested essentially on limiting the tonnages of capital ships in the US, British and Japanese navies in a 5 : 5 : 3 ratio and putting a ceiling on the tonnage of the largest. Later conferences resulting in the 1930 and 1936 London Treaties paid almost equal attention to numbers in each class of ship as to overall tonnages.

It was, arguably, a much simpler age. It was believed that like would fight like at sea. Therefore, although there were strategic asymmetries and these sometimes had to be taken into account,[38] it was at least possible to seek a balance expressed in tonnage and number ratios.

This kind of model no longer applies. Both underwater and above-water warfare provisions in the larger maritime forces form a web of platforms, weapons and types of explosive, made more complex by the fact that various levels of conflict have to be provided for. There are, moreover, asymmetries in superpower naval orders of battle which were undreamed of in the inter-war years.

In an imaginative proposal in the mid-1970s, Blechman[39] attempted to find a way through these difficulties with asymmetrical tonnage limits on four classes of vessel: attack submarines, large aircraft-carriers, medium and small carriers, and other warships. Had they become part of US arms control policy, it seems almost certain that the USSR would have cried 'foul' since, for example, they allowed the USA 1 million tons of large carriers and the USSR none. This example points squarely at the biggest difficulty with tonnage limitation as an arms control measure in this complex age: it is only too easy for either party to play the parity card. Once that is done, all the valuable and stabilizing asymmetries which have grown out of the diverse interests of the parties are removed, and there is substituted an artificial and unstable structure. A linked but separate temptation is to build up to limits after an agreement, even if strategic considerations do not demand it.[40] Finally, there are other obstacles to successful negotiation: the classification or definition of units poses considerable difficulties. It is also possible to install new weapons in old ships or to assign new roles to ships with a different classification, thereby rendering classifications meaningless.

Limitation of weapons

Any attempt to go through each category of naval weapon in order to assess its suitability for limitation would be of book length and unhelpful to this study. This section will deal therefore with two categories: tactical nuclear weapons for use against targets at sea and long-range cruise missiles.

'Tactical' is not a misnomer at sea. While widespread use of the approximately 6500 non-strategic nuclear weapons indicated as deployable[41] would no doubt have a severe impact on the marine environment, its direct effect on populations would be limited. Because this could make the political constraints less than they are in overland use, the tactical effect comes more to the forefront of consideration. This effect is significant. One simple example has been quoted: some Soviet submarines may have the hull strength to withstand conventional explosive charges that are light or imprecisely placed, and it would need a nuclear charge to be sure of eliminating them. Equally, the newly recommissioned US battleships might be able to take a large number of hits from conventional-warhead missiles, but would be incapacitated by a single near-underwater or airburst nuclear explosion.

Thus, even though the plans of both sides probably no longer call for early use, the temptation during higher-level conflict to take the tactical nuclear short cut would become severe the moment one side or the other thought it was losing—perhaps even if it thought it was losing one part of the battle. And while the dangers of escalation from sea to land are not so great as those from early use on land itself, they are still significant.

Maritime tactical nuclear weapons therefore appear to be a prime target for arms control, as are theatre nuclear weapons in Europe. It is suggested that the key concept, at least at the starting-point of the 'virtuous spiral', is that such weapons are 'desperation weapons'. If this is agreed, a much lower level of arsenals at once becomes acceptable, and it might be possible to eliminate certain categories, particularly in the above-water field. Moreover, both sides then have a vested interest in not making the other desperate: a counter-escalation measure of considerable importance.

Such thinking can be linked to the other weapons considered in this section. The cruise missile (CM) has been at sea for several decades, the USA having started with the Regulus in the 1950s and a whole family having been developed by the USSR in the anti-carrier role from the early 1960s. It is more or less impossible to put the clock back on this process, and in any case smaller powers very much rely on such weapons—albeit in the shorter-range brackets and with non-nuclear warheads—to protect their own interests.[42]

Thus, practical limitations can probably only be applied to CMs of very long range—say, over 1000 km—or to nuclear-armed missiles. One is bound to say that even in these categories, given US maritime strategic preoccupations, complete elimination does not seem negotiable in the near future. The ability to strike the Kola complex, which is such an integral part of the Soviet power threatening the Northern Flank, must remain a prized US option, and the ability to do so with nuclear weapons a necessary step, in their eyes, in the 'seamless robe' of deterrence. By the same token as that applying to tactical nuclear weapons, however, it might be possible to reduce considerably Tomahawk nuclear land attack missile holdings in return for similar Soviet concessions in their ability to attack the continental United States.

Limitation of deployments

In one form or another, the limitation of superpower naval deployments has been a frequently voiced arms control idea, particularly from the smaller nations. However, a study of the literature suggests that the most extreme measures, such as confining superpower forces to their own home waters, are seldom suggested, and even the theory that the adoption of exclusive economic zones (EEZs) would, by the extension of economic to security jurisdiction, develop into a form of 'de facto arms control'[43] has not been reflected in any widespread proposals.

The reasons are more apparent than usual at the time of writing, since one superpower is deploying large naval forces in the Gulf, which includes one semi-enclosed sea and several EEZs, and the other's forces are also present though not actively involved. They are there because they regard their vital interests, at and by sea, as being affected. They are also there because they have been drawn into another country's war. This is not uncommon, and the record shows that post-1945 conflict has tended initially to involve non-superpowers. As has been suggested, the direct effect on superpower vital interests is one thing that concerns them; another is the tendency of states in the area, whether directly involved or not, to seek local hegemony. All this makes it difficult for superpowers to accept the concept of 'zones of peace' except as rhetoric— which has its own uses, but is not a basis for specific, workable arms limitation.

However, one area where more specific limitation can be sought, and where the most frequent demands have so far been made,[44] is in the deployment of nuclear weapons at sea. The Treaty of Tlatelolco, and subsequent interpretation of it so far as the sea is concerned, is the subject of extensive literature;[45] its history indicates that the constraints that are put on superpowers by such instruments are more significant than one might think, and the limitations on their practical effect are more severe than their drafters might have hoped (see annexe B).

This brief discussion suggests that the limitation of naval deployments, whether on the Tlatelolco model or in any other form, is not going to be easy to negotiate, even if from a world point of view it was considered desirable. That basic point, it is submitted, is far from proved.

Confidence-building measures

The Document of the Stockholm Conference on Confidence- and Security-Building Measures and Disarmament in Europe of 19 September 1986 was a measure on which all involved expressed a good deal of satisfaction. It was notable, however, that apart from some provisions as to amphibious exercises[46] the sea was excluded. This resulted no doubt from a conscious decision by most of the participants to stick to their 'European' mandate. The Stockholm Document might nevertheless serve as a model for possible confidence-building measures at sea, either between the superpowers or more generally agreed. Such measures would then include the definition of notifiable naval activities; procedures, including time limits, for their notification; the provision of a calendar for the forthcoming year, giving all notifiable activities; provision for the observation of certain naval exercises; and verification arrangements. On the CSBM model, there would also be clauses about no-notice exercises and activities not included in the calendar.

The main practical difficulty concerning naval forces lies in that very mobility and flexibility that is their chief strategic asset. Take, for example, the 13 000-man upper limit for unnotified activities on land: this could conveniently be equated to a CVBG, and normal activities by such groups would therefore be excluded. But what happens when the CVBG makes a rendezvous with an underway replenishment group (URG), which it must do every five days or so to sustain itself at sea? Or when relief on station occurs, and two CVBGs are in the same area at one time? One must conclude that negotiation would need to be intricate in order to take account of such factors, that limits might end rather high and that allowances for unscheduled or alert exercises might need to be generous.

Combining the Stockholm model with another, that of the 1936 Montreux Convention (see paper 1), is a further possibility. In this case, perhaps, it would be made mandatory to declare all excursions by naval forces more than, say, 500 miles (800 km) from the shores of the home country, but the example of the Montreux Convention is far from encouraging to those who wish to limit superpower freedom of action. It has proved relatively simple, by means of phantom declarations that are subsequently cancelled and by very liberal redefinition of warship types,[47] to manage surface ship deployments almost without constraint.

Finally, it must be said that any attempt to establish a regime for declaring the movements of submarines—whether SSBN or other, and however simple or complicated—would almost certainly be opposed by both superpowers. The espousal by both of the Law of the Sea regime of transit passage for straits[48] is sufficient evidence.

It looks as though large set-piece exercises at sea, like the NATO 'Ocean Safari' series or Soviet world-wide exercises on the 'Okean' pattern, could be candidates for notification, but that confidence-building measures involving any activity of smaller-scale or more general application would be in for a rough passage.

VI. Outlook

The most promising and worthwhile arms control initiative at sea appears to be in the field of tactical nuclear weapons. These weapons do not figure so prominently or so early in the operational plans of the superpowers as they once did. It is generally acknowledged that there may be too many of them, and many sea-going officers do not like the prospect of their widespread use because the course of a nuclear war at sea is unpredictable. It may be necessary to keep some in certain categories for the reasons given above, and that outcome may be stabilizing.

Steps could also be taken towards the notification of major naval exercises, using the Stockholm model for CSBMs, but the lower limit would have to be set higher than the land equivalent.

Although limitations on strategic submarine and missile systems at sea are by no means out of the question, they must form a part of any wider pattern of limitation of such systems. This applies also to ballistic missile systems that are held at sea for theatre use.

Finally, perhaps, it is not out of place to say that the employment of forces at sea, particularly in normal conditions or low-confrontational situations, is not by any means the worst way of conducting diplomacy, exerting international pressure or protecting interests. Even when such operations reach the level of conflict, it has generally proved containable and terminable, in marked contrast to action on land whether in terrorist or military form. And it was Schelling and Halperin, prophets of arms control, who said: 'limited war is itself a form of arms control'.[49]

Notes and references

[1] Schelling, T. C. and Halperin, M. H., *Strategy and Arms Control* (first published 1961; Pergamon-Brassey's: Oxford, 1985), pp. 1–5; Bertram, C., *The Future of Arms Control, Part II—Arms Control and Technological Change: Elements of a New Approach*, Adelphi Paper no. 146 (International Institute for Strategic Studies (IISS): London, 1978), pp. 6–8.

[2] Freedman, L., *Arms Control—Management or Reform?*, Chatham House Papers 31 (Routledge & Kegan Paul: London, New York and Henley, 1986), pp. 6–8.

[3] Alford, J. (ed.), *The Future of Arms Control, Part III—Confidence Building Measures*, Adelphi Paper no. 149 (IISS: London, 1979); Holst, J. J., 'Confidence building measures: a conceptual framework', *Survival*, Jan.–Feb. 1983, pp. 2–13.

[4] Schell, J., *The Fate of the Earth* (Picador: London, 1982), pp. 161–62.

[5] See Bertram (note 1), p. 7.

[6] See Freedman (note 2), p. 74.

[7] Kennedy, P. M., *The Rise and Fall of British Naval Mastery* (Allen Lane: London, 1976), p. 157.

[8] Hill, J. R., *Maritime Strategy for Medium Powers* (Croom Helm: Beckenham, 1986), pp. 66–73.

[9] Nitze, P. H., Sullivan, Jr, L. and the Atlantic Council Working Group on Securing the Seas, *Securing the Seas: The Soviet Naval Challenge and Western Alliance Options* (Westview: Boulder, Colo., 1979).

[10] Ranft, B. and Till, G., *The Sea in Soviet Strategy* (Macmillan: London, 1983), p. 152.

[11] Lehman, J. F., 'The 600-ship navy', *Maritime Strategy*, US Naval Institute *Proceedings*, supplement, Jan. 1986, pp. 34–36.

[12] Dismukes, B. and McConnell, J., *Soviet Naval Diplomacy* (Pergamon: Oxford, 1979), pp. 249–50 and 287; Watson, B. W., *Red Navy at Sea: Soviet Naval Operations on the High Seas, 1956–1980* (Arms and Armour: London, 1982), pp. 103 and 170.

[13] O'Connell, D. P., *The Influence of Law on Sea Power* (Manchester University Press: Manchester, 1975), p. 179.

[14] MccGwire, M. K., appears to have coined this expression in papers for the Brookings Institution in the early 1980s. In *Military Objectives in Soviet Foreign Policy* (Brookings Institution: Washington, DC, 1987), p. 112, he suggests that the USSR may in the near future put less reliance on the Barents Sea bastion.

[15] Watkins, J. D. (Admiral), 'The Maritime Strategy', *Maritime Strategy* (note 11), p. 11.

[16] Gorshkov, S. G. (Admiral), *The Sea Power of the State* (Pergamon: Oxford, 1978).

[17] See MccGwire (note 14), p. 47; van Tol, R., 'Soviet naval exercises 1983–85', *Naval Forces*, June 1986, p. 24.

[18] Brooks, L. F. (Captain), 'The nuclear maritime strategy', US Naval Institute *Proceedings*, Apr. 1987, p. 34.

[19] See generally Hill, J. R., *Anti-Submarine Warfare* (Ian Allan: Shepperton, 1984).

[20] Friedman, N., 'Modern torpedoes—a new generation?', *Military Technology*, vol. 9, no. 7 (1985), p. 28; Engelhardt, J. J., 'Soviet sub design philosophy', US Naval Institute *Proceedings*, Oct. 1987, p. 193.

[21] MccGwire (note 14), p. 160.

[22] International Institute for Strategic Studies, *The Military Balance 1986–87* (IISS: London, 1987). ASW capability against sophisticated submarine forces is hard to assess, but the performance of the Argentine Navy in 1982, for example, suggests that it is within the grasp of relatively few maritime forces.

[23] *Jane's Weapon Systems 1986–87* (Jane's: London, 1986) devotes 26 pages to shipborne surface-to-air missile systems and 29 pages to shipborne gun systems.

[24] Friedman, N., 'Real time ocean surveillance', *Military Technology*, vol. 8, no. 9 (1984), p. 76.

[25] See van Tol (note 17), p. 22.

[26] *Statement on the Defence Estimates 1985* (Her Majesty's Stationery Office: London, 1985), Cmnd. 9430-I, p. 6.

[27] See MccGwire (note 14), pp. 153–54.

[28] Byers, R. B. (ed.), *The Denuclearisation of the Oceans* (Croom Helm: Beckenham, 1986), p. 170.

[29] For details and descriptions of these forces see Fieldhouse, R. and Taoka, S., SIPRI, *Superpowers at Sea: An Assessment of the Naval Arms Race*, a Strategic Issue Papers monograph (Oxford University Press: Oxford, 1989), pp. 52–55, 93–105.

[30] Daniel, D. C., IISS, *Anti-Submarine Warfare and Superpower Strategic Stability* (Macmillan: London, 1986).

[31] See Daniel (note 30), p. 205.

[32] For a brief account, see Hill (note 19), pp. 42–43.

[33] The part of unrestricted submarine warfare in bringing the USA into both world wars is well known. Since World War II, the evidence of the escalatory nature of submarine warfare is negative but compelling; see, for example, the extraordinarily low incidence of submarine use in the 144 limited maritime operations described in Cable, J., *Gunboat Diplomacy*, 2nd edn (Macmillan: London, 1981), pp. 222–58.

[34] See Young, E. in Byers (note 28), p. 138.

[35] Heaslip, R. G. (Rear Admiral), 'Submarine warfare', Royal United Services Institute *Journal*, Sep. 1987, p. 23.

[36] *UK Treaty Series* No. 5 (1924), Cmd 2037.

[37] The treaty runs to 25 articles and goes into extensive detail including listing of (and sometimes separate provision for) individual units. Even then, submarines were entirely excluded from the treaty and classes of smaller ships barely mentioned.

[38] These were even more to the fore in the discussion on cruisers in the 1930 London Treaty negotiations; see Roskill, S. W., *Naval Policy between the Wars*, vol. 2 (Collins: London, 1976), pp. 40–44.

[39] Blechman, B. M., *The Control of Naval Armaments* (Brookings Institution: Washington, DC, 1975), pp. 25–30.

[40] See Roskill (note 38), vol. 1, p. 326.

[41] See Fieldhouse and Taoka (note 29).

[42] See *The Military Balance* (note 22), country sections, for the 70 or more navies now equipped with surface-to-surface missile systems.

[43] Young, E., 'New laws for old navies: military implications of the Law of the Sea', *Survival*, Nov.–Dec. 1974, p. 262.

[44] United Nations, *The Naval Arms Race*, Report of the Secretary-General, UN Study series no. 16, UN document A/40/535 (United Nations: New York, 1986), p. 74.

[45] See, among others, Gunnarsson, G., 'Naval arms control', *ADIU Report*, July/Aug. 1986, p. 2; Gallacher, J., 'Article VII, The Treaty of Tlatelolco and colonial warfare in the twentieth century', *Arms Control*, Dec. 1984, p. 75; Quester, G. H., in Byers (note 28), p. 122.

[46] The Stockholm Document is reprinted in SIPRI, *SIPRI Yearbook 1987: World Armaments and Disarmament* (Oxford University Press: Oxford, 1987), pp. 355–69. See especially paras 29–35 and Annex I.

[47] For example, the Soviet classification of their 36 000-ton Kiev Class as 'Large Anti-Submarine Cruisers'; see *Combat Fleets of the World 1986/87* (Arms and Armour Press: London, 1986), p. 493; and for the system of 'contingency declarations' in respect of the Montreux Convention, see Dismukes and McConnell (note 12), p. 167.

[48] UN Convention on the Law of the Sea, 1982, Articles 38 and 39; for the full text, see annexe B.

[49] See Schelling and Halperin (note 1), p. 78.

Part IV
Approaches to naval arms control

Paper 7. Naval arms control and the Convention on the Law of the Sea

Ove Bring

Legal Department, Ministry of Foreign Affairs, Stockholm, Sweden

I. Introduction

On 10 December 1982 the United Nations Convention on the Law of the Sea (UNCLOS) was signed by 117 states in Montego Bay, Jamaica. By May 1989, 41 additional states and other political entities had signed it. As of 1 May 1989, 40 of the signatory states and entities had ratified the Convention. (See annexe B for relevant excerpts of the text of the Convention and the list of states and other entities that have signed and ratified it.) However, 60 states are required to ratify it for it to enter into force, which may prove to be a lengthy process. Several industrial countries find it difficult to accept the Convention's provisions concerning an international exploitation regime for the seabed. The USA, the UK and the Federal Republic of Germany are among the states that have not even signed the UNCLOS. Despite these problems, the Convention has created a new situation with regard to the international law of the sea—a legal starting-point for nations in safeguarding the national, security and economic interests that are at stake in the marine environment.

Although there is profound disagreement on certain provisions of the UNCLOS (e.g., Part XI), there are other provisions—in fact the majority of them—that reflect the general conception of existing law in this area. In many respects, the provisions represent a valuable codification of international customary law, for example, as regards the regime of the high seas, innocent passage and the formerly controversial question of the breadth of territorial seas. In other cases, order has been brought to a confused legal situation in such a way as to indicate that the new rules will soon attain the status of customary law, for example, as regards the breadth of economic zones and the rights pertaining there. In yet other cases, completely new rules have been adopted regarding transit passage in international straits, the delimitation of archipelagic states, routes through archipelagic waters and protection of the marine environment.

It has been said that *one* reason why the US Administration has so far not signed or ratified the Convention on the Law of the Sea is connected with customary law. The United States will be able to benefit from the sections of the Convention that it endorses, for example, the rules with military and strategic implications, even without ratifying the Convention, since these rules will soon acquire, and indeed some have already acquired, the status of customary law.

II. Military aspects of the Convention

The UNCLOS negotiations did not directly discuss military/strategic matters or matters relating to disarmament and arms control at sea. Nor are any of the Convention's 320 articles directly concerned with these matters. However, this is not to say that the question of military utilization of the seas did not play a part during the negotiations. On the contrary, the great powers paid great attention to these aspects and took up their negotiating positions accordingly. Their aim was to ensure maximum naval mobility for their own naval forces. It can be said that they succeeded in this aim; this is witnessed by the provisions on transit passage through international straits.

Several of the Convention's articles have considerable military implications or give rise to problems of interpretation that have such implications. Attention should therefore be paid to the military aspects of the UNCLOS.

The Preamble, setting forth the purposes and spirit of the Convention, emphasizes that its aim is to promote the peaceful utilization of the seas and oceans. This theme is repeated in several articles. According to Article 88, 'the high seas shall be reserved for peaceful purposes', and Article 141 provides that the seabed beyond the limits of national jurisdiction 'shall be open to use exclusively for peaceful purposes'. The term 'peaceful purposes' is not defined in the Convention, and many states may well maintain that any display of military power at sea is against the spirit of the UNCLOS. According to this interpretation, peaceful purposes must be interpreted as non-military purposes. The standing counter-argument of the great naval powers is that the right to individual and collective self-defence presupposes military preparations, and that the principle of the freedom of the seas *ipso facto* legitimizes the use of the seas for military ends.

An interpretation of the term 'peaceful purposes' may in fact be inferred from Article 301 ('Peaceful uses of the seas'). This article provides that 'in exercising their rights and performing their duties in accordance with this Convention, all States Parties shall refrain from any threat or use of force' in conformity with the principles embodied in the UN Charter. This is a reminder of the fact that the virtually absolute prohibition of the use of force laid down in Article 2:4 of the Charter also applies to the seas; at the same time it is, however, recognized that Article 51 of the Charter relating to self-defence is also relevant in this connection. Thus states have the right to use the seas for such military purposes as are related to preparations for self-defence (in peacetime) and the exercise of self-defence (in war).

Article 2:4 of the UN Charter prohibits 'the threat or use of force', whether directed against the territorial integrity or the political independence of another state. The article also protects the equality and self-determination of all states.

The fact that contemporary international law prohibits even the *threat* of force, as well as intervention in the affairs of other states, cannot be over-emphasized. This means that traditional gunboat diplomacy and 'pacific' blockades are illegal under existing international law. The principle of non-intervention also prohibits modern and more subtle forms of power projection, where the purpose is subversive in relation to another state. Today's great powers have a impressive trans-shipment and landing capacity, comprising roll-on, roll-off (ro-ro) vessels and, in the case of the United States, a special Rapid Deployment Force (RDF) which can be used to apply political pressure and for interventions overseas. The UNCLOS, through its reference to the UN Charter, confirms that there do exist certain fundamental restrictions on the utilization of naval capacity.

Innocent passage

Article 19 of the UNCLOS deals with innocent passage. All ships (military as well as non-military) have the right to such passage through the territorial sea of another state. This right does not extend to passage in the zone inside the baselines, the so-called internal waters, for which the permission of the coastal state is always required. Passage through the territorial sea is innocent as long as it is not 'prejudicial to the peace, good order or security of the coastal State'. Article 19 enumerates certain military activities that cannot be considered innocent. The right of passage does not apply, for example, to passage involving the threat or use of force against the coastal state, exercise or practice with weapons, the collecting of information to the prejudice of the defence or security of the coastal state, the launching or landing of aircraft on ships, or the launching or taking on board of military devices.

Aircraft are not embraced by the right of passage; they must have special permission for overflights of national territory, including the territorial sea. Submarines must navigate on the surface and show their flag. Coastal states have certain discretionary means of regulating the extent and exercise of innocent passage, but the Convention does not stipulate any requirements for prior notice, or advance permission, for the passage of naval vessels. However, this issue is a controversial one. Upon signing the Convention, Sweden, Finland, Romania and a number of developing countries indicated that they require prior notice. NATO regards this as verging on an improper restriction of innocent passage. The Soviet attitude to this matter is ambiguous, since the USSR itself traditionally requires advance permission for foreign ships wishing to pass through Soviet territorial seas, while at the same time considering itself, as a great power, entitled to virtually free passage through the waters of other states. Since 1983, however, the Soviet legislation is adapted to the wording of the UNCLOS in the sense that it explicitly requires previous authorization *only* for passage in internal waters of the USSR.

Article 23 provides for innocent passage with nuclear-powered ships and ships carrying nuclear or other noxious substances. The article implies that nuclear passage is not prejudicial in itself, but the need for special safety precautions in connection with such passage is recognized. Nothing is stated in Article 23 about the right for coastal states unilaterally to stipulate conditions for nuclear passage; on the contrary, it is assumed that special safety precautions are laid down in international agreements. The People's Democratic Republic of Yemen (in conjunction with signing) and Egypt (in conjunction with ratification) have stated that they will demand advance permission for nuclear passage; Egypt has said that it will continue to demand this as long as there is no international agreement to this effect.

Article 25 allows coastal states the right, for the protection of their security, to prohibit temporarily the passage of all types of foreign ships in specified zones. On the other hand, Article 24 states that a coastal state shall not hamper the innocent passage of a foreign ship except in accordance with the UNCLOS.

Transit passage

The principle of innocent passage has traditionally applied to straits connecting the high seas or an economic zone with another part of the high seas or another economic zone (international straits). As the Convention would permit nations to extend the breadth of their territorial sea from 3–4 nautical miles up to 12 nautical miles, the great naval powers felt the need, in the course of the negotiations, to guard against the resulting closure of many international straits. Straits that previously had a channel of international water would have been closed if narrower than 24 nautical miles. The United States considers about 125 of these straits to be of strategic importance. Both the USA and the USSR regarded the innocent passage regime, which allowed coastal states to 'interfere with' passage through international straits, as unacceptable. The great powers considered that their SSBNs must be assured maximum freedom of movement. The UN Conference on the Law of the Sea accepted these demands within the framework of a great compromise and established a new regime with practically free passage through international straits.

The new regime ('transit passage') applies only to straits which in practice are used for international passage. While the previous right of innocent passage in international straits did not apply to aircraft—overflights required special permission—the UNCLOS provides that ships and aircraft have an equal right to free passage in international straits. This right applies, in accordance with Article 38, to 'all ships'. Nothing is said about submarines, which means that they can navigate under water. It is a general requirement, however, that passage must be 'continuous and expeditious'. Article 39 prohibits ships in transit passage from threatening or using violence against a coastal state in violation of the provisions of the UN Charter.

The rules of the UNCLOS relating to international straits do not apply to certain 'historical straits', that is, straits regarding which a separate regime of international law has long been established in international agreements (Article 35(c)). The Dardanelles and the Bosphorus, the Öresund, the Magellan and the South Kvarken (the sound between Sweden and the Åland Islands) in the Baltic Sea are examples of such straits.

Another innovation in the Convention is the legitimization of the demands of archipelagic states for enormous areas of water behind generously drawn baselines. Innocent passage applies in the territorial seas of archipelagic states, but in addition a different kind of transit passage has been introduced—the right of free passage through special sea lanes to be specified by the coastal state. The breadth of these sea lanes is 50 nautical miles, which is obviously more than sufficient for merchant marine ships or non-military aircraft in the superjacent air corridor. But 50 nautical miles is a suitable breadth from the point of view of the military requirements of the superpowers. Among other things, the new regime allows submarines to pass under water without announcing their presence.

With respect to the use of the high seas, the UNCLOS confirms the traditional principle of 'reasonable regard' for the activities of other states. In accordance with Article 87:2, the freedom of the high seas (including the militarily important freedom of navigation) shall be exercised with due regard to the interests of other states. The principle of reasonable regard to the interests of others also applies to the seabed (Article 147).

III. Arms control considerations

Hopes that the 1982 Convention on the Law of the Sea might advance 'de facto arms control' have not been fulfilled. On the contrary, the Convention basically confirms the traditionally more or less free military uses of the seas ('non-arms control at sea'). The restrictions that do apply are well adapted to the interests of the superpowers as perceived by these powers themselves. However, the Convention does constitute a legal platform on which future arms control initiatives can be built. The signing of the Convention gave a general indication to the international community of the points of departure which will be relevant to future negotiations. The question of arms control and the restriction of military activities at sea—issues which have previously not ranked high on the international agenda—can now be discussed in a more meaningful manner.

The 1971 Seabed Treaty created a valuable precedent when it entered into force in 1972 (10 years before the UNCLOS was signed). It showed that the principle of the freedom of the seas is compatible with multilateral military restrictions. It is no longer taken for granted that the freedom of the seas means virtually total freedom of action in the marine environment. Military restraints (or environmental safeguards) could be agreed upon as a means to further a progressive development of the law.

This understanding should be remembered in any discussion on arms control at sea. Some will say that future agreements should not be allowed to undermine the principle of the freedom of the seas (in particular the freedom of navigation) as confirmed by the UNCLOS or to impair the military uses of the oceans as legitimized by that principle. Some will even say that proposals for restrictions are in contravention of international law. 'Freedom-oriented' assertions which go that far are, however, based on a complete misapprehension of the legal situation.

It does not follow from the general principle of *mare liberum* that agreed restrictions on military uses of the oceans are in any way inappropriate from a legal point of view. States have the right to *specify* the principle of freedom of the seas and the standard of 'due regard' (taking account of the interests of *all* users of the seas, not only the military).

Since the UNCLOS does not deal with arms control matters *per se*, it follows that such matters could be covered by subsequent agreements. It also follows that any new regulations in this field should not be integrated in the legal system created by the Convention. The peaceful uses regime of the Convention may be amended in the future, but it should not be amended through and disturbed by additional provisions on arms control and confidence-building. Such provisions should be negotiated in separate bilateral or multilateral agreements, as suggested below.

Measures consistent with the Convention

It will be possible to enter into agreements on naval nuclear and non-nuclear disarmament without any complications arising from the law of the sea. The *reduction* of naval forces is unrelated to the principles of *mare liberum* and 'due regard'. It is the *use* (or demanded non-use) of naval forces which relates to the law of the sea and which has to be reconciled with the principles of the 1982 Convention.

The importance of confidence- and security-building measures (CSBMs) has been generally recognized. The objective of such measures is to reduce the dangers of military conflict and of misunderstanding or miscalculation of military activities. These measures should improve predictability by removing to the extent possible such features of military deployment and activities which may be conceived as potentially threatening. Measures relating to exchange of information and greater openness regarding major naval activities and naval armaments could be of importance in this regard. Concrete examples of maritime CSBMs are the existing three bilateral agreements on the prevention of incidents on and over the high seas (see paper 11). A multilateral agreement comparable to those agreements should be negotiated to permit other states to enjoy the same benefits (see paper 12).

Consideration and possible negotiation on maritime CSBMs should be initiated in a global context. The reason for this is that naval operations and activities are global in character and could not easily be the object of geographical limitations.

A suitable forum for negotiations on these issues, including a multilateral agreement on the prevention of incidents at sea, could be the Geneva-based Conference on Disarmament (CD).

Some of the negotiations suggested by the 1986 UN study on the naval arms race will have to take place in other forums.[1] A special review conference is needed for an extension of the nuclear weapon-free regime of the 1959 Antarctic Treaty (Article VI of the treaty has the effect of excluding the high seas in the Antarctic area from some of the military restraints applicable on land). A similar review conference or an amendment procedure through written communications will be needed for a revision/extension of the Seabed Treaty (see paper 10). The Third Seabed Treaty Review Conference is scheduled to be held in September 1989.

The UN study on the naval arms race also suggested a modernization of the laws of naval warfare. For instance, an updating of the 1907 Hague Convention on the Laying of Sea Mines could, if agreed by the major military powers, have considerable confidence-building effects. Because of the humanitarian gains involved in the protection of fishermen and other civilians against the effects of sea mines, it seems that a conference under the auspices of the International Committee of the Red Cross (ICRC) would be an appropriate forum for such negotiations.

All these suggestions on new legal rules in the naval arms control area are in perfect harmony with the UN Convention on the Law of the Sea. There is no lack of ideas for feasible measures of military restraint at sea. There may, however, still be a lack of political will.

Notes and references

This paper is adapted from the author's book *Nedrustningens Folkrätt [The International Law of Disarmament]* (Norstedts: Stockholm, 1987).

[1] United Nations, *The Naval Arms Race*, Report of the Secretary-General, UN Study series no. 16, UN document A/40/535 (United Nations: New York, 1986).

Paper 8. Controlling superpower naval operations

William M. Arkin

Institute for Policy Studies, Washington, DC, USA

I. Introduction

Superpower naval operations are a potential threat to peace. The US and Soviet navies are free to sail virtually anywhere unchecked by international law. Routine peacetime operations and exercises have caused dangerous incidents at sea in the past and could do so again. The US and Soviet navies go beyond the requirements of training, to practice harassment, intimidation and intelligence collection to the detriment of international security. They are free to do so as long as nations accept the superpower interpretation of international rights and freedoms of the seas, which favours global naval powers.

In the 1980s, the US and Soviet navies have increased both the level and the belligerence of their peacetime operations. They have made routine certain practices that are provocative and have gone beyond previous standards of conduct at sea. These operations demonstrate their disregard for naval arms control—particularly on the part of the US Navy. Although significant political and military changes in the USSR have led to a scaling back of its navy and naval operations and to an expressed desire for naval arms control measures, there is no assurance that naval operations will be placed under stricter political control and reasonable restraint or that the situation at sea will improve.

In this paper it is argued that there are two primary explanations for the increased level and belligerence of superpower naval operations in recent years, and the hostility which exists towards naval arms control: (*a*) the unilateralism and autonomy of the US naval establishment; and (*b*) the lack of co-ordination and linkage between the naval arms control and 'law of the sea' processes.

II. The level and dangers of naval operations

The superpower naval arms race is characterized not only by the rapid growth and modernization of naval nuclear and non-nuclear weapons and forces, but also by unprecedented peacetime operations. Admiral James Watkins, former US Chief of Naval Operations (CNO), stated in 1985 that, 'Although technically we are at peace, our operating tempo is about 20 per cent higher than during the Viet Nam War'.[1] Former Secretary of the Navy John F. Lehman told the US Congress the same year that the US Navy was 'spending more time at sea than it had even averaged in the Second World War'.[2] The Soviet Union, with its emerging global naval capability, has been experiencing similar accelerated operations. 'From the Baltic to the Caribbean to the South China Sea', said Lehman, 'our ships and men pass within yards of Soviet naval forces every day'.[3] The current CNO, Admiral Carlisle Trost, wrote in his fiscal year 1988–89 report to Congress: 'We track Soviet submarines trailing our warships and escort Soviet planes flying near our battlegroups on a daily basis'.[4]

The ships, submarines and surveillance aircraft of the superpowers and of the major Western allies regularly operate in dangerous proximity to each other, shadowing each other's movements and activities and performing mock attack drills and manoeuvres. In addition, the increased operating tempo which began in the early 1980s includes unprecedented military exercises, both in terms of their scale and intensity. Because of the locations of these exercises, they are also more and more offensively oriented. Examples of such exercises are the following.

1. In November 1981, a Soviet Whiskey Class attack submarine was stranded inside Swedish territorial waters; the Swedish Government later stated that it believed the submarine was carrying nuclear weapons.[5] Norway, Japan, Indonesia and other countries have experienced similar intrusions, and submarines of both superpowers have been reported to be involved in covert operations that have included violations of territorial waters.[6]

2. In September 1982, the US Navy held its first multiple aircraft-carrier battle group operation in the extreme northern Pacific Ocean (around the western Aleutian Islands) since World War II.[7]

3. During 1982–83, the US Navy held successive operations with two or three aircraft-carrier battle groups in the Norwegian Sea, held large-scale surface exercises in the Sea of Japan (the first such operations in 13 years), and operated attack submarines in the Sea of Okhotsk for the first time ever.[8]

4. In early 1984, the Soviet Navy conducted its largest naval exercise ever in the Atlantic Ocean. More than 200 naval combatants were deployed in the Barents, Norwegian and North Seas. Naval and air force Backfire bombers and other medium and heavy bombers, as well as about 70 Soviet submarines, participated.[9]

5. In November and December 1984, the United States conducted its largest peacetime fleet exercise—'Fleet Ex 85'—since World War II.[10] Five aircraft-carrier battle groups participated in the exercise, and two US aircraft-carriers in the Sea of Japan approached to within 50 miles (80 km) of the Soviet city of Vladivostok.

6. In April 1985, the Soviet Union conducted a large exercise in the Pacific Ocean, described as 'the most extreme and realistic ever conducted by the Soviet Navy in the Pacific'.[11]

7. In July 1985, the Soviet Navy held an unusually long and active naval exercise in the Atlantic Ocean, mobilizing 38 surface warships and 40 submarines, and including over 200 aircraft sorties from land bases, the largest

number of aircraft involved in maritime operations since the 'Okean' exercises in 1975.

8. During August and September 1985, NATO held its largest-ever maritime exercise—'Ocean Safari 85'—in the northern Atlantic Ocean and the Norwegian Sea.[12]

9. In August 1985, the Soviet Navy conducted its first amphibious landing in the Pacific since 1978, as part of an exercise with 21 ships and submarines around the Kurile Islands north of Japan.

10. In August 1986, the Soviet Navy conducted what US Navy officials called a 'sea projection force' exercise in the Pacific east of Japan involving two V/STOL (vertical/short take-off and landing) aircraft-carriers, 14–18 ships and 16–20 submarines.

11. In September 1986, two US aircraft-carrier battle groups and the *USS New Jersey* battleship battle group conducted the largest naval operations ever in the Sea of Japan. The nuclear-capable *New Jersey* and four other warships subsequently entered the Sea of Okhotsk and transited through the Kurile Islands into the Pacific Ocean.

12. In January 1987, the US Marines conducted their first amphibious landing on Shemya Island in the Aleutians since World War II, and their first-ever amphibious landing in the Aleutians during wintertime.

As the intensity and size of the routine military exercises and operations by one side have increased, there have been increasing military (particularly air and submarine) responses from the other side. The September 1982 US exercise in the northern Pacific, for instance, conducted some 500 miles (800 km) from the Soviet coast,[13] provoked simulated anti-ship cruise missile attacks upon US aircraft-carriers by Soviet naval Backfire bombers for the first time.[14] During the NATO exercise 'Northern Wedding 82' in the Norwegian Sea, 102 Soviet aircraft, including Badger and Bear bombers, flew sorties against US and NATO naval forces.[15] The NATO exercise 'Teamwork 84' in the northern Atlantic attracted a sizeable Soviet submarine response.[16] During 'Ocean Safari 85', some 19 Soviet ships and submarines and almost 100 Soviet aircraft sorties operated in response to the NATO forces' presence in northern Atlantic waters and the Norwegian Sea.[17] During the Pacific 'Fleet Ex 85' operations, where US aircraft-carriers came within 50 miles (80 km) of the Soviet coast in December 1985, the Soviet Union responded with over 100 fighter, bomber and reconnaissance overflights, as well as by alerting surface vessels in port.

In addition to accelerated US operations during 1983 and 1984, Lehman reported on a new Soviet development: 'not only did we have two incidents of Soviet nuclear attack submarines actually hitting or inadvertently fouling our surface combatants, but we have now seen a developing pattern of regular deployments of nuclear attack submarines close off our principal naval ports'.[18] More recently, Lehman reported that '"Victor"-class nuclear attack submarines are routinely found lurking near many of our principal naval ports'.[19] 'Their submarines now are deployed regularly among all of our exercises and astride all of our sea lanes.'[20] 'Our most valuable strategic asset, our 10 Trident submarines, are unprotected at Bangor, WA [Washington]. They are right by the Straits of Juan de Fuca, outside which there is a permanently deployed [Soviet] attack submarine presence nearly all the time.'[21]

Dangers of naval operations

The purpose of peacetime military exercises is to practise and test strategies and plans which might be carried out during a crisis or war. This usually includes high-intensity shipboard drills, geared to the ability to operate in unfamiliar environments or to test complex battle group, inter-service and allied interactions and co-ordination. Attaining military readiness is not necessarily tied to the ability to operate under actual wartime conditions but instead stresses the simulation of such an environment. As such, the conduct of naval operations close to adversaries' homelands or the routine operations of naval forces in threatening proximity to adversary forces are political acts for the purpose of harassment or intimidation, rather than a military necessity.

During a crisis, forward naval strategies and aggressive practices could significantly influence the likelihood of exacerbating the crisis or escalating it to a conflict. During war, certain naval operations could autonomously influence the likelihood of a conventional war escalating into a nuclear war.

It is difficult to conceive of a rational decision-making process that would result in political authorization to use nuclear weapons at sea. None the less, it is possible to construct convincing scenarios for purposeful escalation to the use of military force during a superpower crisis. Any direct confrontation between the superpowers inherently increases the risk of the use of nuclear weapons. The routine presence of nuclear weapons in the oceans and their complete integration into the naval formations of the USA and the USSR inherently increase the likelihood that nuclear weapons could be employed in the course of a high-intensity conventional war. Naval operations that could inadvertently accelerate and contribute to such a decision should not be conducted.

If naval operations can inadvertently contribute to escalation either of a crisis or a conventional war, they should be controlled. Several features of current naval operations and strategies seem to create the threat of such escalation.

1. Crisis 'surge deployments' (i.e., sudden surges of submarines out of port into the high seas) of attack and ballistic missile submarines from home ports, with short-notice practice sorties during peacetime exercises for the purpose of practicing 'no-notice' dispersal during a crisis. Such a strategy, adopted by both the United States and the Soviet Union, could precipitate higher levels of mobilization and alert as well as heighten preparations for conflict.

2. Plans for early movement of forces during the 'pre-conflict' period,[22] including deployment of US nuclear-powered attack submarines deep in the 'sea control areas' and 'home waters' of the Soviet Union.[23] These undermine political control of military forces and accelerate the decision-making process as it relates to the use of force.

3. More aggressive electronic warfare operations intended to 'confuse, deceive and disrupt' military decision-makers, including large-scale deception operations by naval forces during peacetime exercises.[24] These create uncertainty and increase the possibility of miscalculation during a crisis or conventional war.

4. A declaratory strategy of intentionally destroying enemy strategic nuclear ballistic missile submarines as part of a conventional naval conflict, and as a means to shift the nuclear balance. This creates the threat of nuclear escalation. The pursuit itself of such anti-submarine operations during a full-scale war would most likely result in significant shifts in the alert levels of strategic nuclear forces.

5. Unclear war termination objectives in wartime—as well as threats to attack enemy homeland bases, amphibious invasions or aggressive covert mining of enemy ports. These could serve to provoke escalation.

The adoption of aggressive maritime strategies and the lack of inhibitions on conducting provocative peacetime operations make the naval arms race an area ripe for arms control. Today there are no constraints on non-strategic naval nuclear weapons or operations; no restrictions on the carriage of nuclear weapons or the operation of nuclear propulsion reactors; almost no prohibited zones (except in territorial seas) for surveillance, cruising or exercises; no universally outlawed manoeuvres or harassment techniques; no geographic restraints; and no proscribed strategies or doctrines. Controls were placed on ballistic missile submarines and their weapons in the SALT agreements, but this was only because strategic nuclear forces happened to be based at sea. In 1972, during the *détente* era, the United States and the Soviet Union did conclude an agreement on preventing incidents at sea (as did the Soviet Union with Great Britain in 1986 and with the Federal Republic of Germany in 1988). Unfortunately, the USA–USSR Incidents at Sea Agreement has had little effect on curtailing provocative naval manoeuvres.

The US Navy (and the other naval powers, particularly Western allies) has a strong aversion to any prohibitions on naval operations. In fact, the United States, Great Britain and France have made the 'right' to conduct unimpeded operations on the high seas a prerequisite for their support for any kind of arms control confidence-building measures (even on land) or for their consent to the existence of nuclear-free zones (see annexe A). To exercise the 'freedoms' of the sea, these naval powers conduct naval operations in sensitive areas. US 'freedom-of-navigation' manoeuvres held near the Soviet Union, however, raise serious questions about the intent behind operations to demonstrate such rights. The seemingly accepted and routine US freedom-of-navigation manoeuvres in the Baltic and Black Seas, for instance, have for no explainable reason been increasing in size and scope in recent years. In September-October 1985, NATO conducted its largest exercise in the Baltic Sea, including participation by the battleship *USS Iowa*, equipped with Tomahawk SLCMs, and ships of the British and West German navies.[25] The United States held three 'Black Sea Ops' during 1986, an unprecedented number. In March 1986, two

US ships (a cruiser and a destroyer) sailed within 6 nautical miles of the Soviet Crimean coast. While the Soviet Union protested the incursion inside its territorial waters, the White House stated that the vessels were merely 'exercising' the 'right of innocent passage'. In February 1988, two US warships—including the *USS Caron*, specially modified for collecting intelligence—again sailed within 6 nautical miles of the Soviet Crimean coast. After warning the US vessels to leave Soviet waters, two Soviet ships collided with the US ships.

III. Unilateralism and autonomy of the US naval establishment

By nature, naval forces are more independent than other military services, and by tradition naval officers have a wider global frame of reference and greater autonomy. Ironically, the current pluralistic world scene—with increasing involvement of independent and non-aligned countries, and a growing international aversion to nuclear weapons—contributes to the view that sea-based forces are growing in importance. This, in turn, heightens the naval sensitivity towards any controls on the freedom of naval forces to operate.

If anything, rather than trying to accommodate new international concerns and attempting to constrain superpower belligerence, the US Navy argues more strongly that it is an ideal agent for unilateralism. Today, according to Admiral Trost, the Navy 'operates in international waters, where no government's permission to base and fly aircraft is required and where U.S. ships, in a perfectly legal way, can signal menace to any potential troublemaker'.[26] A top Navy legal officer explained the situation as follows: 'Since naval forces operate in an international medium—the high seas—they can be moved into an area without the necessity of obtaining overflight or diplomatic clearance'.[27]

The US Navy recognizes that it has an advantage in its ability to conduct operations without the political constraints that affect land-based activities and forces. Referring to the new nuclear-armed Tomahawk SLCM, Admiral Lee Baggett, then Director of Naval Warfare, wrote in May 1984: 'These mobile nuclear weapons are not based on Allied or neutral territory. Our Tomahawk equipped ships can be advanced or withdrawn without inciting hostile demonstration'.[28] Navy spokesmen also point out that if US bases in Spain, Greece or the Philippines were restricted, aircraft-carriers would be the only way of providing a compensating military presence.

Operating without the interference of foreign governments and accustomed to an environment which is out of the focus of the media and the public, the Navy is naturally more secretive than the other military services. This is particularly so when it comes to naval nuclear weapons. One of the better-known secrecy policies of the US Government is that of neither confirming nor denying the presence of nuclear weapons on naval vessels (see paper 9 and the US policy document in annexe A). In October 1985 Sweden raised this matter at the United Nations General Assembly in connection with proposals on naval arms control. The Swedish Disarmament Ambassador stated that the policy to neither confirm nor deny 'creates legitimate concern in many countries, especially when warships of nuclear powers in accordance with international law make use of their right to innocent passage through these countries' territorial waters or call at their harbours. The policy to neither confirm nor to deny does not build confidence between states. Quite the opposite—it is in fact a confidence-blocking practice that should be abandoned'.[29]

Autonomy and secrecy have thus largely removed the US Navy from consideration of arms control and have resulted in a relatively unconstrained acquisition of weapons as well as policies, strategies and practices which could undermine US foreign policy objectives and threaten crisis escalation and the outbreak of war.

Since a navy represents an extension of a government, it should not be an autonomous entity able to influence international relations by itself. Yet one of the fundamental US national security objectives, according to then Secretary of Defense Caspar Weinberger, is to 'ensure US access to critical resources, markets, the oceans, and space'.[30] This is interpreted as requiring that the US Navy enforce its 'inherent right' to transit territorial waters and to navigate and conduct highly provocative operations in disputed waters (e.g., the Gulf of Sidra operations or transit operations in the Black Sea, where on 12 February 1988 two US warships and two Soviet warships collided inside Soviet territorial waters).[31] It is not enough just to repeat that naval forces are merely exercising their right of 'innocent passage'. There are certainly adequate international forums for resolving conflicts which arise when states attempt to exert control beyond the internationally accepted 12-nautical mile limit for territorial waters. Pursuing unilateral military solutions either further undermines the rule of law or threatens the outbreak of conflict.

In addition, the US Navy (and the navies of its allies) undermine Western security interests by assuming that secrecy policies *vis-à-vis* nuclear weapons are more important than the policies of governments or the aspirations of their people. The policy has already created friction with numerous foreign governments (e.g., Denmark, Japan, Iceland, New Zealand, the South Pacific nations, Spain and Sweden). More confrontations will certainly occur in the future and continue to erode goodwill towards the United States throughout the world.

IV. Arms control and the law of the sea

Superpower navies pursue unilateralist policies and reject controls on their operations and weaponry partly because little connection is made between arms control and the international law of the sea. In the nuclear era, there have been only a few examples of naval arms control agreements: the bilateral US–Soviet limitations on ballistic missile submarines and missiles in the SALT I Agreement (1972) and the SALT II Treaty (1979), and the Incidents at Sea

Agreement (1972).[32] In addition, there are five multilateral agreements which affect the seas: (a) the 1959 Antarctic Treaty, which provides for the demilitarization of 'the area south of 60° South Latitude, including all ice shelves'; (b) the 1963 Partial Test Ban Treaty, which prohibits all states parties from conducting any nuclear explosion in or beyond the atmosphere or under water, including territorial waters or high seas; (c) the 1967 Treaty of Tlatelolco, which established a Latin American nuclear weapon-free zone, including a large portion of the Atlantic and Pacific Oceans and the Caribbean Sea;[33] (d) the 1971 Seabed Treaty, which prohibits the emplacement of any nuclear weapon or weapons of mass destruction on the seabed and the ocean floor beyond the outer limit of a certain seabed zone (see paper 10); and (e) the 1985 Treaty of Rarotonga, which established a South Pacific nuclear-free zone from the border of the Latin American zone in the east to the west coast of Australia and from the Antarctic area in the south to roughly the equator in the north. (See annexe B for the texts of these agreements.)

The primary thrust of all these agreements has been against nuclear weapons and not against naval arms or activities as such. In addition, each of these multilateral agreements specifically excludes restrictions on naval operations. The reason is that customary international law of the sea confers the right of 'innocent passage' on naval vessels in territorial waters, a 'right' which the navies would have to forgo in order to achieve arms control restrictions.

Although the nuclear navies have tried to minimize the effects of the conventions and treaties that make up the body of law restricting naval affairs, the international law of the sea should not be considered a total impediment to arms control— it could form the basis for naval arms control if the will existed to look at broader security concerns and create a counter to naval autonomy.

As far back as the 1958 Geneva Convention on the High Seas, the freedom of navigation and overflight required that such rights be exercised 'with reasonable regard to the interests of other states in their exercise of the freedom of the high seas'[34] including the freedom of fishing and the freedom of navigation. The 1982 United Nations Convention on the Law of the Sea (UNCLOS) includes the right of innocent passage for ships in the territorial seas and of transit passage in international straits. Innocent passage, according to paragraph 1, Article 19 of the Convention, is defined as passage which is not 'prejudicial to the peace, good order or security of the coastal state' (see annexe B). In addition, Article 23 of the UNCLOS provides that: 'Foreign nuclear-powered ships and ships carrying nuclear or other inherently dangerous or noxious substances shall, when exercising the right of innocent passage through the territorial sea, carry documents and observe special precautionary measures established for such ships by international agreements'.

This provision regarding innocent passage of nuclear-powered ships and those carrying radioactive and other inherently dangerous or noxious substances seems logically to apply also to ships carrying nuclear weapons. Thus weapons on board vessels, including nuclear weapons, could be said to violate the two

Conventions if: (*a*) they impede the fishing or shipping activities of other states; or (*b*) they create marine pollution resulting from radioactive or hazardous substances.[35]

Without an invitation—or permission—from a coastal state, the presence of naval vessels in the territorial waters of another state is limited to innocent passage. The presence must conform to international law governing innocent passage, in that it must be *passage* ('navigation through the territorial sea for the purpose either of traversing that sea without entering territorial waters, or of proceeding to internal waters, or of making for the high seas from internal waters'), and it must be *innocent* ('innocent so long as it is not prejudicial to the peace, good order or security of the coastal state').[36] Article 39 of the UNCLOS requires, in addition, that ships and aircraft exercising the right of transit passage 'refrain from any threat or use of force against the sovereignty, territorial integrity or political independence of States bordering straits'.[37]

These various restrictions could form the basis for international constraints on potentially dangerous naval operations and on the presence of nuclear weapons. Yet these principles have been used by the naval powers to reaffirm a presumed right to conduct unlimited military operations at sea. Thus the Antarctic Treaty, for instance, in Article VI, does not restrict naval operations on the high seas within its demilitarized zone. The 1985 Rarotonga Treaty, in Article 2, does not limit any existing 'freedom of the seas' (see annexe B).

Perhaps the best example of how control of naval arms and operations has been avoided is in the way the subject of transit is handled in the Treaty of Tlatelolco.[38] The United States and France, in pledging to respect the status of the treaty by acceding to Protocol II, filed reservations to the extension of arms control measures into high sea areas referring to 'recognized international law'. On 7 February 1967, the Preparatory Commission for the Denuclearization of Latin America placed on record the reason why any mention of the transit of nuclear weapons through the zone was omitted:

The Commission deems it unnecessary to include the term 'transit' in Article 1, concerning 'Obligations', for the following reasons:

1. If the carrier is one of the Contracting Parties, transport is covered by the prohibitions expressly laid down in the remaining provisions of article 1 and there is no need to mention it expressly, since the article prohibits 'any form of possession of any nuclear weapon, directly or indirectly, by the Parties themselves, by anyone on their behalf or in any other way'.

2. If the carrier is a State not a Party to the Treaty, transport is identical with 'transit' which, in the absence of any provision in the Treaty, must be understood to be governed by the principles and rules of international law; according to these principles and rules it is for the territorial State, in the free exercise of its sovereignty, to grant or deny permission for such transit in each individual case, upon application by the State interested in effecting the transit, unless some other arrangement has been reached in a treaty between the states.[39]

One naval observer has stated: 'The relative lack of interest in naval forces with regard to arms control is hardly due to lack of appreciation for their importance but rather the fact that the legal regime at sea was not until recently defined in a clear way'.[40] But the environment is changing. Soon after signing the UNCLOS, the UN General Assembly undertook an expert study on the naval arms race which was completed in 1985. Naval arms control is now an increasingly interesting issue within multilateral disarmament bodies.

In addition, since 1980, the USSR has made consistent proposals for naval restraints. At the 1982 UN Second Special Session on Disarmament the USSR made a number of recommendations dealing with naval limitations, including 'removal of missile submarines from extensive areas of combat patrol, and confinement of their cruises within agreed limits', limitation of new submarine missiles, renunciation of deployment of sea-based long-range cruise missiles, and regional measures in the Mediterranean Sea and the Persian Gulf.[41]

In April 1984, Soviet Foreign Minister Andrei Gromyko wrote to the UN Secretary-General saying that the USSR was ready for multilateral talks on naval disarmament.[42] In his Vladivostok speech in July 1986 and during the Soviet–Indian summit meeting in November 1986, General Secretary Gorbachev stated the USSR's readiness to conduct negotiations on confidence-building measures in the Pacific and Indian Oceans. Proposals were put forward on notification of transfers and manoeuvres of naval forces.[43] Concerning the Pacific, Gorbachev proposed in Vladivostok 'to start talks on the reduction of the activity of naval forces in the Pacific, in particular, nuclear-armed ships'.[44] The response from the USA and its nuclear allies has been consistently negative. Whether the USSR is serious or not is unknown, but the West's re-luctance to take the issue seriously has been the major impediment to progress.

V. Prospects for control of naval operations

Naval autonomy and unilateralism, and the refusal to accept legal constraints on naval operations, are two prime contributors to the current naval arms race. The result has been uncontrolled modernization of naval forces, increasing nuclearization of the oceans, and provocative and potentially destabilizing operations and strategies. One additional problem is that, for several reasons, these conditions have also created an environment which encourages the increased movement of nuclear weapons to sea.

First, basing nuclear weapons at sea is seen by some as a way to avoid political controversy and constraints on the operations and use of land-based nuclear weapons. Soon after it became clear that Pershing II and ground-launched cruise missiles might be removed from Europe as part of an arms control agreement, many defence analysts were arguing to shift the theatre nuclear arsenal to sea.

Second, some sea-based nuclear weapons are developed to affect land warfare (sea-launched cruise missiles and gravity bombs on aircraft-carriers) but are not allowed to be subject to alliance controls or consultation. The Carter Administration, for instance, discouraged critics of the NATO 1979 nuclear modernization decision from viewing the Tomahawk sea-launched cruise missile as an alternative to land-based 'Euromissiles'. At the time of the December 1979 decision, according to former Defense Department official Walter B. Slocombe, 'we were concerned that if we . . . pushed ahead [with Tomahawk deployment], European critics would say, "Why don't we do SLCMs instead of the agreed deployment"'.[45]

Finally, the pursuit of strategic defences by both superpowers may create an incentive for sea-based systems to be pursued more aggressively in the future because their mobility and stealth would facilitate circumvention of defences against land-based ballistic missiles.

No doubt the navies of the United States and the Soviet Union learn a great deal from their war games. But if a real confrontation arose, or one or the other of the nuclear navies experienced a miscue or made a miscalculation about the intentions of the other side, the result could be disastrous. On 21 March 1984, while on what was described as 'routine' night manoeuvres observing the annual US–South Korean 'Team Spirit' exercise, a Soviet nuclear-powered Victor Class attack submarine collided with the US aircraft-carrier *USS Kitty Hawk* 150 miles (240 km) east of the Korean Peninsula. The *Kitty Hawk* sustained a ruptured fuel tank, and the submarine was so damaged that it had to be towed back to base. Just a few weeks after this incident (on 2 April), the Soviet aircraft-carrier *Minsk* fired eight signal flares at the US Navy frigate *USS Harold E. Holt* when the latter ship disregarded a request from the *Minsk* to stand clear and passed within 300 metres of the *Minsk*.[46] According to former Navy Secretary Lehman, about 40 'potentially dangerous incidents' took place during 1982 between the US and Soviet navies.[47] There is no evidence to suggest that this rate has since declined.

Given the US Navy's attitude towards Soviet responses to exercises, one could think that they were intentionally trying to goad the Soviets by their manoeuvres. Vice Admiral James A. Lyons, Deputy Chief of Naval Operations for Plans, Policy and Operations, testified before the Senate Armed Services Committee in 1985:

We can always count on the fact that when we do these exercises, there are going to be Soviets intermingled. Quite frankly, as a fleet commander, I used to welcome their participation for two reasons. First, the services that they provided were free, we didn't have to pay for them. Second, we had a message to send, and the message was—if we operate with obvious proficiency in front of them then in effect we have improved the deterrence equation without firing a shot.[48]

As Admiral Watkins testified in 1984: 'The Soviets actually act as our target forces, our orange forces, as we call them. They provide very effective exercise services to our forces because we can really see what we are up against'.[49]

As long as the navies of the superpowers and their allies are in close proximity to each other (such as they are routinely in the Mediterranean Sea, or as they become during exercises), their deployments could have the effect of accelerating decision-making relating to the use of force during crisis of war. Large-scale operations in the northern Atlantic or Pacific during the outbreak of a crisis could require Soviet forces to concentrate on neutralizing adversary aircraft-carriers and anti-submarine warfare forces in order to safeguard their strategic submarine holding areas in the Barents Sea and the Arctic Ocean, or the Sea of Okhotsk and the Bering Sea. The highest Soviet priority would probably be the early establishment of a Soviet submarine barrier in the Norwegian Sea or the northern Pacific south of Kamchatka, with air attacks on surface naval forces and land bases a secondary mission. The question is how quickly these operations (or movements and preparations for such operations) would get under way, and how the crisis response strategies of the United States and the Soviet Union would contribute to increasing the intensity and seriousness of such a crisis.

The priority for international security must be to eliminate those weapons, practices and operations which may be provocative and destabilizing. How do maritime operations and strategies that merely encourage the other side to increase their military capabilities and intensify their defensive efforts lead to better conditions in the long run?

There is certainly no lack of potential controls which could be considered in pursuit of either national arms control interests or multilateral interests in reducing the risks of confrontation which could arise from naval operations:[50] (a) regulation of dangerous manoeuvres and restraints on different forms of harassment at sea; (b) special codes of conduct for submarines, other submerged activities, and anti-submarine warfare forces; (c) banning of the deployment of certain naval nuclear weapons, such as long-range sea-launched cruise missiles or nuclear bombs on aircraft-carriers; (d) prohibitions on carrying nuclear weapons aboard naval vessels except aboard specifically recognized units; (e) restrictions on the freedom of navigation of ships and submarines carrying nuclear weapons and nuclear materials; (f) pre-notification of military exercises in sea areas; (g) restrictions on navigation of naval forces in areas remote from home ports or close to coasts of other states; (h) restrictions on access to certain regions for certain types of unit; (i) strengthening nuclear-free zones, such as giving full effect to the Antarctic Treaty by including the sea areas within its area of application; (j) prohibitions on the establishment of new military bases; and (k) preservation of the difficulty in converting conventional weapons to nuclear weapons through the use of new technologies such as 'insertable nuclear components'.

There is widespread recognition of the fact that arms control is a trade-off between a purely military view of what promotes security and competing political objectives. In the United States, theoretically, the trade-off is not merely tolerated; the necessity to control destabilizing weapons and military capabilities elevates arms control to a 'major US national security objective'.[51]

In the naval field, however, the acceptance of this trade-off is lacking. The US Navy has determined, largely by itself, whether it should be subject to controls, and has so far concluded that it should not. This evasion is due primarily to a tradition of autonomy and unilateralism and the pursuit of 'freedom of the seas'. What is becoming increasingly clear is that unrestricted naval activities neither enhance US foreign relations nor increase global security. They may be part of a tradition that should be abandoned in favour of a more important objective.

Notes and references

[1] US Congress, House Appropriations Committee, *Department of Defense Appropriations for FY 1986*, Part 2, Hearings (hereafter referred to as HAC, FY 1986 DOD), p. 710.

[2] HAC, FY 1986 DOD, p. 649.

[3] Lehman, J. F., 'The 600-ship navy', US Naval Institute *Proceedings*, Jan. 1986, supplement, p. 32.

[4] US Navy, *Report to Congress by Admiral C. A. H. Trost, Chief of Naval Operations, on the Posture and Fiscal Year 1988–89 Budget of the United States Navy*, p. 20.

[5] Swedish Ministry of Defence, *Countering the Submarine Threat: Submarine Violations and Swedish Security Policy* (Submarine Defence Commission: Stockholm, 1983).

[6] See, for example, Woodward, B., *Veil: The Secret Wars of the CIA 1981–1987* (Simon & Schuster: London, 1987), pp. 30, 87, 448 ff.

[7] In Mar.–Apr. 1983, the US Navy operated three aircraft-carriers in the northern Pacific near the Aleutian Islands during 'Fleet Ex 83', an even larger exercise.

[8] US Congress, House Armed Services Committee, *FY 1984 Department of Defense Authorization for Appropriations*, Hearings (hereafter referred to as HASC, FY 1984 DOD), Part 3, pp. 111–12.

[9] HAC, FY 1986 DOD, Part 2, p. 648.

[10] HAC, FY 1986 DOD, Part 2, p. 293.

[11] Daniel, D. and Tarleton, G., 'The Soviet Navy in 1985', US Naval Institute *Proceedings*, May 1986 (annual 'Naval Review' issue), pp. 98–108.

[12] HAC, FY 1987 DOD, Part 1, p. 293; and US Navy, 'Statement of Vice Admiral James A. Lyons, Jr, Deputy Chief of Naval Operations for Plans, Policy and Operations before the Seapower and Force Projection Subcommittee of the Senate Armed Services Committee on the US Navy's Global Commitments', 28 Feb. 1985, p. 18.

[13] HAC, FY 1984 DOD, Part 2, p. 454.

[14] US Congress, Senate Armed Services Committee, *FY 1984 Department of Defense Authorization for Appropriations* (hereafter referred to as SASC, FY 1984 DOD), Part 2, p. 1008; 'Statement of Rear Admiral John L. Butts, US Navy, Director of Naval Intelligence, before the Subcommittee on Seapower and Force Projection of the Senate Armed Services Committee on the Naval Threat', Mar. 1983.

[15] SASC, FY 1985 DOD, Part 8, pp. 3885–86.

[16] Lyons (note 12), p. 18.

[17] Lehman (note 3), p. 36.

[18] Lehman (note 3), p. 36.

[19] HAC, FY 1987 DOD, Part 1, p. 284; see also US Congress, House Armed Services Committee, *The 600-Ship Navy and the Maritime Strategy*, Hearings (US Government Printing Office: Washington, DC, 1986), p. 277.

[20] HAC, FY 1986 DOD, Part 2, p. 648.

[21] SASC, FY 1987 DOD, Part 3, p. 1204.

[22] 'Statement of Admiral Ronald J. Hays, USN, Commander in Chief, US Pacific Command, before the House Appropriations Defense Subcommittee on FY 1988-89 Defense Budget', 21 Apr. 1987, p. 6; see also 'Statement of Rear Admiral Hugh L. Webster, USN, Director of Logistics and Security Assistance, US Pacific Command before the Readiness, Sustainability and Support Subcommittee of the Senate Armed Services Committee', p. 5.

[23] HASC, *The 600-Ship Navy*, p. 137.

[24] During 'Northern Wedding', for instance, the USA used sophisticated deception techniques to operate a cruiser north of Norway for a number of days undetected by the USSR. See HASC, *The 600-Ship Navy*, p. 49. In 1986, the aircraft-carrier *Ranger* also operated in a similar manner in the Bering Sea for 9 days without being found by Soviet surveillance. See Arkin, W. M., 'Red Herring in the Pacific', *Bulletin of the Atomic Scientists*, Apr. 1987, pp. 6–7.

[25] Towards the end of the NATO exercises, the Swedish intelligence ship *Orion* was rammed by a Soviet minesweeper near Gotland Island in the Baltic Sea.

[26] Trost, C. A. H., 'Higher, faster, farther, deeper: the U.S. Navy in the 21st century', *Seapower*, Apr. 1987, p. 7; see also Admiral Watkins in HASC, *The 600-Ship Navy*, p. 44.

[27] Commander Dennis R. Neutze, USN, 'Bluejacket diplomacy: a juridical examination of the use of naval forces in support of United States foreign policy', *JAG Journal* [US Navy], summer 1982, p. 85.

[28] Department of the Navy, Director, Naval Warfare, 'Colloquy in Opposition: Proposed Amendment on Sea-Launched Cruise Missiles', 22 May 1984, released under the Freedom of Information Act, 27 Feb. 1987.

[29] United Nations document A/C.1/40/PV.4, 15 Oct. 1985, p. 11.

[30] Department of Defense, *Annual Report to the Congress, Fiscal Year 1988* (US Government Printing Office: Washington, DC, 1987), p. 42.

[31] Previous operations in the Black Sea were held in Nov. 1984 and Mar. 1986.

[32] The UK and the USSR concluded a similar agreement on prevention of incidents at sea on 15 July 1986, as did the USSR and the Federal Republic of Germany on 25 Oct. 1988.

[33] The Tlatelolco Treaty was signed in 1967 and has entered into force for 23 Caribbean, Central American and South American states. Protocol II (the guarantee protocol) is in force for all nuclear weapon states.

[34] Geneva Convention on the High Seas, 29 Apr. 1958, Article 2.

[35] Monica Pinto and Rear Admiral Fernando A. Milia, Argentine Navy, 'Argentine Council on International Relations Study on the Naval Arms Race', Buenos Aires (mimeo), 1984, p. 15.

[36] See note 27, p. 146.

[37] See note 27, pp. 154–55.

[38] This discussion is taken from Pinto and Milia (note 35), pp. 18–20.

[39] This material is cited by Pinto and Milia; see note 35.

[40] Prawitz, J., 'Naval arms and naval arms control', in eds J. Maas and R. Stewart, *Toward a World of Peace: People Create Alternatives* (University of the South Pacific: Suva, Fiji, 1987).

[41] United Nations document A/S-12 /AC.1/11, 17 June 1982.

[42] 'Soviets seek naval arms talks', *Baltimore Sun*, 15 Apr. 1984.

[43] USSR Academy of Sciences, Institute of World Economy and International Relations (IMEMO), *Disarmament and Security: 1986 Yearbook*, vol. 2 (Novosti Press Agency Publishing House: Moscow, 1987), pp. 61–62.

[44] *Security in the Asia–Pacific Region: The Soviet Approach, Documents and Materials,* (Novosti Press Agency Publishing House: Moscow, 1988), p. 25.

[45] Quoted in Gordon, M. R., 'Deployment of Tomahawk cruise missiles stirs arms control controversy', *National Journal* (Washington, DC), 26 May 1984.

[46] *Washington Post*, 8 June 1984.

[47] US Department of Defense, 'News Briefing by Secretary of the Navy John Lehman at the Pentagon', 10 June 1983.

[48] SASC, FY 1985 DOD, Part 8, p. 4417.

[49] SASC, FY 1985 DOD, Part 8, p. 3881.

[50] Several of these ideas are from Prawitz (note 40), p. 56.

[51] See note 30.

Paper 9. Naval nuclear arms control

Richard Fieldhouse
SIPRI

I. Introduction

Naval nuclear weapons should be brought under control. This is the basic premise of this paper. Between one-quarter and one-third of all the nuclear warheads in the world are for naval nuclear weapons—more than 16 000 warheads in all, of which 9700 are for strategic ballistic missiles carried by submarines and roughly 6500 are for non-strategic weapons.[1] Only the submarine-launched ballistic missiles (SLBMs) of the USA and the USSR are under any arms control constraints; none of their other 6300 naval nuclear weapons—nor any of those of France, the UK or China—are included in any arms control agreements. These facts alone suggest good reason to consider controls.

There are a great number of other reasons why naval nuclear weapons, especially the non-strategic ones, should be given special attention in arms control considerations. The political and military limitations of these weapons are seldom acknowledged by officials of the nations in question. It is argued here that non-strategic naval nuclear weapons are not necessary for any naval mission—deterrence or war-fighting—nor are they usable or credible as weapons. As Vice Admiral Henry Mustin, former Deputy Chief of Naval Operations for Plans, Policy and Operations, stated in 1989: 'The concept of a nuclear war at sea is a concept whose time has passed. It is in the interest of [the USA] to persuade the Soviets that the time has passed.'[2] Consequently the risks and dangers posed by the widespread nuclearization of the Soviet and US fleets could be reduced or removed without diminishing the two nations' security; quite the opposite would be achieved. Furthermore, both nations could have compelling military and political reasons to take such steps.

This paper concentrates on *non-strategic* (non-SLBM) naval nuclear arms control. This is because US and Soviet SLBMs and the submarines that carry them have been included in past arms control talks (SALT) and are the subject of current negotiations (START), albeit not in a naval context. Consequently, much more consideration has been given to the question of arms control for strategic naval nuclear forces than for non-strategic ones. Practically speaking, however, SLBMs are not particularly 'naval' except for the fact that the navies operate the submarines that carry them. Otherwise, SLBMs have little to do with naval warfare but are strategic forces at sea. Unless otherwise stated, in this paper the term 'naval nuclear weapons' refers to non-SLBM nuclear forces, or the non-strategic naval nuclear forces.

This paper fills an important void in the discussion of naval nuclear arms control and puts forward ideas and proposals for debate on this neglected subject. The focus is primarily on the USA and the USSR—the two largest naval nuclear powers—beginning with an explanation of why naval nuclear weapons should be controlled. Following a brief description of the types and categories of such systems, possible measures of control are examined—from confidence-building measures (CBMs) to operational controls to limits and bans, using unilateral and multilateral approaches. Section V contains a discussion of two major difficulties inherent in attempts to control non-strategic naval nuclear forces. The paper concludes with suggestions for future action.

II. Why control naval nuclear weapons?

Navies do not need non-strategic, or tactical, nuclear weapons. This is the assumption made and argued in this paper. Nuclear weapons are not necessary for the US or Soviet navies—or any other navy—to carry out their combat missions.[3] These missions can only be achieved using conventional (non-nuclear) weapons for two reasons. First and foremost, any use of a nuclear weapon would create the risk of escalation to a massive nuclear war. Such a risk is unacceptably high for any nation. Second, although there are military reasons why the use of nuclear weapons might possibly seem expedient in a war, there are also a great number of stronger reasons weighing heavily against their use.[4]

This assumption is supported by the fact that the US Navy decided in 1988–89 to retire three of its ageing non-strategic nuclear weapon systems designed for sea combat (see also section III). This decision demonstrates a recognition within the Navy that these short-range nuclear weapons have little utility for war at sea, and that they are not necessary for any deterrent purpose.[5]

Naval nuclear weapons do not necessarily solve the problems that naval planners worry about, namely, the complex tactical problems of naval warfare—such as locating or destroying an adversary's submarine (see paper 6). Furthermore, navies would have to be concerned that any use of nuclear weapons at sea would quickly lead to widespread escalation and to their own rapid destruction. Neither superpower appears to believe that the other relies on nuclear weapons to fight a war at sea, nor that the other plans to use them early in such a war. Thus, simply stated, nuclear weapons do not offer a rational or credible alternative to conventional weapons.

None the less, the argument is made in the West that naval nuclear weapons are necessary for deterrence at sea, that is, to dissuade other nations from using nuclear weapons against one's own naval forces by having the capability to retaliate in kind.[6] This argument fails on several grounds. The USA does not itself believe that naval nuclear weapons would deter the USSR from initiating the use of nuclear weapons at sea. US policy is to 'not permit the Soviet Union to confine a nuclear war to the sea', which means that the USA threatens to respond to nuclear attacks against its navy by attacking Soviet land targets with nuclear weapons.[7] This is corroborated by the fact that the US Navy is removing three types of nuclear weapon for sea combat, partly because they are seen to have no deterrent value. In this connection, Admiral Mustin stated: 'If you want to deter [the USSR], you have to deter them with a weapon that scares them the most. We now see that the thing that the Soviets are most concerned about is attacks on Mother Russia.'[8] Thus the US Navy is moving towards a nuclear force dominated by land-attack weapons (semi-strategic weapons) that merely duplicate the weapons and functions of the US strategic nuclear arsenal.

If navies do not need nuclear weapons either to carry out their missions or to deter other navies, then there is no justification for having non-strategic nuclear weapons in their fleets. Given that strategic nuclear forces (ICBMs, SLBMs and bombers) can suffice for posing a retaliatory threat to an adversary's homeland, there is no need for semi-strategic naval weapons, such as sea-launched cruise missiles or gravity bombs carried aboard aircraft-carriers. This logic leads to the conclusion that there should be no political or military obstacle to arms control measures regarding naval nuclear weapons.

Incentives for controlling naval nuclear weapons

There are many reasons why the nations that possess naval nuclear weapons might have an interest in reducing them or including them in a co-operative arms control regime. Naval nuclear weapons present special risks and dangers that nations would probably like to reduce or eliminate. The greatest risk is that a crisis involving nuclear-armed naval forces could escalate out of control and inadvertently erupt into a nuclear war. These risks and dangers are discussed in detail in the companion volume to this book; a number of the problems that contribute to such risks are: military incentives for using nuclear weapons at sea; perceptions of reduced risks of escalation; command and control problems; and pressures to shoot first in a war at sea.[9]

The basic point for the superpowers is that naval nuclear arms control would serve their national interests, increase their security, reduce certain risks inherent in nuclearized naval operations, and make their navies more efficient and survivable. Navies would be relieved of the burdensome special handling and procedures that greatly complicate all naval nuclear activities. It is possible that certain costs associated with naval nuclear weapons and operations could also be reduced, although this possibility requires further study.[10]

If non-strategic naval nuclear weapons were greatly reduced or eliminated, this could have far-reaching and positive effects. For the USA, the most important point is that not only would the navy retain its strong margin of advantage over the Soviet Navy, but its ability to carry out its missions would also be enhanced. The only way that the Soviet Navy could destroy the US Navy is with nuclear weapons; without such a capacity the Soviet Navy poses a much smaller threat to its superior rival. If the USSR retains its large naval nuclear arsenal, then all US naval advantages—which apply only to conventional forces—are put at greater risk. As stated by Admiral Mustin, 'There is a recognition that if there is a nuclear war at sea, we have got more to lose than the Russians'.[11]

For the USSR, the most important point is that it would reduce the considerable nuclear threat to its territory and to its Navy from the US Navy, a security enhancement which is of paramount interest. The US Navy has more than 1400 nuclear bombs for its carrier-based aircraft and plans to have more than 750 nuclear land-attack SLCMs by 1995. This is a considerable force of nuclear weapons that could be used to attack the USSR.

In addition to enhancing US–Soviet mutual security, placing controls on naval nuclear weapons might also increase the possibilities of concluding arms control agreements that are held up by the issue of naval nuclear weapons, such as the issue of SLCMs at the START negotiations.

Other security-enhancing advantages in having few or no non-strategic naval nuclear weapons would be apparent to both nations (and their navies):

1. There would be less risk of nuclear incidents or accidents between the two navies.

2. There would be less risk of being a nuclear target and of a miscalculation that the other navy is preparing to use nuclear weapons.

3. There would be little reason to prepare for or respond quickly to a massive 'first salvo' nuclear attack, thus reducing nuclear crisis pressures.

4. There would be no need to stockpile nuclear weapons throughout the fleets to deter the use of nuclear systems by an adversary.

A ship operating without nuclear weapons aboard could be preferred by a commanding officer (CO) and crew for several reasons. It would give the CO more flexibility and freedom of operation and decision in peacetime, crisis and war, since there would be no need to be restricted by or to consider the question or procedures of using nuclear weapons. Both the safety risks involved in handling, transporting and maintaining nuclear weapons aboard vessels and the time-consuming and cumbersome paperwork and bureaucracy that accompany nuclear weapons would be avoided. There would be fewer problems with command, control and communications to and from higher military and political authorities. There would be no problems with port calls to nations that do not permit nuclear weapons in their territorial waters or ports. Finally, there would be more space available on his vessel for non-nuclear weapon systems and ammunition, which are the only kind a CO can be sure will be usable for self-defence.

These features and more might logically appeal to naval professionals and political leaders as compelling reasons to consider positively the reduction or elimination of the nuclear weapons in their navies.

To summarize the above arguments, there is no military or political need for navies to have non-strategic nuclear weapons, for war-fighting or for deterrence; there are undesirable risks and dangers that arise from the nuclearization of navies; there are reasons why nations and navies might want to place controls on naval nuclear weapons; and there should be no political or military objections to such controls. These are the necessary ingredients for nations to begin serious work on naval nuclear arms control. Before considering the possibilities it is useful to review the weapon systems and activities that might be included in such a process.

III. What should be controlled?

This section provides a brief overview of the naval nuclear weapon systems and activities that might be subject to arms control measures. Naval nuclear forces can be described in various ways, basically according to their capabilities and purposes. For arms control purposes it is important to understand the composition, capabilities and characteristics of naval nuclear forces. (A full review of these forces is provided in the companion volume to this book.[12])

Naval nuclear weapons can be divided into strategic and non-strategic categories, with the exception of some grey-area 'semi-strategic' systems—namely, sea-launched cruise missiles and aircraft-delivered nuclear weapons for attacking land targets.[13] These semi-strategic weapon systems do not fit easily into the traditional arms control categories for weapons because, although their range is less than intercontinental, their mission is basically strategic; they are clearly not non-strategic, but are not clearly strategic. Future nuclear arms control negotiations will most likely have to go beyond considering a weapon's range as the primary criterion for inclusion or exclusion to overcome a number of inadequacies in that traditional approach.

Sea-launched cruise missiles are certainly analogous to air-launched cruise missiles (ALCMs) in their mode of operation (i.e., they are carried by a long-range platform within range of the target) but, unlike ALCMs, were not included in US–Soviet strategic nuclear arms control negotiations until late 1987, when the USSR persuaded the USA that they could not be excluded from the prospective START treaty. Carrier-based attack aircraft are somewhat analogous to cruise missiles in operation but have never been included in any arms control negotiations. Nuclear SLCMs and gravity bombs on aircraft-carriers are, in fact, assigned strategic missions by the USA.

Strategic naval nuclear forces are the SLBMs carried in the submarines (SSBNs) of the USSR, the USA, France, the UK and China. These SLBMs have ranges of 3000–8000 km, which is sufficient to strike targets on the territory of their adversaries. The major feature of these systems is that they carry nearly 9700 nuclear warheads and are thus a central component of the nuclear arms race. Strategic submarines are the least vulnerable nuclear forces because they can be extremely difficult for an adversary to locate and destroy. Ballistic missiles are not carried by surface ships.

Non-strategic naval nuclear weapons can be divided into two major categories based on their primary purpose: those for war *at sea* and those for attacks on *land targets* (semi-strategic systems). Thousands of nuclear weapons exist for the three types of warfare at sea: anti-submarine warfare (ASW), anti-surface warfare (ASUW) against ships, and anti-air warfare (AAW) against aerial targets such as aircraft and missiles. The ranges of these weapons vary from a few kilometres to more than 500 km. They can also be used to attack targets other than their primary targets. For example, many Soviet anti-ship cruise missiles (ASCMs) are believed to have ranges of 250–550 km. Most of these could be used to attack land targets if the carrier platform (ship, submarine or aircraft) is within range of a land target. Similarly, US nuclear gravity bombs for carrier-based aircraft have a secondary mission to attack surface ships. British and French carrier-based attack aircraft could be used in either anti-ship or anti-shore roles.

Nuclear weapons for the three types of sea warfare exist in many forms and are carried by ships, submarines and aircraft of many classes. There are more than 25 different kinds of such nuclear weapons deployed in the navies of the USSR, the USA, the UK and France, including torpedoes, depth bombs, surface-to-surface missiles (SSMs), surface-to-air missiles (SAMs), air-to-surface missiles (ASMs) and variations on these basic systems. The USSR alone has 21 types of nuclear weapons for war at sea.

Land-attack naval nuclear weapons are somewhat more complicated to place in the non-strategic or strategic categories because they have a variety of capabilities and missions. For example, the US Tomahawk SLCM comes in three basic varieties: a conventionally armed anti-ship missile with a range of some 450 km, two conventionally armed land-attack versions (with either high-explosive or sub-munition warheads) with a range of about 1250 km, and the nuclear-armed land-attack variant with a range of 2500 km. These Tomahawk SLCMs are deployed on ships and submarines, and the plan is for nearly 4000 missiles to be deployed on almost 200 vessels of 8 classes. Any Tomahawk-capable vessel can fire any of the three different varieties.

Nuclear arsenals

A snapshot of the nuclear forces of the five nuclear navies (as of June 1988) is as follows.[14] The navies of the USA, the USSR, the UK, France and China possess some 16 200 nuclear weapons among them, of which 9700 are strategic warheads for SLBMs. Four of these navies (those of the USSR, the USA, the

UK and France) are estimated to possess a combined total of about 6500 non-strategic naval nuclear weapons. The five nuclear navies consist of more than 3700 nuclear-capable naval platforms, comprised of 500 ships of 59 classes, 447 submarines of 49 classes and 2750 aircraft of 20 classes.

The USSR has the greatest variety of weapons deployed (more than 20 types) on more than 45 types of platform: ships, submarines and aircraft. In all, there are estimated to be more than 2700 Soviet non-strategic nuclear warheads. The USA has the greatest quantity of weapons (some 3600), also spread throughout its naval vessels: 25 classes of ship and submarine (as well as the support and logistics ships that can carry weapons) and 8 types of aircraft. Britain and France each operate nuclear-capable naval aircraft for which nuclear warheads are deployed at sea. Each nation's nuclear navy is briefly summarized below.

The Soviet Navy is the most nuclearized navy in the world. Including the strategic submarine forces, Soviet naval nuclear-capable forces have: 77 ballistic missile submarines, 63 cruise missile submarines, 199 attack submarines, 6 V/STOL (vertical/short take-off and landing) aircraft-carriers, 39 cruisers, 69 destroyers, 118 frigates and 56 patrol craft. In addition, Soviet naval aircraft include 370 attack aircraft and 390 anti-submarine warfare (ASW) aircraft capable of using nuclear weapons. Thus, the Soviet nuclear Navy is comprised of some 627 ships and submarines and 760 aircraft.

The nuclear-capable ships and submarines of the US Navy include: 36 ballistic missile submarines, 89 attack submarines, all 14 active aircraft-carriers, 5 V/STOL aircraft-carriers, 3 battleships, all 36 cruisers, all 64 destroyers and 65 frigates—312 vessels in all. The US Navy also operates land- and sea-based nuclear-capable aircraft. For use aboard surface ships there are 1129 aircraft, 187 fixed-wing ASW aircraft and 128 ASW helicopters; there are 347 active land-based ASW aircraft or 1791 nuclear-capable aircraft in all.

The nuclear component of the British Royal Navy consists of 4 ballistic missile submarines, 3 aircraft-carriers, 12 destroyers and 8 frigates. The Royal Navy operates nuclear-capable aircraft from ships (34 attack aircraft and 134 ASW helicopters). France has 6 ballistic missile submarines and 2 aircraft-carriers. Nuclear-capable naval aviation consists of 36 attack aircraft for the carriers and 31 on land. China has 3 ballistic missile submarines, 1 of which has been officially declared operational. It is possible that some of China's stockpile of nuclear bombs may be available for its naval bomber force. It is estimated that these three smaller naval nuclear powers have some 578 naval nuclear warheads among them although this number will grow considerably in the 1990s.

Changes to the US arsenal

In April 1989 it was revealed that the USA had decided to unilaterally retire three of its ageing non-strategic nuclear weapon systems: the ASROC (anti-submarine rocket) and SUBROC (submarine rocket) ASW missiles and the Terrier SAM.[15] No replacements are currently planned for these forces, which will be retired by 1992, earlier than the weapons' original retirement schedule. If the planned retirement proceeds as reported it will have a significant effect on the US naval nuclear arsenal and its fleet of nuclear weapon-capable vessels, removing the nuclear capability of 140 ships and submarines, about 45 per cent of the Navy's nuclear-capable vessels, including SSBNs.

Together, the three systems account for about 1144 non-strategic warheads deployed (out of a total of 3645) on 140 ships and submarines (out of 312 vessels) of more than 23 classes. The ASROC system is the most widely deployed nuclear weapon in the US Navy; it is present on 18 classes of warship. There are 574 warheads stockpiled for the ASROC. The SUBROC system is deployed on all 5 classes of attack submarine, with 285 warheads stockpiled. The Terrier, an anti-air warfare missile, is deployed aboard 6 classes of warship; 285 nuclear warheads are stockpiled. This partial denuclearization will remove roughly one-third of the US Navy's stockpile (as of 1989) of non-strategic warheads.

After the 'triple zero' retirement is complete, there will be three types of non-strategic (i.e., non-SLBM) naval nuclear weapon in the US arsenal: Tomahawk sea-launched cruise missiles (SLCMs) for attack against land targets, gravity bombs for use against land targets by jets on aircraft-carriers, and nuclear depth bombs for use against submarines by land-based and sea-based anti-submarine aircraft. Tomahawk SLCMs will be the only nuclear weapon system carried by most nuclear-capable surface warships; only aircraft-carriers (14) carry the gravity bombs and anti-submarine depth bombs. By 1995 the US Navy plans to have Tomahawk SLCMs deployed aboard 198 vessels: 91 surface ships and 107 submarines.

After the three sea combat weapons are retired, the US Navy will have a predominently land-attack orientation for its non-strategic nuclear weapons, with nuclear depth bombs (900 stockpiled in 1989) remaining as the only tactical weapons for war *at sea*. Nuclear SLCMs and gravity bombs will form the core of the Navy's modern nuclear weapons, which will change the complexion of naval arms control considerations somewhat. The focus will largely be on SLCMs and on the nuclear bombs aboard aircraft-carriers. The Soviet Union has already expressed strong interest in limits on SLCMs and has a long-standing concern about US aircraft-carriers because they carry a formidable arsenal of nuclear bombs capable of being dropped on Soviet territory.

General characteristics

In order to consider naval nuclear arms control seriously, it is important to understand the characteristics of naval nuclear weapon systems. Most of these systems follow a general pattern of deployment and operation that can be important for designing and assessing arms control proposals.

A nuclear warhead is contained in a weapon system (missile, torpedo, bomb, etc.) which in turn is carried by a naval platform (ship, submarine or aircraft). There are several combinations possible, such as an aircraft-carrier with aircraft that can carry nuclear weapons. Many of the nuclear weapon systems are 'dual-capable', that is, able to use either nuclear or conventional warheads. It is not currently possible (or practical) for navies to exchange nuclear and conventional warheads on a weapon system; navies generally carry both conventional and nuclear versions of dual-capable systems. Certain missiles, particularly those in vertical launch systems (VLSs), are loaded with their warheads in their launchers and cannot be altered without disabling the weapon. Some weapon systems are capable of using only nuclear warheads, such as the US SUBROC anti-submarine system or several Soviet anti-ship missile systems. It is generally known which weapon systems are nuclear or nuclear-capable, although there are notable Soviet exceptions. The presence of these systems, or their launchers or other associated equipment, is often the only guide to a platform's nuclear capability.

Because of their excessively destructive capabilities, all nuclear weapon systems and warheads are presumed to be under various forms of strict political and/or physical control. In most cases naval nuclear weapons require special communications systems to pass on political and military authorization and special codes required to permit their use. (US naval nuclear weapons have one exception to this general rule; they do not carry the electromagnetic control devices called Permissive Action Links, or PALS, that are present on all other US nuclear weapons.) Consequently, nuclear weapon-capable platforms often have dedicated or distinct equipment for nuclear weapons, such as special fire-control systems (radar and computer systems used to fire a weapon) or communications equipment.

According to the US Navy: 'There is no aspect of navy operations that gets more emphasis, more attention, than the safety, training, operational procedures and material condition surrounding Navy nuclear weapons and reactors.'[16] As nuclear weapons require special handling and procedures, many naval vessels have facilities, practices and personnel that are unique to those weapons. For example, nuclear weapons are usually stored in special, secured lockers or vaults. These are normally guarded by a security detail, and only certain designated personnel are permitted access to these areas, normally in pairs to ensure that no individual could take control of a warhead or weapon. Any naval platform that carries nuclear weapons has specially trained personnel who are responsible for the weapons. Some non-strategic nuclear weapons and especially their warheads can be transferred (loaded on and off ships) at sea. This is a standard practice for the US Navy. Such loading at sea requires certain equipment, usually helicopters and ships to carry and store nuclear weapons or warheads.

These and other features and characteristics are important both because they are signs of nuclear weapon-related activities and, as such, because they are elements which may be monitored, controlled or changed in some future agreement. It must be said, however, that the secrecy that surrounds virtually all naval nuclear weapon activities prevents observers from knowing all the details that should be known in order to design naval nuclear weapon controls. This observation in itself may suggest one objective for arms control efforts.

IV. Possible measures

If nations wish to pursue naval nuclear arms control, what sort of measures would be possible? In order to answer this question it is important to clarify what is meant by the term 'arms control'. As elaborated in the introduction to this book, it is useful to take a broad view of arms control as a process of self-restraint and co-operation among nations to improve mutual security and reduce the risk of military confrontation. Many possible actions, decisions or agreements can be pursued in this process. Thus, as used in this paper, the concept of arms control is not limited to the traditional idea of placing limits on particular weapon systems or technologies. It includes the general area of confidence-building measures (CBMs)—also called CSBMs to include *security*-building measures.[17]   For analytical purposes we shall use the three categories of arms control described in Part I of this book: CBMs, operational and structural. The measures presented can be applied to particular nuclear forces and activities as appropriate.

Obviously, any national decision to pursue (or not pursue) arms control will be based on an assessment of a variety of related factors that are often called 'national interest', that is, what outcome a nation wants, how important it is relative to other objectives, how it will affect the nation's overall security situation, whether it is politically and militarily feasible, and so on. With respect to naval nuclear arms control, nations would have to assess *inter alia* the need for or desirability of controls, the problems or risks to be addressed, the utility (if any) of the forces or activities in question, whether there are suitable alternatives available, what sacrifices it would make in order to secure controls on other nations' forces, and whether desired controls are acceptably and adequately verifiable.

If, as suggested in this paper, nations decide that they do not need naval nuclear weapons this would create the most, and the most significant, possibilities for arms control. Somewhere between wanting some controls and not wanting any naval nuclear weapons lie many other possible measures.

Confidence-building measures

All arms control measures should have the effect of building confidence, but some measures are designed expressly for that purpose and have no other operational or structural effects. There is considerable opportunity for confidence-building in several areas of naval nuclear weapons and operations. Such CBMs could be designed to create understanding and overcome some of the negative effects of the excessive secrecy surrounding naval nuclear weapons. They could also serve as the mechanism for providing an exchange of information required before certain agreements could be negotiated or signed— such as the data exchanged before the USA–USSR INF Treaty was signed. Some of the measures outlined below could be applied to other aspects of naval forces and operations as well, and would most probably be part of a larger framework of naval CBMs. All arms limitation agreements have confidence-building or -assuring provisions, such as suitable arrangements for verifying compliance with the terms of the agreement. After all, adequate verification is itself an essential CBM.

Dialogue and information exchange

Possible measures could include such seemingly simple acts as instituting discussion among navies about their nuclear forces and exchanging information about such systems. Such talks could aim to establish a base of exchanged information about the weapons as well as the official national perspectives on their role. This could include official acknowledgement of which weapon systems are in fact nuclear or nuclear-capable and which are not, the designations of the nuclear-related sytems and their basic functions and characteristics, which platforms carry which nuclear-capable systems, what associated equipment has a nuclear or nuclear-related function, and so on. Nuclear navies could also inform each other of the safety and control measures they take to prevent the accidental or unauthorized use of nuclear weapons. For the USA and the USSR this could be done in accordance with Article 7 of their Accidents Measures Agreement.[18]

Although much information is known about US naval nuclear weapons, the USSR has never revealed even basic facts about its own weapon systems.[19] The USA does not know most facts about Soviet naval non-strategic nuclear weapons but makes intelligence estimates that are prone to considerable error. It should also be said that, although much is made of the notion that the USSR can know almost everything about the USA and its military (including nuclear weapon) programmes because of the open nature of US society and its great press freedoms, the USSR cannot depend on Western newspaper reports for its intelligence estimates of US military capabilities. The paucity of hard, official information concerning naval nuclear weapons is a major difficulty both for debating the issue and for attempting to negotiate agreements. Reflecting on this naval nuclear information shortage, Admiral Richard Hill writes that 'it is quite likely that the lack of a firm intelligence base from which to start a negotiation is the biggest single factor militating against arms control in this field'.[20] If this is true, it would require a considerable exchange of information to permit negotiation. This sort of information exchange should therefore be considered an essential prerequisite to negotiation, as well as a valuable CBM in its own right.

Information exchanges could have an important effect on the degree of understanding about otherwise inscrutable systems. This would remove the guesswork and incorrect estimates about other navies' nuclear forces. It might also lead to the possibility of exploring the doctrinal and tactical questions that are seldom discussed concerning these weapons. Each superpower might learn that the other had little interest in or need for its naval nuclear weapons, but felt obliged to deploy them because the other did so. Such understandings, were they possible, could lead to agreements on restricting or limiting the weapons in question.

Naval nuclear openness

Secrecy is a tradition with nuclear navies. Even in the case of the US Navy's unilateral 'triple zero' retirement of tactical naval nuclear weapon systems, the decision was made secretly, and its implementation was not made public by the Navy. Only after the fact was revealed and documented by a private analyst did the Navy confirm the fact.[21] This is despite the fact that, as Admiral Mustin acknowledged, 'it is in the interest of [the USA] to persuade the Soviets that the time has passed' for the concept of a nuclear war at sea. This traditional secrecy needs to be removed in order to proceed with naval nuclear arms control.

One of the most obvious CBMs possible would be for the nuclear navies to change or abandon their 'neither confirm nor deny' (NCND) policy concerning the presence of nuclear weapons aboard naval vessels. The NCND policy has several effects that do not promote security or confidence but instead cause a considerable amount of international controversy while stifling public and governmental debate on the subject of naval nuclear weapons and their control. The policy is given such prominence and weight by the USA that it may also be a major obstacle to nuclear arms control efforts—including a prospective START treaty.[22] Concerning SLCMs, a senior US State Department official testified to Congress in April 1989 that 'verification schemes would also have to be designed so as not to disturb naval operational plans or interrupt our policy to "neither confirm nor deny" the presence or absence of nuclear weapons on ships'.[23] Unyielding insistence on neither confirming nor denying the presence of nuclear weapons aboard ships or submarines would make it exceedingly difficult to negotiate or implement agreements limiting these systems. As such, the policy is an impediment to arms control and will have to be altered or somehow overcome if naval nuclear weapons—including SLCMs—are to be included in arms control agreements.

It appears that the NCND policy is entirely unnecessary and could be changed without any loss of security but with some increase in operational flexibility and international acceptability for the nuclear navies (see also section V).

This leads to one more possible CBM regarding the NCND policy. The nuclear navies could publicly declare which vessels or units do *not* have a nuclear weapon capability. This could be done according to the class or model of the platform (ship, submarine or aircraft) and would provide an official guide to knowing which platforms are nuclear-weapon free. This information is not classified for the US Navy, nor presumably for those of the UK or France; its public release should present no difficulty. The USSR should, of course, also make such an official list public. This would have a considerable confidence-building effect on the public and might be a good start to nuclear information exchanges between navies.

Other CBMs

The nuclear navies could make a practice of providing each other (and the public) with information about planned or actual changes to their nuclear forces. This would include information about programmes planned or in research and development (R&D) phases, as well as changes in existing force structure—such as the retirement or withdrawal of a nuclear weapon system. Under the SALT agreements, the USA and the USSR have agreed to procedures for observing the dismantling of strategic submarines, but they could enhance the process by notifying each other of planned dismantlement or conversion work and then confirm that the changes have been made. The USA could have informed the USSR about its plan to retire the three nuclear weapon systems described above and should have done so if it wishes to convince the USSR that such nuclear weapons are not desirable.

Finally, if they do not already do so, all the nuclear navies could place electromechanical locks—like the Permissive Action Links which the USA has on its other nuclear weapons—on their non-strategic nuclear weapons. This certainly should be done by the US Navy. Despite naval arguments about the difficulty of communications to naval forces, there is no good reason for excluding PALS from naval nuclear weapons. In fact, in their 1971 Accidents Measures Agreement, the USA and the USSR each committed itself to 'maintain and to improve, as it deems necessary, its existing organizational and technical arrangements to guard against the accidental or unauthorized use of nuclear weapons under its control'.[24] This commitment could be translated into placing naval nuclear weapons under the same rigid controls as all other US nuclear weapons.

Operational measures

Operational measures are those which affect the operations or activities of military forces, rather than their force structure (number and type of forces). Some military activities or the potential for certain destabilizing activities have been considered dangerous or as causing fear or worry among other nations. The three bilateral Incidents at Sea agreements (those concluded between the USA and the USSR, between the UK and the USSR, and between the Federal Republic of Germany and the USSR) are good examples of operational measures that constrain certain undesired behaviour and establish procedures for avoiding or resolving incidents (see papers 11 and 12). As they pertain to naval nuclear weapons, operational measures would focus on naval deployments or practices that are of the greatest concern to other nations. These measures basically fall into three categories: rules of behaviour, geographical limits and deployment limits, although there is certainly some overlap.

Rules of behaviour

Nations can enter into agreements restricting behaviour that is deemed dangerous or requiring certain precautionary actions to prevent unecessary danger. This was the motivation behind the Incidents at Sea Agreements, as well as the USA–USSR Agreement on the Prevention of Dangerous Military Activities of 12 June 1989. There are some possible agreements that take into account the risks of routine nuclear weapon deployments and are logical additions to existing agreements. These could proscribe behaviour that could be indicative of or misinterpreted as preparations for the use of naval nuclear weapons. For example, the USA and the USSR could agree not to use nuclear-related systems (fire control radars, nuclear communications networks, loading of launchers, etc.), either as a general rule or under certain conditions. Such measures might help alleviate doubts or fears that a nuclear attack was imminent and would obviate the need for countermeasures that might be interpreted as a similar threat. This would be consistent with both the 1971 Accidents Measures Agreement and the 1989 Prevention of Dangerous Military Activities Agreement, and would constitute a basic set of rules of engagement covering nuclear weapons

Geographical limits

Some nations, primarily the USSR, have called for limits on the cruising areas of nuclear-armed vessels.[25] The basic thrust of this idea is that naval vessels should not approach land areas within range of their nuclear weapons in peacetime. Considering the high mobility of naval forces, this proposal is intended to remove the possibility of nations being threatened by naval nuclear weapons, as well as to discourage naval nuclear arms from being brought into otherwise non-nuclearized regions. Thus, a ship carrying a nuclear weapon of range x should be required to sail more than distance x from the shores of foreign nations. Proposals have also been made which are variations on this theme, such as limits on the sea areas where nuclear-armed vessels may operate: international straits, areas of heavy commercial shipping or fishing, territorial waters, and so on.

Such geographic restrictions present many principle and practical difficulties and would be excessively difficult to implement under current conditions. Nor is it clear that such restrictions would be worth pursuing. Naval forces are fundamentally global and free to sail the high seas without any geographic restriction. The legal regime of the oceans is based on the concept of the freedom of the seas, and maritime nations will not easily accept any measure that contradicts this principle. In the words of Floyd Kennedy, a prominent US naval commentator, 'the absolute freedom of international waters is a tenet for which the United States has fought wars since the creation of the republic'.[26] Such measures could not be considered for ballistic missile submarines, since they can carry missiles with intercontinental ranges. Long-range SLCMs also present a problem in this regard; they are often capable of flying more than 2000 km, which does not leave much room for operating the carrier platform. Furthermore, the difficulty of knowing the location of submerged submarines makes it exceedingly difficult to consider such restrictions on nuclear-capable submarine forces.

The one instance in which geographical restraints are feasible is the case of port visits by foreign nuclear-capable naval vessels. These are visits to a nation's sovereign territory and not operations in international waters. Any nation that wishes to *guarantee* that nuclear weapons are not brought to its ports—as distinct from merely declaring a prohibition on such visits—can do so, as has New Zealand. But, because of the policy of the nuclear navies to neither confirm nor deny the presence of nuclear weapons, this can be done only by banning their visits outright—at great political cost to nations that wish to maintain friendly relations with them (see also section V).

Deployment limits

The final category of operational measures is limits on deployments of non-strategic nuclear weapons. Although this could arguably be considered a structural measure, it would not necessarily affect the number or type of nuclear weapons held by a navy—only their deployment. Here the idea would be to denuclearize naval operations and to restrict or prohibit naval vessels from carrying nuclear weapons in peacetime. Such limits could, in addition, accomplish many of the objectives of other proposed measures. If the USA and the USSR (and preferably also the UK and France) agreed to leave their naval nuclear weapons ashore, this would reduce the risks of naval incidents or confrontations, remove the potential for nuclear threats against coastal nations, eliminate the risk of nuclear weapon accidents at sea, permit more flexible and safer naval operations, eliminate the controversy over port calls, and generally achieve much of what an outright ban on naval nuclear weapons would achieve.

It might be possible for nuclear navies to agree to leave nuclear weapons ashore altogether in peacetime, and to have the option to return to port to load nuclear weapons in a crisis or war if it were deemed necessary. This would be analogous to the operations of nuclear-capable aircraft, which basically do not carry nuclear weapons (at least not the warheads) in peacetime but could do so in a crisis. Nations have long recognized the dangers of having air forces routinely carry nuclear weapons, so they have devised alternative methods of practising and training for nuclear missions—mostly with dummy weapons that can simulate the physical characteristics of real nuclear weapons. If nuclear nations believed that there is no need to carry nuclear weapons at sea, they might be able to devise international agreements prohibiting such deployments.

Such agreements would require less stringent verification measures than structural measures, since the only condition is that nuclear weapons not be present aboard naval vessels (excluding SLBMs on SSBNs) in peacetime. Given the practice of arming submarines only in port and their covert operating nature, nations might wish to exclude them from deployment limits, at least at their initial stage. But surface ships could all be included in a ban on nuclear weapons at sea. Presumably this would require nations to accept so-called intrusive or on-site inspections, at least on a challenge basis.

Structural measures

Structural nuclear arms control concerns either the limitation of nuclear weapon systems under some ceiling or their complete elimination. This discussion will therefore consider two types of measure: limits that permit the possession of some nuclear weapons and a comprehensive ban on such weapons. As with the possible measures mentioned above, what can be achieved depends on what result nations want and how far they are willing to go to achieve it.

Banning all naval nuclear weapons

If the USA and the USSR agreed that their naval nuclear weapons were superfluous for deterrence and combat, they could pursue a ban on all such weapons, leaving SLBMs as their only nuclear weapons at sea. An overall ban on naval nuclear weapons is appealing for a number of reasons. First, it reduces the greatest number of dangers connected with these weapons; it is a comprehensive approach and offers a potential security enhancement for everyone. Banning naval nuclear weapons would require a much-desired and unprecedented degree of openness and co-operation among the nations involved. In addition to the benefits listed in this paper, it would clear a considerable log-jam in the START negotiations concerning SLCMs.[27] It would obviate the supposed need for the obsolete 'neither confirm nor deny' policy, as well as much of the inflated secrecy surrounding naval nuclear weapons. It would be a great international confidence-building measure that would help to demonstrate to other nations the seriousness of the superpower commitment to Article VI of the Non-Proliferation Treaty, and thereby reinforce the treaty and act as a disincentive to further nuclear proliferation. Because of its comprehensive nature, it would be the simplest kind of naval nuclear agreement to verify; no nuclear weapon activity would be permitted.

In 1988 Paul Nitze, President Reagan's senior arms control adviser and former Secretary of the Navy, informally raised the possibility of a total ban on naval nuclear weapons as a way to break the deadlock on SLCMs at the START negotiations. According to Strobe Talbot, Secretary of Defense Carlucci and the Joint Chiefs of Staff (JCS) 'vetoed the idea. . . . He and the Chiefs concluded that the United States must preserve the option of deploying ship-to-shore (or "land-attack") nuclear-armed SLCMs as a means of bolstering nuclear deterrence on behalf of NATO, particularly West Germany, now that the Pershing IIs and ground-launched cruise missiles were going to be removed as a result of the INF treaty'.[28] This is a sad comment on the state of thinking about any need to 'bolster deterrence', as well as a stark reminder of the level of political thinking concerning the need to somehow compensate for NATO INF systems that would no longer have any justification or targets deployed in Eastern Europe.

Unlike the INF Treaty, a naval nuclear treaty could not ignore the question of warheads and focus only on launchers and associated equipment. In an agreement banning all naval non-strategic nuclear weapons, the parties would presumably have to concentrate on the elimination of warheads since many of the launcher systems (dual-capable ones) would be permitted for conventional weapons. To satisfy concerns about secret stockpiling of nuclear warheads, land facilities—such as ports, weapon factories and weapon storage areas—would have to be monitored, in addition to some inspections of ships and submarines. This would require a great degree of co-operation and openness by the parties involved.

Numerical limits

If nations chose not to pursue a total ban they could still aim for limits on naval nuclear weapons. Such limits, while not comprehensive, could reduce certain risks associated with individual types of weapon or could aim to reduce the overall level of naval nuclearization. For example, SLCMs were included in the START negotiations at Soviet insistence because their unconstrained proliferation could effectively nullify the intended effects of the prospective treaty.[29] Reflecting their mutual view that there are simply too many nuclear weapons, the USA and the USSR have agreed on the principle of 50 per cent reductions in strategic offensive nuclear forces.[30] Admiral Richard Hill has suggested a possible goal of 50 per cent reductions in naval nuclear arsenals.[31] There are still other possibilities that have not been explored.

In the category of controlling specific types of weapon several possibilities arise. Most of the ideas in this field have concerned SLCMs, which are a central hurdle to a START treaty and which may be the most difficult type of weapon to control. But other nuclear weapons may also be considered worthy of controls or individual elimination. For example, several varieties of weapon may be considered particularly undesirable because they heighten the risk of inadvertent escalation to nuclear war. Knowing that an adversary has nuclear-tipped ASMs or SAMs may force commanders in a crisis situation to believe that they are about to be attacked by such nuclear weapons. The decision time permitted is very short before some method of self-defence is chosen.[32] In such a situation the odds are higher that nuclear weapons would be used than if the attack could only be made with non-nuclear weapons. Therefore, it might be advisable to negotiate the elimination or limitation of those types of weapon which are considered most destabilizing in a crisis.

Efforts to limit SLCMs provide the best example of the general complexity and possibilities involved in the field of numerical limits. At the US–Soviet summit meeting in December 1987, both nations committed themselves to limiting SLCMs. According to the joint summit statement of 10 December 1987:

The sides shall find a mutually acceptable solution to the question of limiting the deployment of long-range, nuclear-armed SLCMs. Such limitations will not involve counting long-range, nuclear-armed SLCMs within the 6000 warheads and 1600 strategic offensive delivery systems limits. The sides committed themselves to establish ceilings on such missiles, and to seek mutually acceptable and effective methods of verification of such limitations, which could include the employment of national technical means, cooperative measures and onsite inspection.[33]

Several proposals have been made for SLCM limits. One Soviet proposal would reportedly limit both nations to a total of 1000 long-range SLCMs, of which 400 could be nuclear and 600 conventionally armed.[34] Another component of this proposal would be to limit the deployment of long-range SLCMs to only a few classes of vessel, either two classes of submarine or an additional class of surface ship (see annexe A). Such limits would require considerable verification provisions because the sides would want to have an assured count of the total number of SLCMs deployed, stored and manufactured, plus some means of assurance that the ceilings on nuclear and conventional models were adhered to. This might or might not require a capability to distinguish between conventional and nuclear warheads on missiles.

An alternative approach would be to ban all nuclear-armed SLCMs, regardless of their range. This idea, which appears to have Soviet support, would eliminate the large Soviet nuclear-armed anti-ship cruise missile (ASCM) force deployed at sea as well as the US nuclear Tomahawk programme.[35] It would also ease somewhat the verification tasks of a SLCM agreement because no nuclear wearheads would be permitted, thus obviating the need to account for each warhead.

The methods possible for verifying SLCM limits include such activities as: exchanging and verifying data on missile characteristics and locations, monitoring missile production and assembly, monitoring the fitting of warheads to missiles and assuring that the combination cannot be changed, monitoring missile storage facilities, observing the loading of missiles aboard ships and submarines in port, boarding and inspecting ships or submarines to establish that limits are not exceeded, and so on. Some of these methods have been used for the INF Treaty; similar ones are being negotiated for a START treaty. Others are new but not dissimilar.

Numerous ideas have been proposed in the academic community for ways to determine the number and type of existing warheads (deployed and not deployed) and to ensure that they are not changed. These include various schemes for tagging warheads, using tamper-proof seals on missiles once they have been fitted with warheads, using radiation detecting equipment and other similar methods of accounting for each warhead. Such schemes have not been used in any existing treaty, but the USA and the USSR have agreed to the principle of inspections of missiles to count the number of warheads for a START treaty. Although more work is required to develop the technologies and methods of application for warhead accountability, there is no reason to believe that verifying such limits is technologically impossible (see paper 5). But the conclusion is clearly that negotiated numerical limits pose the greatest complexites to naval nuclear arms control.

Unilateral measures

Some mention must be made of unilateral measures for several reasons. First, nations are vastly more disposed to making decisions unilaterally than through negotiation. As the example of the US Navy 'triple zero' retirement plan illustrates, nations may be able to decide unilaterally what they will not or cannot do bilaterally. Furthermore, although unilateral measures have had a poor reputation for many years, they are coming to play an important role in East–West arms control (conventional and nuclear) and may be increasingly important in the future. Given the asymmetry of forces and conditions facing the USA and the USSR, it may be necessary or helpful for one or both sides to make unilateral concessions or cuts to permit progress. The USSR has recognized this possibility and has taken some significant unilateral initiatives, particularly concerning its land-based forces. There is certainly great capacity for unilateral cuts in the large Soviet naval nuclear inventory. If verification problems are intractable, unilateral measures may offer a partial alternative. Finally, although unilateral measures are not normally considered to be measures of arms control, they are in fact a way of controlling, reducing or eliminating arms. The challenge is to create and implement unilateral measures in such a way as to build confidence and encourage co-operation and reciprocal self-restraint. This area will require much greater attention and imagination in the future.

Particularly with naval nuclear forces, some technical difficulties may be overcome by unilateral measures. For example, as regards the verification problems associated with SLCMs and other naval nuclear systems, it is entirely conceivable that the USA and the USSR might not be able to find workable or mutually acceptable bilateral solutions. Reflecting this possibility, the USA has proposed an alternative unilateral measure at the START negotiations. In April 1989 a senior State Department official told Congress: 'Because we have been unable to identify an effective verification regime for SLCMs, our START position does not limit these weapons. Instead, our approach is to adopt non-binding declarations of our respective plans for nuclear-armed SLCMs'.[36] This approach, which is uncharacteristic of the recent US preoccupation with strict verification and which suggests a lack of interest in limiting SLCMs, does not solve the basic problem. Nor does it appeal to the USSR.

A new approach might help overcome such problems. It could be possible to have each side present a plan for a unilataral measure of control (possibly including limitation or elimination) and an accompanying plan for assuring the other side that the measure is satisfactorily implemented. This second part would be the CBM component—a form of invited assurance—and could be negotiated so as to satisfy both sides that the measure is not phony or easily reversible. Some unilateral measures—such as scrapping ships and submarines—would need little if any invited assurance component. This kind of co-operation is a logical extension of the possibilities now emerging in US–Soviet relations and in the CSCE process. If initial attempts were judged to be successful this might open the way for new possibilities.

V. Difficulties

There are obviously many inherent difficulties involved in any attempt at naval nuclear arms control—some minor and some major. It is not within the scope of this paper (nor perhaps is it yet possible) to consider them all. Several problems stand out as the most significant in the long run; chief among them are: the national motivations for wanting to have and keep naval nuclear weapons, secrecy and the 'neither confirm nor deny' policy and verification. Verification issues are treated in paper 5 of this volume. Other difficulties are considered more easily solvable. If the major difficulties are overcome, the minor ones should be manageable.

Options

One of the most difficult topics to address in naval nuclear arms control considerations is why nations have and apparently want to keep nuclear weapons. The problem is that governments are reluctant to discuss the subject beyond general (and generally vague) statements about deterrence and the perceived need for naval nuclear weapons. It is a topic surrounded by secrecy and perceptions, which makes it difficult to research, debate or document. It is argued here that the major reason can be summed up in one word: options. Political leaders of the nuclear naval nations apparently want to have the nuclear option, just in case: 'Better to have too many options than too few'. This is a natural and understandable position, especially given the unprecedented risks and uncertainties that nuclear weapons present. But the central fact remains that nuclear weapons cannot be *used* without risking unimaginable and unacceptable destruction.

Thus the supposed military options provided by tactical nuclear weapons are illusory. The basic situation perceived of as nuclear deterrence cannot be bolstered or enhanced. Nations are either terrified of nuclear war or they are not; in either case, amending nuclear force structures will not make a difference in calculations of nuclear risk. The evidence of the nuclear era suggests that nations are indeed terrified of nuclear war, and for good reason. In this regard, it is dismaying that the idea of banning SLCMs could have been vetoed by the US Secretary of Defense and JCS because they 'concluded that the United States must preserve the option of deploying ship-to-shore (or "land-attack") nuclear-armed SLCMs as a means of bolstering nuclear deterrence on behalf of NATO'.[37] As long as such considerations prevail in international politics they will make improved mutual security much more difficult than it already is inherently. It is possible that if East–West security and political relations continue to improve and if nations come to understand each other better and gain confidence in each other, the desire for nuclear options will fade away. But this will require a willingness to overcome the secrecy associated with nuclear weapon issues and discuss them openly.

Secrecy and 'neither confirm nor deny'

Secrecy is one of the chief obstacles to naval nuclear arms control because it prevents a full debate on the issue and makes it difficult for people to learn enough facts to be well-informed. Its most obvious and pernicious manifestation is the 'neither confirm nor deny' (NCND) practice of the nuclear weapon nations. A full treatment of this subject would require a book (perhaps several), but it needs some examination here because it is important for naval arms control and because it is a controversial and insufficiently debated issue.

The USA, the UK and France each has a policy of not acknowledging whether its naval vessels are or are not carrying nuclear weapons at any given moment, including when they are visiting foreign ports in nations that prohibit nuclear weapons. It is not clear what the Soviet position is on the subject, but traditional Soviet secrecy has prevented any specific discussion of its naval nuclear weapons in the past.[38] The USSR has not espoused an NCND policy, and recent actions indicate that it is willing to deny or confirm the presence of nuclear weapons as it sees fit.[39]

As mentioned above, the one instance in which nations *can* exert control on the deployment of naval nuclear weapons is when foreign warships visit their ports. Because of the NCND policy, nuclear-capable ship visits have caused considerable international controversy. In 1985 New Zealand adopted a policy prohibiting foreign ships from visiting its harbours if they were nuclear-powered or nuclear-armed. This caused a serious strain in US–New Zealand relations, and led the USA to suspend its military obligations to New Zealand under the 1951 ANZUS (Australia–New Zealand–United States) Treaty. In 1987 the Swedish Social Democratic Party Congress passed a resolution that gave an ultimatum to the Swedish Government, saying that if Sweden could not find some acceptable compromise before the next Party Congress in 1990 that ensured that its non-nuclear policy was respected by visiting navies then it would ban such visits.

In 1988 the Danish Parliament passed an opposition-sponsored resolution calling on the government to inform each visiting ship of the long-standing Danish policy prohibiting nuclear weapons on Danish territory in peacetime. This caused a political crisis for the government, which fell and called for a snap election. (Ironically, the resolution did not call for any confirmation or denial from visiting naval captains, and was very similar to the government-sponsored resolution.) After the resolution was passed, the USA and the UK pressed harsh criticism on the Danish Government and threatened to cut back their military co-operation.[40] The election was inconclusive, and a 'compromise' was worked out between Denmark and the USA and the UK, permitting their naval vessels to visit Denmark without any mention of nuclear weapons.

It is important to put the issue of port calls in perspective. What is a port visit? It is meant to be a goodwill visit, subject to the permission (or invitation) of the host country and involving special privileges and responsibilities for the visiting warship.[41] Permission is granted on the understanding that visiting vessels and their crews will respect and observe *all* policies, regulations and laws of the host state, including those concerning nuclear weapons. Otherwise the ships would not be upholding their responsibilities and would have absolutely no business calling at ports while knowingly disregarding host-country national policies. Nations presumably would not welcome ships that do not respect their laws and policies. In those nations which have policies prohibiting nuclear weapons on visiting warships, as in all the Nordic countries, the public is angered by the arrogance of the nuclear navies wanting to visit with nuclear-capable ships but not being willing to assure them publicly that their non-nuclear policy is respected and that no nuclear weapons are present on visiting warships.

If the nations with NCND policies continue this practice and offer no possibility for compromise, it may provoke a number of countries to deny them permission to make port calls, as New Zealand did. This could considerably restrict the access of nuclear navies, particularly the US Navy, to ports of nations with non-nuclear policies. This would be seen by the USA as a serious impediment to its political and military flexibility—the opposite result of what the NCND policy is meant to achieve. Protests against naval nuclear weapons are not directed only at the USA, the most active of the nuclear navies, but have also been aimed at the UK and the USSR.[42]

Official explanations of the various NCND policies are not easily available to the public. In response to a SIPRI request to the five nuclear weapon nations for information on their policies concerning NCND, only the USA and France acknowledged that they have such policies and offered some explanation for them. The USSR, the UK and China did not respond. This hinders a full examination of the topic.

US policy

The US NCND policy is so important to the USA that one would expect to find solid, well-reasoned explanations for its existence. However, it is considered so sensitive an issue that the policy itself is not open for discussion. This may simply be a feature of self-preservation, as any full debate about the policy could well end in the conclusion that there is no clear or reasonable rationale for it. Several requests to the US Government for information yielded brief explanations of its policy, the most eloquent of which is as follows:

The United States maintains a longstanding policy of neither confirming nor denying (NCND) the presence or absence of nuclear weapons at any general or specific location, including aboard any US military station, ship, vehicle or aircraft. This policy, which is common among the Western nuclear allies, has as its fundamental purpose the military security of nuclear weapons.

By neither confirming nor denying the presence or absence of nuclear weapons, those who would threaten the weapons, including terrorists and saboteurs, are denied important information. Potential adversaries therefore find it more difficult to attack US forces effectively.

By denying a potential adversary accurate information on our military forces, we complicate his military planning and reduce his chance for a successful attack. The greater the uncertainty an aggressor faces, the greater the risks in a preemptive attack, and the more likely deterrence will be sustained.

The Western policy of deterrence is based on a strategy of flexible response. By reducing a potential adversary's chances of differentiating between nuclear and non-nuclear units, we have a greater flexibility in deploying all units and a greater chance of successfully employing them if the need should ever arise.

NCND is thus an essential component of our policy of deterrence.[43]

This official explanation leaves much to be desired. It makes a number of unsupported assertions, confuses the issue of security threats from terrorists, saboteurs and adversary militaries and, in the author's view, greatly overstates the effects of denying one simple piece of information. Of course, the INF Treaty disproved the supposedly all-encompassing scope of the NCND policy. The USA and the USSR provided each other with complete lists of the exact locations and numbers of every system limited by the treaty. Presumably, when it comes to port visits by US Navy ships in nuclear-free harbours, the only permissible possibility is that they are not carrying any nuclear weapons. Otherwise they would be infringing on the sovereignty of the host state. So, why does the USA refuse to assure those nations with non-nuclear policies that it respects their policies on ship visits?

The USA has tried to make the issue the acid (and acidic) test of alliance and international relations, implying that *good* allies and friends will not question its policy. The US presumption is that its global nuclear deployments are essential to the maintenance of peace, and that through such 'effective deterrence' all states benefit from its so-called 'nuclear umbrella'. In 1985, in one of the few public explanations of the official US view of this situation, Admiral James Watkins, then Chief of Naval Operations, wrote:

By banning port access to U.S. Navy ships, New Zealand has demonstrated unwillingness to accept basic alliance support responsibilities. As a member of the Western alliance, New Zealand is protected by, and benefits from, the United States' nuclear umbrella. By accepting the benefits of this security, New Zealand cannot choose selectively to support some portions of the allied defense strategy while opting out of others and ignoring the realities of the nuclear age.[44]

This approach puts the blame on allied nations that stray from unquestioning faith in US nuclear weapons as the ultimate guarantor of peace and from willingness to support the nuclear infrastructure that is supposedly an indivisible component of their security. Watkins went on to suggest a military reason for US behaviour, stating that 'U.S. naval ships must be prepared to go anywhere at any time to carry out any of a variety of defensive and offensive missions, among which is employment of a nuclear weapons capability. We cannot tailor forces to accommodate New Zealand's nuclear sensitivities because New Zealand is only one element of the global strategic equation'.[45] The NCND policy is used both to prevent 'nuclear sensitivity' from becoming more widespread and to avoid recognizing that it is already a global phenomenon.

As ships might be called on at any time to go to war there is a general notion that they must always be fully prepared for all types of war. However, the suggestion that nuclear weapons must actually be aboard every nuclear-capable ship at all times, including during port calls to nations that prohibit nuclear weapons, cannot be taken seriously. The US Navy has the capability and the practice of transferring many of its nuclear weapons on and off ships at sea.[46] A fleet of ammunition and supply ships exists just for that purpose. Aircraft-carriers also serve as nuclear weapon storage ships. The non-strategic nuclear weapons most common aboard US surface warships can be off-loaded before ships go into port; this may well be US practice for a variety of political and military reasons regardless of the nuclear policy of host nations. In this sense the USA *can* tailor the forces that visit ports in countries with non-nuclear policies and, by international law, should be required to do so. There is simply no need to have nuclear weapons in foreign harbours.

Furthermore, ships do not sail from normal peacetime deployments (including foreign port calls) and charge directly into battle alone. They can only function as units within a larger force of interdependent ships, submarines and aircraft. Before sailing to war it is necessary to regroup with the other forces, refuel, resupply, take on weapons (possibly including nuclear weapons) and co-ordinate plans before sailing in harm's way. This is a process that could take weeks. The NCND policy precludes any debate that would make these practices and facts known.

There appear to be two possible means for foreign nations with non-nuclear policies to resolve the NCND dilemma. These possibilities would not, however, require a fundamental change in the NCND policy and would not, therefore, help solve the basic arms control dilemma. They might be a first required step towards deflating the NCND issue and thus permitting progress towards negotiated arms control.

The first solution would be for host nations to require a *public* assurance that visiting warships will observe and respect *all* their laws, policies and regulations. Such an assurance could be made once for the record and need not be reissued with each ship visit. It need not—and given the 'nuclear sensitivity' of the nuclear navies, probably should not—refer to nuclear weapons. This would serve as an implicit acknowledgement that nuclear weapons are not present on visiting warships. The assurance must be public because private assurances do not create public confidence. Secret understandings among top-level cabinet officials cannot substitute for public confidence that national policies are respected.

The second possible solution will arise when the US Navy has retired the three ageing nuclear weapon systems described above. Assuming that the Navy does not introduce new nuclear weapon systems to the vessels in question, this partial denuclearization will create a fleet of about 115 ships and 25 submarines without any nuclear weapon capability. None of these vessels is planned to be equipped with the Tomahawk SLCM system, which will be virtually the only non-strategic nuclear weapon carried by surface combatants after 1992. The exception to this pattern are aircraft-carriers, which normally carry many nuclear warheads (perhaps 100), but which do not make many port visits because of their large size. Consequently, the US Navy will have a large selection of non-nuclear ships that could be available for port calls to countries with non-nuclear policies. Under these circumstances, it would almost be more difficult to send a nuclear-capable ship than a non-nuclear ship to such ports. The USA could finesse the NCND issue by sending ships that are acknowledged to have no nuclear weapon capability.

The final irony on the NCND issue is that the US and other nuclear navies may indeed already respect the non-nuclear policies of foreign nations where their ships call, albeit secretly. If this is the case, then the nuclear nations have created the problem that prevents other nations from having confidence in nuclear-capable ship visits. Confidence-building is entirely in order; the NCND policy is not.

VI. Conclusions

If the USA and the USSR wish to co-operate on measures of naval nuclear arms control, a number of possibilities appear to be worth pursuing. If they and the two smaller nuclear naval powers—Britain and France—come to recognize that non-strategic naval nuclear weapons are not essential for fighting wars or for deterrence, then it may be possible to pursue major reductions or even the elimination of all such weapons. For reasons explained in this paper, if the task is possible, nations should strive for a comprehensive ban as the goal. But regardless of which goal or measure might be chosen, naval nuclear arms control will require a greater degree of openness and co-operation than has so far been shown.

It seems that, as a first step, the USA and the USSR could begin on some of the measures listed above in the confidence-building category as part of their expanding programme of military-to-military contacts and exchanges.

Four specific measures are suggested.

1. Place PALs on all naval nuclear weapons, including SLBMs.
2. Alter and eventually abandon the NCND policy and practice.
3. Inform other nations and the public of changes to naval nuclear force structures.
4. Begin a bilateral dialogue and exchange of information concerning naval forces, including nuclear weapons.

Even if they do not find it possible to proceed beyond this stage for the foreseeable future they could accomplish significant results. This would also serve as a basis for building the confidence, openness and co-operation required for the more ambitious efforts which they might wish to make. In the end, if nations have the requisite political will to control naval nuclear weapons they should be able to design equitable measures and overcome verification complexities. Unilateral measures may be a useful or necessary part of this process.

Although the problems of naval nuclear arms control are complex and not amenable to sudden solutions, one need not (and indeed cannot) have all the answers to the difficult questions of exactly how to devise equitable agreements before they are negotiated. After all, that is what negotiations are for. Under the proper conditions many of the arms control and security ideas being discussed today on a theoretical level might be practical and feasible. The USA and the USSR have committed themselves to solving the nuclear SLCM problem; they should be devoting considerable energy to finding solutions, not simply making excuses and leaving the job to others. The challenge is to determine what goal is desirable and work hard to achieve it. The requirement is to open these issues to a full and public debate.

Notes and references

[1] The figures for nuclear weapons in this paper are taken from the companion volume to this book: Fieldhouse, R. and Taoka, S., SIPRI, *Superpowers at Sea: An Assessment of the Naval Arms Race*, a Strategic Issue Papers monograph (Oxford University Press: Oxford, 1989), pp. 83–132.

[2] Gordon, M. R, 'Navy phasing out nuclear rockets for close combat', *New York Times*, 30 Apr. 1989, p. 1.

[3] For a description of the missions and capabilities of the US and Soviet navies, see Fieldhouse and Taoka (note 1).

[4] See Hill, R., *Arms Control at Sea* (Routledge: London, 1989), pp. 108–109.

[5] See Gordon, M. R., 'Navy phasing out nuclear rockets for close combat', *New York Times*, 30 Apr. 1989, p. 1.

[6] See Fieldhouse and Taoka (note 1), pp. 140–42.

[7] See Fieldhouse and Taoka (note 1), pp. 139–40; and US policy explanation in US Congress, Senate Armed Services Committee (SASC), *Department of Defense Authorization for Appropriations for Fiscal Year 1984* (DOD Hearings FY 1984), Part 5, p. 2463.

[8] Gordon (note 5), p. 28.

[9] For a full discussion of these issues, see Fieldhouse and Taoka (note 1), pp. 133–40.

[10] The cost factor was one of several reasons cited for the US Navy decision to retire the ASROC, SUBROC and Terrier nuclear weapon systems ahead of schedule. See Gordon (note 5), p. 1.

[11] Gordon (note 5), p. 1.

[12] For a full description of naval nuclear weapon systems, see Fieldhouse and Taoka (note 1), pp. 83–132.

[13] Both the USA and the USSR have nuclear SLCMs that are either intended for or capable of attacking targets ashore. The US Navy has more than 1000 nuclear-capable attack aircraft aboard its aircraft-carriers; they are intended *inter alia* to drop nuclear bombs on the USSR.

[14] These figures are taken from Fieldhouse and Taoka (note 1), pp. 83–132.

[15] Gordon (note 5), p. 1.

[16] Rosenthal, A., '50 warheads lie on seabed, study asserts', *International Herald Tribune*, 8 June 1989, p. 3.

[17] The term 'confidence- and security-building measure' (CSBM) is used in the Conference on Security and Co-operation in Europe (CSCE) process where 35 states are pursuing increased confidence and decreased risk of military confrontation in Europe.

[18] Agreement Between the USA and the USSR on Measures to Reduce the Risk of Outbreak of Nuclear War, signed and entered into force on 30 Sep. 1971. Article 1 states: 'Each Party undertakes to maintain and to improve, as it deems necessary, its existing organizational and technical arrangements to guard against the accidental or unauthorized use of nuclear weapons under its control'. Article 7 states: 'The Parties undertake to hold consultations, as mutually agreed, to consider questions relating to the implementation of the provisions of this Agreement, as well as to discuss possible amendments thereto aimed at further implementation of the purposes of this Agreement'. The two nations later agreed to use the Standing Consultative Commission (SCC) created for the ABM Treaty as the forum for such consultations. For the texts of the relevant agreements see Goldblat, J., SIPRI, *Agreements for Arms Control: A Critical Survey* (Taylor & Francis: London, 1982), pp. 192–933, 198 and 206–207.

[19] There are encouraging signs that *glasnost* is reaching into Soviet nuclear weapon issues. For example, after the Soviet Mike Class submarine *Komsomolets* sank off Norway in Apr. 1989, the Soviet Government acknowledged that it was carrying two nuclear-armed torpedoes. Additionally, since 1987 the USSR has been making considerable information publicly available concerning its nuclear forces, including their names and ranges. This was obviously necessary for the INF Treaty Data Exchange and will be even more so for any START agreement. These and other public disclosures indicate that the USSR recognizes the need for openness in military information if confidence-building or arms control are to be achieved.

[20] Hill (note 4), p. 125.

[21] See Gordon (note 5); '3 shipboard nuke missiles to be mothballed by navy', *Stars and Stripes* (European edn), 1 May 1989, p. 4; 'The navy's arms control step', *Boston Globe*, 3 May 1989, p. 18.

[22] In 1989 Captain Linton Brooks, deputy head of the US START delegation in Geneva, stated that the USA opposes proposals 'that would violate our long-standing policy of neither confirming nor denying the presence or absence of nuclear weapons' aboard ships. Brooks, L., in Newman, R., 'US views START round as "businesslike", "productive"', *Wireless File*, US Information Service, US Embassy, Stockholm, Sweden, 31 July 1989, p. 13.

[23] 'Testimony of Roger Harrison, Deputy Assistant Secretary of State for Arms Control, Bureau of Politico-Military Affairs, before the House Armed Services Committee, Subcommittee on Seapower, Strategic Minerals and Critical Materials', 27 Apr. 1989, mimeo, p. 5.

[24] The text of the agreement appears in Goldblat (note 18), pp. 192–93.

[25] For example, in his July 1987 interview with the Indonesian newspaper *Merdeka*, General Secretary Gorbachev stated: 'We could agree to restrict the areas where naval vessels carrying nuclear weapons move so that they would not be able to approach the coastline of the other side within range of their onboard nuclear systems'. *Security in the Asia–Pacific Region: The Soviet Approach: Documents and Materials* (Novosti Press Agency Publishing House: Moscow, 1988), pp. 37–38.

[26] Kennedy, F., 'Naval arms control', *National Defense*, July–Aug. 1988, p. 10.

[27] For an enlightening account of the SLCM issue, see Talbot, S., *The Master of the Game: Paul Nitze and the Nuclear Peace* (Alfred A. Knopf: New York, 1988), pp. 378–81.

[28] Talbot (note 27), p. 380.

[29] The USA could potentially deploy more than 10 000 Tomahawk SLCMs. See Sloan, S. R., Bowen, A. M. and O'Rourke, R., 'The implications for strategic arms control of nuclear armed sea launched cruise missiles', Congressional Research Service, Report no. 86-25F, 10 Dec. 1985, esp. pp. 18–23.

[30] Although both nations refer to 50 per cent reductions, the outline of the draft START agreement made public in 1988 would not reduce strategic weapons by such a margin but more likely by 35–45 per cent.

[31] Hill (note 4), pp. 118–23.

[32] Even in a completely different situation, the crew aboard the USS Vincennes believed it was about to be attacked by a hostile aircraft in the Persian Gulf and chose to fire two anti-aircraft missiles for self-defence. Only afterwards did they discover that they had destroyed a commercial Iranian flight on schedule and on the proper route.

[33] 'Joint Summit Statement, 10 December 1987', Department of State Bulletin, Feb. 1988, p. 13.

[34] Gordon, M. R., 'Soviets seek limits on sea-based missiles', International Herald Tribune, 15 Feb. 1988, p. 2.

[35] In July 1989 several senior Soviet arms control officials acknowledged that the USSR would be willing to include all nuclear-armed SLCMs in an elimination agreement. See Remnick, D. and Smith, R. J., 'Moscow shifts on missiles', International Herald Tribune, 14 July 1989, p. 1.

[36] See note 23.

[37] Talbot (note 27), p. 380.

[38] In 1981 the USSR would neither confirm nor deny the presence of nuclear weapons aboard a Whiskey Class attack submarine (No. 137) stranded on Swedish territory. Until glasnost entered the realm of Soviet military affairs in the late 1980s, the USSR did not discuss any aspect of its naval nuclear weapons. See Prawitz, J., 'Neither confirming nor denying: thoughts on a principle', paper prepared for the 52nd Pugwash symposium on Naval Forces: Arms Restraint and Confidence-Building, June 1988, Oslo, Norway.

[39] The Soviet Government has stated that it would reveal the presence or absence of nuclear weapons aboard its warships in foreign ports if the Western nations change their NCND policy, a prospect so unlikely at present as to make the Soviet offer seem almost irrelevant. However, the fact that the USSR acknowledged that its Mike Class attack submarine Komsomolets was carrying two nuclear-armed torpedoes when it sank off Norway in Apr. 1989, demonstrations of new openness with regard to military and nuclear weapon information—including an experiment in which US and Soviet scientists measured radiation from a nuclear warhead aboard the Soviet cruiser Slava—several public denials of nuclear weapon presence aboard visiting warships, and conversations with Soviet naval officers indicate that the USSR is more flexible than might be expected.

[40] Gordon, M. R., 'Denmark agrees on nuclear policy', New York Times, 8 June 1988.

[41] For a description of the unique status of warships in foreign port visits, see Brittin, B. H., International Law for Seagoing Officers, 5th edn (Naval Institute Press: Annapolis, Md., 1986), pp. 123–35.

[42] See Ross, M., 'The "nuclear allergy" is still spreading', International Herald Tribune, 6–7 Aug. 1988, p. 4.

[43] US Department of State official explanation of the reasons for the NCND policy, 'Neither Confirm Nor Deny Policy', transmitted to SIPRI via the US Embassy, Stockholm, Sweden, 3 Oct. 1988. Further attempts by SIPRI to obtain any more detailed explanation, or a historical summary of the policy, ended in failure. This is the most detailed explanation the State Department offers.

[44] Watkins, J. D., 'New Zealand's nuclear policy', Foreign Affairs, fall 1985, p. 169.

[45] Watkins (note 44), p. 170.

[46] The same is true for the UK and France. Soviet at-sea transfer capabilities are not publicly known.

Paper 10. The Seabed Treaty and arms control

Jozef Goldblat

SIPRI

I. Introduction

In addition to the 1972 bilateral Agreement on the Prevention of Incidents on and over the High Seas between the ships of the armed forces of the United States and the Soviet Union, five multilateral treaties have been concluded in the post-World War II period restricting, to varying degrees, the military uses of the seas. (For the texts or relevant articles of these and other agreements, see annexe B.)

The 1961 Antarctic Treaty declared the Antarctic as an area to be used for peaceful purposes only. This declaration was reinforced by the prohibition of any measures of a military nature, such as the establishment of military bases and fortifications, the carrying out of military manoeuvres, and the testing of weapons. Nuclear explosions of any kind have been explicitly prohibited. The provisions of the treaty apply south of latitude 60°S. Thereby, in addition to the Antarctic continent, the ice shelves which surround the continent and occupy an area estimated at 800 000 square miles have been put under the demilitarized regime.

The 1963 Partial Test Ban Treaty (PTBT) banned nuclear weapon tests in three environments. One of the environments prohibited for testing is the underwater environment including 'territorial waters or high seas'. High seas were singled out to remove the possibility of an argument being put forward that these parts of the seas were not under the jurisdiction or control of any party and thus were not covered by the prohibition. In fact, all bodies of water are included in the ban, both inland waters, lakes and rivers, and the seas.

The treaty prohibiting nuclear weapons in Latin America, the Treaty of Tlatelolco, was signed on 14 February 1967. It has been in effect since 22 April 1968 for each state that ratified it and waived the requirements for the entry into force of the treaty, as specified in one of its articles. The zone of application of the treaty embraces the territory, territorial sea, airspace and any other space over which the zonal state exercises sovereignty 'in accordance with its own legislation'. The treaty also provides that the zone will eventually cover an area between longitude 150°W and longitude 20°W, extending hundreds of kilometres off the coast of the states party to the treaty, and thereby covering large portions of the Atlantic and Pacific Oceans, over which no state has claimed jurisdiction.

Most extra-continental and continental states which are internationally responsible for territories lying within the limits of the geographical zone established by the treaty have formally undertaken to apply the statute of military denuclearization to these territories, while all the nuclear weapon states are now under the obligation not to contribute to violations of the treaty.

The 1985 Treaty of Rarotonga, which established the South Pacific nuclear-free zone, bans the presence of nuclear weapons within the territories of South Pacific states up to the 12-nautical mile territorial sea limit. In contrast to the Treaty of Tlatelolco, it does not seek to have nuclear weapon prohibitions applied to the larger ocean area, but invites the nuclear weapon powers not to test nuclear explosive devices in the South Pacific zone, and to apply the denuclearization measures in respect of their territories in the zone.

These four treaties treated the seas merely as one of the environments covered by their arms control provisions. The only multilateral arms control treaty focusing exclusively on the seas is the 1971 Treaty on the Prohibition of the Emplacement of Nuclear Weapons and Other Weapons of Mass Destruction on the Seabed and the Ocean Floor and in the Subsoil Thereof (the Seabed Treaty). It is useful to review this unique treaty in considering existing measures of military restraint in the seas, as well as to discuss possible steps to improve it or to enlarge its scope. The following sections of this paper review the negotiating history of this treaty, the scope and the geographical coverage of its prohibitions, as well as the means provided for verification of compliance. The implementation of the Seabed Treaty and its value as an arms limitation measure are also discussed. In the final section, suggestions are made for further action with a view to controlling the arms race in the seas.

II. History

Arms control measures concerning the seabed began to receive attention in 1967, when the United Nations decided to engage in a thorough examination of the possibility of reserving exclusively for peaceful purposes the seabed, the ocean floor, and the subsoil thereof, underlying the high seas beyond the limits of present national jurisdiction and the use of their resources in the interest of mankind.[1]

In 1968, the Soviet Union suggested that the Eighteen-Nation Disarmament Committee (ENDC) should consider the prohibition of the use for military purposes of the seabed beyond the limits of the territorial waters.[2] The United States proposed to take up the question of arms limitation on the seabed with a view to preventing the use of this environment for the emplacement of weapons of mass destruction.[3] Negotiations in the ENDC began in the spring of 1969 with the presentation by the Soviet Union of a draft treaty which provided for total demilitarization of the seabed and the ocean floor.[4] The United States, in opposing the Soviet comprehensive approach, submitted its own draft calling only for denuclearization of the seabed environment.[5]

It soon became evident that no comprehensive ban on the military use of the seabed would be achieved in the foreseeable future. In October 1969, following the concessions made by the USSR, the Soviet and the US co-chairmen of the Conference of the Committee on Disarmament (CCD),[6] which succeeded the ENDC, tabled a joint draft treaty under which the parties would undertake not to place nuclear weapons or other weapons of mass destruction on the seabed beyond a zone defined in the draft. The text of the joint draft was found by many nations to be inadequate. In the light of their criticisms, three further revised joint drafts were submitted by the United States and the Soviet Union.[7] The resulting text was judged acceptable by the Committee on Disarmament (CD) and was commended by the UN General Assembly at its twenty-fifth session in a resolution of 7 December 1970.[8] However, in agreeing that the treaty should be opened for signature and ratification, many UN representatives made it clear that their affirmative votes for the resolution did not prejudge the positions which their governments would eventually adopt. The reasons for this reserve were explained in the course of the UN debate.

Several nations, including France,[9] considered the scope of the treaty prohibition to be too narrow, restricted as it was to activities of little military interest. The treaty was also found insufficient as a denuclearization measure, since it exempted from the ban a portion of the seabed. Peru considered the exemption to be an 'unjustifiable discrimination' in favour of the nuclear weapon powers.[10] An amendment to enlarge the geographical extent of the prohibition to cover the entire seabed and ocean floor[11] was not accepted; but, significantly, out of 99 delegations participating in the vote on the amendment, as many as 39 (i.e., over one-third) abstained. The provisions on verification, although rather elaborate, proved unsatisfactory to France and Pakistan,[12] in that no genuinely international control system was established.

Even more objectionable than these omissions, in the view of some states, were the imputed 'sins of commission'. It was charged, especially by some Latin American countries, that the reference in Article II of the treaty to the 1958 Geneva Convention on the Territorial Sea and the Contiguous Zone was meant to set an international precedent in support of the 12-nautical mile territorial water limit, which at that time most of these countries strongly opposed. The language of the treaty was criticized for lack of precision; Ecuador did not hesitate to call it a network of ambiguities and errors.[13]

Nevertheless, since the misgivings of coastal states were allayed by a disclaimer clause stating that nothing in the treaty should be interpreted as supporting or prejudicing the position of the parties with respect to existing international conventions, many of them saw no harm in endorsing an agreement covering an environment of marginal military importance. It was also appreciated that the treaty, which in essence represented a bilateral US–Soviet self-limitation, had been negotiated and finalized multilaterally. Consequently, only two delegations (El Salvador and Peru) opposed the UN

General Assembly resolution commending the treaty, and two abstained (Ecuador and France), while 19 delegations were absent during the vote.

III. Scope of the prohibitions

UN resolutions calling for the reserved use of the seabed and ocean floor and the subsoil thereof exclusively for peaceful purposes[14] formed a framework for possible arms control measures. However, a controversy arose over the meaning of the phrase 'exclusively for peaceful purposes'.

The non-aligned countries contended that the United Nations had invariably understood the use of a given environment for exclusively peaceful purposes to mean the prohibition of all military activities, whatever their purpose, and that there should be no departure from this approach in the case of the seabed. Some of them reasoned that, since the seabed must be used for the benefit of all states (as stated in the above resolutions), any military use of it represented an unjustified usurpation hampering peaceful exploitation of the environment.

The Soviet Union also equated 'peaceful purposes' with 'non-military purposes'. Its approach was similar to that applied to Antarctica under the Antarctic Treaty. Accordingly, the first Soviet draft treaty aimed at completely demilitarizing the seabed and the ocean floor as well as the subsoil thereof.[15]

The United States interpreted the phrase 'peaceful purposes' as not barring military activities generally. It argued that specific limitations of certain military activities would require detailed agreements and that activities not precluded by such agreements would continue to be conducted in accordance with the principle of the freedom of the seas. It saw an analogy with the 1967 Outer Space Treaty, which does not provide for the use of outer space exclusively for peaceful purposes but specifically prohibits the placing in orbit around the earth of objects carrying nuclear weapons or other kinds of weapon of mass destruction. Accordingly, the United States proposed that states undertake not to emplant or emplace fixed nuclear weapons or other weapons of mass destruction or associated fixed launching platforms on, within or beneath the seabed and ocean floor.[16] In advocating these measures, the United States asserted that only weapons of mass destruction could have enough significance militarily to justify the expense of stationing them on the seabed. It expressed the belief that realistic possibilities did not and would not soon exist for such conventional military uses of the seabed as would be threatening to the territories of states. Some non-nuclear but clearly military uses of the seabed (e.g., devices for detection and surveillance of submarines) were considered essential to the security of states and therefore indispensable. In the opinion of the United States, complete demilitarization would, moreover, raise verification problems by imposing the task of deciding whether each object or installation emplaced on the seabed was of a military nature. In any event, the United States was not prepared to accept a ban on all military activities on the seabed.

The text eventually agreed upon provides for an undertaking by states parties to the treaty not to emplant or emplace on the seabed and the ocean floor and in the subsoil thereof any nuclear weapons or any other types of weapon of mass destruction as well as structures, launching installations or any other facilities specifically designed for storing, testing or using such weapons. The parties also undertake not to assist, encourage or induce any state to carry out activities prohibited by the treaty and not to participate in any other way in such actions (Article I). The term 'other types of weapon of mass destruction' is to be understood, in accordance with the 1948 UN definition,[17] as including biological, chemical and radiological weapons.

When asked for more precision, the sponsors of the treaty explained that the treaty prohibits, *inter alia*, nuclear mines anchored to or emplaced on the seabed. It does not apply to facilities for research or for commercial exploitation not specifically designed for storing, testing or using weapons of mass destruction, but facilities specifically designed for using such weapons could not be exempted from the prohibitions of the treaty on the grounds that they could also use conventional weapons. The prohibitions are not intended to affect the use of nuclear reactors or other non-weapon applications of nuclear energy, consistent with the treaty obligations. It was also explained that, while submersible vehicles able to navigate in the water above the seabed would be viewed as any other ships and would not violate the treaty when anchored to or resting on the bottom, bottom-crawling vehicles which could navigate only when in contact with the seabed and which were specifically designed to use nuclear weapons would be banned. Thus, the prohibition embraces not only fixed facilities (as was originally provided for in the US draft) but also certain mobile facilities.

IV. Geographical coverage

There was a general understanding that, as indicated in several UN resolutions,[18] seabed disarmament measures were to include the area underlying the high seas beyond the limits of national jurisdiction. The vague language reflected the disagreement existing at that time as to where these limits actually lay. However, a view prevailed that a precise boundary, devised specifically for arms control purposes and expressed in terms of distance from the coast, should be agreed upon.

Under the Soviet draft treaty the prohibition was to cover an area beyond a 12-mile maritime zone of the coastal states.[19] The US draft provided for a prohibition beyond a 3-mile band adjacent to the coast.[20] The area of prohibition was eventually defined (Articles I and II) as lying beyond the outer limit of a seabed zone coterminous with the 12-mile outer limit of the zone referred to in part II of the Convention on the Territorial Sea and the Contiguous Zone, signed at Geneva on 29 April 1958. It should be noted that only a minority of nations have ratified the Geneva Convention. Some states qualified its provisions as highly controversial and antiquated and thus considered it inappropriate to invite non-parties to an agreement to accept its formulations in defining new obligations. Indeed, there was no need to refer to this convention. A simple and self-sufficient formula would have served the same purpose.

The undertakings by states parties to the treaty are applicable also to the 12-nautical mile seabed zone, except that within such a zone they shall not apply either to the coastal state (which is free to place any object there) or to the seabed beneath its territorial waters (Article I, para. 2). In other words, since the treaty does not contain an absolute prohibition on the placement of weapons of mass destruction beyond the parties' *own* seabed zone, and since an exception has been made with regard to territorial waters, states have the right, according to the language of the treaty, to install weapons of mass destruction on the seabed beneath the territorial waters within the 12-nautical mile seabed zone of *other* states, presumably with the consent and authorization of the states concerned ('allied option'). This would not be permitted in the band between the outer limit of the territorial sea and the 12-nautical mile limit of the seabed zone in cases where the breadth of the territorial waters is narrower than 12 nautical miles. The United States and the Soviet Union pointed out that the exception regarding the seabed beneath the territorial waters within the seabed zone left unaffected the sovereign authority and control of the coastal state within its territorial sea.[21]

The 1979 SALT II Treaty prohibited the development, testing or deployment of fixed ballistic or cruise missile launchers for emplacement in any area of the ocean floor and the seabed, or on the beds of internal waters and inland waters, or in the subsoil thereof, or mobile launchers of such missiles, which move only in contact with the ocean floor, the seabed, or the beds of internal waters and inland waters, or missiles for such launchers (Article IX, para. 1(b) with an agreed statement). This treaty never entered into force, but there is no evidence that the parties acted, or intend to act, contrary to its provisions concerning the seabed.

V. Verification

The problem most extensively discussed was how to verify compliance with the prohibitions. In the first drafts the question was dealt with rather cursorily. The Soviet Union proposed that all installations and structures on the seabed and the ocean floor and in the subsoil thereof should be open, on the basis of reciprocity, to representatives of other states parties to the treaty for verification of the fulfilment of the obligations.[22] The United States proposed that the parties should be free to observe activities of other states on the seabed and ocean floor, without interfering with the activities or otherwise infringing rights recognized under international law, including the freedom of the high seas.[23]

Neither proposal proved acceptable. It was pointed out that, while verification must protect the interests of all, a mere proclamation of the right to verify would be meaningless for states with less developed undersea technology—that is, for the overwhelming majority of states. Such countries would be unable to exercise the right of verification even if they suspected that they were threatened by weapons or military installations in adjacent areas of the seabed, unless they were guaranteed assistance in carrying out the necessary operations by the technologically more advanced states.

The USA and the USSR refused to commit themselves formally to assisting any complaining state in conducting verification. The United States said that, given the present state of technology, heavy expenses as well as hazards were involved in performing major underwater searches, the equipment and personnel for these specialized activities being in short supply. Besides, varying political relations among countries that might become parties to the treaty made it impossible for the USA to accept a firm obligation in this respect. Some countries felt that in seeking direct aid from a nuclear weapon power they would compromise their policy of non-alignment. A clause dealing with the subject was nevertheless inserted in the treaty, stipulating that verification may be undertaken by any state party using its own means or with the full or partial assistance of any other party (Article III, para. 5).

The reluctance to resort to the optional aid of the technologically advanced states and to rely for security on such uncertain factors as good will, availability of equipment, or the changing circumstances of the world situation brought about demands from many states for the internationalization of control. Some urged the setting up of a special body responsible for the observance of the Seabed Treaty prohibitions. Others envisaged the use of existing international organizations for channelling verification requests. Canada suggested recourse to good offices, including those of the UN Secretary-General, in identifying the state responsible for activities giving rise to concern relating to compliance with the treaty, as well as in arranging assistance in carrying out verification procedures.[24] Still others understood internationalization only as providing a possibility to call upon the UN Security Council to settle disputes over verification.

The USA and the USSR considered it needless and in any event premature and wasteful of resources to require special international arrangements for carrying out control or the turning over of verification functions to the United Nations. They believed that reliance should be placed on consultation and co-operation but conceded that, if consultation and co-operation had not removed the doubts and there remained a serious question concerning fulfilment of the obligations assumed under the treaty, a state party might refer the matter to the UN Security Council for action in accordance with the UN Charter (Article III, para. 4). Nevertheless, the non-aligned countries continued to insist on the inclusion in the text of at least some reference to the possibility of international verification. This insistence was probably not directly related to the requirements of the Seabed Treaty. No one expected that there would be much need for verification. What appeared to matter was the establishment of a principle to be followed in arms control agreements of greater importance. Finally, it was agreed that verification might be undertaken also 'through appropriate international procedures within the framework of the United Nations' (Article III, para. 5).

As regards the nature of verification, the right of each state to observe was taken for granted, but it was felt that the right to verify would be deprived of substance if it were limited to observation. A number of countries insisted on access without restriction, so that dubious installations may be not only 'looked at' but also 'looked into'. They also asked that the parties be obliged to disclose their activities on the seabed.

The Soviet Union was in favour of access to the relevant facilities, similar to access provided under the Antarctic Treaty. The United States maintained that a right to go into a facility emplaced on the seabed or to open up equipment for the purpose of verifying whether nuclear weapons had not been installed there would be both difficult to exercise and unnecessary. Under the freedom of the high seas, parties could approach the area of a facility or an object, as long as they did not interfere with the activities of the states concerned. Emplacements for nuclear weapons on the scale required to be of significant military value would be difficult to build without the knowledge of other countries. The placement of such installations would require a great deal of sophisticated material, unusual engineering activities and a highly visible support effort also on the surface of the sea. In addition, the deploying country would obviously try to develop security systems to protect the military secrets of such installations. All this would attract the attention of other maritime countries. The USA held that the configuration and operation of facilities specifically designed for nuclear weapons and other weapons of mass destruction would be conspicuous and identifiable.

Following compromise proposals made by Brazil, Canada[25] and a number of other countries, the USA and the USSR agreed on and wrote into the treaty a procedure which can be summarized as follows. Each party shall have the right to verify through observation the activities of other parties on the seabed and the ocean floor and in the subsoil thereof beyond the seabed zone, provided that observation does not interfere with such activities. If after such observation reasonable doubts remain concerning the fulfilment of the obligations assumed under the treaty, the party having such doubts and the party responsible for the activities giving rise to the doubts shall consult with a view to removing them. If the doubts persist, the party having such doubts shall notify other parties, and the parties concerned shall co-operate on such further procedures for verification as may be agreed, including appropriate inspection of objects, structures, installations or other facilities that reasonably may be expected to be of a kind prohibited by the treaty. If the state responsible for the activities giving rise to the reasonable doubts is not identifiable by observation of the object, structure, installation or other facility, the party having such doubts 'shall notify and make appropriate inquiries of States Parties in the region of the activities and of any other State Party. If it is ascertained through these inquiries that a particular State Party is responsible for the activities, that State Party shall consult and cooperate with other Parties' as provided above. If the identity of the state responsible for the activities cannot be ascertained through these inquiries, then further verification procedures, including inspection, may be undertaken by the inquiring party (Article III, paras 1–3).

The extent of inspection envisaged in the treaty has not been spelled out. The formula employed poses a problem of how to proceed if the identity of the state responsible for the activities giving rise to doubts became known only after the inspection had been initiated, and if the state in question proved to be a non-party to the treaty.

VI. Implementation

The Seabed Treaty entered into force on 18 May 1972, and by 1 June 1989 had been joined by 82 nations and other political entities. (For the list of parties, see annexe B.)

Upon signing or ratifying the treaty, certain states made reservations to ensure that their rights under the law of the sea were not adversely affected, or to reiterate the points of view that had not been taken into account during the negotiating process.[26] Thus, Argentina stated that, in its understanding, the reference to the rights of exploration and exploitation by coastal states over their continental shelves (Article III, para. 6) was included solely because these could be the rights most frequently affected by verification procedures; it precluded any possibility of strengthening, through the Seabed Treaty, certain positions concerning continental shelves to the detriment of others based on different criteria. Brazil stressed that nothing in the treaty should be interpreted as prejudicing in any way its sovereign rights in the area of the sea, the seabed and the subsoil thereof adjacent to its coasts; in its understanding, the word 'observation', appearing in connection with verification (Article III, para. 1), refers only to observation that is incidental to the normal course of navigation in accordance with international law.

Yugoslavia made an interpretative declaration a few months after the deposit of its instrument of ratification. In its view, the article which deals with verification through observation should be interpreted in such a way that a state exercising its right under this article is obliged to notify in advance the coastal state, in so far as its observations are to be carried out 'within the stretch of the sea extending above the continental shelf of the said State'. The USA and the UK rejected this interpretation and placed on record their formal objection to the Yugoslav reservation on the grounds that it was incompatible with the object and purpose of the Seabed Treaty. The Federal Republic of Germany stated that the declaration by Yugoslavia is not of a nature to confer on the government of this country more far-reaching rights than those to which it is entitled under current international law.

In joining the treaty, Canada, India and Mexico reserved the right to verify, inspect, remove or destroy any weapon, structure, installation, facility or device placed by other countries on or beneath their continental shelves beyond the outer limit of the seabed zone.

Italy pointed out that, in the case of agreement on further measures in the field of disarmament relating to the seabed, the question of the delimitation of the area within which these measures would find application would have to be examined and solved in each instance in accordance with the nature of the measures to be adopted. This was a reference to the proposal which had been put forward by Italy during the negotiations on the Seabed Treaty but which was not accepted—namely, that weapon-emplacement prohibitions should apply beyond a curve corresponding to a depth of 200 metres.

The Seabed Treaty provides for a periodic review of its operation with a view to ensuring that its purposes and provisions are being realized; the review must take into account the 'relevant technological developments'. As a matter of fact, the main task of the first two review conferences (held in 1977 and 1983) has been to examine the effects of developments in underwater and weapon technology on the military uses of the ocean floor and the implications of such developments for efforts aimed at controlling all types of arms on the seabed. However, such examination has proved impossible. The superpowers which both possess sophisticated underwater technologies and military resources, and which are in a position to identify developments that might affect the purposes and provisions of the treaty, have not made available such information.

The participants in the review conferences stated that the parties had 'faithfully' observed their obligations. However, since no charges of treaty violation had been made, the effectiveness and practicability of the verification procedures, as set out in the treaty, have remained untested.

VII. Assessment

The Seabed Treaty binds only the superpowers. A prohibition on placing nuclear weapons on the bottom of the sea cannot be a restraint on the military activities of countries which have formally renounced acquisition of such weapons under the 1968 Non-Proliferation Treaty, or of those other countries which, while having nuclear weapons, may not have the means to conduct the banned nuclear activities on a significant scale. Neither do these countries possess resources to place other weapons of mass destruction on the seabed, even if such activities made military sense, which could hardly be the case. One issue that directly engages non-nuclear weapon states is the question of non-nuclear military installations. However, this question has not been covered by the treaty.

The arms control value of the Seabed Treaty is rather low. Nuclear installations on the seabed, once considered a possibility, have proved to be unattractive to the military. They would be extremely costly, very difficult to maintain and control and, above all, vulnerable and redundant. The placing of other weapons of mass destruction on the seabed is even less probable. The treaty banned something which did not exist and which, even without a prohibition, was not likely to be developed. In view of its limited scope and geographic coverage, it is much less important as a preventive or non-armament measure than the Antarctic Treaty, the Treaty of Tlatelolco or the Treaty of Rarotonga, described in section I of this paper. And since it permits the use of the seabed for facilities servicing free-swimming nuclear weapon systems, it presents no obstacle to a nuclear arms race in the entire sea environment.

VIII. Possible further action

The parties to the Seabed Treaty have undertaken to continue negotiations 'in good faith' concerning further measures in the field of disarmament for the prevention of an arms race on the seabed, the ocean floor and the subsoil thereof (Article V). No such negotiations have as yet taken place.

A first and relatively easy step to render the Seabed Treaty more meaningful would be to extend the prohibitions it contains to the entire seabed environment 'from shore to shore'. For it is precisely beneath the territorial waters, where nuclearization of the seabed is still allowed, that the technological and other restrictions that have impeded plans for missile deployment on the seabed are less severe. The area of application could even be enlarged to comprise the beds of all inland waters. This would amount to transforming the bilateral US–Soviet commitment in the unratified SALT II Treaty into a multilateral obligation and could be achieved by amending the Seabed Treaty or by adding a protocol to it.

Several proposals were made related to conventional underwater armaments. In 1969 Canada advanced a concept of a 200-nautical mile zone extending from the outer limits of a 12-nautical mile coastal band in which only the coastal state, or another state acting with its explicit consent, would be able to perform the defensive activities not prohibited by the Seabed Treaty. Nigeria preferred a 50-nautical mile zone for similar purposes. In the UN Seabed Committee, a few Latin American states in 1973 expressed the view that the emplacement of any kinds of facility on the seabed of the 'adjacent area' should be subject to authorization and regulation by the coastal state; and at the 1974 Law of the Sea Conference in Caracas, Kenya and Mexico, with the support of some other countries, formally proposed that no state should be entitled to construct, maintain, deploy or operate on or over the continental shelf of another state any military installations or devices or any other installations for whatever purposes without the consent of the coastal state. None of these suggestions became the subject of negotiations.

Considering the ban on the emplacement of nuclear weapons and other weapons of mass destruction beyond a 12-nautical mile seabed zone under the Seabed Treaty, it is difficult to see what kinds of conventional weapon could be safely emplanted on the continental shelf of other states. Shore-bombardment weapons and installations from which manned incursions could be mounted against a coastal state were mentioned in the debate on the Seabed Treaty, but the military value of such costly offensive systems would be doubtful, given their detectability and the need to protect them. Devices monitoring communications of the coastal state and/or capable of disrupting them, submarine navigation systems, devices monitoring the entrance or exit of submarines and surface ships to and from harbours as well as instruments designed to render ineffective the surveillance and defences of another state would appear to be more useful. These devices and instruments would be more autonomous than weapon systems but would still pose problems of information transmission and power supply. They would also be sensitive to possible countermeasures. Nevertheless, technical difficulties can be overcome, and it might be found worthwhile, under certain circumstances, to take the risks inherent in operations conducted far from the shores of the emplanting state.

Military installations in the proximity of other states cannot be justified on the grounds that they serve the defence interests of the state emplacing them, even if the installations are not of a patently offensive nature. It would therefore seem useful to establish a seabed security zone adjacent to the coast, in which the coastal state would have the exclusive right to mount military equipment or other devices for military purposes without obstructing international navigation. The zone would have to be sufficiently large to generate a sense of security among nations.

A related arms control measure which appears to be overdue concerns sea mines. It is clear that sea mines can be employed both for offensive and defensive purposes; their complete prohibition outside the context of general disarmament is therefore hardly conceivable. However, their use is regulated by the general principles of international customary law, which are supplemented by specific norms of the conventional humanitarian law of armed conflict. The relevant principles of customary law are those regarding the protection of the civilian population, including those prohibiting action expected to cause incidental losses or injuries, as well as damage to civilian objects, or denial of objects which are indispensable for the survival of the population. As regards conventional law, there is only one international multilateral treaty dealing with sea mines: Hague Convention VIII of 1907.

This Hague Convention forbids the laying of unanchored mines, except when they are so constructed as to become harmless 'one hour at most after the person who laid them ceases to control them'. It also prohibits laying anchored mines which do not become harmless as soon as they have broken loose from their moorings, or laying them off the coast and ports of the enemy with the 'sole object' of intercepting commercial shipping. The Hague rules refer only to 'automatic contact mines', one of the two types in existence at the turn of the century, the other being mines for close-in protection of harbours, controlled and detonated from a shore facility, and comparatively non-controversial. An updating of these rules would seem to be in order. There is no good reason why the scope of restrictions should not be widened to cover modern mines (including nuclear ones), those relying on magnetic, acoustic or pressure effects, or a combination thereof. It would be essential to provide for a careful recording of location and technical characteristics of the deployed sea mines to facilitate subsequent clearance operations. The new norms could be introduced through an additional protocol to the 1981 Convention Prohibiting or Restricting Conventional Weapons Deemed to be Excessively Injurious or to Have Indiscriminate Effects (the 'Inhumane Weapons' Convention). Protocol II of this convention restricts the use of land mines. The anti-submarine warfare potential of states with respect to submarines carrying strategic ballistic missiles would also eventually have to be curbed so as not to upset the present strategic stability among the nuclear weapon powers.

Because of the rapid militarization of the seas, arms control measures limited to the seabed may lose their attraction. It is becoming increasingly evident that in order to devise significant restrictions on military activities in the oceans, with due account being taken of the security requirements of all states, the ocean environment must be treated as an indivisible whole.

Notes and references

[1] General Assembly Resolution 2340 (XXII) of 18 Dec. 1967.

[2] See the summary records of the *Ad Hoc* Committee to Study the Peaceful Use of the Seabed and the Ocean Floor beyond the Limits of National Jurisdiction, third session, 13th to 26th meetings (A/AC.135/SR.13–26, pp. 98–108; in particular A/AC.135/SR.20). See also United Nations, General Assembly, *Letter Dated 5 July 1968 from the Permanent Representative of the Union of Soviet Socialist Republics to the United Nations, addressed to the Secretary-General*, 8 July 1968.

[3] United Nations document A/AC.135/SR.13–26 (note 2), pp. 157–71.

[4] Conference of the Eighteen-Nation Committee on Disarmament, Union of Soviet Socialist Republics, *Draft Treaty on Prohibition of the Use for Military Purposes of the Seabed and the Ocean Floor and the Subsoil Thereof* (ENDC/240 of 18 Mar. 1969).

[5] Conference of the Eighteen-Nation Committee on Disarmament, United States of America, *Draft Treaty Prohibiting the Emplacement of Nuclear Weapons and Other Weapons of Mass Destruction on the Seabed and Ocean Floor* (ENDC/249 of 22 May 1969).

[6] In the summer of 1969 the membership of the Eighteen-Nation Committee on Disarmament was enlarged, and it was decided that the new name of the negotiating body would be the Conference of the Committee on Disarmament (CCD).

[7] Conference of the Committee on Disarmament, Union of Soviet Socialist Republics and United States of America, *Draft Treaty on the Prohibition of the Emplacement of Nuclear Weapons and Other Weapons of Mass Destruction on the Seabed and the Ocean Floor and in the Subsoil Thereof* (CCD/269 of 7 Oct. 1969), and revisions 1, 2 and 3; and CCD/317, annex A.

[8] General Assembly Resolution 2660 (XXV), annex, of 7 Dec. 1970.

[9] See *Official Records of the General Assembly, Twenty-fifth Session, First Committee*, 1754th meeting.

[10] See *Official Records of the General Assembly* (note 9), 1763rd meeting.

[11] United Nations document A/C.1/L.528.

[12] See note 9.

[13] See *Official Records of the General Assembly* (note 9), 1763rd and 1764th meetings.

[14] See note 1; and General Assembly Resolution 2467 (XXIII) of 21 Dec. 1968.

[15] See note 4.

[16] See note 5.

[17] UN document S/C.3/32.

[18] See notes 1 and 14; and General Assembly Resolution 2574 (XXIV) of 15 Dec. 1969.

[19] See note 4.

[20] See note 5.

[21] Conference of the Committee on Disarmament document CCD/PV.492.

[22] See note 4.

[23] See note 5.

[24] United Nations documents A/7741, annex A; and A/C.1/992.

[25] See note 24; and United Nations document A/C.1/993/Rev.1/Corr.1.

[26] See the *SIPRI Yearbooks* for such statements and reservations, e.g., SIPRI, *SIPRI Yearbook 1989: World Armaments and Disarmament* (Oxford University Press: Oxford, 1989), annexe A, esp. pp. 495–503.

Part V
Confidence-building measures

Paper 11. Applying and extending the USA–USSR Incidents at Sea Agreement

Sean M. Lynn-Jones

Center for Science and International Affairs, Harvard University, Cambridge, Massachusetts, USA

I. Introduction

The 1972 USA–USSR Agreement on the Prevention of Incidents on and over the High Seas[1] is widely regarded as a success. In its 18 years of operation, the agreement has reduced the frequency and severity of superpower naval incidents while building greater trust and confidence at sea. It has served as the model for two similar bilateral agreements—one in 1986 between the USSR and the UK, and one in 1988 between the USSR and the Federal Republic of Germany. At a time when improved US–Soviet relations, economic constraints and progress in ongoing arms control efforts all have focused renewed attention on the question of naval arms control, it is appropriate to consider how this agreement might serve as a useful precedent for further agreements.

This paper examines the question of extending the USA–USSR Incidents at Sea Agreement to cover other countries. After a brief review of the problems posed by naval incidents, it discusses the negotiation and operation of the agreement. The 1986 UK–USSR Incidents at Sea Agreement is also considered, as is the 1988 FRG–USSR Agreement. Finally, the possibilities for multilateral or bilateral extensions or applications of the USA–USSR Agreement are examined and assessed.

II. The 1972 USA–USSR Incidents at Sea Agreement

The risks of naval incidents

The 1972 USA–USSR Incidents at Sea Agreement was negotiated to reduce the number of potentially dangerous confrontations between the US and Soviet navies. As the Soviet Navy grew during the 1960s, incidents involving US and Soviet warships became increasingly frequent. These incidents included various dangerous manoeuvres in which ships violated the letter or the spirit of the International Regulations for Preventing Collisions at Sea (Rules of the Road).[2] In such incidents, US or Soviet warships would engage in what former US Chief of Naval Operations Admiral Elmo Zumwalt has called 'an extremely dangerous, but exhilarating, running game of "chicken"',[3] attempting to force other vessels to take evasive action to avoid imminent collisions. Soviet vessels would frequently disrupt flight operations of US aircraft-carriers by manoeuvring in front of a carrier as it launched or landed aircraft. Such actions often exploited ambiguities in the Rules of the Road, which were designed to govern civilian vessels, not military operations. Other incidents at sea included close air surveillance ('buzzing'), simulated attacks with weapons or sensor systems, harassment with flares or searchlights and accidental firing on vessels during naval exercises.

In some cases, naval incidents may be politically motivated, serving in effect as a form of gunboat diplomacy. Soviet harassment of US vessels, for example, may be intended to demonstrate Soviet naval capabilities to the US Navy or to signal displeasure over US naval deployments in areas close to Soviet waters (see paper 2). More frequently, however, incidents probably have been the result of the excessive zeal or incompetence of naval officers.[4] Admiral Zumwalt has argued that ship captains bear the primary responsibility for naval incidents: 'It was always my opinion that the leadership on both sides was less anxious to play the kind of game I have described than peppery young ship captains were'.[5]

Regardless of the motivation behind or cause of naval incidents, the 1972 Agreement to prevent them was based on a shared perception of their dangers. Although the US and Soviet navies have not made public the exact number of incidents in the late 1960s or early 1970s, there were probably at least 100.[6] Dangerous manoeuvres create the possibility of collisions in which ships and/or lives could be lost. Former US Secretary of the Navy John Warner has said that the two superpowers 'were just waiting for an accident to happen during this period'.[7] Luckily, few US–Soviet incidents seemed to have led to loss of life or the sinking of ships.[8] Nevertheless, US naval officers have stressed the threat to human life and ships when discussing the risks of incidents at sea.[9]

Naval incidents also have the potential to raise US–Soviet tensions and the risk of war. Even if it were a relatively minor event in itself, an ill-timed incident could needlessly disrupt negotiations, much as the U-2 incident of 1960 forced the cancellation of a Khrushchev–Eisenhower summit meeting. During a crisis or conditions of extreme tension, a naval incident could even escalate to actual combat if some form of harassment were to be interpreted as a sign of imminent attack. The proximity of US and Soviet naval forces during a crisis would enable either to launch an attack from point-blank range without advance warning. A nervous naval commander might view actions such as the training of fire-control radars on his vessel as the prelude to an attack. Under conditions of extreme tension, he might resort to countermeasures or a pre-emptive attack. A dangerous spiral of escalation could be initiated by various forms of harassment and counter-harassment. Confusion and uncertainty—both of which could be widespread during an acute crisis—might lead to inadvertent hostilities in which shots were fired and ships sunk or damaged. Although such a scenario is unlikely, it may be more probable that US–Soviet war could erupt at sea rather than on land.[10]

Provisions of the agreement

Recognition of these dangers eventually led the United States and the Soviet Union to negotiate their Incidents at Sea Agreement in 1971–72. The USA originally proposed negotiations in 1967, but the USSR did not respond until 1970. After the Moscow and Washington negotiating sessions involving high-level US and Soviet naval delegations, the agreement was signed at the 1972 Moscow summit meeting.[11] The agreement seeks to limit the number and dangers of naval incidents through (a) regulation of dangerous manoeuvres, (b) restriction of other forms of harassment, (c) increased communication at sea, and (d) convening regular naval consultations and exchanges of information.

1. *Regulation of dangerous manoeuvres.* The agreement reaffirms the Rules of the Road, and Article II specifically requires ships to remain well clear of one another to avoid hindering the evolution of formations, and to show particular care in approaching ships engaged in launching or landing aircraft, as well as ships engaged in underway replenishment.

2. *Restriction of other harassment.* Articles II and IV of the agreement also prohibit simulated attacks[12] or the launching of objects in the direction of passing ships of the other party, the use of searchlights to illuminate navigation bridges, the performance of 'various aerobatics'[13] over ships and the dropping of various objects that would be hazardous to ships or constitute a hazard to navigation. This last provision apparently reflects Soviet concern over the US practice of dropping sonar buoys from aircraft,[14] but the ambiguous wording probably allows the United States to continue to act as it did before the agreement. It is always possible to claim that the sonar buoys did not actually endanger safe navigation.

3. *Increased communication at sea.* Article III of the agreement requires the use of internationally recognized signals to convey information about operations and intentions and to warn ships of the presence of submarines in an area. Article V requires both parties to use signals to announce the commencement of flight operations and mandates that aircraft flying over the high seas display navigation lights 'whenever feasible'. Finally, Article VI requires three to five days' advance notification of actions (naval exercises or missile test launches) on the high seas that represent a danger to navigation or to aircraft and requires increased use of special informative signals to signify intentions of vessels manoeuvring in close proximity to one another. These signals convey messages such as 'I am testing my gun systems' and 'dangerous operations in progress'.[15] These provisions reduce the danger of accidental attacks during exercises and limit the possibility of collisions arising from misunderstanding or misinterpretation.

4. *Regular consultations and information exchanges.* Article VII stipulates that the Soviet and US naval attachés in each other's capitals shall serve as the channel for the exchange of information concerning incidents and collisions. This provision may help to minimize the diplomatic consequences of incidents

at sea by ensuring that such matters are handled quietly and primarily by the two navies.[16] During the negotiations the USSR was apparently pleased that incidents could be discussed between 'brothers at sea'; this type of attitude may provide a basis for fruitful exchanges on the details of any incidents. Article IX provides that the United States and the Soviet Union shall conduct annual reviews of the agreement. Article X specifically establishes a committee to meet within six months to 'consider the practical workability of concrete fixed distances to be observed in encounters between ships, aircraft, and ships and aircraft'.[17]

US and Soviet negotiators did not reach any agreement on a distance formula, although the USSR continues to raise the issue, and both countries have agreed to study it further at the annual reviews of the agreement.[18] Subsequent negotiations did, however, produce a Protocol to the original agreement on 22 May 1973.[19] The Protocol extends some applicable provisions of the 1972 Agreement to non-military ships. Article I states that measures shall be taken to notify non-military ships of each party of the provisions of the agreement directed at mutual safety. Article II prohibits simulated attacks on non-military ships and the dropping of objects near them in a hazardous manner. The Protocol seems to be a logical extension of the original agreement, as several US–Soviet incidents at sea have involved merchant or fishing vessels. Although the Protocol obviously is meant to safeguard the non-military ships of both parties, it may confer somewhat greater benefits on the Soviet Union. Its provisions could serve to protect Soviet trawlers or other non-military vessels that actually serve some military purpose, particularly intelligence collection and surveillance. Moreover, the large and growing Soviet merchant fleet is more exposed to Western harassment. The bulk of Soviet merchant and fishing vessels operate in waters that can be controlled by the West, whereas only an insignificant portion of US shipping is usually found in Soviet-controlled waters.[20]

Assessing the agreement

Most observers, including the US Navy, regard the Incidents at Sea Agreement as a success.[21] The Soviet Navy has expanded since the early 1970s, and the US Navy has engaged in more forward operations near the Soviet coasts. As a result, superpower fleets now conduct operations in close proximity to one another on every ocean. In 1983, John Lehman, then US Secretary of the Navy, noted that 'the Soviet fleet now is virtually everywhere our operations are, where our exercising is. We are also where they do most of their exercising and deploying'.[22] Nevertheless, the number and severity of incidents appear to have declined. US officials have pointed out that 'each year we've seen basically a decrease in the number of incidents'.[23] The most dangerous manoeuvres and attempts to disrupt formations are no longer commonplace.

Numbers alone, however, may not tell the whole story. The USA–USSR Agreement is also intended to resolve questions about incidents, as well as to prevent them. When incidents do occur, they are resolved by the US and Soviet navies through the channels established by the agreement. Naval commanders are less likely to retaliate on their own, thereby provoking further incidents. The existence of established channels also reduces the likelihood that incidents will become diplomatic controversies. Lehman has said that the annual meetings to review the accord have produced a 'stable pattern' of dealing with incidents and that they provide 'pretty good resolution'[24] of any disputes in a 'rather businesslike' manner.[25]

US–Soviet naval interaction in the October 1973 Arab–Israeli War provides a good example of the rapid positive impact of the agreement. The USSR deployed a peak of 96 vessels during the war, confronting a slightly smaller number of US ships.[26] Despite the heightened political tensions and the increased probability of incidents owing to the proximity of so many hostile vessels, incidents were relatively rare. Some Soviet warships trained guns or searchlights on US vessels, fired flares near US aircraft or engaged in close manoeuvring. However, as Stephen Roberts notes, these actions were probably 'clumsy efforts at reconnaissance' or were performed for 'operational reasons'. The 'gun movements (which tended to occur around 8:00 AM)' may have been 'routine checks of equipment'. On the whole, Soviet ships observed the agreement and avoided harassment of their US counterparts.[27] Admiral Worth Bagley, Commander-in-Chief of US Naval Forces in Europe at the time, remarked that the 'Soviets weren't overly aggressive. It looked as though they were taking some care not to cause an incident'.[28]

Soviet assessments of the agreement also indicate that it has been a success. In 1981, Captain Valentin Serkov wrote in *Morskoy Sbornik*:

Nine years have elapsed since the aforesaid agreement was signed and put into effect. In that comparatively short time the safety of sea navigation and overflight has noticeably improved, and the role of the norms and principles of international law has grown greater in dealings between the two Navies on the high seas. The number of serious incidents between ships and aircraft of the two countries have been curtailed.[29]

Although Serkov went on to note that 'regular, professional contact has been established between representatives of the two Navies', he also pointed out that 'there have been certain negative phenomena' and reiterated the Soviet belief that a distance formula would be effective. He concluded that naval commanders needed to display 'undeviating observance of the provisions of the said Agreement'.[30]

The agreement was never entirely insulated from the overall state of US–Soviet relations. US naval commanders report that the Soviet Union tends to engage in more harassment when superpower relations deteriorate. Nevertheless, the agreement has continued to function despite the decline of the *détente* that provided the atmosphere for the negotiation of the agreement. The

1980 annual review took place in Moscow, despite the suspension of most other US–Soviet contacts after the Soviet invasion of Afghanistan.

Events of the mid-1980s, however, seemed to suggest that the agreement was not faring so well. A spate of incidents received widespread media attention in 1983 and 1984. Soviet vessels interfered with salvage operations by US and allied vessels in the Sea of Japan following the downing of the Korean airliner in 1983, making low passes over ships, dashing at US salvage vessels to force them to change course and running parallel to them to drown out signals from US underwater listening equipment.[31] A Soviet guided-missile frigate apparently attempted to disrupt flight operations of the US aircraft-carrier *Ranger* in the Arabian Sea before colliding with the US frigate *Fife* in November 1983.[32]

Additional incidents were reported in early 1984. In March, a Soviet Victor-I Class submarine running without lights collided with the US carrier *Kitty Hawk* in the Sea of Japan. Although the carrier was not seriously damaged, the submarine was apparently disabled. The US Navy began an inquiry to determine whether the Soviet submarine was at fault, although Lehman indicated that the collision appeared to be 'inadvertent'.[33] Several days later, the Soviet carrier *Minsk* fired eight flares at the US frigate *Harold E. Holt*. Three hit the US vessel, including one that passed within 3 feet of the captain. The *Holt* was within 30 yards of the *Minsk*, which had stopped for unexplained reasons. The *Holt* had apparently signalled that it planned to pass the *Minsk* on the starboard side and did so despite several warnings from the Soviet vessel. The US Navy decided to raise the incident at the annual meeting in May 1984.[34]

These incidents do not necessarily signal the demise of the agreement. Soviet vessels in the Sea of Japan may have been reacting to the extraordinary tension that followed the downing of the Korean airliner, or they may have been attempting to prevent the United States from recovering the aircraft's flight recorder. US naval officials believe that the harassment was politically motivated, at least in part because of the proximity to Soviet borders and bases. Even under these circumstances, the agreement apparently helped to limit Soviet harassment. Admiral Sylvester R. Foley, Jr, then Commander of the US Pacific Fleet, recalls that during the search the Soviets 'gave us trouble and hassled us, and we said, "If the Incidents at Sea Agreement means anything, cut it out," and they did'.[35] The collisions with the *Fife* and the *Kitty Hawk* and the firing of flares at the *Holt* were all potentially dangerous incidents, but Lehman stated that he believed that relations between the US and Soviet fleets are still 'very professional and workmanlike'. Commenting on the *Minsk* incident, he said: 'I don't see anything sinister in the incident with the *Minsk*. Let's say there are two plausible sides to that story. The *Minsk* skipper may not have been all on the wrong side'.[36] Other senior US officials have reaffirmed that the incidents of 1983 and 1984 have not changed their interpretation of Soviet behaviour, arguing that the 'Soviets have made it very clear that they believe in the Incidents at Sea agreement. They want it to continue. They want it to work. They want to live up to it'.[37]

The May 1984 meeting in Moscow of US and Soviet representatives to review the agreement provided further evidence of its success. The talks were reportedly conducted in an open, frank and professional manner. Admiral James Watkins, then US Chief of Naval Operations, said that the session was 'well run' and drew a 'higher caliber' of Soviet officer.[38] Each side acknowledged the concerns of the other and avoided political rhetoric and unreasonable demands. A State Department participant is said to have been amazed by the contrast between the frankness and professionalism of the naval talks and normal US–Soviet diplomatic intercourse.[39] US naval officers, who said that the sessions were the best such meetings in memory, and their Soviet counterparts formally renewed the agreement for three years.[40] Announcing this renewal to a conference on US–Soviet exchanges, President Ronald Reagan described the agreement as 'useful'. In addition, the Soviet delegation reportedly proposed extending the principles of the agreement to cover additional activities of military aircraft.[41]

Ironically, the successful 1984 meeting was followed by the postponement of the 1985 meeting for political reasons. The annual meeting was scheduled to be held in Washington, but US Secretary of Defense Caspar Weinberger decided to shorten the meeting and cancel all its social events in retaliation for the killing of US Major Arthur Nicholson by a Soviet sentry in the German Democratic Republic. The USSR then informed the US State Department that it would not attend. Several Reagan Administration officials reported that Weinberger's decision was taken without consulting Secretary of State George Shultz or the then National Security Adviser, Robert McFarlane.[42] Senator John Warner, who had signed the agreement in 1972 when he was Secretary of the Navy, argued: 'We should not link the operation of the agreement to problems elsewhere in the world'.[43] The US Navy also opposed the changes in the schedule of the meetings, suggesting that Weinberger's decision reflected political considerations, not any problems with the agreement itself. Admiral Watkins later said: 'We like the sessions. They like the sessions. . . . It is important that we get back to the table'.[44] The two countries reached agreement in November 1985 on resuming the annual meetings and held the delayed meeting that month. The annual meetings since 1986 have been held on schedule (the 1986 and 1988 meetings in Moscow and the 1987 and 1989 meetings in Washington), without incident and without publicity. The general atmosphere of these meetings has improved along with the general improvement in US–Soviet relations.

Explaining the success of the agreement

The relative ease with which the USA–USSR Agreement was negotiated can be attributed in large measure to the climate of *détente* that prevailed in the early

1970s. This general state of good relations probably increased the US and Soviet incentives for an agreement, although it is difficult to find specific connections between the negotiations and the political atmosphere. The improvement in US–Soviet relations may have influenced the Soviet decision to accept the US offer to negotiate in 1970—more than two years after the United States had made its initial proposal. Senior officers of both navies may have believed that negotiating the agreement not only served their interests but also enabled them to demonstrate their support for the general strategy of *détente* pursued by the political leadership in both countries. Finally, the emergence of *détente* may have encouraged high-level political involvement in the preparations for the talks and support for an agreement.

The negotiation of the agreement may also be attributable to complementary US and Soviet interests that emerged in the early 1970s. The Soviet Union may have seen the agreement as a recognition of its status as the equal of the US Navy on the high seas.[45] After a period of marked inferiority in which they harassed US vessels to make their presence felt,[46] the Soviet Navy may have decided to seek the agreement as a symbolic recognition of parity on the world's oceans. The United States, on the other hand, would have no need for a recognition of its status but would have an interest in reducing Soviet harassment of US vessels. As the location of US allies and naval bases makes it more likely that US warships will find themselves operating in or near Soviet 'home waters', the United States may have had a greater interest in restricting dangerous manoeuvres and harassment.

Although the fortuitous circumstances of the early 1970s may have contributed to the negotiation and signing of the Incidents at Sea Agreement, the shared US–Soviet interest in avoiding the dangers of accidents or escalation has unquestionably played the major role in sustaining the agreement. Given that the United States and the Soviet Union each have large, ocean-going navies, there will be frequent encounters between their fleets on the high seas. Increases in the size of the fleets of the two superpowers and the tendency of both to conduct naval operations further from their own shores have in recent years strengthened their incentives for adherence to the agreement. In 1987, US Chief of Naval Operations Admiral Carlisle Trost told the US Congress that US Navy ships and aircraft 'track Soviet submarines trailing our warships and escort Soviet planes flying near our battlegroups on a daily basis'.[47]

The successful operation of the agreement has also been helped by the navy-to-navy nature of its implementation. One US admiral points out that the professional officers of each navy may be able to communicate more effectively with one another than with other agencies of their own governments.[48] Another claims that 'mariners have a common bond'.[49] Because the agreement is implemented largely by the two navies, it can generally be insulated from political considerations. Neither the US nor the Soviet Navy has an interest in exploiting the agreement for propaganda purposes. Indeed, the US

Navy appears to believe that the absence of publicity contributes to the success of the agreement and has done little to call attention to it since 1972.[50]

Both navies appear to have internalized and institutionalized the norms reaffirmed by the agreement. The regime for naval incidents appears to have acquired its own momentum. Representatives of the US and Soviet navies reaffirm the agreement from time to time and, at least in the USA, the Navy now seems to be the most vigorous defender of the agreement. Both navies have published the agreement and circulated it among their fleets. The special signals devised by the agreement are posted on the bridge of every US and Soviet surface naval vessel.

The prominent role of the US Navy in negotiating and implementing the agreement probably accounts for the absence of some of the usual obstacles to arms control in the United States. The extensive and high-level participation of US naval representatives in the actual negotiations may have helped to reduce any fears that the agreement might prevent the US Navy from performing what it sees as its vital missions. Although the US Navy initially feared that the Soviet offer to open negotiations was a ruse to establish zones in which anti-submarine warfare (ASW) would be prohibited, naval representatives were able to ensure that the US stance in the talks would rule out any such accord. The US delegation refused to entertain the possibility of any agreement that might restrict the traditional principle of freedom of the seas by limiting the geographical scope of submarine or surface deployments. Naval satisfaction with the process and outcome of the negotiations may have helped the Incidents at Sea Agreement to avoid the domestic controversy provoked by the SALT agreements and other US attempts to negotiate arms control with the Soviet Union. Moreover, because the agreement is not a treaty but an executive agreement, it was not subjected to a public ratification debate in the US Senate.

Limits of the agreement

Although the 1972 USA–USSR Incidents at Sea Agreement has generally been successful, it is not without limits. First, it has not prevented incidents entirely. Naval confrontations continue to involve actions that appear to violate the agreement. For example, in February 1988 two Soviet Navy ships collided with two US ships in the Black Sea in a dispute over innocent passage in Soviet territorial waters. Even if the US and Soviet navies have been able to resolve questions arising from such incidents, the threat of accident or escalation still exists. Nevertheless, a few naval incidents do not mean that the agreement has failed. There are important benefits from reducing the number of incidents and from providing regular procedures to deal with incidents that do arise. The agreement itself operates on the implicit assumption that some possible violations will occur and provides a set of procedures for their resolution.

Second, the agreement does little to prevent incidents such as the 1987 Iraqi attack on the *USS Stark* or the 1967 Israeli attack on the *USS Liberty*. If a

Soviet ship or aircraft incorrectly identified a US vessel, the Incidents at Sea Agreement would not prevent the US ship from coming under a possible attack. The question of how to react to potential threats of imminent hostilities is a question of rules of engagement.[51] The Incidents at Sea Agreement can regulate only actions that might seem hostile or give rise to a misunderstanding; it does not eliminate the possibility of misidentification. Fortunately, however, US and Soviet naval commanders generally have acted with extreme prudence and remain subject to central control.[52]

Third, the USA–USSR Agreement does not apply to submarines when they are submerged. Because the essence of many—if not all—submarine operations is stealth, they were excluded from the agreement. Even if the US and Soviet negotiators had wanted to regulate submarine encounters, it is hard to imagine how systems of signals could be devised, as they were for surface ships. Several US–Soviet underwater incidents have taken place. There have been a number of collisions between US and Soviet submarines, some of which were carrying nuclear weapons. Some of these collisions even have been in Soviet territorial waters.[53]

III. Extending the Incidents at Sea Agreement

Given the apparent success of the USA–USSR Incidents at Sea Agreement, it has been argued that the agreement should be extended to cover the naval forces of other countries. Collisions, near-misses and other incidents have not been confined to the US and Soviet navies. In 1970, the British aircraft-carrier *Ark Royal* collided with a Soviet destroyer in the Mediterranean Sea, killing at least two Soviet seamen.[54] In June 1987, the West German Navy tender *Neckar* was hit by shells from a Polish naval vessel while observing Warsaw Pact manoeuvres in the Baltic Sea.[55] Incidents involving navies other than those of the United States and the Soviet Union may not pose the same dangers of escalation as superpower incidents, but they have the potential to cause damage and loss of life, to heighten political tensions and to increase the chances of inadvertent hostilities in a crisis.

There are two ways in which the USA–USSR Incidents at Sea Agreement could be extended to other states. The first is the establishment of a multilateral regime that any state could join. The second would be the negotiation of additional bilateral agreements between pairs of maritime countries.

Towards a multilateral regime for incidents at sea?

A UN report prepared in 1985 on the naval arms race argued that 'consideration should be given to making multilateral the existing bilateral agreement between the Soviet Union and the United States'.[56] The Swedish Delegation to the UN General Assembly has conducted consultations and circulated a draft multilateral treaty on incidents at sea (see paper 12).[57] A multilateral regime might be established by opening the USA–USSR Agreement (or a similar document) for accession by other countries.[58] All states signing the agreement would agree to abide by its provisions regulating dangerous manoeuvres, restricting harassment and establishing better means of communication at sea. The special signals for US and Soviet vessels could be used by the navies of all states party to the agreement, thereby establishing a uniform system of communications for military vessels. Naval attachés or other diplomatic channels could be used to communicate protests, and annual meetings could be scheduled to discuss incidents between two particular countries.

A multilateral regime for incidents at sea might reduce the number of naval incidents. It also would have a norm-building function. A multilateral agreement incorporating restrictions on dangerous manoeuvres and harassment would probably give such regulations the same status as the Rules of the Road. The overall effect would be to build confidence on the high seas.

Nevertheless, a multilateral agreement would also suffer from some problems not experienced by the USA–USSR Agreement. The most basic problem with a multilateral regime is that the USA and the USSR would have reasons not to agree to it. The size, strength and frequent interaction of the US and Soviet navies have given both superpowers good reason to regulate their naval confrontations. Similar incentives would not exist between either superpower and many—perhaps most—smaller naval powers. Although they would be reluctant to admit it publicly, the United States and the Soviet Union might also want to retain the option of harassing vessels of other countries. It is difficult to imagine that the United States would want to enter into an incidents at sea agreement that included countries such as Libya and Cuba. However, the superpower navies might want to restrict third-country harassment of their vessels. The USA and the USSR would face a trade-off between restricting their freedom of action and limiting the potentially dangerous activities of smaller navies. Given the preponderance of the US and Soviet fleets, the two navies are not likely to favour limits on their actions, even if there is a strong political case to be made for applying the same standards of behaviour to all navies.[59]

A multilateral incidents at sea regime also would probably not provide all of the benefits of bilateral US–Soviet consultations. US naval officers have argued that the regular professional contact between the US and Soviet navies at the annual reviews of the USA–USSR Agreement has generated a greater sense of trust and understanding between the two navies. Such an atmosphere might be more difficult to attain in the absence of frequent and regular contact. Scheduling meetings to discuss a small number of incidents with a variety of countries would be a cumbersome, time-consuming process. If a multilateral regime followed the US–Soviet model, in which the naval attaché channel is used only to raise issues which would then be dealt with in detail at the annual meetings, such meetings would be necessary to resolve questions arising from incidents. The US–Soviet annual reviews have included frank exchanges of information on standard operating procedures.[60] It is doubtful whether either superpower would want to share such information with any country that happened to be involved in an incident with one of its ships. (Some countries might even provoke incidents on the grounds that achieving a meeting with the US or Soviet Navy would confer prestige or other political benefits.) A multilateral conference would probably offer a more convenient forum for discussing incidents, but the actual discussion would be constrained by the presence of representatives of many other countries. The US Navy would probably fear that a large conference would focus on attempts to limit superpower naval forces and activities.

Instead of a universal incidents at sea regime, regional agreements might be negotiated for areas in which incidents are frequent. In the Baltic Sea, for example, littoral states could regulate naval encounters. Such an arrangement would offer the potential for reducing dangerous incidents while avoiding some of the political problems that might accompany a universal agreement. In some cases, the United States and the Soviet Union might join a regional agreement for an area far from their own shores, but such agreements might also work without the participation of one or the other of the superpowers if much of the naval interaction were confined to vessels from states in the region.

Some advocates of a multilateral regime may hope that such an agreement would lead to additional naval arms control measures. In general, confidence-building measures such as incidents at sea agreements may help to produce later arms limitations, although the historical record does not support any clear conclusions on this point.[61] No US–Soviet naval arms control agreement followed in the wake of their bilateral Incidents at Sea Agreement, however. In 1972 the US and Soviet navies apparently were more interested in finding a solution to the problem of naval incidents than in seeking a broader naval arms control regime. Indeed, the fact that neither navy seemed interested in more sweeping arms control agreements may have increased their confidence in the negotiation and implementation of the Incidents at Sea Agreement, which they probably see more as naval *traffic* control than naval *arms* control.

Bilateral agreements

The principles of the Incidents at Sea Agreement might be extended to other countries through the negotiation of additional bilateral agreements. Such agreements would build on the precedent of the USA–USSR Agreement by regulating dangerous activities and establishing procedures for communication between navies. As of 1989, there have been two additional bilateral agreements, with more reported to be under discussion.

An Incidents at Sea Agreement was signed by the UK and the USSR in 1986.[62] While it is modelled on the USA–USSR Agreement, it also covers non-military vessels, thereby combining the original 1972 Agreement and the 1973 Protocol.[63] The UK–USSR Agreement also incorporates as an annex special signals for communication at sea. The signals are the same as those agreed upon by the United States and the Soviet Union but explicit reference is made to them in the agreement, whereas the USA–USSR Agreement left the actual discussion of signals to the two navies. The *Financial Times* acclaimed the agreement as 'perhaps the most significant accord' to emerge from Soviet Foreign Minister Eduard Shevardnadze's 1986 visit to the United Kingdom.[64]

The UK–USSR Agreement served as the model for an agreement between the USSR and the Federal Republic of Germany which was signed in 1988.[65] It is virtually identical to the UK–USSR Agreement and was motivated by the June 1987 West German–Polish naval incident. It took three days for Poland to communicate with the FRG about the incident and to admit responsibility.[66] The agreement provides for a standard communication link between the Navy of the Federal Republic of Germany and the WTO navies that was previously lacking.

The UK–USSR and FRG–USSR Agreements could serve as models for additional bilateral accords. By incorporating the same rules and signals used in the USA–USSR Agreement, they avoid the possible confusion that would arise from the negotiation of bilateral agreements with different terms. There is reportedly some discussion of a similar agreement between the Soviet Union and France.[67] A Sino-Soviet agreement might also be useful; Soviet and Chinese vessels have been involved in several near-collisions and have exchanged warning shots,[68] and both navies would appear to have an incentive to regulate this type of behaviour. Many bilateral agreements, however, would serve little purpose if the naval interaction between the two parties did not pose significant risks. Agreements entered into for purposes of political symbolism would not follow the precedent of the USA–USSR Agreement, which was a response to a real and growing problem. Even in the case of the existing UK–USSR Agreement, one wonders whether the political symbolism of such an accord was a factor in British and Soviet desires for an agreement, regardless of the level of risk posed by naval incidents.

IV. Conclusions

Not all of the factors that have contributed to the successful operation of the USA–USSR Incidents at Sea Agreement would exist in a universal naval incidents regime. Close navy-to-navy contacts would be more difficult to maintain. A global agreement would, however, have an important normative function in delegitimizing dangerous manoeuvres and harassment. Regional multilateral agreements would have a more limited normative function, but they might still be useful if they are negotiated between navies that frequently interact in the same area.

Bilateral agreements on naval incidents may have more direct utility, especially when they are between those naval powers that have large fleets that frequently interact. The USA–USSR Agreement has succeeded in part because of relatively unpublicized navy-to-navy contacts. Such a pattern of communication could best be replicated in a bilateral agreement.

The USA–USSR Incidents at Sea Agreement is both a model and an exception. In at least some cases, additional bilateral agreements can play a useful role in reducing the number and risks of naval incidents. A universal agreement, however, would be unlikely to incorporate the depoliticized, professional naval contacts that have characterized the USA–USSR Agreement. It could, however, lead to more widespread observance of the restrictions on dangerous activities that are included in the USA–USSR Agreement. For most countries, the problem of naval incidents will be of a much lesser order of magnitude than it was for the United States and the Soviet Union. Additional regional or bilateral agreements should not be expected to generate additional naval arms control agreements, but they may be useful when they address specific problems of naval interaction. On balance, there are many multilateral and bilateral approaches to regulating dangerous naval incidents that are worth pursuing.

Notes and references

[1] The complete text appears in annexe B.

[2] The Rules of the Road govern nautical lighting, manoeuvring and signalling procedures to ensure safe navigation.

[3] Zumwalt, Jr, E. R., *On Watch* (Quadrangle: New York, 1976), p. 391.

[4] It is difficult to assess the extent to which the seamanship of Soviet officers and crews played a role in naval incidents during the 1960s and early 1970s, but it is reasonable to assume that inexperience led to some incidents. Soviet captains must have lacked the ocean-going experience of their US counterparts, if only because the Soviet Navy had not had the capability to operate for long periods on the high seas. Many assessments of the Soviet Navy continue to emphasize that the quality and training of officers and crews fall below US standards. See, for example, Miller, C. E. and Papp, R. G., 'Soviet naval personnel and schools', eds B. W. Watson and S. M. Watson, *The Soviet Navy: Strengths and Liabilities* (Westview: Boulder, Colo., 1986), pp. 42–44.

[5] Zumwalt (note 3), p. 394.

[6] Transcript of news briefing by Secretary of the Navy John Lehman, 10 June 1983, mimeograph, p. 2.

[7] Quoted in Gordon, M. R., 'At sea', *National Journal*, 6 July 1985, p. 159.

[8] In May 1968, however, a Soviet Tu-16 bomber attempting to buzz US vessels crashed into the Norwegian Sea. See Wolfe, T. W., 'Soviet naval interaction with the United States and its influence on Soviet naval developments', ed. M. MccGwire, *Soviet Naval Developments: Capability and Context* (Praeger: New York, 1973), p. 268.

[9] See Hilton, Sr, R. P., 'The US–Soviet Incidents at Sea treaty', *Naval Forces*, vol. 6, no. 1 (1985), p. 37; and Zumwalt (note 3), p. 393. The amount of property damage obviously will vary from incident to incident, but one 1976 US–Soviet collision caused $500 000 in damage to a US frigate in the Ionian Sea. See 'US ship crash blamed on Russia', *International Herald Tribune*, 16 Mar. 1977. In the absence of the USA–USSR Incidents at Sea Agreement, this incident doubtless would have had serious political consequences.

[10] See Ball, D., 'Nuclear war at sea', *International Security*, vol. 10, no. 3 (winter 1985/86), pp. 3–31. Donald Daniel argues that using nuclear weapons at sea might offer advantages to the Soviet Navy, but that any such decision would not be made independently of a decision for using nuclear weapons on land; see 'The Soviet Navy and tactical nuclear war at sea', *Survival*, vol. 24, no. 4 (July/Aug. 1987), pp. 318–35.

[11] For discussions of the actual process of negotiating the agreement, see Lynn-Jones, S. M., 'A quiet success for arms control: preventing incidents at sea', *International Security*, vol. 9, no. 4 (spring 1985), pp. 169–74; and Wolf, A. F., 'Agreement at sea: the United States–USSR agreement on incidents at sea', *Korean Journal of International Studies*, vol. 9, no. 3 (1978), pp. 57–80.

[12] The definition of simulated attacks has included the illumination of vessels with fire-control radars and other sensor systems.

[13] In practice, this provision has meant that the US and Soviet aircraft fly no lower than 1000 feet (300 m) and do not pass directly overhead, according to van der Aart, D., *Aerial Espionage* (Airlife: Shrewsbury, UK, 1985), p. 144. The USSR apparently objects to lower overflights. In July 1981 a Soviet destroyer fired a warning shot at an aircraft chartered by the Columbia Broadcasting System (CBS) carrying cameramen and flying at 800 feet (240 m) near Cyprus. See 'Soviet ship fires at cameramen off Cyprus', *The Times*, 7 July 1981.

[14] This issue arose in the negotiations leading to the 1972 Agreement. See Lynn-Jones (note 11), p. 172. A 1983 incident in the Atlantic Ocean in which a Soviet submarine was apparently disabled and forced to surface after US sonar equipment became entangled in its propeller demonstrates the validity of Soviet concerns, although that sonar array was towed by a surface ship, not dropped from the air. Even if buoys and cables do not become entangled in Soviet submarines, they may be extremely irritating. According to a US official, when such buoys are dropped near submarines, 'the pinging really drives them crazy'. See 'High seas diplomacy continuing', *Washington Post*, 8 June 1984, p. A15.

[15] Naval officers report that these special signals had a significant impact. See Hilton (note 9), p. 33.

[16] The channel is used relatively often. Between June 1982 and June 1983, for example, the US Government called in the Soviet naval attaché for consultations seven times, while the US attaché was summoned to the Soviet Ministry of Foreign Affairs eight times. See Lehman briefing (note 6), p. 1.

[17] The issue of a distance formula was an important sticking point in the negotiations leading to the agreement. See Lynn-Jones (note 11), pp. 170, 172–73.

[18] Hilton (note 9), p. 33.

[19] Protocol to the Agreement between the Government of the United States of America and the Government of the Union of Soviet Socialist Republics on the Prevention of Incidents on and over the High Seas, signed on 22 May 1973. The English text can be found in annexe 2.

[20] MccGwire, M., 'Soviet naval policy for the seventies', in MccGwire (note 8), p. 509.

[21] For arguments that the agreement has been successful, see Hilton, (note 9), p. 33; Nunn, S. and Warner, J., 'A nuclear risk reduction system', excerpts from the Report of the Nunn/Warner Working Group on Nuclear Risk Reduction, *Survival*, vol. 26, no. 3 (May/June 1984), p. 135; Ury, W. L. and Smoke, R., *Beyond the Hotline: Controlling a Nuclear Crisis* (Nuclear Negotiation Project, Harvard Law School: Cambridge, Mass., 1984), p. iv; and Wolfowitz, P. D., 'Preserving nuclear peace', *Naval War College Review*, vol. 36, no. 2 (Mar.–Apr. 1983), p. 78.

[22] Lehman (note 6), p. 1.

[23] *Washington Post* (note 14), p. A15.

[24] ABC-TV *Nightline*, 3 Apr. 1984.

[25] CBS radio news, 8:12 AM Eastern Standard Time, 4 Apr. 1984.

[26] See Weinland, R. G., 'Superpower naval diplomacy in the October 1973 Arab–Israeli War: a case study', in E. N. Luttwak and R. G. Weinland, 'Sea power in the Mediterranean: political utility and military constraints', *Washington Papers*, no. 61 (Sage/Center for Strategic and International Studies: Beverly Hills, Calif., 1979), pp. 68–88.

[27] Roberts, S., 'The October 1973 Arab–Israeli War', eds. B. Dismukes and J. McConnell, *Soviet Naval Diplomacy* (Pergamon: New York, 1979), p. 196. The USSR did, however, simulate attacks after the US alert. See Roberts (this note), p. 210.

[28] Quoted in Caldwell, D., *American–Soviet Relations: From 1947 to the Nixon–Kissinger Grand Design* (Greenwood: Westport, Conn., 1981), p. 228.

[29] Quoted in Hilton (note 9), p. 33. *Morskoy Sbornik* is a professional naval journal intended primarily for Soviet naval officers.

[30] Quoted in Hilton (note 9), pp. 33–34. Fleet Admiral Vladimir Nikolayevich Chernavin, Commander-in-Chief of the Soviet Navy, echoed this assessment in 1989. See 'Chernavin responds', US Naval Institute *Proceedings*, Feb. 1989, pp. 77–78.

[31] See 'Soviets harass searches for 747 debris', *Aviation Week & Space Technology*, 12 Sep. 1983, p. 28; and 'Race for the black box', *Time*, 3 Oct. 1983, p. 26.

[32] 'Soviet warship, US Navy vessel collide in Mideast', *Boston Globe*, 18 Nov. 1983, p. 6.

[33] See 'Soviet sub bumps into US carrier', *Washington Post*, 22 Mar. 1984, p. A28; and 'Soviet sub and US carrier collide in Sea of Japan', *New York Times*, 22 Mar. 1984, p. A7. If the submarine was underwater at the time of the collision, the Incidents at Sea Agreement probably would not even apply.

[34] 'Moscow's muscle flexing', *Time*, 16 Apr. 1984, pp. 28–30. On these incidents and others, in the mid-1980s, see Arkin, W. M., *The Nuclear Arms Race at Sea*, Neptune Papers, no. 1 (Greenpeace and Institute for Policy Studies: Washington, DC, Oct. 1987).

[35] Quoted in Gordon (note 7), p. 159.

[36] *Washington Post* (note 14), p. A15.

[37] See note 36.

[38] Quoted in Gordon (note 7), p. 159.

[39] Hilton (note 9), p. 37.

[40] Article 8 of the agreement provides for renewal 'without further action', but the US and Soviet delegations made this step official with an announcement.

[41] Beecher, W., 'Election clouds weapons talks', *Boston Globe*, 17 July 1984, p. 4. The full text of Reagan's speech appears in *Weekly Compilation of Presidential Documents*, vol. 20, no. 26 (2 July 1984), pp. 944–46.

[42] Gelb, L. H., 'U.S.–Soviet session on '72 naval accord canceled', *New York Times*, 19 June 1985, p. A1.

[43] Gelb (note 42), p. A1.

[44] Quoted in Gordon (note 7), p. 159.

[45] See Wolf (note 11), pp. 76–77; Mitchell, D. W., *A History of Russian and Soviet Sea Power* (Macmillan: New York, 1975), p. 554; and Admiral Gorshkov's claim that the United States had obtained a recognition of parity from Great Britain at the inter-war naval conferences and that the USSR may have achieved the same in 1972, in Shulsky, A. N., 'Gorshkov on naval arms limitations: KTO KOGO?', ed. P. J. Murphy, *Naval Power in Soviet Policy* (US Government Printing Office: Washington, DC, 1978), p. 250.

[46] An article in the Sep. 1967 *Morskoy Sbornik* even urged Soviet captains to act 'boldly, energetically, and decisively, without fear of responsibility dictated by the situation'. Quoted in Martin, T. C., 'Dangerous maneuvering—the Russian view', US Naval Institute *Proceedings*, vol. 95, no. 2 (Feb. 1969), p. 145.

[47] Quoted in Arkin, W. M., 'Navy autonomy thwarts arms control', *Bulletin of the Atomic Scientists*, Sep. 1987, p. 15.

[48] Hilton (note 9), p. 37.

[49] Former US Chief of Naval Operations Admiral James Watkins, quoted in Gordon (note 7), p. 159.

[50] Hilton (note 9), p. 37.

[51] For a discussion of this issue, see Bunn, G., 'International law and the use of force in peacetime: do US ships have to take the first hit?', *Naval War College Review*, vol. 39, no. 3 (May–June 1986), pp. 69–80.

[52] The actions of the US Navy during the Cuban missile crisis are a possible exception. At the height of the crisis, US naval forces reportedly dropped small depth charges on Soviet submarines to force them to surface. See Sagan , S. D., 'Nuclear alerts and crisis management', *International Security*, vol. 9, no. 4 (spring 1985), pp. 113–18.

[53] The collisions in Soviet territorial waters involved US submarines on intelligence missions. Such missions entailed monitoring Soviet submarines and plugging into underwater communication cables. On one occasion a US submarine surfaced under a Soviet ship during naval exercises. In another incident a US submarine was temporarily grounded beneath Vladivostok harbour. Other incidents have doubtless occurred as US and Soviet submarines have played a running game of cat and mouse under the high seas. See 'Operation Holystone',

Nation, 19 July 1975, pp. 35–36; Caldwell (note 25), p. 128; Ball (note 10), pp. 4–6; 'Critics of US spy subs offer mission details', *International Herald Tribune*, 26 May 1975, p. 1; and Coates, J. and Fuller, J., 'US, Soviet subs treading dangerous waters', *Chicago Tribune*, 4 Dec. 1977, p. 1. US cable-tapping operations, code-named 'Ivy Bells', continued until at least 1981, when they were revaled to the USSR by Ronald Pelton, who was later convicted of spying for the Soviet Union. See Woodward, B., *Veil: The Secret Wars of the CIA, 1981–1987* (Simon and Schuster: New York, 1987), pp. 30, 87, 448–63; and Woodward, B. and Tyler, P., 'Eavesdropping system betrayed: high-technology device disclosed by Pelton was lost to Soviets', *Washington Post*, 21 May 1986, p. 1. Whether intelligence missions in Soviet waters continue remains unclear, but submarine collisions still occur. US and Soviet submarines collided in international waters near Gibraltar in Oct. 1986, causing $2.7 million in damage to the US vessel. See 'Deadly game of hide-and-seek', *US News & World Report*, 15 June 1987, p. 39.

54 Fairhall, D., *Russia Looks to the Sea* (Andre Deutsch: London, 1971), p. 217.

55 'Errant shells hit a German ship', *New York Times*, 16 June 1987, p. A14.

56 United Nations, *The Naval Arms Race*, Report of the Secretary-General, UN Study series no. 16, UN document A/40/535 (United Nations: New York, 1986), p. 83.

57 Personal communication to the author from Ambassador Anders Ferm, Permanent Representative of Sweden to the United Nations, 16 Sep. 1987.

58 Various modifications to the US–Soviet Agreement could be proposed. For example, additional provisions to cover the use of lasers for harassment would extend the agreement to an area in which technology has advanced. Soviet warships have used lasers to irradiate US aircraft. For a report of one such incident, see 'Russian lasers reported aimed at US planes', *New York Times*, 3 Oct. 1987, pp. 1, 6. See also Fridling, B. E., 'Blinding lasers: the need for control', US Naval Institute *Proceedings*, Oct. 1988, p. 151. Restrictions on the use of lasers are already included in the June 1989 USA–USSR Agreement on the Prevention of Dangerous Military Activities, which applies many of the principles of the USA–USSR Incidents at Sea Agreement to military incidents in general. See 'US, Soviets vow accidents won't lead to warfare', *Boston Globe*, 7 June 1989, pp. 1, 7; Woodward, B. and Smith, R. J., 'US–Soviet pact aims to avert clashes', *International Herald Tribune*, 8 June 1989, p. 1.

59 It is worth pointing out, however, that the US Navy initially had reservations about the Incidents at Sea Agreement but has become its strongest supporter.

60 Lehman briefing (note 6), p. 6.

61 The Agreement between the USA and the USSR on Measures to Reduce the Risk of Outbreak of Nuclear War (known as the Accidents Measures Agreement) of 30 Sep. 1971 preceded the SALT I Agreement and the Anti-Ballistic Missile (ABM) Treaty. For the full text of the agreement, see Goldblat, J., SIPRI, *Agreements for Arms Control: A Critical Survey* (Taylor & Francis: London, 1982), pp. 192–93. It seems possible that the Helsinki and Stockholm confidence-building measures (CBMs) for Europe will lead to conventional arms limitations in that theatre since the Negotiation on Conventional Forces in Europe (CFE) began in Mar. 1989 with that objective.

62 The text can be found in annexe B.

63 The UK–USSR Agreement also refers to 'beyond the territorial sea' instead of 'high seas', reflecting the fact that the 1982 UN Convention on the Law of the Sea establishes other categories such as the 200-nautical mile exclusive economic zone (EEZ), which is neither the high seas nor the territorial seas.

64 'Anglo-Soviet manoeuvres', *Financial Times*, 17 July 1986.

65 The English text can be found in annexe B.

66 Personal communication to the author from a naval officer of the FRG, Jan. 1988.

67 As this book was going to press, it was learned that France signed an Incidents at Sea Agreement with the USSR in Moscow on 4 July 1989. The text of the agreement was not available for publication in this book.

68 Personal communication to the author from a US naval commander, 11 May 1985.

Paper 12. A multilateral regime for prevention of incidents at sea

Jan Prawitz

Swedish Ministry of Defence, Stockholm, Sweden

I. Introduction

On 25 May 1972 the United States and the Soviet Union signed an Agreement on the Prevention of Incidents on and over the High Seas.[1] This is one of several agreements in the category of confidence-building measures that were concluded as forerunners to the SALT I Agreement concluded the same year.

The objective of the agreement was to avoid the risk of collisions and other dangerous incidents, which had been occurring in increasing numbers when the naval forces of both powers mixed with and watched each other at sea. It was technically a complement to the International Regulations for Preventing Collisions at Sea (Rules of the Road).[2] A table of special signals was later annexed to the USA–USSR Incidents at Sea Agreement to permit the reliable communication of predetermined specialized messages.

One year later the parties signed a protocol to the US–Soviet agreement, which prohibited confrontation between the warships of one of the parties and the non-military ships of the other party.[3] On 3 May 1979, the parties agreed to amend articles containing a reference to the 1965 Rules of the Road regulations by referring instead to the 1972 regulations which were then in force.[4]

The implementation of this agreement is considered a great success in general as well as in comparison with other arms control agreements. Various aspects of the agreement and its implementation are analysed by Sean Lynn-Jones in paper 11 in this volume.

On 15 July 1986 a second bilateral agreement on incidents at sea was signed—this time between the UK and the USSR.[5] That same year the USA and the USSR added two signals to the annex of their 1972 agreement, thus making it identical to the table of signals annexed to the 1986 UK–USSR Incidents at Sea Agreement (see annexe B). On 25 October 1988 an agreement was signed in Moscow between the Federal Republic of Germany and the USSR which is nearly identical to the UK–USSR Incidents at Sea Agreement.[6] On 4 July 1989 another nearly identical agreement was signed in Moscow between France and the USSR.[7] On 21 September 1989 the Government of Norway announced its intention to initiate negotiations with the USSR on a bilateral Incidents at Sea Agreement. The draft agreement is based on the earlier ones but includes an additional provision for information about 'other maritime events', such as single accidents at sea.[8]

The success of the USA–USSR Incidents at Sea Agreement was noted in a report on the naval arms race, prepared in 1985 by an expert panel appointed by the Secretary-General of the United Nations. The report summarized most of the measures of naval arms control that had been proposed up to that time. While it did not assign priorities to the measures, the report singled out four measures for special consideration. One of these was the suggestion to make 'multilateral the existing bilateral agreement between the Soviet Union and the United States on the Prevention of Incidents on and over the High Seas'.[9] Both the success of the bilateral agreement and the need for similar rules felt by many other countries with negative experience of incidents at sea provided the basis for the recommendation by the Secretary-General's expert panel.

This recommendation later raised concern that multilateralization of the agreement could be the end of its success. Therefore, when the matter was discussed at the 1986 session of the United Nations Disarmament Commission, it was relabelled a 'multilateral agreement corresponding to the existing bilateral agreement between the USSR and the USA on the Prevention of Incidents on and over the High Seas'.[10] A multilateral agreement was thus suggested not to supersede the bilateral agreement but rather to coexist with it.

At the 1987 session of the UN Disarmament Commission the same recommendation was described as 'negotiating a multilateral agreement concerning the prevention of incidents at sea beyond the territorial sea in addition to existing agreements', taking into account the 1986 UK–USSR Incidents at Sea Agreement concluded between the sessions.[11]

At the 1988 session it was added that states 'with particular concerns may prefer' to conclude bilateral agreements, thus accommodating ongoing bilateral negotiations between France and the USSR.[12]

At the 1989 session little was added to earlier conclusions. However, Sweden tabled a working paper on a multilateral agreement for preventing incidents at sea.[13]

It thus seems clear that the international community is interested in a multilateral prevention of incidents at sea agreement *in addition* to the existing bilateral agreements. Naturally, the political reasons vary for individual states to contribute to the wide support for pursuing the proposal.

The recommendation by the Secretary-General's expert panel certainly played an important role for many governments. Some countries have had negative experiences with incidents and wanted to be part of an apparently successful process. Many states entertained an interest in naval arms control in general and, while not concerned with actual, specific incidents, felt that a multilateral prevention of incidents agreement would facilitate development towards something more important (the 'snowball idea'). The expected confidence-building effect of the proposed measure was also referred to with appreciation.

II. Elements of a multilateral agreement

This section describes a possible set of principles and rules for such a multilateral agreement, aimed at meeting the requirements of being both effective and negotiable.

Principles

1. The scope of the agreement shall generally be the same as that of the USA–USSR, the UK–USSR and the FRG–USSR Incidents at Sea Agreements. There should be no special rules for submarines or for ships or aircraft carrying nuclear weapons.

2. The agreement shall be a complement to the Rules of the Road, that is, the 1972 International Regulations for Preventing Collisions at Sea ('1972 Collision Regulations'). It is relevant to make a comparison with the special rules which apply to sailing races.

3. The terminology of the agreement should be in harmony with the 1982 UN Convention on the Law of the Sea and other relevant international agreements. The treaty language should be as similar as possible to the existing bilateral agreements, thus avoiding future differences of interpretation. The USA–USSR Incidents at Sea Agreement was concluded long before the conclusion of the Third UN Law of the Sea Conference, while the UK–USSR and the FRG–USSR Agreements were concluded after the Convention on the Law of the Sea was adopted.

4. Technological features and terms could be updated to cover recent developments.

5. Prescribed consultation procedures in case of incidents should be primarily between the parties immediately concerned.

6. Where a separate bilateral agreement exists on the prevention of incidents at sea between two parties to a multilateral agreement, that bilateral agreement could take precedence as far as the bilateral relationship is concerned.

Rules

The main multilateral rules based on these principles can be summarized as follows.

1. In all cases ships operating in proximity to each other, except when required to maintain course and speed under the 1972 Collision Regulations, shall remain well clear to avoid risk of collision.

2. Ships meeting or operating in the vicinity of a formation of another party shall, while conforming to the 1972 Collision Regulations, avoid manoeuvring in a manner which would hinder the evolutions of the formation.

3. Formations shall not conduct manoeuvres through areas of heavy traffic where internationally recognized traffic separation schemes are in effect.

4. Ships engaged in surveillance of other ships shall stay at a distance which avoids the risk of collision and shall avoid executing manoeuvres which embarrass or endanger the ships under surveillance. Except when required to maintain course and speed under the 1972 Collision Regulations, both the surveillant and the surveilled shall take positive early action so as, in the exercise of good seamanship, not to embarrass or endanger ships surveilling or under surveillance.

5. When ships of parties manoeuvre in sight of one another, such signals (flag, sound and light) as are prescribed by the 1972 Collision Regulations or the International Code of Signals or other mutually agreed signals shall be adhered to for signalling operations and intentions.[14] Existing bilateral agreements include instructions for the use of special signals that might be adopted for multilateral use.

6. Ships of the parties shall not simulate attacks by aiming guns, missile launchers, torpedo tubes and other weapons in the direction of a passing ship or aircraft of another party or let fire-control radars lock on such ships or aircraft, nor launch any object or substance (natural or artificial) in the direction of passing ships or aircraft of another party in such a manner as to be hazardous to those ships or aircraft or to constitute a hazard to navigation, safe operation, or a hindrance to visibility (such as artificial fog), and not use searchlights or other powerful illumination devices to illuminate the navigation bridges of passing ships or aircraft of another party.

7. When conducting exercises with submerged submarines, exercising ships shall show appropriate signals prescribed by the International Code of Signals to warn ships of the presence of submarines in the area.

8. Ships of one party, when approaching ships of another party conducting operations as set forth in Rule 3(g) of the 1972 Collision Regulations, particularly ships engaged in launching or landing aircraft as well as ships engaged in replenishment underway, shall take appropriate measures not to hinder manoeuvres of such ships and shall remain well clear.

9. Commanders of aircraft of the parties shall use the greatest caution and prudence in approaching aircraft and ships of other parties operating on and over the sea beyond the territorial sea, in particular, ships engaged in launching or landing aircraft, and in the interest of mutual safety shall not permit: simulated attacks by the simulated use of weapons against aircraft and ships, or performance of various aerobatics over ships, or dropping various objects, including chaff, near them in such a manner as to be hazardous to ships or to constitute a hazard to navigation.

10. Ships and aircraft of the parties shall not make simulated attacks by aiming guns, missile launchers, torpedo tubes and other weapons at non-military ships of another party, nor launch nor drop any objects or chaff near

non-military ships of another party in such a manner as to be hazardous to these ships or to constitute a hazard to navigation.

11. Ships of parties operating in sight of one another shall raise proper signals concerning their intent to begin launching or landing aircraft.

12. Aircraft of parties flying over the sea beyond the territorial sea in darkness or under instrument conditions shall, whenever feasible, display navigation lights.

13. Parties shall provide through the established system of radio broadcasts of information and warning to mariners, not less than five days in advance as a rule, notification of actions on the sea beyond the territorial sea which represent a danger to navigation or to aircraft in flight.

14. Parties shall make timely and prudent use of the informative signals contained in the International Code of Signals or other mutually agreed signals to communicate the intentions of their respective ships when manoeuvring in proximity to one another. At night, or in conditions of reduced visibility, or under conditions of lighting and such distances when signal flags are not distinct, flashing light or radio, should be used to inform ships of manoeuvres which may hinder the movements of others or involve a risk of collision.

15. Parties involved in instances of collision, incidents which result in damage, or other incidents at sea between ships and aircraft of the parties shall promptly exchange appropriate information concerning such occurrences through their respective naval attachés or other diplomatic channels, as appropriate.

16. Any two states parties to the agreement may, if deemed necessary, hold consultations to review the implementation of the terms of the agreement by the two parties at a mutually agreed time or interval.

III. Final remarks

While the 16 rules listed in the section above are drafted with the intention of serving as background to possible future negotiations on the issue, there are of course a variety of other possibilities. It is possible that those countries which have solved their main incidents at sea problems through bilateral agreements would prefer to continue with those agreements, particularly their consultation clauses. If so, their participation in a multilateral agreement would probably be limited to solving problems of specific incidents with other countries.

The existing bilateral agreements would therefore probably remain in effect, and a multilateral agreement should be as similar as possible to avoid confusion in practical situations at sea. The same should also apply to the system of special signals.

Negotiations will not start automatically; this will depend on the appreciation by many states of the confidence-building effect prevailing over the concern by some about the snowball effect. The probable procedure would then be a decision by the UN General Assembly to refer the issue for negotiation to the Conference on Disarmament in Geneva.

Notes and references

[1] Agreement between the USA and the USSR on the Prevention of Incidents on and over the High Seas, signed in Moscow and entered into force on 25 May 1972. For the text, see annexe B.

[2] The International Regulations for Preventing Collisions at Sea are produced by the International Maritime Organization, a specialized United Nations agency with more than 130 member nations. The Regulations govern nautical lighting, manoeuvring and signalling procedures to ensure safe navigation and avoid collision. For a discussion of recent revisions, see Cutler, T. J., 'More changes to the Rules of the Road', US Naval Institute *Proceedings*, vol. 109, no. 6 (June 1983), pp. 89–93.

[3] Protocol to the Agreement between the USA and the USSR on the Prevention of Incidents on and over the High Seas, signed in Geneva and entered into force on 22 May 1973. For the text, see annexe B.

[4] The 1979 amendment of the USA–USSR agreement meant that reference to Rule 4(c) of the 1965 Regulations was replaced by reference to Rule 3(g) of the 1972 Regulations (see Article III.8).

[5] Agreement between the Government of the United Kingdom of Great Britain and Northern Ireland and the Government of the Union of the Soviet Socialist Republics concerning the Prevention of Incidents at Sea beyond the Territorial Sea, signed in London and entered into force on 15 July 1986. For the text, see annexe B.

[6] Agreement between the Federal Republic of Germany and the USSR concerning the Prevention of Incidents at Sea beyond the Territorial Sea, signed in Moscow on 25 Oct. 1988. The signal annex was signed in Bonn on 18 Nov. 1988. For the unofficial English translation of the text, see annexe B; the agreement exists officially in only the German and Russian languages.

[7] The text of this agreement was not available for publication in this book.

[8] Norwegian Ministry of Foreign Affairs press release no. 68/89.

[9] United Nations, *The Naval Arms Race*, Report of the Secretary-General, UN Study series no. 16, UN document A/40/535 (United Nations: New York, 1986), paragraph 322.

[10] Disarmament Commission Document A/CN.10/83.

[11] Disarmament Commission Document A/CN.10/102.

[12] Disarmament Commission Document A/CN.10/113.

[13] UN Document A/CN.10/121, 10 May 1989.

[14] The International Code of Signals is promulgated by the International Maritime Organization (see note 2).

Paper 13. Naval confidence-building measures: a CSCE perspective

Patrick Howard

Embassy of Denmark, Stockholm, Sweden

I. Introduction

Naval confidence-building measures (CBMs) are in this paper discussed in the context of the Conference on Security and Co-operation in Europe (the CSCE process). The topic is limited to the problem areas involved in reaching an agreement among some or all of the 35 CSCE participating states[1] in the conventional (i.e., non-nuclear) field of naval forces.

The paper examines the desirability and feasibility of implementing naval CBMs along the model of the 1986 Final Document of the Stockholm Conference on Confidence- and Security-Building Measures and Disarmament in Europe (CDE), also known as the Stockholm Document.[2] After focusing on the possibilities and problems associated with the exchange of information and prior notification of naval activities, the paper suggests two other areas where naval CBMs might play a useful role: constraints on provocative exercises with strategic implications and improved CBMs for amphibious activities.

Ideally, the issue of naval CBMs should be considered in a global context, but it is also important to assess the merit and value of such measures in a regional context. Although naval units can in principle sail the high seas all over the world, the confidence- and security-building aspect of naval activities is limited mainly to specific, relevant regions. Thus it cannot be taken for granted that CBMs agreed in one area can be transferred to another political and military environment. After the Middle East, the European region covered in the CSCE process can be considered one of the most significant areas with regard to the elimination of the causes of tension between East and West and the increase of stability and security in the world.

One sensitive issue concerning naval CBMs is their possible application to submarine operations. A great number of the ocean-going submarines carry SLBMs and are thus elements of strategic nuclear deterrence forces. These units would not normally be included in a CSCE regime covering naval CBMs. However, a large number of conventionally and nuclear-powered attack submarines also operate in the European region. These units would probably be deployed early in a crisis or a period of tension and thus act as an important warning indicator.[3] They are therefore significant factors in any discussion of naval CBMs and are discussed in this paper.

II. Desirability of naval CBMs

The discussion in this paper is based on the following two assumptions.

1. CBMs, in general, are valid only in peacetime. When two states or alliances reach a period of serious tension or political crisis, a CBM agreement would probably be overruled by the preservation of the security interests of the states or alliances involved. It will naturally be a major problem for a state to be the first to violate such an agreement, but from a military point of view it will most probably have to be done sooner or later in such a situation.

2. CBMs are fundamentally based on the concept of openness or transparency, in other words, on exchange of information. However, a second concept is considered to be of value by some states, that is, the concept of constraining military activities.

In order to set the issue of naval CBMs in a useful CSCE perspective, it is important to emphasize the justification for limiting the confidence- and security-building measures (CSBM) regime in the Stockholm Document to land activities. If the aim of the Stockholm Document CSBMs was to reduce the risk of military confrontation in Europe by reducing the risk of misunderstanding or miscalculation of military activities that could give rise to apprehension, then it was justified to focus first on the huge number of conventional land forces and activities concentrated in Europe. Even though naval forces should not be underestimated as a military and political factor, there is one important difference which should be stressed when comparing them with land forces: naval surface combatants, that is, ships cannot *occupy* or *conquer* territory.

Looking back at the history of modern naval warfare, it is difficult to find many cases of peacetime naval operations—apart from the strategic attack on Pearl Harbor—which in themselves were the first signs of the outbreak of war (*casus belli*). Naval units have naturally been deployed in times of crisis to local conflict areas for political purposes (gunboat diplomacy) but, unlike land forces, have not been considered as the first indicators of a major hostile act or the first step towards a major aggression. Submarine operations in this context are mentioned in section IV.

Before entering into a discussion of the feasibility of naval CBMs, several questions must be posed concerning the need for naval CBMs.

1. What kind of confidence are we trying to create, and on whose part?

2. Is there really a need for naval CBMs? Can naval operations and deployments in peacetime be interpreted as an indication of hostile intent or surprise attack? Are naval surface ships (combatants) threatening by themselves? Do they have an offensive capability? Can they be used for military intimidation?

3. Can an incident at sea trigger a crisis which could escalate to war?

It is important to discuss the purpose of naval CBMs and the kind of confidence they are intended to create. First of all, the level of ambition must be defined.

All the CSCE participating states seem to acknowledge the principle of peaceful coexistence and claim that their military forces exist only for reasons of self-defence. In the Stockholm Document, the CSCE member states accepted that a confidence-building regime should 'give effect and expression to the duty of states to refrain from the threat or use of force in their mutual relations as well as their international relations in general'.[4] As agreed in Vienna in January 1989, all 35 CSCE states wish to increase confidence and 'reduce the risk of military confrontation in Europe' by adopting new and improved CSBMs, negotiation of which began in March 1989.[5] The 23 states members of the NATO and WTO alliances also agreed in Vienna to the Negotiation on Conventional Armed Forces in Europe (CFE) within the CSCE process and in parallel to the CSBM negotiations. It should be stated that if these CFE negotiations succeed in bringing about a major reduction of armed forces in a stable manner it would have a most significant confidence-building impact.

It is apparent that confidence can be created on various levels, bilaterally and multilaterally, depending on the kind of confidence which is needed. In the field of stability and security in Europe, it is valid to distinguish between CBMs which are 'nice to have' and CBMs which 'contribute to reducing the dangers of armed conflict and of misunderstanding or miscalculation of military activities'.[6] Naval CBMs in the CSCE process should apply to the latter category, while less significant CBMs could be agreed bilaterally and still be appropriate.

Looking at the threat potential of naval surface ships, the question of whether naval units have a threatening or offensive capability must first be answered. In general, they do not. However, several types do have threatening or destructive capabilities. Aircraft-carriers with fixed-wing aircraft have the capability to launch attacks on land targets and to inflict considerable damage, including nuclear devastation. The recent introduction of long-range, land-attack sea-launched cruise missiles (SLCMs) on naval ships is also an augmentation of an offensive naval capability. However, the conventional damage and destruction which surface combatants can inflict on land targets will be local if not limited and, outside the context of a co-ordinated land or amphibious activity, could not act as a warning indicator for a large-scale hostile act. Moreover, any damage which could be inflicted by a surface ship could, to the same extent, be carried out by a missile—probably more accurately and with a greater degree of surprise. Finally, there are amphibious warfare forces which can also be used offensively as a rapid buildup of combat power ashore. (Amphibious forces are discussed in section IV.)

As to the question of incidents at sea, it is difficult to envisage an incident (collision, provocative 'tattletailing', etc.) in peacetime that, by misunderstanding or miscalculation, could lead to a military confrontation between East and West. Only if a number of incidents create a pattern can it be recognized as a policy of a state or an alliance to provoke a confrontation. It is interesting to note in this context the lack of rising political tension or military response when the *USS Stark* was damaged by an Iraqi missile in the Persian Gulf in May 1987. However, this was not a case of East–West tension, but rather part of a complicated war between Iraq and Iran.

This does not mean that bilateral agreements such as that between the USA and the USSR on the prevention of incidents on and over the high seas are not valuable but that they are simply in a different category than naval CBMs in a regional context, such as in the CSCE process.

III. Feasibility of CBMs at sea

Leaving the discussion about the justification for naval CBMs, this section looks at the feasibility of transferring the well-established Stockholm Document CSBMs to the maritime environment. In accordance with the Stockholm Document, the information to be given on *naval* activities to be included in prior notification of a land activity is the following:[7] (*a*) naval ship-to-shore gunfire; (*b*) indication of other naval ship-to-shore support; (*c*) level of command, organizing and commanding the naval force participation; (*d*) total number of amphibious troops involved in notifiable amphibious landings; and (*e*) in the case of a notifiable amphibious landing, the point or points of embarkation in the zone of application.

It should be noted that much time was spent during the negotiations at the Stockholm Conference in discussing whether independent naval operations in the so-called 'adjoining sea area' to Europe were to be included in the new CSBM regime.

The NATO group argued that its interpretation of the Madrid mandate for the Stockholm Conference[8] was clear and was based on the so-called 'functional approach'; that is, there had to be a functional link between the naval activities in the adjoining sea area and the notifiable activity on land. However, although the Warsaw Treaty Organization states and some neutral states did not fully agree with this interpretation, it was finally tacitly agreed upon, obviously in order to proceed in the negotiations. It was also understood that this issue would be pursued by some neutral and WTO countries in a future phase of the CSCE/CDE conference. The zone of application was thus understood as the land mass of Europe extending to the coastline. The adjoining sea area, which in principle had no limit, was to be included only if the naval activity had the above-mentioned functional link to a land activity which was notifiable, that is, above the agreed threshold.

Concerning the potential area of application of naval CBMs, it is important to define the area explicitly. In the CSCE process—in which the USA and Canada also participate—the whole of the northern Atlantic Ocean might have to be included, as there are no natural boundaries or limits that separate part of this ocean from Europe.

The criteria for adoption of CSBMs for land activities at the Stockholm Conference were that they should be: (a) militarily significant, (b) politically binding, (c) verifiable and (d) balanced. These are important criteria and should also apply to naval CBMs if they are to be seen in the context of the CSCE process.

The basic concept in the field of confidence-building has been to improve transparency and openness by exchanging information and accepting observation and inspection of relevant military activities. However, it is not clear whether this concept is viable for naval forces and operations; nor is it clear whether naval CBMs would have the same effect as land CBMs.

Another fundamental criterion for all CSBMs was that they should not impair the freedom of states or members of an alliance to train and modernize their forces to the extent needed to maintain a credible defence and to react to events which threaten their security. For this reason, any measure which constrains military activities and at the same time has an adverse effect on the training capacity of a state or an alliance may be difficult for them to accept.

There are, however, three basic areas where one could argue that the Stockholm Document concept of CSBMs could apply to naval forces: (a) exchange of so-called static information on inventory, base facilities and command organization; (b) prior notification of exercises, transits and deployments; and (c) constraints on exercise activities.

Information exchange

Exchanging information on the military force structure, including the naval command organization, would be extremely important for assessing the defensive nature of the armed forces and the scope of military exercise activities, and would be a significant step forward in the field of confidence-building. The NATO proposal at the Stockholm Conference to exchange information concerning land forces was rejected by the WTO as being too intrusive. However, in 1989 the WTO states agreed in the mandate for the CFE negotiations to exchange sufficient information to compare capabilities and to help verify an agreement.[9] Such information exchanges might lead to the possibility for further exchanges, including information on naval forces.

Another area where the exchange of information may be valid is that on, for example, shipbuilding programmes and the operational status of existing ships. Such information could assist in the evaluation of force levels and trends in shipbuilding. The positive effect it could have is to prevent a naval arms race based on incorrect intelligence. However, it could also have the opposite effect, which would result in states finding it necessary to respond with countermeasures or by starting new shipbuilding projects in order to maintain a military balance.

It has often been stated that the idea or concept of exchanging military information has lost some of its value because of the technological development of so-called 'national technical means'—intelligence systems used for verification—especially in the field of satellite reconnaissance and ocean-surveillance systems. However, only a few nations have such capabilities and other nations' access to this kind of information is still limited. The small and the neutral and non-aligned (NNA) states would benefit most from such a measure.

Prior notification

While prior notification of activities such as exercises, deployments and transits might seem useful for promoting openness, advance information on various activities might also result in other states conducting similar activities in the same area as a response and thus trigger incidents which might not otherwise have taken place. However, a great number of NATO's major naval exercises are well structured, planned long in advance and take place, for example, in the North Atlantic more or less regularly every second year ('Ocean Safari') or every fourth year (the 'Northern Wedding' and 'Teamwork' series). There should be no problem in notifying major exercises such as these, especially as some information is given in press releases prior to these exercises. The problem lies in defining the threshold that triggers the notification and the level of detail which is required in the notification.

It is difficult to compare the naval surface units of different countries. The size (tonnage/displacement) of the ship or the crew is not a fair indication of the ship's potential. Furthermore, weapon systems such as guns and missiles are not comparable. A threshold in which an aircraft-carrier task group itself triggers a notification would, of course, be unacceptable to NATO, as carriers form the core of many ship groupings and would require virtually continuous notification of all aircraft-carrier movements in the North Atlantic and Mediterranean.

A greater problem would be the prior notification of deployments and transits which are carried out either as political demonstrations or simply as routine movements which are not necessarily linked to any exercise activity. In this case there is no similarity to land forces. Transits on the high seas and innocent passage are basic rights laid down in the Law of the Sea (see paper 7). Here again, the role of naval units is unique and can in no way be compared with land forces.

All maritime nations have the right to exercise sovereignty over their territory, and many have an interest in 'showing the flag' on the high seas, often combined with port visits. This is part of an overall political maritime strategy and is a necessary training requirement. A measure that imposes undue restrictions on states and limits the freedom to exercise their forces to maintain a credible defence touches upon the fundamental security interests of these states. It would therefore probably be difficult to reach an agreement which denies maritime nations these fundamental rights.

Observation and verification of naval activities

According to the Stockholm Document, the purpose of observation is 'to confirm that the notified activity is non-threatening in character and that it is carried out in conformity with the appropriate provisions of the notification'.[10] The issue of inviting observers to naval exercises—if it were agreed upon— deserves further study. However, there is no merit in a measure that will restrict observers to certain areas of a ship and give them the opportunity to observe visually only the activities which take place within their line of sight. Access to restricted areas such as operations rooms or combat information centres (CICs) where the overall picture is displayed must probably be considered as too intrusive. Because major naval exercises are so large, visual observation alone would not fulfil its intended purpose. The use of fixed-wing aircraft and helicopters is not a suitable alternative, since they are limited in endurance and seldom available in required numbers during exercises.

In order to get a comprehensive picture of the activity, observers could be spread out among different naval units and meet after the exercise to discuss the scope and purpose of the exercise. This would, however, be a somewhat different concept from that in the Stockholm Document, as observers would be given different functions. The assessment of the activity would thus take place long after the activity has taken place and would be based on information from various sources.

Owing to the space limitations on board ships and the number of observers that would probably have to be invited under a CSCE regime—the Stockholm Document permits two from each of the other CSCE states—such a measure might be more beneficial if it were implemented on a bilateral basis, for example, between neighbouring states.

Balance and reciprocity

The final CSCE criteria for any confidence-building measure is that it should be balanced. It should require the same amount of 'give and take' from all parties to an agreement. The Madrid mandate clearly stated that the Stockholm Conference should work out CSBMs 'on the basis of equality of rights, balance and reciprocity'.

In the field of prior notification, the naval CBMs mentioned above could pose more of a burden on NATO than on the WTO because NATO is a maritime alliance and consequently conducts more naval operations (including exercises) than the WTO.

NATO is to a great extent a maritime alliance completely dependent in peacetime on oceanic trade routes (sea lines of communication) and in time of crisis on the transfer of external military reinforcement and re-supply from the continental USA and Canada to Europe via the seas. Sea control and anti-submarine warfare must therefore be exercised regularly in the northern Atlantic Ocean and the Mediterranean Sea, especially since so many members of the Alliance are involved in this maritime task.

This is not the case for the WTO, whose naval forces have a different role. They fulfil a global political purpose or are earmarked to protect the 'homeland' and to support military land activities. The fundamental disparities and asymmetries between WTO and NATO naval strategy and forces could thus make it difficult to design balanced CBMs in the field of prior notification and exchange of information.

In conclusion, it is difficult to believe that it is either appropriate or feasible to transfer the traditional CSBMs from the Stockholm Document to naval activities—unless a balance is achieved in other areas, such as exchange of information on land forces and land activities, or reductions/limitations on conventional arms. However, given the developments at the Vienna CSCE and CFE negotiations by June 1989, there is reason to believe that some form of mutually acceptable and desirable CBMs could be applied to naval forces in the future.

IV. Potentially useful CBMs

There are two areas where naval confidence-building measures might be significant: (*a*) 'strategic behaviour', offensive and provocative war scenarios; and (*b*) amphibious activities, assault landings and their verification. Both of these areas are discussed below.

Strategic behaviour

An important aspect of the US–NATO forward Maritime Strategy is the philosophy of strategic offence. This is often called a deterrent strategy. It is difficult to question the justification for a forward and offensive strategy, but it is also difficult to see what one gains in deterrence compared with what one loses in confidence when *exercising* such offensive activities in certain areas.

It is possible that peacetime naval activities or exercises conducted in certain areas could be considered provocative if they are conducted in the scenario of a strategic offensive intended to destroy the military forces or occupy the territory of another state.

Peacetime naval deployments and exercises related to a forward offensive strategy can have a destabilizing effect and provoke countermeasures that increase the risk of tension and therefore do not add to confidence. The following are examples of such activities.

1. WTO exercises in the North Atlantic with a war scenario which clearly indicate simulated attacks on Western shipping lines or sea lines of communication (SLOCs), can only increase NATO's sense of insecurity, since NATO is totally dependent on the integrity of these SLOCs.

2. US exercise activities which include operations in the Norwegian and Barents Seas could be assessed as exercising offensive operations not far from Soviet strategic units (SSBNs) and facilities on the Kola Peninsula and are likely to provoke an adverse Soviet reaction.

3. WTO amphibious assault landing exercises in the western Baltic Sea could create the impression that the offensive operations were being rehearsed against other littoral states and give rise to great concern.

4. Peacetime deployment of US attack submarines (SSNs) to areas in the Barents Sea or of Soviet SSNs off the eastern coast of the continental USA, which would be potential attack positions against the other side's SSBNs in times of crisis and war, could be interpreted as an extremely serious signal and thus have both a military and political impact.

Similar examples could apply to other key areas, such as the Mediterranean and Black Seas. The importance of the Soviet trade routes in the Mediterranean are often underestimated. These sea routes from the Suez Canal to the Black Sea are more important for the USSR than most people in the West appreciate.[11] The size and composition of the Soviet Mediterranean squadron are undoubtedly influenced by the presence of the US Sixth Fleet which, apart from securing certain strategic interests, could be assessed as a threat to these SLOCs and Soviet interests in the Black Sea.

The deployment of NATO surface combatants in the Baltic and Black Seas are often characterized as offensive and provocative, especially by the Soviet Union. However, these deployments should be seen in the context of Soviet claims that these seas should be so-called 'seas of peace' or closed seas (*mare clausum*). It is thus necessary for NATO to demonstrate regularly the right of any ship to sail on the high seas and in international waters in these areas.

Confidence-building measures might not necessarily apply only to NATO and Soviet naval forces. Such measures could become increasingly important in, for example, the Aegean Sea, for reducing the risk of tension between Greece and Turkey.

In conclusion, measures must be defined which would constrain nations from exercising in peacetime certain offensive and provocative activities in specific forward key areas. The purpose is not to argue for a so-called 'defensive defence structure' or 'non-offensive defence strategy' but simply to promote an agreement which precludes provocative exercise behaviour in peacetime. In practical terms this would entail a change in the exercise policy of maritime forces.

The deterrence factor should be based on the uncertainty of the offensive application of these forces and should not necessarily have to be demonstrated in peacetime. This could be done without jeopardizing the overall security interests and strategic objectives of any state, but it could prove difficult to convince admirals that they cannot exercise an agreed offensive forward strategy.

Amphibious activities and verification

The second area which could be pursued in order to create more confidence at sea is an improvement of the Stockholm Document CSBMs concerning notification of amphibious activities and their verification.

As mentioned above, amphibious forces are considered as the most offensive units in naval warfare since they can conquer (and reconquer) territory. Discussions of amphibious operations concern amphibious assault landings where troops and equipment are landed from the sea directly on the beach.

In accordance with the Stockholm Document, the point or points of embarkation are to be included in the notification if they take place in the zone of application. Amphibious landings are subject to observation whenever the number of troops engaged equals or exceeds 5000 troops. However, this measure lacks one important element to be credible—adequate verification provisions. First of all, the threshold is numerical and is based on the personnel strength of the landing force. The special configuration of amphibious units makes it very difficult to observe visually the cargo (i.e., equipment) embarked and personnel strength on board the ships as they are mostly carried below deck.

If an amphibious activity is not notified, it is difficult to verify whether the personnel strength exceeds the agreed personnel threshold and consequently whether a violation of the agreement has occurred.

The only way to verify an amphibious activity is to observe or inspect the embarkation of personnel on to the landing ships. However, this is unrealistic, since observers or inspections will probably not be allowed at military bases or installations where such embarkations normally take place.

The fundamental reason for notifying a military exercise activity is to inform that the activity is a *training* activity and not an act or threat of aggression under the guise of an exercise activity. If it is to have a confidence-building effect, however, it must be adequately verifiable.

Even if an amphibious activity is notified, in accordance with the Stockholm Document, verification is, as mentioned above, based on observation of the landing. Transit of the amphibious force is not included in the notification. If the amphibious force selects another landing area, this would prevent adequate observation, as observers would be waiting at the wrong location. Besides, if the number of personnel exceeds the notified number it would be too late to discover this fact at the landing if the 'exercise' is actually some form of aggression.

If an amphibious activity is not notified and it is claimed that it will not terminate in a landing within the zone of application and that the personnel strength is below the agreed threshold, such a force could be deployed in sensitive or vulnerable areas—in principle close to another country's territorial sea—and states would be in no position to verify the exact nature of this activity.

If, instead of a personnel threshold, a *capacity threshold* were applied to amphibious activities, a number of advantages could be obtained, especially regarding the verification of such an activity.

Practically all landing ships are officially known by type. Most states have accurate intelligence information on the lifting capacity of amphibious units. By adopting a capacity threshold, an amphibious activity would have to be notified when the ship capacity of the participating units exceeded a certain displacement or cubic content, regardless of the actual number of personnel who embarked. The activity would thus be immediately verifiable by direct visual observation of the number and type of ships departing from the embarkation area as well as during transit to the planned landing site.

One possibility for circumvention which could have a significant threatening character would be to carry out amphibious activities 'close to each other in time and space'. A number of amphibious forces—each below the notifiable threshold—could rendezvous immediately before the planned hostile landing, thus giving a very short warning time.

A supplementary measure to the capacity threshold would be to include a distance formula in the notification clause. This would mean that amphibious activities which take place within x nautical miles of another country's territorial sea would automatically be subject to the capacity threshold. This should also include amphibious activities 'close to each other in time and space' in order to preclude circumvention.

V. Conclusion

In Europe there is definitely a need to remove the grounds for suspicion and mistrust, to reach a better understanding of other nations' intentions, and to ensure that the military understanding and doctrines of states are based on defensive principles. Naval arms control can certainly help in this field. The two areas proposed could be pursued but will certainly meet with some opposition. There is one other area of interest for naval CBMs—nuclear weapons aboard ships—but this topic will not be addressed in the CSCE/CDE process.[12]

If, as stated in the Helsinki Final Act, the aim of CBMs in the CSCE/CDE process is to reduce the risk of military confrontation in Europe, time and energy would, from an overall CBM point of view, be more beneficially spent on either improving the existing Stockholm Document CSBMs for land activities or reducing conventional forces in Europe, as are the respective aims of the CSCE and CFE negotiations that commenced in Vienna in March 1989.

With respect to these important tasks, naval CBMs seem to have diminishing and secondary significance compared with the real concern in connection with a possible military confrontation in Europe: the concentration of a large number of conventional ground forces in Central Europe.

Notes and references

[1] The 35 participating states of the Conference on Security and Co-operation in Europe (CSCE) are: Austria, Belgium, Bulgaria, Canada, Cyprus, Czechoslovakia, Denmark, Finland, France, the Federal Republic of Germany, the German Democratic Republic, Greece, the Holy See, Hungary, Iceland, Ireland, Italy, Liechtenstein, Luxembourg, Malta, Monaco, the Netherlands, Norway, Poland, Portugal, Romania, San Marino, Spain, Sweden, Switzerland, Turkey, the Union of Soviet Socialist Republics, the United Kingdom, the United States of America and Yugoslavia.

[2] For the text of the Stockholm Document, see SIPRI, *SIPRI Yearbook 1987: World Armaments and Disarmament* (Oxford University Press: Oxford, 1987), pp. 355–69. In the CDE context, the term CSBM is used instead of CBM.

[3] Mearsheimer, J. J., 'A strategic misstep: the Maritime Strategy and deterrence in Europe', *International Security*, vol. 11, no. 2 (autumn 1986), pp. 3–57.

[4] Stockholm Document, para. 6. See note 2.

[5] The Concluding Document of the 1986–89 Vienna CSCE follow-up meeting states: 'The participating States have agreed that Negotiations on Confidence- and Security-building Measures will take place in order to build upon and expand the results already achieved at the Stockholm Conference with the aim of elaborating and adopting a new set of mutually complementary confidence- and security-building measures designed to reduce the risk of military confrontation in Europe.' See SIPRI, *SIPRI Yearbook 1989: World Armaments and Disarmament* (Oxford University Press: Oxford, 1989), p. 419.

[6] Helsinki Final Act, Chapter 2.

[7] Stockholm Document, paras 35.1.10–35.2.2. See note 2.

[8] On 6 Sep. 1983, at the second CSCE follow-up meeting in Madrid, the 35 CSCE states agreed on a mandate for the Stockholm Conference, known as the Madrid mandate. See SIPRI, *World Armaments and Disarmament: SIPRI Yearbook 1984* (Taylor & Francis: London, 1984), pp. 570–71.

[9] The CFE negotiating mandate states: 'Information shall be exchanged in sufficient detail so as to allow a meaningful comparison of the capabilities of the forces involved. Information shall also be exchanged in sufficient detail so as to provide a basis for the verification of compliance.' See *SIPRI Yearbook 1989* (note 5), p. 421.

[10] Stockholm Document, para. 53. See note 2.

[11] Westwood, J. T., 'Soviet maritime strategy and transportation', *Naval War College Review*, Nov.–Dec. 1985, p. 47.

[12] The uncertainty of storage aboard ships and the control of these weapons are of some concern. This is a field which will have to be brought into focus in some other arms control forum. The CFE mandate specifically excludes both nuclear weapons and naval forces from the negotiations. See *SIPRI Yearbook 1989* (note 5), p. 421.

Annexes

Annexe A. Official Soviet and US views on naval arms control, 1988–89

One of the more important tasks in this field is to understand the differing views of the two largest and most important naval powers—the United States and the Soviet Union. Their perspectives and policies play the largest role in determining the prospects for arms control of naval forces. This annexe presents a selection of the best material available.

I. The Soviet view

The following article appeared in the 5 September 1988 issue of Pravda. *This translation is taken from the Foreign Broadcast Information Service (FBIS) Daily Report, a translation service of the US Department of Commerce. It is therefore not an official translation, but it is the best English-language version available. This article, written by the then Chief of the Soviet Armed Forces General Staff, was the most authoritative official Soviet statement on the subject of naval forces and arms control published at the time of writing.*

NAVAL FORCES AND UNIVERSAL SECURITY

by Marshal Sergey Akhromeyev

As a result of persistent efforts by the USSR and the allied socialist countries and—it would be only fair to say—corresponding countersteps by the United States and its allies, there has been success in easing military tension and achieving positive results in the sphere of nuclear arms reduction. There have been positive changes in reducing the level of military confrontation in Europe, which is seeing the development of processes leading to increased mutual trust and creating the prerequisites for achieving measures in the disarmament sphere. There are, however, other trends that are also clearly visible. The efforts by the United States and its allies are aimed at not conducting talks on arms in which the NATO bloc states enjoy superiority.

The United States is making especially great efforts to prevent talks on the reduction of naval forces and their armaments, to prevent verification of naval activity. A totally unrestricted arms race is still continuing in the open oceans and seas; a gigantic destructive potential of nuclear and conventional weapons is concentrated on surface ships and submarines. The US Navy controls all oceans and most seas. This creates an atmosphere of tension and threatens the security of socialist states and other countries alike.

Why is that the United States refuses talks on reducing naval forces and disagrees on any restrictions on their military activity? Could it be that the assessment of these forces as dangerous for the cause of peace and the demand for their reduction are unobjective? Let us try to answer these questions.

I.

Addressing the professorial and tutorial staff of the USSR Armed Forces General Staff Military Academy on 1 August 1988, in the course of his official visit to the Soviet Union, US Secretary of Defense F. Carlucci frankly declared that the United States does not intend to reduce its naval forces nor in any way to restrict their activity since these forces perform, in his words, purely defensive functions to defend shipping lanes, communications, and links with allies. They and their activity are not, apparently, dangerous for other countries. F. Carlucci declared that to demand a reduction of naval forces by the United States would be tantamount to the Americans demanding that the

Soviet Union dismantle its railroad and high-ways networks.

This statement does not stand up to critical examination. Nobody is asking the United States to leave its sea communications un-defended. It has all it needs to offer such defense. Furthermore, the Soviet Union is proposing to start talks and reduce (on a re-ciprocal basis, of course) those elements of the USSR Navy that worry the United States. But the United States stubbornly rejects this.

The US naval forces today are much in excess of the levels required for defense. Despite this, the Navy's proportion in the country's overall military potential is steadily growing. The Navy and the Air Force are the most powerful components in the structure of the US Armed Forces. In terms of numerical strength they each represent 35 percent (a total of 70 percent), and the ground forces another 30 percent, of the total armed forces potential. Such a situation prevails in virtually no other army in the world, with the Navy and Air Force being numerically stronger than the ground forces and representing the bulk of a state's might.

The US Navy's main purpose is not defense but the conduct of active offensive operations in the totally unrestricted ocean expanses. A dominant position in its structure is occupied by strike means: nuclear submarines, major surface ships including battleships (all armed with long-range cruise missiles with a range of 2600 km and more), a numerically strong naval aviation apparatus, and powerful am-phibious forces capable of simultaneously transporting Marine Corps expeditionary units over long distances.

Particular mention ought to be made of the aircraft carriers and carrier task forces. They possess a huge might. The US Navy has 15 strike aircraft carriers, 5 of which are nuclear powered. Each one of these carriers represents a floating aviation division. They provide base facilities for up to 100 combat aircraft with an operational range of 1000 km and more, more than 40 of which carry nuclear weapons. Such a ship carries on board 15 mil-lion liters of aircraft fuel and almost 1000 tonnes of combat munitions. Their crews consist of about 6000 men. Each aircraft carrier is escorted by support combat ships.

Open publications in the United States bluntly state that carrier task forces must be in a state of permanent readiness to perform combat tasks and to strike immediately at selected targets 'anywhere on the globe and in any un-declared wars'. These are not just empty words. Libya, Lebanon, and Grenada have already experienced strikes by these forces.

Therefore, the US Navy's strike force—no matter how much people might try to con-vince us to the contrary—is incalculably greater than is necessary to meet US defense requirements. Moreover, it is long-range offensive weapons that are being built up, and new aircraft carriers are under con-struction.

The so-called 'new naval strategy' provides the basis for the building and operational use of the US Navy. Its demands boil down to en-hancing the Navy's offensive potential still further within the overall structure of the armed forces, securing its superiority at sea by the further growth of strike means, and es-tablishing control in all 'vitally important' parts of the world—the North Atlantic, Pacific, and Indian Oceans, in the Norwegian Sea, and in the Mediterranean. The main point, according to former US Secretary of the Navy J. Lehman, one of the authors of this strategy, is to ensure that the US naval forces are ready to conduct offensive operations against the USSR in its littoral seas and to strike targets situated deep inside Soviet terri-tory. According to the 'new naval strategy', the Navy's objectives are to gain advantage through preventive measures, capture the initiative at the start of a conflict, deliver strikes, and destroy the enemy. This is the essence of US naval strategy. There is no talk here about defense of shipping lanes and communications.

The tenets of the 'naval strategy' are re-hearsed in exercises and maneuvers involving the systematic concentration of strike forces, equivalent to wartime forces, in the immediate vicinity of USSR territory.

The US naval forces are the main instrument of pressure used to pursue the US policy 'from a position of strength'. There is no need to look very far for examples. The United States and its allies have concentrated in the Persian Gulf region an armada that is without equal in peacetime (more than 60 warships, over one-half of which are US ships). This dangerous demonstration of naval power (military operations between Iraq and Iran have ceased) is attributed to an alleged desire to secure freedom of navigation in the Persian Gulf. The true purpose is to consolidate the US Navy's permanent presence there. No secret is made of this by Washington officials. US Secretary of Defense F. Carlucci, speaking in a US television interview 9 August, bluntly declared that the United States will remain in the Gulf even after the normalization of the situation there.

The US presence is being built up virtually everywhere in the world's oceans.

The scale of exercises conducted in the North Atlantic and the northern seas of Europe is expanding. US nuclear submarines are intensively establishing themselves in the Arctic. There has been increased activity by ASW forces and military aircraft.

Ships and combat aircraft of the 6th Fleet are permanently stationed in the Mediterranean. The United States maintains more than 170 bases and other military facilities there, which constitute a bridgehead posing a permanent military threat to the Soviet Union and the socialist countries in the Balkan Peninsula, and are used as a staging base for the movement of US Rapid Deployment Forces in the Near and Middle East.

The scale of naval activity and the presence of forward-based forces close to the Soviet Union's Far East borders are expanding. The number of ships fitted with Tomahawk cruise missiles is growing within the 7th Fleet which operates there. Large-scale exercises involving aircraft carriers, battleships, and landing ships take place in waters close to the Soviet Union's borders from the Sea of Japan to the Bering Sea, and their intensity and scope have increased recently. The offensive nature of these exercises can be seen in the fact that they are held as part of a single plan, with similar NATO exercises in the Atlantic and in Europe, to rehearse in the course of these exercises seaborne strikes against Soviet territory.

In an interview with the newspaper *Tagesspiegel*, US General J. Galvin, NATO supreme allied commander in Europe, spoke again of the 'Soviet military threat' posed to Europe by the Soviet Union. In fact, such a threat does not exist. But in order to relieve the West European countries' concern, we are prepared to talk on the entire package of questions of armed forces and armaments in Europe, including their reduction.

Is the United States prepared for talks with the Soviet Union in reducing the sides' naval forces? So far it has been rejecting such talks.

II.

In order to somehow explain the true scale and offensive spirit of their navies' activity, people in the West recently started spreading a story about an alleged 'buildup of Soviet naval forces', about 'a greater Soviet presence in different parts of the oceans'. All this is a fabrication. It does not conform with the real state of affairs. In reality the Soviet Navy is not only not building up but is actually reducing its presence in the oceans.

It is true that the Soviet Navy's combat composition includes both defensive and strike means. Its main strike force comprises nuclear-powered missile-carrying submarines armed with ballistic missiles. It is, however, well known that this type of naval arms is covered by the USSR–US talks on reducing strategic offensive arms. We also have (quite a few at that) multipurpose nuclear- and diesel-powered submarines carrying missile and torpedo arms. We are asking the United States to start talks on the reduction of the sides' naval forces. This reduction will also cover these submarines of ours. As for the remaining forces of our Navy, they are basically for coastal operations and designed to defend our shores. Let us show, for comparison purposes, the warship structure of the USSR and US navies.

Warship Structure of the USSR and US Navies (in percentages)

Type of ship	USSR	USA
Nuclear-powered missile-carrying submarines	6	8
Submarines, other types	30	21
Ocean-going ships	12	65
Coastal operations ships	52	6

The Soviet Union and our allies also have to take into account the naval forces of the other NATO bloc countries. The overall correlation of naval forces is as follows: NATO's is superior to the Warsaw Pact in naval personnel strength by a factor of 4.5; in numbers of ocean-going ships by a factor of 7.6; in total tonnage of ships by a factor of 3; and in naval combat aircraft by a factor of 2.4. The Warsaw Pact has a certain superiority in submarines—by a factor of 1.2—and in ships for coastal operations by a factor of 1.6. But the overall superiority of the US and NATO navies over the USSR and the Warsaw Pact navies is considerable.

The figures cited above on the ship structure and correlation of the sides' naval forces confirm the defensive nature of the USSR and the Warsaw Pact navies and the offensive thrust of the US and NATO bloc navies.

This conclusion is also confirmed by the correlation of US and USSR amphibious forces. The Americans enjoy an almost sixfold superiority over us in total tonnage of landing ships, a fourfold superiority in amphibious assault troops accommodation, and are many times superior to us in terms of naval infantry strength.

As regards regional imbalances, the United States is again superior to the USSR in almost all naval force components in all main parts of the world's oceans—the Atlantic, the Mediterranean, the Asia–Pacific region, and the Indian Ocean.

This is precisely why the United States is unwilling to embark on a reduction of the sides' naval forces and on reciprocal restrictions on their activity. To maintain superiority, to keep other states subject to tension from the seas and oceans—then the answer is 'yes'. But the United States does not consent to a reciprocal reduction of the military danger from the oceans.

The arms race at sea, which has been unleashed by the United States and some other NATO countries, and the sharp increase of their navies' activity are leading to an increased military danger and render the world's oceans the most likely place for the emergence of conflict situations involving the use of weapons. This situation cannot continue.

The problem of disarmament in the seas and oceans is becoming an inalienable factor of the development of East–West relations as a whole. In line with the development of the process of reducing strategic offensive arms and armed forces and armaments on the European Continent and with the expansion and deepening of verification measures concerning military activity by ground forces, the question of limiting and reducing naval arms and of extending confidence-building measures to the independent activity of naval forces is emerging to the fore. These forces are becoming an increasingly destabilizing factor of the international situation, both globally and regionally.

The question is: How does the US side intend to solve the problem of limiting naval arms and restraining the activity of its naval forces? The United States must give a specific answer to this question.

III.

The Soviet Union and the other countries of the Warsaw Pact have no intention of infringing on the security interests of the United States and NATO. They propose the adoption of effective measures aimed at lowering the level of the military presence and the intensity of military activity in the various areas of the world oceans. For many years in succession now at conferences of the Warsaw Pact states' Political Consultative Committee the socialist countries have been advocating examination of the question of limiting and reducing the level of the military presence and military activity in the relevant regions—be it the Atlantic, Indian, or Pacific Oceans, the Mediterranean, or the Persian Gulf.

A specific program for resolving naval problems was set out in M. S. Gorbachev's speech in Vladivostok (1986), in the interview with the Indonesian paper Merdeka (1987), and in his speeches in Murmansk (1987) and Yugoslavia (1988). We have proposed the convening of a special international conference to discuss issues of limiting the activity of and reducing naval forces. We have declared the Soviet Union's readiness to convene a special sitting of the UN Security Council to discuss these issues.

All these constructive proposals have been passed over in silence by the United States and the NATO bloc as a whole. Their logic is, simply, surprising. They are seeking the further extension of confidence-building measures to the activities of ground forces in Europe, yet as soon as the issue of naval armaments—in which they possess an advantage—is raised, suddenly there is a multitude of excuses. For instance, it is asserted that the proposed Soviet measures on curbing naval activity as a consequence of the US superiority in naval armaments (particularly in ocean-going ships) are 'unbalanced' (for the United States has more of these forces!) and are therefore, they say, unacceptable. How would US representatives react to such 'logic' from our side in relation, say, to the combat strength of the armored forces?

The Soviet Union believes that the achievement of the goals of limiting and reducing naval armament is possible in practice. Moreover, this can be accomplished stage by stage, beginning with the achievement of accords on the simplest measures on which elements of mutual understanding already exist—for example, the provision of guarantees of the security of maritime communications and the extension of confidence-building measures to naval forces.

Why not agree on the extension of confidence-building measures defined by the Stockholm document to the independent activity of the sides' naval forces? In particular, prior notification of major naval exercises, the invitation of observers to them, the mutual inspection of naval exercises, and the limitation of the number of major exercises in each ocean and sea theater of military operations. Reciprocal notification could also embrace major transfers of those naval forces that possess the potential for sudden attack (for example, the transfer of naval infantry or ground forces by sea and by air).

We also consider completely realistic the adoption of measures curbing the most dangerous activity of naval fleets. We propose, for example, the establishment of agreed security areas for missile-carrying submarines (as a means of retaliatory strike) in which the activity of ASW forces is to be prohibited; the prohibition of naval activity in agreed zones of international gulfs and areas of intensive shipping and fishing; limitation of the sailing of nuclear-armed ships in such a way as to prevent their approaching the other side's seaboard to within the range of their own onboard nuclear means; limitation of the deployment areas of the sides' amphibious forces in order to reduce the threat of a sudden seaborne attack. It would be possible to agree on other issues related to curbing naval activity and reducing naval armaments to within limits of reasonable sufficiency. The Soviet side is prepared here to examine all aspects of the problem of limiting and reducing fleets' naval activity and armaments to any level and within the framework of any forum.

In a word, given the sides' political will for this, it is possible to do much in the sphere of reducing naval armaments, increasing confidence and the openness of fleets' activities, and reducing the threat of a sudden seaborne attack. Does the United States have such political will, responsibility, and consideration for the security requirements of the other side? I believe that in the new world that will take shape in the climate of disarmament it will be increasingly difficult to evade the problem of reducing naval forces. Sooner or later the political decisions that take mutual interests into consideration will have to be made.

As for the Soviet Union and the other Warsaw Pact countries, they are doing everything incumbent on them to transform the world's oceans from a zone of war danger into a zone of peace and cooperation, into a sphere of further development of the political and economic ties of the peoples of all countries of the world community. We call upon the United States and its NATO allies to support us in this. If both sides adopt such an approach then this will make possible the most decisive advance in yet another area of disarmament—the sphere of naval armaments.

Source: FBIS, *Daily Report: Soviet Union*, FBIS-SOV-88-172, 6 Sep. 1988, pp. 6–10.

II. The US view

Until 1989 there were very few official US statements concerning naval arms control. This section presents one of the first such pieces, an article by Admiral Carlisle Trost, Chief of Naval Operations, as well as two relevant policy statements and the prepared testimony of Admiral Larson, Deputy Chief of Naval Operations, at the first congressional hearing on naval arms control, held in April 1989.

NORTHERN SEAS ARE VITAL FOR NATO'S DEFENSE

by Admiral Carlisle A. H. Trost

While public attention remains captivated by the recent INF Treaty and nuclear arms control issues, a less dramatic Soviet diplomatic initiative is underway—a new 'peace offensive' that has thus far escaped the careful evaluation which it merits. In a major speech delivered recently in the Arctic city of Murmansk, General Secretary Mikhail Gorbachev reiterated previous Soviet calls for the creation of a northern 'zone of peace'. He proposed East–West talks aimed at curtailing military activity in the Baltic, North, Norwegian, and Greenland Seas, areas vital to the defense of NATO and the United States.

Gorbachev's proposal to eliminate naval and air presence in these northern waters was echoed by Soviet representatives at the Stockholm International Peace Research Institute's conference on naval arms control. It is clear that the Soviets are moving forward with a comprehensive program to undermine the West's successful deterrent strategy for northern Europe.

The program outlined by Gorbachev has widespread appeal, particularly to some segments of the Nordic population. While most European leaders have reacted to his diplomatic initiative with caution, expressing concern that any such maritime accord would work to the advantage of the Soviet Union, some have responded with enthusiasm. At least one NATO member has welcomed the proposal and announced its intention to raise the matter within NATO councils.

Would Gorbachev's diplomatic thrust serve the cause of peace or is it merely part of a broad-based propaganda effort by Soviet leaders to cast the USSR in the role of preeminent peacemaker?

A long-held objective of Soviet ocean policy has been to limit the mobility of US naval and air forces. In various conventional arms control negotiations, the Soviets have proposed confidence-building measures which would place constraints on the freedom of these forces to operate on the high seas.

The United States and our NATO Allies have successfully resisted these efforts on the grounds that any enhancement of security provided by such measures would be marginal, while restrictions on naval and air activity at sea would benefit the Warsaw Pact. Alliance consensus has long supported the position that negotiations to enhance security and stability in Europe are properly confined to the land mass of Europe. It is the potential confrontation on land, where the conventional balance favors the East, that could threaten peace between NATO and the Warsaw Pact.

One issue is whether the Soviets sincerely believe that restrictions on maritime forces will reduce East–West tensions and enhance stability, or if they are diplomatic ploys to tilt the military balance to Soviet advantage. Some observers suggest that Gorbachev is attempting to drive a wedge into NATO solidarity by isolating the Nordic members of the alliance. Others see these efforts as an attempt to use negotiations to offset the western advantage in maritime forces.

From the strategic perspective, the purity of Soviet motives is not really the key question. What matters is whether NATO's deterrent posture would be strengthened or diluted by accepting constraints on our naval mobility in exchange for similar Soviet concessions.

NATO's military strategy and the effectiveness of western deterrence depend upon the ability to reinforce Europe during a crisis, before war could be initiated on Soviet terms. Agreement to a demilitarized northern region would handicap NATO's ability to exercise early reinforcement, thus weakening deterrence and complicating our ability to attain a maximum conventional defense.

Acquiescence to the Soviet proposal would sacrifice one of the West's greatest competitive strengths. As a great land power opposing a maritime coalition, the Soviet Union could achieve its territorial aims in the event of war without dependence on the sea. NATO, on the other hand, absolutely requires use of the high seas and international air space for reinforcement and sustainment. Our competitive advantage lies in maximizing the mobility and flexibility of our maritime forces.

The Soviets' latest proposals for northern Europe clearly reveal that Soviet leaders understand that their continental military superiority cannot guarantee success as long as NATO naval and air forces can operate without restrictions in northern European waters.

If this initiative succeeds, stability will be reduced and our ability to deter Soviet aggression in Europe will be degraded. We must not allow ourselves to be maneuvered into taking such a dangerous step while the conventional balance in European land forces continues to favor the Soviet Union.

Source: *Long Island Newsday*, 28 Mar. 1988, p. 50.

THE NEITHER CONFIRM NOR DENY (NCND) POLICY

Highlights

US policy is neither to confirm nor to deny presence or absence of nuclear weapons aboard any US military station, ship, or aircraft.

Policy necessary to:
- Enhance the deterrence value of having nuclear weapons deployed on ships and aircraft.
- Impede potential adversaries from identifying weapon deployment patterns, and determining distribution and numbers of weapons.
- Withhold from a potential enemy information that could be used against US forces in the event of a conflict.

- Complicate an enemy's tactical problem by forcing all nuclear capable platforms to be treated as if they were fully nuclear armed.
- Contribute to security of weapons especially against terrorist and saboteur threats.
- Reduce potential for release of classified technical information relating to nuclear weapon design, stowage and handling.
- Avoid handing adversaries data of intelligence value which would permit rechanneling intel [intelligence] resources to other targets.

Due to the perishability of intelligence information, a security breach at a specific location at a specific time does not vitiate our national security interest in protecting information as to that location at other times.

Breach of policy in response to specific concerns at individual locations could result in assumptions about presence of weapons whenever NCND response is given and invite endless pressure to vary the policy elsewhere.

The ability of an enemy to assess probable weapons locations is not a reasonable justification for breach of the policy.
- Enemy uncertainty is maintained.
- The information he derives to a large extent is perishable.
- He must tie up his intelligence resources to make the assessment.

Source: US Navy, Office of the Chief of Naval Operations, background materials provided to SIPRI, 1988.

THE US POSITION ON NUCLEAR WEAPON FREE ZONES (NWFZ)

The US supports the concept of NWFZs as a non-proliferation measure when consistent with the following criteria:
- The initiative for the creation of the NWFZ should come from the states in the region concerned.
- All states whose participation is deemed important should participate in the zone.

- The zone arrangement should provide for adequate verification of compliance with the zone's provisions.
- The establishment of the zone should not disturb existing security arrangements to the detriment of regional and international security.
- The zone arrangement should effectively prohibit its parties from developing any nuclear explosive device, for whatever purpose.
- The zone arrangement should not seek to impose restrictions on the exercise of rights recognized under international law, particularly the principle of freedom of navigation on the high seas, in international airspace, and in straits used for international navigation and the right of innocent passage through territorial seas.
- The establishment of a zone should not affect the existing rights of its parties under international law to grant or deny transit privileges, including port calls and overflight, to other states.

Source: US Navy, Office of the Chief of Naval Operations, background materials provided to SIPRI, 1988.

STATEMENT OF VICE ADMIRAL CHARLES R. LARSON, US NAVY, DEPUTY CHIEF OF NAVAL OPERATIONS (PLANS, POLICY AND OPERATIONS), BEFORE THE HOUSE ARMED SERVICES COMMITTEE, ON NAVAL ARMS CONTROL

I welcome the opportunity to present the Navy's views on arms control.

We recognize that arms control, both as a process and a goal, is a prominent feature of today's international security environment, and is likely to remain one of the dominant security issues of the 1990s. Increasingly in the current political and economic climate, arms control is seen by some policy-makers as an attractive method for countering the threat to national security interests at reduced levels of defense spending. Coupled with the view of arms control as means for reducing tensions, this has created significant public enthusiasm for negotiated arms reductions.

While arms control offers opportunities to enhance security and stability, it also poses dangers if outcomes are not carefully evaluated in advance of agreement. For instance, a smaller, more mobile, highly technical Soviet military may pose a far more capable and ominous threat than the one we face now. Additionally, there is no guarantee that arms control will necessarily bring about lower levels of defense spending, as we are learning in the context of the INF treaty and the costly verification programs associated with its execution.

Of particular concern to the US Navy are the Soviet arms control proposals of the past two years which focus on naval forces and capabilities, an area of traditional Western strength and Soviet weakness, or to put it in other terms, an area in which we enjoy the advantage of a 'competitive strategy'. The US Navy supports the US and allied position of excluding naval forces from the current conventional armed forces negotiations, and has grave reservations about the inclusion of Sea-Launched Cruise Missiles (SLCM) in the Strategic Arms Reduction Talks.

Requirements of US security

In formulating our position on arms control we sought to identify the national security objectives and supporting strategy which we want arms control to support. In this context, we considered both the long-term competition with the Soviet Union, and various security interests outside that competition.

The United States is an island nation, in the sense that oceans separate us from principal allies and trading partners. Indeed, we are in fact the leader of a global coalition, linked by mutual security and economic interests. Elements of US national security strategy have been remarkably consistent for over four decades:
- deterrence of war as the primary strategic objective;
- global, forward presence to support deterrence in peace, and to provide flexible response options in crisis;
- coalition defense to defeat any attack if deterrence fails.

Given the current force structure of the US Navy, as well as developments in military technology, these enduring characteristics of the national strategy necessitate a particular naval posture and required set of capabilities. To contribute effectively to deterrence, naval forces must be visible, maintained at a high state of readiness and be perceived by allies and potential adversaries alike to be capable of carrying out assigned missions across the entire spectrum of conflict, from peacetime presence to global war. For a nation dependent on use of the sea for survival, this translates to the necessity to maintain a militarily significant number of combat-ready, forward-deployed naval forces which are available and usable as an instrument of diplomacy, particularly as a visible symbol of commitment to allies and friends throughout the world.

In addition to the basic tenets of US national strategy (and the resulting maritime capabilities and posture which these tenets dictate) our approach to arms control must also take into account the differing geographic factors characterizing the US and Soviet Union that have produced different world views, as well as different military requirements.

The United States is the world's most dominant maritime power. We have the ability to command critical ocean areas and sea lines of communication to maintain access to allies, to reinforce and sustain alliance forces globally, and ensure our economic survival. This ability assumes a robust Navy, with free and unimpeded access to all international waters.

The Soviet Union, on the other hand, is a dominant land power, physically located on the Eurasian land mass, with contiguous allies and internal lines of communication for its economic and security interests. Soviet security depends far less on control of the seas than does that of the United States.

Regardless of how the overall military force structure in Europe is altered through arms control, the Soviet Union will always be able to field land forces sufficient to protect its territorial integrity and, if desired, threaten domination of the Eurasian land mass. Prevention of such domination, by the Soviet Union or any other hostile power, or coalition of powers, is an explicit security objective of the United States.

Maritime superiority assures the ability to support our allies and reinforce forward-deployed forces early enough to counter the relative speed and concentration of mass on the Eurasian continent that the Soviet Union and its allies inherently possess. This ability rests upon a number of factors, including a forward maritime posture and superior naval capabilities which must be preserved as we seek to lower the level of military confrontation through arms control. To ensure Western security, the US must maintain fully capable forward-deployed naval forces, which ensure the ability to rapidly reinforce our overseas allies.

Finally, there is one further factor in the interlocking set of strategic requirements that must be considered in evaluating arms control proposals. The current arms control efforts are focused on the NATO–Warsaw Pact military balance in Europe. US arms control strategy must also account for the capabilities needed to ensure a variety of vital US interests which are not directly related to the U.S.–Soviet military balance.

While the Soviet threat will remain our worst case concern, more probable challenges face us in low intensity conflicts. Regional conflicts in the Persian Gulf, the Middle East, and Latin America, as well as non-state actions, such as international terrorism and drug trafficking, will require US military actions. These low intensity conflict requirements frequently determine the peacetime location and mission of naval forces. These requirements will not disappear simply because the Soviets might reduce their military efforts.

We believe the arms control dialogue must be a logical step by step process if it is to maintain stability while addressing complex security issues. We should first address land forces in Europe because the vast asymmetry in NATO–Warsaw Pact land force capabilities poses the most immediate threat to East–West stability and security. NATO maintains, and the Warsaw Pact agrees, that these forces must be considered destabilizing because of their ability to take and hold territory. Limiting these forces will, if properly structured, enhance stability. Current proposals call for reduction of Soviet forces in Europe to parity with those maintained by NATO and a phased reduction thereafter to an agreed upon level. Given the dynamic of the current negotiations, it would be a grave error to complicate this process by drawing independent naval forces into the equation. Once a mutually agreed upon arms control regime for land forces has been established that enhances stability in Europe, then the Western allies can examine the possibility of limitations on naval forces as they would affect the European balance of military power.

The issue of a changing Soviet Union

One of the dominant themes in current arms control thinking centers on the well-publicized 'Gorbachev revolution' in the Soviet Union. Soviet/Warsaw Pact announcements of a 'defensive' military doctrine, and proclaimed adoption of the principle of 'reasonable sufficiency' in military capabilities, have convinced some observers that the fundamental Soviet view of world politics and national security has changed. The corollary of this belief is that new opportunities for arms control exist, offering a window for 'building down' the confrontation between East and West.

To quote the Chief of Naval Operations, Admiral Trost, 'regarding the Soviet threat, and the supposed doctrine of reasonable sufficiency, now apparently to be authenticated by a substantial cut in the number of Soviet troops, we must be careful not to mistake trends with realities, or stated intentions with capabilities . . . Let's remember that to date there have been no reductions in Soviet capability except those mandated by treaty; that Soviet military spending continues to absorb a disproportionate amount of their gross national product and continues to grow; that their forces retain an offensive character; and that having achieved numerical superiority over the West, they are making every effort, legal and otherwise, to acquire new technology, and thus achieve qualitative superiority as well. In short, while they project an attractive new image, the old reality has yet to catch up'.

By raising the issue of naval arms control, the Soviets seem to have two immediate goals. First, they seek to create dissension within the West through diplomacy and propaganda that has great appeal to certain segments of the public:
  - by declaring, and then exploiting, linkages between naval arms limitations and other

arms control negotiations, as exemplified by their insistence that no START agreement is possible without limits on SLCM;
  - by declaring, and then exploiting, linkages between proposed naval operational restrictions and existing political issues, such as regional nuclear free zones.

Then, they hope to force naval issues onto the formal arms control agenda, in order to negate the West's maritime advantages through negotiated limits and constraints.

Over the past several years, a wide variety of *apparently plausible* naval arms control proposals have been offered by the Soviets in furtherance of these goals. On close examination, these proposals have two common objectives. First, they would significantly degrade the ability of the United States to maintain the lines of communications and sustain alliance forces in the event of war, or a war-threatening crisis. Second, they would dramatically decrease the defense burden on the Soviet forces by reducing the threat to the Soviet homeland from the surrounding seas, thereby allowing the Soviets to shift resources from or within the military sector without appreciably reducing their own security. They would also significantly reduce the complexities which Soviet planners must resolve as they consider future military operations, either in the context of global war or in support of national wars of liberation. As we consider potential naval arms control agreements, we must remember these Soviet perspectives on the advantages which naval arms control can confer on them.

The Soviet leadership claims that Western naval forces are inherently destabilizing. This view seems grounded in the position that naval forces are relatively independent from controlling authorities and that their mobility allows them to use their power projection capability to alter the correlation of forces. Of course naval forces have only a limited capability to take and hold territory. The reality is that the mobility of naval forces enhances Western security. A tenet of the US National Strategy is that demonstrated capability and forward presence establishes a deterrent to aggression. Our naval forces possess outstanding command and control capabilities which allow them to precisely execute the policy of the National Command Authority in times of crisis or war.

Arms control negotiations

Pressure to accede to naval arms control measures in one of the specific arms control negotiations already in progress, or which the US and NATO will undertake in 1989, will come from the Soviets, some allies, and selected arms control proponents in the United States. Of particular concern to the Navy are START, CFE, and the Confidence- and Security-Building Measures follow-up conference which will examine possible CSBMs to increase openness and transparency on both sides.

A. START

The Strategic Arms Reduction Talks (START) have as a goal the development of a more stable alignment of strategic offensive and defensive forces. As such, it is important to understand that survivability of forces, under all potential nuclear warfare scenarios, is the key to effective deterrence and crisis stability. The sea-based leg of the Triad, comprised of the TRIDENT submarine and D-5 missile, is the force that provides this assured survivability and, therefore, must be preserved within the framework of any START agreement. Although an exact force structure has yet to be determined, we have concluded that our survivable SSBNs must provide a significant share of our future deterrent capability. With START negotiations still in progress, it is to our advantage to carry out the President's Strategic Modernization Program by continuing to build one Trident submarine per year and to resist pressure to decide upon an ultimate force level for Trident submarines now.

The SSBN force will be undergoing significant changes throughout the 1990s: Our aging POSEIDON SSBN force will be retired as we continue simultaneous production of TRIDENT submarines at one per year. If we continue to build at this rate our force size will shrink to 21 SSBNs in the year 2000. It is, therefore, critical that we support fully this key element of our nation's strategic forces.

Sea Launched Cruise Missiles (SLCM) are vital to US national security because of their diverse capabilities, flexible employment, and the inherent stability resulting from dispersal onboard many surface combatants and submarines.

- The *deterrent* value of widely dispersed, nuclear SLCM severely complicates Soviet planning and raises the risk and uncertainty in making a decision to start a war.
- Failing deterrence, the *expanded strike capability* of SLCM, augmenting and in concert with carrier based air power, is an unmatchable force multiplier.
- The key contribution that nuclear SLCM makes today to the flexible response capability of theater commanders provides essential deterrence without basing problems.
- The *global utility* of conventional SLCM for low intensity conflicts should not be sacrificed for the sake of arms control agreements with the Soviets. This capability is becoming increasingly important as access to foreign bases and overflight rights shrink, creating ever-greater demands for power projection from the sea.

From the beginning of the negotiations the Soviet Union has attempted to include limitations on SLCM within the structure of the START Treaty. The United States has been just as firm in our position that SLCM should *not* be considered in START. The Soviets propose to constrain both conventional and nuclear variants and limit the number and type of naval vessels from which they can be deployed. The US position has consistently been:
- it is unacceptable to place limits on conventional SLCM;
- it is unacceptable to designate particular classes of warships as carriers of nuclear armed SLCM;
- it is unacceptable to permit on-site inspection of US naval forces not subject to the START agreement.

US negotiating strategy has consistently maintained that SLCM does not belong in START. It is clearly a case of Soviet attempts to negotiate systems of lesser importance to them in return for systems and technologies of critical value to a maritime coalition. Furthermore, the covert possibilities for production, storage and deployment, as well as difficulty in distinguishing between nuclear and conventional variants, all make verification impossible. It is absolutely vital that we protect our long-range nuclear and conventional capabilities at sea, and above all, ensure that future technologies and options are not foreclosed.

If a START agreement which would reduce both sides' strategic arsenals stands on its own merits, and serves the interests of both the United States and the Soviet Union, the exclusion of SLCM should not bar such an agreement.

Nevertheless, US desires for a START agreement and Soviet intransigence until a 'meaningful' control regime on SLCMs is achieved, should not force compromise for reasons of expediency or public perception. The Soviets could use this issue on which the US has been unyielding to showcase their willingness to reduce arms and the lack of US responsiveness. They may also view the internal US debate and recent reduction in SDI funding as indicators of success for their negotiating strategy, and increase propaganda efforts to blame SLCM for lack of progress in START. The Navy will carefully analyze all SLCM proposals for limits and verification, and will continue to weigh the importance of all SLCM variants to US national security, as well as the dangers of losing this system in asymmetrical reductions.

B. Negotiation on Conventional Armed Forces in Europe (CFE)

Begun in March this year, these negotiations on reductions in conventional forces have superseded the moribund MBFR negotiations. Because these talks focus on the Atlantic-to-the-Urals (ATTU) zone, naval forces are excluded from the negotiations by mandate. The potential impact on naval forces in CFE appears to be a long-term contingency: if agreement is reached on land forces, or if the talks stalemate until asymmetries can be eliminated, the focus of negotiations could shift, first to air, then to naval forces.

For example, the Soviet Union could use unilateral reductions in its own naval forces (taken for economic reasons or because of force obsolescence) to pressure the West to follow suit. Such reciprocal reductions in naval forces would appeal to some proponents of arms control, and would be enticing to governments faced with severe fiscal constraints. While this pressure is not likely to cause significant reductions in naval forces directly, it could indirectly foster an environment conducive to early retirements, or delays and cancellations in future acquisitions. It is especially likely that the Soviets will retire some of their older and less capable ships (e.g. Mirka FF, Kotlin DD, and Whiskey SS classes) claiming such retirements as a 'testimony of good faith', and seeking compensatory cuts in the generally more capable Western naval forces.

In the context of CFE, challenges to the Navy are more likely to come from the associated arms control 'theater'. The Soviets will continue to hammer away at the theme that elimination of their asymmetrical advantages in ground forces in Eastern Europe must be reciprocated by elimination of NATO advantages which, according to the Soviets, lie in naval and air power. This is seductive logic, which appeals to those who have not thought through the potential consequences of agreement to this rationale.

The Soviets have an inherent capability to regenerate forces from the East, regardless of their maintaining forward-stationed land and air forces. To counter this advantage, NATO must maintain a countervailing force based on the capability for rapid reinforcement from the US and secure lines of communication among NATO's Central, Northern and Southern regions. This requires an assured ability to control the Atlantic Ocean and European seas.

The ultimate threat to the sovereignty of any state is the occupation of its territory, which can only be accomplished on a permanent basis by Army forces, not naval ships, naval aircraft or their embarked marine units. Accordingly, conventional reductions should focus on the land forces which provide the ability to undertake large-scale offensive operations for the purpose of permanently occupying territory.

Confidence- and Security-Building Measures

Also derived from the current CSCE conference in Vienna, the next round of the Conference on Disarmament in Europe to expand the confidence and security-building measures (CSBM) of the Stockholm Agreement began concurrently with CFE. The 12 Neutral and Non-Aligned (NNA) states will participate directly in this conference, along with the members of NATO and the Warsaw Pact, bringing the number of participants to 35.

It is in this arms control forum that we expect the Soviets to make their most direct challenge to US general-purpose naval forces. The Soviets have stated, both privately and publicly, that in view of the 'great concession' which they made in agreeing to exclude naval forces from CFE, they expect NATO to be forthcoming in CSBM, specifically to be ready to discuss extension of confidence-building measures to independent naval and air activities. The fact is that these negotiations are the most complex set of discussions ever attempted by the two alliances. Expansion of the scope and application of CSBMs after the fact, to include independent naval forces with global responsibilities, would substantially add to the complexity of an already difficult process and may preclude the possibility of any subsequent agreement.

Soviet CSBM proposals range from pre-notification of independent naval activities to limitations on exercises and exchange of observers. More extreme proposals, which may be offered more for propaganda value than in any realistic expectation of agreement, include nuclear-free zones, SSBN havens or ASW-free zones, and prohibition of naval activity in international straits and major shipping routes.

The US and our NATO allies have consistently opposed extension of CSBMs to naval forces and activities. Prior notification of, or constraints upon, naval activities in international waters would impinge upon the internationally accepted doctrine of freedom of the seas. This doctrine underwrites the basic attribute of naval forces: their flexibility. CSBMs would substantially inhibit this flexibility. To many, naval CSBMs are an appealing type of arms control, because they have the role of easing tensions and ensuring a crisis situation does not get out of control. This rationale fails to consider fully the reasons why CSBMs are counter to Western security interests in detail:

- Western naval forces have global responsibilities, and therefore should not be restricted in a regional arms control regime, such as CSBMs for Europe and adjacent areas.
- Naval forces in port are easily observed by national technical means. Underway and on the high seas they may be observed by a variety of tactical reconnaissance means.

Such precautions as advance notification, inspectors, and similar CSBMs are not required for stability.
- Although subject to external intelligence monitoring, naval units do not lend themselves to close observation or on-site (i. e. shipboard) inspections (fundamental elements of a CSBM regime) without an unacceptable level of intrusiveness.
- Confidence-building measures could force the US into more predictable or disadvantageous deployment patterns, thus presenting the Soviets with a less effective deterrent posture.
- The US need to operate naval forces, globally and unconstrained, is analogous to the Soviet need to maintain the freedom to reposition armed forces within their borders. The SLOCs defended by the Navy have exactly the same vital importance to the West as the railway system defended by the Soviet Army.
- To expand CSBMs to include naval forces would establish an undesirable precedent for their inclusion in other conventional arms control negotiations. Because of the West's much greater dependence on the sea, CSBMs which have been proposed to date, or the possible constraints to which they might lead, would favor the Soviet Union over the West.
- Any type of CSBMs which would limit access to certain geographic areas would pose a problem of international law.
- Naval CSBMs are a difficult issue to address, their effect is subtle, but they have potentially significant implications for national defense. In short, any arms control agreement restricting naval flexibility or capabilities would weaken the West's deterrent posture and consequently decrease Western security.

Even so, we are likely to face increasing pressure from both the Soviets and some arms control proponents in the West to agree to naval confidence-building measures. Currently, naval activities which are in direct support of reportable land exercises are notified and subject to limited observation. We accept this limitation because it is actually the land exercise being reported and the supporting naval forces involved are functionally linked. An expansion of this regime will almost certainly be considered in [the] CSBM negotiations. The Navy strongly urges the rejection of such an expansion on the grounds that independent naval forces would be captured by a regional agreement to the detriment of our global deterrent posture.

Issues related to arms control

The foregoing discussion of START, CFE, and CSBM [negotiations] summarizes the arms control challenges which we face. Beyond these arms control negotiations, there are a variety of related issues, addressed in the following paragraphs, which may be affected by arms control, and which must be considered in order to avoid pitfalls.

Maintaining the cohesion of the western alliance is one of the greatest challenges in the arms control arena. This is particularly important in the two multilateral negotiations (CFE and CSBM). Western governments face tremendous public pressure for progress in arms control, both to improve their perceived security and to accommodate reductions in defense spending. Yet political pressure is not good justification to abandon the interests of Western security. Those interests require maritime superiority.

A key characteristic of arms control agreements is that once they are made, they affect strategic options and force structure for the foreseeable future. As we evaluate Soviet proposals for naval arms control, we should think through not only the immediate consequences, but also potential long-term implications.

The most cogent issue in this regard is the durability of the apparent change in Soviet policy. Will they still be talking of 'defensive defense' and 'reasonable sufficiency' in 20 years? Some Soviet sources indicate that 'reasonable sufficiency' may result in stronger military capabilities through an influx of Western technology. What would be the results for Western security if their intentions turn more aggressive, especially if Western capabilities have substantially decreased? Would we be willing and able to undertake a new defense build-up?

Historically, the reaction time for democracies has been slow or uncertain, often with tragic consequences. For example, the Anglo–German Disarmament Treaty in the 1930s restricted the British from building capital ships while permitting a Nazi building rate greater than their production capacity. This allowed the German submarine building program that contributed so effectively to the Battle for the Atlantic. Unlike some forces, which can be built up rapidly, naval ships and systems are capital intensive. Consider that it requires seven years to build a modern aircraft carrier. We now have a maritime advantage that meets our commitments and deters aggression against us. Allowing the Soviets to eliminate that advantage through naval arms control may well be a mistake from which it will be difficult if not impossible to recover.

In the process of thinking through long-term impacts of arms control, the US must ensure that whatever agreements we make do not endanger our ability:
  - to respond to crises in a flexible manner, whether in Europe or any other part of the world far removed from any Soviet threat or direct involvement.
  - to reinforce our own and allied forces in Europe in the event that the Soviet Union threatens direct aggression against NATO Europe.

To meet these long-term requirements, the US will continue to require maritime strength based on modern naval forces ready and capable of sustained operations far forward on a global basis. *This* does not necessarily imply that the Navy must remain forever excluded from the arms control process. It simply means that any agreement we sign must not imperil these required capabilities.

Conclusion

In summary, recognizing that our responsibilities to national security are global, we should be careful not to adopt any policy that recognizes, implicitly or explicitly, any connection between Soviet force levels in Europe and naval force levels at sea. As the leader of a maritime alliance, our need for credible power at sea is not related solely to the capabilities of the Soviet Union, although we must not lose sight of the fact that the Soviets will remain the single greatest threat our nation must face well into the next century. Given the uncertainty of domestic politics within the Soviet Union, the historical nature of Soviet defense policy, the enduring geographical asymmetries between the defense needs of NATO and the Warsaw Pact, and our global needs as a maritime nation, we should not waiver in our position that naval forces not be considered in the context of ongoing arms control negotiations. If the security concerns being discussed today are ameliorated by the current negotiations, then and only then the United States and its allies may consider a naval arms control dialogue with the Eastern Bloc to be advantageous.

Source: US Congress, House Armed Services Committee, 'Statement of Vice Admiral Charles R. Larson, US Navy, Deputy Chief of Naval Operations (Plans, Policy and Operations), before the Seapower Subcommittee of the House Armed Services Committee, on Naval Arms Control', mimeo, 27 Apr. 1989.

Annexe B. Current international agreements relevant to naval forces and arms control

This annexe is divided into two sections for ease of use. The Incidents at Sea agreements are presented together in section I so that they can be easily compared. Other agreements are presented in section II. Within these sections, the agreements appear in chronological order; each agreement is listed in the table of contents at the front of this book. Parties to the multilateral agreements are given below the texts. For some agreements, only the relevant excerpts which apply to naval forces and arms control are presented. The complete texts of those excerpted agreements concluded before 1982 may be found in Goldblat, J., SIPRI, Agreements for Arms Control: A Critical Survey (Taylor & Francis: London, 1982) or Arms Control Agreements, A Handbook (Praeger: New York, 1983). For the statements and reservations made by states upon signing agreements, see the annual SIPRI Yearbooks.

I. Incidents at Sea agreements

AGREEMENT BETWEEN THE USA AND THE USSR ON THE PREVENTION OF INCIDENTS ON AND OVER THE HIGH SEAS (USA–USSR INCIDENTS AT SEA AGREEMENT)

Signed in Moscow on 25 May 1972
Entered into force on 25 May 1972

The Government of the United States of America and the Government of the Union of Soviet Socialist Republics,

Desiring to assure the safety of navigation of the ships of their respective armed forces on the high seas and flight of their military aircraft over the high seas, and

Guided by the principles and rules of international law,

Have decided to conclude this Agreement and have agreed as follows:

Article I

For the purposes of this Agreement, the following definitions shall apply:

1. 'Ship' means:

(a) A warship belonging to the naval forces of the Parties bearing the external marks distinguishing warships of its nationality, under the command of an officer duly commissioned by the government and whose name appears in the Navy list, and manned by a crew who are under regular naval discipline;

(b) Naval auxiliaries of the Parties, which include all naval ships authorized to fly the naval auxiliary flag where such a flag has been established by either Party.

2. 'Aircraft' means all military manned heavier-than-air and lighter-than-air craft, excluding space craft.

3. 'Formation' means an ordered arrangement of two or more ships proceeding together and normally maneuvered together.

Article II

The Parties shall take measures to instruct the commanding officers of their respective ships to observe strictly the letter and spirit of the International Regulations for Preventing Collisions at Sea, hereinafter referred to as the Rules of the Road. The Parties recognize that their freedom to conduct operations on the high seas is based on the principles established under recognized international law and codified in the 1958 Geneva Convention on the High Seas.

Article III

1. In all cases ships operating in proximity to each other, except when required to maintain course and speed under the Rules of the Road, shall remain well clear to avoid risk of collision.

2. Ships meeting or operating in the vicinity of a formation of the other Party shall,

while conforming to the Rules of the Road, avoid maneuvering in a manner which would hinder the evolutions of the formation.

3. Formations shall not conduct maneuvers through areas of heavy traffic where internationally recognized traffic separation schemes are in effect.

4. Ships engaged in surveillance of other ships shall stay at a distance which avoids the risk of collision and also shall avoid executing maneuvers embarrassing or endangering the ships under surveillance. Except when required to maintain course and speed under the Rules of the Road, a surveillant shall take positive early action so as, in the exercise of good seamanship, not to embarrass or endanger ships under surveillance.

5. When ships of both Parties maneuver in sight of one another, such signals (flag, sound, and light) as are prescribed by the Rules of the Road, the International Code of Signals, or other mutually agreed signals, shall be adhered to for signalling operations and intentions.

6. Ships of the Parties shall not simulate attacks by aiming guns, missile launchers, torpedo tubes, and other weapons in the direction of a passing ship of the other Party, not launch any object in the direction of passing ships of the other Party, and not use searchlights or other powerful illumination devices to illuminate the navigation bridges of passing ships of the other Party.

7. When conducting exercises with submerged submarines, exercising ships shall show the appropriate signals prescribed by the International Code of Signals to warn ships of the presence of submarines in the area.

8. Ships of one Party when approaching ships of the other Party conducting operations as set forth in Rule 4(c) of the Rules of the Road, and particularly ships engaged in launching or landing aircraft as well as ships engaged in replenishment underway, shall take appropriate measures not to hinder maneuvers of such ships and shall remain well clear.

Article IV

Commanders of aircraft of the Parties shall use the greatest caution and prudence in approaching aircraft and ships of the other Party operating on and over the high seas, in particular, ships engaged in launching or landing aircraft, and in the interest of mutual safety shall not permit: simulated attacks by the simulated use of weapons against aircraft and

ships, or performance of various aerobatics over ships, or dropping various objects near them in such a manner as to be hazardous to ships or to constitute a hazard to navigation.

Article V

1. Ships of the Parties operating in sight of one another shall raise proper signals concerning their intent to begin launching or landing aircraft.

2. Aircraft of the Parties flying over the high seas in darkness or under instrument conditions shall, whenever feasible, display navigation lights.

Article VI

Both Parties shall:

1. Provide through the established system of radio broadcasts of information and warning to mariners, not less than 3 to 5 days in advance as a rule, notification of actions on the high seas which represent a danger to navigation or to aircraft in flight.

2. Make increased use of the informative signals contained in the International Code of Signals to signify the intentions of their respective ships when maneuvering in proximity to one another. At night, or in conditions of reduced visibility, or under conditions of lighting and such distances when signal flags are not distinct, flashing light should be used to inform ships of maneuvers which may hinder the movements of others or involve a risk of collision.

3. Utilize on a trial basis signals additional to those in the International Code of Signals, submitting such signals to the Intergovernmental Maritime Consultative Organization for its consideration and for the information of other States.

Article VII

The parties shall exchange appropriate information concerning instances of collision, incidents which result in damage, or other incidents at sea between ships and aircraft of the Parties. The United States Navy shall provide such information through the Soviet Naval Attache in Washington and the Soviet Navy shall provide such information through the United States Naval Attache in Moscow.

Article VIII

This Agreement shall enter into force on the date of its signature and shall remain in force for a period of three years. It will thereafter be renewed without further action by the

Parties for successive periods of three years each.

This Agreement may be terminated by either Party upon six months written notice to the other Party.

Article IX

The Parties shall meet within one year after the date of the signing of this Agreement to review the implementation of its terms. Similar consultations shall be held thereafter annually, or more frequently as the Parties may decide.

Article X

The Parties shall designate members to form a Committee which will consider specific measures in conformity with this Agreement. The Committee will, as a particular part of its work, consider the practical workability of concrete fixed distances to be observed in encounters between ships, aircraft, and ships and aircraft. The Committee will meet within six months of the date of signature of this Agreement and submit its recommendations for decision by the Parties during the consultations prescribed in Article IX.

Source: *Treaties and Other International Acts, Series 7379* (US Department of State: Washington, DC, 1972)

PROTOCOL

Signed in Geneva on 22 May 1973
Entered into force on 22 May 1973

The Government of the United States of America and the Government of the Union of Soviet Socialist Republics, herein referred to as the Parties;

Having agreed on measures directed to improve the safety of navigation of the ships of their respective armed forces on the high seas and flight of their military aircraft over the high seas,

Recognizing that the objectives of the Agreement may be furthered by additional understandings, in particular concerning actions of naval ships and military aircraft with respect to the non-military ships of each Party,

Further agree as follows:

Article I

The Parties shall take measures to notify the non-military ships of each Party on the provisions of the Agreement directed at securing mutual safety.

Article II

Ships and aircraft of the Parties shall not make simulated attacks by aiming guns, missile launchers, torpedo tubes and other weapons at non-military ships of the other Party, nor launch nor drop any objects near non-military ships of the other Party in such a manner as to be hazardous to these ships or to constitute a hazard to navigation.

Article III

This Protocol will enter into force on the day of its signing and will be considered as an integral part of the Agreement between the Government of the United States of America and the Government of the Union of Soviet Socialist Republics on the Prevention of Incidents On and Over the High Seas which was signed in Moscow on May 25, 1972.

Source: *Treaties and Other International Acts, Series 7624* (US Department of State: Washington, DC, 1973)

AGREEMENT BETWEEN THE UK AND THE USSR CONCERNING THE PREVENTION OF INCIDENTS AT SEA BEYOND THE TERRITORIAL SEA (UK–USSR INCIDENTS AT SEA AGREEMENT)

Signed in London on 15 July 1986
Entered into force on 15 July 1986

The Government of the United Kingdom of Great Britain and Northern Ireland and the Government of the Union of Soviet Socialist Republics;

Desiring to ensure the safety of navigation of the ships of their respective armed forces, and of the flight of their military aircraft beyond the territorial sea;

Acknowledging that actions prohibited by this Agreement should also not be taken against non-military ships of the Parties;

Guided by the principles and rules of international law;

Have agreed as follows:

Article I

For the purposes of this Agreement the following definitions shall apply:

1. 'ship' means:

(*a*) a warship belonging to the armed forces of the Parties bearing the external marks distinguishing warships of its nationality, under the command of an officer duly commissioned by the Government and whose name appears in the appropriate service list or its equivalent, and manned by a crew who are under regular armed forces discipline; and

(*b*) auxiliary ships belonging to the armed forces of the Parties, which include all ships authorised to fly the auxiliary ship flag where such a flag has been established by either Party;

2. 'aircraft' means all military manned heavier-than-air and lighter-than-air craft, excluding space craft;

3. 'formation' means an ordered arrangement of two or more ships proceeding in company and normally manoeuvring together.

This Agreement shall apply to ships and aircraft operating beyond the territorial sea.

Article II

The Parties shall take measures to instruct the Commanding Officers of their respective ships to observe strictly the letter and spirit of the 1972 International Regulations for Preventing Collision at Sea, hereinafter referred to as 'the 1972 Collision Regulations'. The Parties recognise that their freedom to conduct operations beyond the territorial sea is based on the principles established under recognised international law and codified in the 1958 Geneva Convention on the High Seas.

Article III

1. In all cases ships of the Parties operating in proximity to each other, except when required to maintain course and speed under the 1972 Collision Regulations, shall remain well clear to avoid risk of collision.

2. Ships meeting or operating in the vicinity of a formation of the other Party shall, while conforming to the 1972 Collision Regulations, avoid manoeuvring in a manner which would hinder the evolutions of the formation.

3. Formations shall not conduct manoeuvres through areas of heavy traffic where internationally recognised traffic separation schemes are in effect.

4. Ships engaged in surveillance of ships of the other Party shall stay at a distance which avoids the risk of collision and shall also avoid executing manoeuvres embarrassing or endangering the ships under surveillance. Except when required to maintain course and speed under the 1972 Collision Regulations, a surveillant shall take positive early action so as, in the exercise of good seamanship, not to embarrass or endanger ships under surveillance.

5. When ships of both Parties manoeuvre in sight of one another, such signals (flag, sound and light) as are prescribed by the 1972 Collision Regulations, the International Code of Signals and the Table of Special Signals set forth in the Annex to this Agreement shall be adhered to for signalling operations and intentions. At night or in conditions of reduced visibility, or under conditions of lighting and at such distances when signal flags are not distinct, flashing light or Very High Frequency Radio Channel 16 (156.8 MHz) should be used.

6. Ships of the Parties shall not simulate attacks by aiming guns, missile launchers, torpedo tubes and other weapons in the direction of passing ships of the other Party; nor launch any object in the direction of passing ships of the other Party in such a manner as to be hazardous to those ships or to constitute a hazard to navigation; nor use searchlights or other powerful illumination devices for the purpose of illuminating the navigation bridges of passing ships of the other Party.

Such actions shall also not be taken by ships of each Party against non-military ships of the other Party.

7. When conducting exercises with submerged submarines, supporting ships shall show the appropriate signals prescribed by the International Code of Signals, or in the Table of Special Signals set forth in the Annex to this Agreement, to warn ships of the presence of submarines in the area.

8. Ships of one Party when approaching ships of the other Party conducting operations which in accordance with Rule 3(g) of the 1972 Collision Regulations are restricted in their ability to manoeuvre, and particularly ships engaged in replenishment underway, shall take appropriate measures not to hinder

manoeuvres of such ships and shall remain well clear.

Article IV

1. Commanders of aircraft of the Parties shall use the greatest caution and prudence in approaching aircraft and ships of the other Party, in particular ships engaged in launching or landing aircraft, and, in the interest of mutual safety, shall not permit simulated attacks by the simulated use of weapons against aircraft and ships of the other Party, or the performance of aerobatics over ships of the other Party, or dropping objects near them in such a manner as to be hazardous to ships or to constitute a hazard to navigation.

Such actions shall also not be taken by aircraft of each Party against non-military ships of the other Party.

2. Aircraft of the Parties flying in darkness or under instrument conditions shall, whenever feasible, display navigation lights.

Article V

The Parties shall take measures to notify the non-military ships of each Party about the provisions of this Agreement directed at securing mutual safety.

Article VI

The Parties shall provide through the established system of radio broadcasts of information and warning to mariners, normally not less than three to five days in advance, notification of actions beyond the territorial sea which represent a danger to navigation or to aircraft in flight.

Article VII

The Parties shall exchange in a timely manner appropriate information concerning instances of collisions, incidents which result in damage, and other incidents at sea between ships and aircraft of the Parties. The Royal Navy shall provide such information through the Soviet Naval or other Military Attaché in London and the Soviet Navy shall provide such information through the British Naval or other Military Attaché in Moscow.

Article VIII

This Agreement shall enter into force on the date of its signature. It may be terminated by either Party giving six months' written notice of termination to the other Party.

Article IX

Representatives of the Parties shall meet within one year after the date of the signing of this Agreement to review the implementation of its terms, as well as possible ways of promoting a higher level of safety of navigation of their ships and flight of their aircraft beyond the territorial sea. Similar consultations shall be held thereafter annually, or more frequently as the Parties may decide.

In witness whereof the undersigned, duly authorised thereto by their respective Governments, have signed this Agreement.

ANNEX

TABLE OF SPECIAL SIGNALS[1]

YANKEE VICTOR ONE (YV1)

The following signals are to be preceded by the above group:

Signal	Meaning of Signals
IR1	I am engaged in oceanographic operations.
IR2 (...)	I am streaming/towing hydrographic survey equipment...meters astern.
IR3	I am recovering hydrographic survey equipment.
IR4	I am conducting salvage operations.
JH1	I am attempting to retract a grounded vessel.
MH1	Request you not cross my course ahead of me.
NB1 (...)	I have my unattached hydrographic survey equipment bearing in a direction from me as indicated...(Table 3 of ICS).
PJ1	I am unable to alter course to my starboard.
PJ2	I am unable to alter course to my port.
PJ3	Caution, I have a steering casualty.

---

[1] Both Parties will issue mutually agreed instructions for the use of the signals of this Table. The representatives of the Parties may by mutual agreement introduce into this Table necessary alterations and additions.

PP8 (...) Dangerous operations in progress. Request you keep clear of the direction indicated from me...(Table 3 of ICS).

QF1 Caution, I have stopped the engines.

QS6 (...) I am proceeding to anchorage on course...

QV2 I am in a fixed multiple leg moor using two or more anchors or buoys fore and aft. Request you remain clear.

QV3 I am anchored in deep water with hydrographic survey equipment streamed.

RT2 I intend to pass you on your port side.

RT3 I intend to pass you on your starboard side.

RT4 I will overtake you on your port side.

RT5 I will overtake you on your starboard side.

RT6 (...) I am manoeuvring (or the formation is manoeuvring). Request you keep clear of the direction indicated from me...(Table 3 of ICS).

RT7 (...) I shall approach your ship on starboard side to a distance of...100's of meters (yards).

RT8 (...) I shall approach your ship on port side to a distance of...100's of meters (yards).

RT9 (...) I shall cross astern at a distance of ...100's of meters (yards).

RU2 (...) I am beginning a port turn in approximately...minutes.

RU3 (...) I am beginning a starboard turn in approximately...minutes.

RU4 The formation is preparing to alter course to port.

RU5 The formation is preparing to alter course to starboard.

RU6 I am engaged in manoeuvring exercises. It is dangerous to be inside the formation.

RU7 I am preparing to submerge.

RU8 A submarine will surface within two miles of me within 30 minutes. Request you remain clear.

SL2 Request your course speed and passing intention.

TX1 I am engaged in fisheries patrol.

UY1 (...) I am preparing to launch/recover aircraft on course...

UY2 (...) I am preparing to conduct missile exercises. Request you keep clear of the direction indicated from me...(Table 3 of ICS).

UY3 (..:) I am preparing to conduct gunnery exercises. Request you keep clear of the direction indicated from me...(Table 3 of ICS).

UY4 I am preparing to conduct/am conducting operations employing explosive charges.

UY5 (...) I am manoeuvring in preparation for torpedo launching exercises in a direction from me as indicated...(Table 3 of ICS).

UY6 (...) I am preparing to conduct/am conducting underway replenishment on course...Request you remain clear.

UY7 I am preparing to conduct extensive small boat and ship to shore amphibious training operations.

UY8 I am manoeuvring to launch/recover landing craft/boats.

UY9 I am preparing to conduct/am conducting helicopter operations over my stern.

UY10 I am checking gunnery systems.*

UY11 I am checking rocket systems.*

UY12 I am preparing to conduct/I am conducting/gunnery exercises/bombing/by aircraft of the towed target. Request you keep clear of the direction indicated from me...(Table 3 of ICS).

ZL1 I have received and understood your signal.

ZL2 Do you understand? Request acknowledgement.

---

* Those signals are transmitted by ships when they conduct their routine checking work and testings of gunnery and rocket rotating mechanisms, the activities provided for by certain technical requirements.

Source: UK, *Treaty Series No. 5 (1987)*, (Her Majesty's Stationery Office: London, 1986), Cm 57

AGREEMENT BETWEEN THE FEDERAL REPUBLIC OF GERMANY AND THE USSR CONCERNING THE PREVENTION OF INCIDENTS AT SEA BEYOND THE TERRITORIAL SEA (FRG–USSR INCIDENTS AT SEA AGREEMENT)

Signed at Moscow on 25 October 1988
Entered into force on 25 October 1988

The FRG–USSR Incidents at Sea Agreement is official only in its original German and Russian texts. The English-language text below is not official but gives an accurate account of the official agreement, which differs only slightly from the UK–USSR Agreement of July 1986.

The Government of the Federal Republic of Germany and the Government of the Union of Soviet Socialist Republics;

Desiring to ensure the safety of navigation of the ships of their respective armed forces, and of the flight of their military aircraft beyond the territorial sea;

Desiring to contribute to the strengthening of peace and security in Europe and the world in accordance with the expressed wish of the Treaty Between the Federal Republic of Germany and the Union of Soviet Socialist Republics of 12 August 1970;

Acknowledging that actions prohibited by this Agreement should also not be taken against non-military ships of the Parties;

Guided by the principles and rules of international law;

Have agreed as follows:

Article I

For the purposes of this Agreement the following definitions shall apply:

1. 'ship' means:

(a) a warship belonging to the armed forces of the Parties bearing the external marks distinguishing warships of its nationality, under the command of an officer duly commissioned by the Government and whose name appears in the appropriate service list or its equivalent, and manned by a crew who are under regular armed forces discipline; and

(b) auxiliary ships belonging to the armed forces of the Parties, which include all ships authorised to fly the auxiliary ship flag where

such a flag has been established by either Party;

2. 'air vehicle' means all military manned heavier-than-air and lighter-than-air craft, excluding space craft;

3. 'formation' means an ordered arrangement of two or more ships normally operating together.

Article II

The Parties shall take measures to instruct the Commanding Officers of their respective ships to observe strictly the letter and spirit of the 1972 International Regulations for Preventing Collision at Sea, hereinafter referred to as 'the 1972 Collision Regulations'. The Parties recognise that their freedom to conduct operations beyond the territorial sea is based on the principles established under recognised international law and codified in the 1958 Geneva Convention on the High Seas.

Article III

1. In all cases ships of the Parties operating in proximity to each other, except when required to maintain course and speed under the 1972 Collision Regulations, shall remain well clear to avoid risk of collision.

2. Ships meeting or operating in the vicinity of a formation of the other Party shall, while conforming to the 1972 Collision Regulations, avoid manoeuvring in a manner which would hinder the evolutions of the formation.

3. Formations shall not conduct manoeuvres through areas of heavy traffic where internationally recognised traffic separation schemes are in effect.

4. Ships engaged in surveillance of ships of the other Party shall stay at a distance which avoids the risk of collision and shall also avoid executing manoeuvres embarrassing or endangering the ships under surveillance. Except when required to maintain course and speed under the 1972 Collision Regulations, a surveillant shall take positive early action so as, in the exercise of good seamanship, not to embarrass or endanger ships under surveillance.

5. When ships of both Parties manoeuvre in sight of one another, such signals (flag, sound and light) as are prescribed by the 1972 Collision Regulations, the International Code of Signals and the Table of Special Signals set forth in the Annex to this Agreement shall be

adhered to for signalling operations and intentions. At night or in conditions of reduced visibility, or under conditions of lighting and at such distances when signal flags are not distinct, flashing light or Very High Frequency Radio Channel 16 (156.8 MHz) shall be used.

6. Ships of the Parties shall not simulate attacks by aiming guns, missile launchers, torpedo tubes and other weapons in the direction of passing ships of the other Party; nor launch any object in the direction of passing ships of the other Party in such a manner as to be hazardous to those ships or to constitute a hazard to navigation; nor use searchlights or other powerful illumination devices for the purpose of illuminating the navigation bridges of passing ships of the other Party.

Such actions shall also not be taken by ships of each Party against non-military ships of the other Party.

7. When conducting exercises with submerged submarines, supporting ships shall show the appropriate signals prescribed by the International Code of Signals, or in the Table of Special Signals set forth in the Annex to this Agreement, to warn ships of the presence of submarines in the area.

8. Ships of one Party when approaching ships of the other Party conducting operations which in accordance with Rule 3(g) of the 1972 Collision Regulations are restricted in their ability to manoeuvre, and particularly ships engaged in replenishment underway, shall take appropriate measures not to hinder manoeuvres of such ships and shall remain well clear.

Article IV

1. Commanders of aircraft of the Parties shall use the greatest caution and prudence in approaching aircraft and ships of the other Party, in particular ships engaged in launching or landing aircraft, and, in the interest of mutual safety, shall not permit simulated attacks by the simulated use of weapons against aircraft and ships of the other Party, or the performance of aerobatics over ships of the other Party, or dropping objects near them in such a manner as to be hazardous to ships or to constitute a hazard to navigation.

Such actions shall also not be taken by aircraft of each Party against non-military ships of the other Party.

2. Aircraft of the Parties flying in darkness or under instrument conditions shall, whenever feasible, display navigation lights.

Article V

The Parties shall take measures to notify the non-military ships of each Party about the provisions of this Agreement directed at securing mutual safety.

Article VI

The Parties shall provide through the established system of radio broadcasts of information and warning to mariners, normally not less than five days in advance, notification of actions beyond the territorial sea which represent a danger to navigation or to aircraft in flight.

Article VII

The Parties shall exchange without delay appropriate information concerning instances of collisions, incidents which result in damage, and other incidents at sea between ships and aircraft of the Parties. The Royal Navy shall provide such information through the Soviet Naval or other Military Attaché in London and the Soviet Navy shall provide such information through the British Naval or other Military Attaché in Moscow.

Article VIII

This Agreement shall enter into force on the date of its signature. It may be terminated by either Party giving six months' written notice of termination to the other Party.

Article IX

Representatives of the Parties shall meet within one year after the date of the signing of this Agreement to review the implementation of its terms, as well as possible ways of promoting a higher level of safety of navigation of their ships and flight of their aircraft beyond the territorial sea. Similar consultations shall be held thereafter annually, or more frequently as the Parties may decide.

In witness whereof the undersigned, duly authorised thereto by their respective Governments, have signed this Agreement.

PROTOCOL

Signed in Bonn on 18 November 1988

On 17 and 18 November 1988 in Bonn negotiations took place between a delegation of the FRG and a delegation of the USSR elaborating the Table of Special Signals as provided for in Article 3, paragraph 5 and paragraph 7 of the Agreement Between the

FRG and the USSR Concerning the Prevention of Incidents at Sea Beyond the Territorial Sea (Annex to the Agreement).

The Head of Delegation for the FRG was Assistant Undersecretary Dr Hofstetter.

The Head of Delegation for the USSR was Vice Admiral D. M. Komarov.

As a result of the negotiations the attached text of the Table of Special Signals (Annex to the Agreement) was agreed upon in the German and Russian languages.

Signed in Bonn on 18 November 1988.

ANNEX: *Identical to the Annex to the UK–USSR Incidents at Sea Agreement of July 1986; see above.*

Source: Copy of the original document: Abkommen zwischen der Regierung der Bundesrepublik Deutschland und der Regierung der Union der Sozialistischen Sowjetrepubliken über die Verhütung von Zwischenfällen auf See außerhalb der Hoheitsgewässer.

II. Other agreements

ANTARCTIC TREATY

Signed in Washington on 1 December 1959
Entered into force on 23 June 1961
Depositary: US Government

Excerpts

The Governments of Argentina, Australia, Belgium, Chile, the French Republic, Japan, New Zealand, Norway, the Union of South Africa, the Union of Soviet Socialist Republics, the United Kingdom of Great Britain and Northern Ireland, and the United States of America,

Have agreed as follows:

Article I

1. Antarctica shall be used for peaceful purposes only. There shall be prohibited, *inter alia*, any measures of a military nature, such as the establishment of military bases and fortifications, the carrying out of military maneuvers, as well as the testing of any type of weapons.

Article V

1. Any nuclear explosions in Antarctica and the disposal there of radioactive waste material shall be prohibited.

Article VI

The provisions of the present Treaty shall apply to the area south of 60° South Latitude, including all ice shelves, but nothing in the present Treaty shall prejudice or in any way affect the rights, or the exercise of the rights, of any State under international law with regard to the high seas within that area.

Article VII

1. In order to promote the objectives and ensure the observance of the provisions of the present Treaty, each Contracting Party whose representatives are entitled to participate in the meetings referred to in Article IX of the Treaty shall have the right to designate observers to carry out any inspection provided for by the present Article. Observers shall be nationals of the Contracting Parties which designate them. The names of observers shall be communicated to every other Contracting Party having the right to designate observers, and like notice shall be given of the termination of their appointment.

2. Each observer designated in accordance with the provisions of paragraph 1 of this Article shall have complete freedom of access at any time to any or all areas of Antarctica.

3. All areas of Antarctica, including all stations, installations and equipment within those areas, and all ships and aircraft at points of discharging or embarking cargoes or personnel in Antarctica, shall be open at all times to inspection by any observers designated in accordance with paragraph 1 of this Article.

4. Aerial observation may be carried out at any time over any or all areas of Antarctica by any of the Contracting Parties having the right to designate observers.

5. Each Contracting Party shall, at the time when the present Treaty enters into force for it, inform the other Contracting Parties, and thereafter shall give them notice in advance, of

(*a*) all expeditions to and within Antarctica, on the part of its ships or nationals, and all expeditions to Antarctica organized in or proceeding from its territory;

(b) all stations in Antarctica occupied by its nationals; and

(c) any military personnel or equipment intended to be introduced by it into Antarctica subject to the conditions prescribed in paragraph 2 of Article I of the present Treaty.

Parties as of 1 June 1989: Argentina, Australia, Austria, Belgium, Brazil, Bulgaria, Canada, Chile, China, Cuba, Czechoslovakia, Denmark, Ecuador, Finland, France, German Democratic Republic, Federal Republic of Germany, Greece, Hungary, India, Italy, Japan, Democratic People's Republic of Korea, Republic of Korea, Netherlands, New Zealand, Norway, Papua New Guinea, Peru, Poland, Romania, South Africa, Spain, Sweden, UK, Uruguay, USA, USSR

Source: *Treaty Series*, vol. 402 (United Nations: New York)

TREATY BANNING NUCLEAR WEAPON TESTS IN THE ATMOSPHERE, IN OUTER SPACE AND UNDER WATER (PARTIAL TEST BAN TREATY)

Signed in Moscow on 5 August 1963
Entered into force on 10 October 1963
Depositaries: UK, US and Soviet
  Governments

Excerpts

The Governments of the United States of America, the United Kingdom of Great Britain and Northern Ireland, and the Union of Soviet Socialist Republics, hereinafter referred to as the 'Original Parties',
Have agreed as follows:

Article I

1. Each of the Parties of this Treaty undertakes to prohibit, to prevent, and not to carry out any nuclear weapon test explosion, or any other nuclear explosion, at any place under its jurisdiction or control:

(a) in the atmosphere; beyond its limits, including outer space; or under water, including territorial waters or high seas; or

(b) in any other environment if such explosion causes radioactive debris to be present outside the territorial limits of the State under whose jurisdiction or control such explosion is conducted.

2. Each of the Parties to this Treaty undertakes furthermore to refrain from causing, encouraging, or in any way participating in, the carrying out of any nuclear weapon test explosion, or any other nuclear explosion, anywhere which would take place in any of the environments described, or have the effect referred to, in paragraph 1 of this Article.

Parties as of 1 June 1989: Afghanistan, Antigua and Barbuda, Argentina, Australia, Austria, Bahamas, Bangladesh, Belgium, Benin, Bhutan, Bolivia, Botswana, Brazil, Bulgaria, Burma (Myanma), Byelorussia, Canada, Cape Verde, Central African Republic, Chad, Chile, Colombia, Costa Rica, Côte d'Ivoire, Cyprus, Czechoslovakia, Denmark, Dominican Republic, Ecuador, Egypt, El Salvador, Fiji, Finland, Gabon, Gambia, German Democratic Republic, Federal Republic of Germany, Ghana, Greece, Guatemala, Guinea-Bissau, Honduras, Hungary, Iceland, India, Indonesia, Iran, Iraq, Ireland, Israel, Italy, Japan, Jordan, Kenya, Republic of Korea, Kuwait, Lao People's Democratic Republic, Lebanon, Liberia, Libya, Luxembourg, Madagascar, Malawi, Malaysia, Malta, Mauritania, Mauritius, Mexico, Mongolia, Morocco, Nepal, Netherlands, New Zealand, Nicaragua, Niger, Nigeria, Norway, Pakistan, Panama, Papua New Guinea, Peru, Philippines, Poland, Romania, Rwanda, Western Samoa, San Marino, Senegal, Seychelles, Sierra Leone, Singapore, South Africa, Spain, Sri Lanka, Sudan, Swaziland, Sweden, Switzerland, Syria, Taiwan, Tanzania, Thailand, Togo, Tonga, Trinidad and Tobago, Tunisia, Turkey, Uganda, UK, Ukraine, Uruguay, USA, USSR, Venezuela, People's Democratic Republic of Yemen, Yugoslavia, Zaire, Zambia

Signatories as of 1 June 1989: Algeria, Burkina Faso, Burundi, Cameroon, Ethiopia, Haiti, Jamaica, Mali, Paraguay, Portugal, Somalia, Yemen Arab Republic

Source: *Treaty Series*, vol. 480 (United Nations: New York)

TREATY FOR THE PROHIBITION OF NUCLEAR WEAPONS IN LATIN AMERICA (TREATY OF TLATELOLCO)

Signed in Mexico, Distrito Federal, on 14 February 1967
Entered into force on 22 April 1968
Depositary: Mexican Government

Excerpts

In the name of their peoples and faithfully interpreting their desires and aspirations, the Governments of the States which sign the Treaty for the Prohibition of Nuclear Weapons in Latin America,

Have agreed as follows:

Article 1. *Obligations*

1. The Contracting Parties hereby undertake to use exclusively for peaceful purposes the nuclear material and facilities which are under their jurisdiction, and to prohibit and prevent in their respective territories:

(*a*) The testing, use, manufacture, production or acquisition by any means whatsoever of any nuclear weapons, by the Parties themselves, directly or indirectly, on behalf of anyone else or in any other way, and

(*b*) the receipt, storage, installation, deployment and any form of possession of any nuclear weapons, directly or indirectly, by the Parties themselves, by anyone on their behalf or in any other way.

2. The Contracting Parties also undertake to refrain from engaging in, encouraging or authorizing, directly or indirectly, or in any way participating in the testing, use, manufacture, production, possession or control of any nuclear weapon.

Article 2. *Definition of the Contracting Parties*

For the purposes of this Treaty, the Contracting Parties are those for whom the Treaty is in force.

Article 3. *Definition of territory*

For the purposes of this Treaty, the term 'territory' shall include the territorial sea, air space and any other space over which the State exercises sovereignty in accordance with its own legislation.

Article 4. *Zone of application*

1. The zone of application of this Treaty is the whole of the territories for which the Treaty is in force.

2. Upon fulfilment of the requirements of article 28, paragraph 1, the zone of application of this Treaty shall also be that which is situated in the western hemisphere within the following limits (except the continental part of the territory of the United States of America and its territorial waters): starting at a point located at 35° north latitude, 75° west longitude; from this point directly southward to a point at 30° north latitude, 75° west longitude; from there, directly eastward to a point at 30° north latitude, 50° west longitude; from there, along a loxodromic line to a point at 5° north latitude, 20° west longitude; from there, directly southward to a point at 60° south latitude, 20° west longitude; from there, directly westward to a point at 60° south latitude, 115° west longitude; from there, directly northward to a point at 0 latitude, 115° west longitude; from there, along a loxodromic line to a point at 35° north latitude, 150° west longitude; from there, directly eastward to a point at 35° north latitude, 75° west longitude.

Article 25. *Signature*

1. This Treaty shall be open indefinitely for signature by:

(*a*) All the Latin American Republics, and

(*b*) All other soverign States situated in their entirety south of latitude 35° north in the western hemisphere; and, except as provided in paragraph 2 of this article, all such States which become sovereign, when they have been admitted by the General Conference.

2. The General Conference shall not take any decision regarding the admission of a political entity part or all of whose territory is the subject, prior to the date when this Treaty is opened for signature, of a dispute or claim between an extra-continental country and one or more Latin American States, so long as the dispute has not been settled by peaceful means.

Article 28. *Entry into force*

1. Subject to the provisions of paragraph 2 of this article, this Treaty shall enter into force among the States that have ratified it as soon as the following requirements have been met:

(*a*) Deposit of the instruments of ratification of this Treaty with the Depositary Government by the Governments of the States mentioned in article 25 which are in existence on the date when this Treaty is opened for signature and which are not affected by the provisions of article 25, paragraph 2;

(*b*) Signature and ratification of Additional Protocol I annexed to this Treaty by all extra-continental or continental States having *de jure* or *de facto* international responsibility for territories situated in the zone of application of the Treaty;

(*c*) Signature and ratification of the Additional Protocol II annexed to this Treaty by all powers possessing nuclear weapons;

(*d*) Conclusion of bilateral or multilateral agreements on the application of the Safeguards System of the International Atomic Energy Agency in accordance with article 13 of this Treaty.

ADDITIONAL PROTOCOL I

Excerpts

The undersigned Plenipotentiaries, furnished with full powers by their respective Governments,

Have agreed as follows:

Article 1

To undertake to apply the statute of denuclearization in respect of warlike purposes as defined in articles 1, 3, 5 and 13 of the Treaty for the Prohibition of Nuclear Weapons in Latin America in territories for which, *de jure* or *de facto*, they are internationally responsible and which lie within the limits of the geographical zone established in that Treaty.

Article 2

The duration of this Protocol shall be the same as that of the Treaty for the Prohibition of Nuclear Weapons in Latin America of which this Protocol is an annex, and the provisions regarding ratification and denunciation contained in the Treaty shall be applicable to it.

Article 3

This Protocol shall enter into force, for the States which have ratified it, on the date of the deposit of their respective instruments of ratification.

ADDITIONAL PROTOCOL II

Excerpts

The undersigned Plenipotentiaries, furnished with full powers by their respective Governments,

Have agreed as follows:

Article 1

The statute of denuclearization of Latin America in respect of warlike purposes, as defined, delimited and set forth in the Treaty for the Prohibition of Nuclear Weapons in Latin America of which this instrument is an annex, shall be fully respected by the parties to this Protocol in all its express aims and provisions.

Article 2

The Governments represented by the undersigned Plenipotentiaries undertake, therefore, not to contribute in any way to the performance of acts involving a violation of the obligations of article 1 of the Treaty in the territories to which the Treaty applies in accordance with article 4 thereof.

Article 3

The Governments represented by the undersigned Plenipotentiaries also undertake not to use or threaten to use nuclear weapons against the Contracting Parties of the Treaty for the Prohibition of Nuclear Weapons in Latin America.

Article 4

The duration of this Protocol shall be the same as that of the Treaty for the Prohibition of Nuclear Weapons in Latin America of which this Protocol is an annex, and the definitions of territory and nuclear weapons set forth in articles 3 and 5 of the Treaty shall be applicable to this Protocol, as well as the provisions regarding ratification, reservations, denunciation, authentic texts and registration contained in articles 26, 27, 30 and 31 of the Treaty.

Article 5

This Protocol shall enter into force, for the States which have ratified it, on the date of the deposit of their respective instruments of ratification.

Parties as of 1 June 1989: Antigua and Barbuda, Bahamas, Barbados, Bolivia,

Colombia, Costa Rica, Dominican Republic, Ecuador, El Salvador, Grenada, Guatemala, Haiti, Honduras, Jamaica, Mexico, Nicaragua, Panama, Paraguay, Peru, Suriname, Trinidad and Tobago, Uruguay, Venezuela

Signatories as of 1 June 1989: Argentina, Brazil, Chile

Protocol I: Netherlands, UK, USA

Protocol II: China, France (not ratified), UK, USA, USSR

———

Source: *Treaty Series*, vol. 634 (United Nations: New York)

———

TREATY ON THE PROHIBITION OF THE EMPLACEMENT OF NUCLEAR WEAPONS AND OTHER WEAPONS OF MASS DESTRUCTION ON THE SEABED AND THE OCEAN FLOOR AND IN THE SUBSOIL THEREOF (SEABED TREATY)

Signed in London, Moscow and Washington on 11 February 1971
Entered into force on 18 May 1972
Depositaries: UK, US and Soviet Governments

The States Parties to this Treaty,
Recognizing the common interest of mankind in the progress of the exploration and use of the seabed and the ocean floor for peaceful purposes,
Considering that the prevention of a nuclear arms race on the seabed and the ocean floor serves the interests of maintaining world peace, reduces international tensions and strengthens friendly relations among States,
Convinced that this Treaty constitutes a step towards the exclusion of the seabed, the ocean floor and the subsoil thereof from the arms race,
Convinced that this Treaty constitutes a step towards a treaty on general and complete disarmament under strict and effective international control, and determined to continue negotiations to this end,
Convinced that this Treaty will further the purposes and principles of the Charter of the United Nations, in a manner consistent with the principles of international law and without infringing the freedoms of the high seas,

Have agreed as follows:

Article I

1. The States Parties to this Treaty undertake not to emplant or emplace on the seabed and the ocean floor and in the subsoil thereof beyond the outer limit of a seabed zone, as defined in article II, any nuclear weapons or any other types of weapons of mass destruction as well as structures, launching installations or any other facilities specifically designed for storing, testing or using such weapons.
2. The undertakings of paragraph 1 of this article shall also apply to the seabed zone referred to in the same paragraph, except that within such seabed zone, they shall not apply either to the coastal State or to the seabed beneath its territorial waters.
3. The States Parties to this Treaty undertake not to assist, encourage or induce any State to carry out activities referred to in paragraph 1 of this article and not to participate in any other way in such actions.

Article II

For the purpose of this Treaty, the outer limit of the seabed zone referred to in article I shall be coterminous with the twelve-mile outer limit of the zone referred to in part II of the Convention on the Territorial Sea and the Contiguous Zone, signed at Geneva on April 29, 1958, and shall be measured in accordance with the provisions of part I, section II, of that Convention and in accordance with international law.

Article III

1. In order to promote the objectives of and insure compliance with the provisions of this Treaty, each State Party to the Treaty shall have the right to verify through observation the activities of other States Parties to the Treaty on the seabed and the ocean floor and in the subsoil thereof beyond the zone referred to in article I, provided that observation does not interfere with such activities.
2. If after such observation reasonable doubts remain concerning the fulfillment of the obligations assumed under the Treaty, the State Party having such doubts and the State Party that is responsible for the activities giving rise to the doubts shall consult with a view to removing the doubts. If the doubts persist, the State Party having such doubts shall notify the other States Parties, and the Parties

concerned shall cooperate on such further procedures for verification as may be agreed, including appropriate inspection of objects, structures, installations or other facilities that reasonably may be expected to be of a kind described in article I. The Parties in the region of the activities, including any coastal State, and any other Party so requesting, shall be entitled to participate in such consultation and cooperation. After completion of the further procedures for verification, an appropriate report shall be circulated to other Parties by the Party that initiated such procedures.

3. If the State responsible for the activities giving rise to the reasonable doubts is not identifiable by observation of the object, structure, installation or other facility, the State Party having such doubts shall notify and make appropriate inquiries of States Parties in the region of the activities and of any other State Party. If it is ascertained through these inquiries that a particular State Party is responsible for the activities, that State Party shall consult and cooperate with other Parties as provided in paragraph 2 of this article. If the identity of the State responsible for the activities cannot be ascertained through these inquiries, then further verification procedures, including inspection, may be undertaken by the inquiring State Party, which shall invite the participation of the Parties in the region of the activities, including any coastal State, and of any other Party desiring to cooperate.

4. If consultation and cooperation pursuant to paragraphs 2 and 3 of this article have not removed the doubts concerning the activities and there remains a serious question concerning fulfillment of the obligations assumed under this Treaty, a State Party may, in accordance with the provisions of the Charter of the United Nations, refer the matter to the Security Council, which may take action in accordance with the Charter.

5. Verification pursuant to this article may be undertaken by any State Party using its own means, or with the full or partial assistance of any other State Party, or through appropriate international procedures within the framework of the United Nations and in accordance with its Charter.

6. Verification activities pursuant to this Treaty shall not interfere with activities of other States Parties and shall be conducted with due regard for rights recognized under international law, including the freedoms of the high seas and the rights of coastal States with respect to the exploration and exploitation of their continental shelves.

Article IV

Nothing in this Treaty shall be interpreted as supporting or prejudicing the position of any State Party with respect to existing international conventions, including the 1958 Convention on the Territorial Sea and the Contiguous Zone, or with respect to rights or claims which such State Party may assert, or with respect to recognition or nonrecognition of rights or claims asserted by any other State, related to waters off its coasts, including, *inter alia*, territorial seas and contiguous zones, or to the seabed and the ocean floor, including continental shelves.

Article V

The Parties to this Treaty undertake to continue negotiations in good faith concerning further measures in the field of disarmament for the prevention of an arms race on the seabed, the ocean floor and the subsoil thereof.

Article VI

Any State Party may propose amendments to this Treaty. Amendments shall enter into force for each State Party accepting the amendments upon their acceptance by a majority of the States Parties to the Treaty and, thereafter, for each remaining State Party on the date of acceptance by it.

Article VII

Five years after the entry into force of this Treaty, a conference of Parties to the Treaty shall be held at Geneva, Switzerland, in order to review the operation of this Treaty with a view to assuring that the purposes of the preamble and the provisions of the Treaty are being realized. Such review shall take into account any relevant technological developments. The review conference shall determine, in accordance with the views of a majority of those Parties attending, whether and when an additional review conference shall be convened.

Article VIII

Each State Party to this Treaty shall in exercising its national sovereignty have the right to withdraw from this Treaty if it decides that extraordinary events related to the subject matter of this Treaty have jeopardized the supreme interests of its country. It shall give notice of such withdrawal to all other States

Parties to the Treaty and to the United Nations Security Council three months in advance. Such notice shall include a statement of the extraordinary events it considers to have jeopardized its supreme interests.

Article IX

The provisions of this Treaty shall in no way affect the obligations assumed by States Parties to the Treaty under international instruments establishing zones free from nuclear weapons.

Article X

1. This Treaty shall be open for signature to all States. Any State which does not sign the Treaty before its entry into force in accordance with paragraph 3 of this article may accede to it at any time.

2. This Treaty shall be subject to ratification by signatory States. Instruments of ratification and of accession shall be deposited with the Governments of the United States of America, the United Kingdom of Great Britain and Northern Ireland, and the Union of Soviet Socialist Republics, which are hereby designated the Depositary Governments.

3. This Treaty shall enter into force after the deposit of instruments of ratification by twenty-two Governments, including the Governments designated as Depositary Governments of this Treaty.

4. For States whose instruments of ratification or accession are deposited after the entry into force of this Treaty, it shall enter into force on the date of the deposit of their instruments of ratification or accession.

5. The Depositary Governments shall promptly inform the Governments of all signatory and acceding States of the date of each signature, of the date of deposit of each instrument of ratification or of accession, of the date of the entry into force of this Treaty, and of the receipt of other notices.

6. This Treaty shall be registered by the Depositary Governments pursuant to Article 102 of the Charter of the United Nations.

Article XI

This Treaty, the English, Russian, French, Spanish and Chinese texts of which are equally authentic, shall be deposited in the archives of the Depositary Governments. Duly certified copies of this Treaty shall be transmitted by the Depositary Governments to the Governments of the States signatory and acceding thereto.

Parties as of 1 June 1989: Afghanistan, Antigua and Barbuda, Argentina, Australia, Austria, Belgium, Benin, Botswana, Brazil, Bulgaria, Byelorussia, Canada, Cape Verde, Central African Republic, Congo, Côte d'Ivoire, Cuba, Cyprus, Czechoslovakia, Denmark, Dominican Republic, Ethiopia, Finland, German Democratic Republic, Federal Republic of Germany, Ghana, Greece, Guinea-Bissau, Hungary, Iceland, India, Iran, Iraq, Ireland, Italy, Jamaica, Japan, Jordan, Lao People's Democratic Republic, Lesotho, Luxembourg, Malaysia, Malta, Mauritius, Mexico, Mongolia, Morocco, Nepal, Netherlands, New Zealand, Nicaragua, Niger, Norway, Panama, Poland, Portugal, Qatar, Republic of Korea, Romania, Rwanda, Sao Tome and Principe, Saudi Arabia, Seychelles, Singapore, Solomon Islands, South Africa, Spain, Swaziland, Sweden, Switzerland, Taiwan, Togo, Tunisia, Turkey, UK, Ukraine, USA, USSR, Viet Nam, People's Democratic Republic of Yemen, Yugoslavia, Zambia

Signatories as of 1 June 1989: Bolivia, Burma (Myanma), Burundi, Cameroon, Colombia, Costa Rica, Equatorial Guinea, Gambia, Guatemala, Guinea, Honduras, Kampuchea (Cambodia), Lebanon, Liberia, Madagascar, Mali, Paraguay, Senegal, Sierra Leone, Sudan, Tanzania, Uruguay, Yemen Arab Republic

———

Source: *Treaties and Other International Acts, Series 7337* (US Department of State: Washington, DC, 1972)

INTERIM AGREEMENT BETWEEN THE USA AND THE USSR ON CERTAIN MEASURES WITH RESPECT TO THE LIMITATION OF STRATEGIC OFFENSIVE ARMS (SALT I AGREEMENT)

Signed in Moscow on 26 May 1972
Entered into force on 3 October 1972

Excerpts

The United States of America and the Union of Soviet Socialist Republics, hereinafter referred to as the Parties,
Have agreed as follows:

Article III

The Parties undertake to limit submarine-launched ballistic missile (SLBM) launchers and modern ballistic missile submarines to the numbers operational and under construction on the date of signature of this Interim Agreement, and in addition to launchers and submarines constructed under procedures established by the Parties as replacements for an equal number of ICBM launchers of older types deployed prior to 1964 or for launchers on older submarines.

PROTOCOL

Excerpts

The Parties understand that, under Article III of the Interim Agreement, for the period during which that Agreement remains in force:
The US may have no more than 710 ballistic missile launchers on submarines (SLBMs) and no more than 44 modern ballistic missile submarines. The Soviet Union may have no more than 950 ballistic missile launchers on submarines and no more than 62 modern ballistic missile submarines.
Additional ballistic missile launchers on submarines up to the above-mentioned levels, in the US—over 656 ballistic missile launchers on nuclear-powered submarines, and in the USSR—over 740 ballistic missile launchers on nuclear-powered submarines, operational and under construction, may become operational as replacements for equal numbers of ballistic missile launchers of older types deployed prior to 1964 or of ballistic missile launchers on older submarines.

The deployment of modern SLBMs on any submarine, regardless of type, will be counted against the total level of SLBMs permitted for the US and the USSR.

AGREED INTERPRETATIONS AND UNILATERAL STATEMENTS

Excerpts

1. Agreed interpretations
   [E]
The Parties understand that dismantling or destruction of ICBM launchers of older types deployed prior to 1964 and ballistic missile launchers on older submarines being replaced by new SLBM launchers on modern submarines will be initiated at the time of the beginning of sea trials of a replacement submarine, and will be completed in the shortest possible agreed period of time. Such dismantling or destruction, and timely notification thereof, will be accomplished under procedures to be agreed in the Standing Consultative Commission.

Source: *Treaties and Other International Acts, Series 7504* (US Department of State: Washington, DC, 1972)

TREATY BETWEEN THE USA AND THE USSR ON THE LIMITATION OF STRATEGIC OFFENSIVE ARMS (SALT II TREATY)

Signed in Vienna on 18 June 1979
Not in force by 1 June 1989

Excerpts

The United States of America and the Union of Soviet Socialist Republics, hereinafter referred to as the Parties,
Have agreed as follows:

Article III

1. Upon entry into force of this Treaty, each Party undertakes to limit ICBM launchers, SLBM launchers, heavy bombers, and ASBMs to an aggregate number not to exceed 2,400.

Article IV

12. Each Party undertakes not to flight-test or deploy SLBMs with a number of re-entry vehicles greater than the maximum number of re-entry vehicles, with which an SLBM of either party has been flight-tested as of 1 May 1979, that is, 14.

Article V

1. Within the aggregate numbers provided for in paragraphs 1 and 2 of Article III, each Party undertakes to limit launchers of ICBMs and SLBMs equipped with MIRVs, ASBMs equipped with MIRVs, and heavy bombers equipped for cruise missiles capable of a range in excess of 600 kilometres to an aggregate number not to exceed 1,320.

2. Within the aggregate number provided for in paragraph 1 of this Article, each Party undertakes to limit launchers of ICBMs and SLBMs equipped with MIRVs, and ASBMs equipped with MIRVs to an aggregate number not to exceed 1,200.

Article VII

1. The limitations provided for in Article III shall not apply to ICBM and SLBM test and training launchers or to space vehicle launchers for exploration and use of outer space. ICBM and SLBM test and training launchers are ICBM and SLBM launchers used only for testing or training.

Article IX

1. Each Party undertakes not to develop, test, or deploy:

(a) ballistic missiles capable of a range in excess of 600 kilometres for installation on waterborne vehicles other than submarines, or launchers of such missiles;

(b) fixed ballistic or cruise missile launchers for emplacement on the ocean floor, on the seabed, or on the beds of internal waters and inland waters, or in the subsoil thereof, or mobile launchers of such missiles, which move only in contact with the ocean floor, the seabed, or the beds of internal waters and inland waters, or missiles for such launchers;

(e) SLBMs which have a launch-weight or throw-weight greater than that of the heaviest, in terms of either launch-weight or throw-weight, respectively, of the light ICBMs deployed by either Party as of the date of signature of this Treaty, or launchers of such SLBMs.

Agreed Statement to subparagraph (b). The obligations provided for in subparagraph 1(b) of Article IX of the Treaty shall apply to all areas of the ocean floor and the seabed, including the seabed zone referred to in Article I and II of the 1971 Treaty on the Prohibition of the Emplacement of Nuclear Weapons and Other Weapons of Mass Destruction on the Seabed and the Ocean Floor and in the Subsoil Thereof.

Source: Committee on Disarmament documents CD/28, 27 June 1979 and CD/29, 2 July 1979.

UNITED NATIONS CONVENTION ON THE LAW OF THE SEA (UNCLOS CONVENTION)

Signed in Montego Bay, Jamaica, on 10 December 1982
Not in force by 1 June 1989
Depositary: Secretary-General of the United Nations

Excerpts

The States Parties to this Convention,
Have agreed as follows:

Part II, Section 3. INNOCENT PASSAGE IN THE TERRITORIAL SEA

Article 17. *Right of innocent passage*

Subject to this Convention, ships of all States, whether coastal or land-locked, enjoy the right of innocent passage through the territorial sea.

Article 18. *Meaning of passage*

1. Passage means navigation through the territorial sea for the purpose of:

(a) traversing that sea without entering internal waters or calling at a roadstead or port facility outside internal waters; or

(b) proceed to or from internal waters or a call at such roadstead or port facility.

2. Passage shall be continuous and expeditious. However, passage includes stopping and anchoring, but only in so far as the same

are incidental to ordinary navigation or are rendered necessary by *force majeure* or distress or for the purpose of rendering assistance to persons, ships or aircraft in danger or distress.

Article 19. *Meaning of innocent passage*

1. Passage is innocent so long as it is not prejudicial to the peace, good order or security of the coastal State. Such passage shall take place in conformity with this Convention and with other rules of international law.

2. Passage of a foreign ship shall be considered to be prejudicial to the peace, good order or security of the coastal State if in the territorial sea it engages in any of the following activities:

(*a*) any threat or use of force against the sovereignty, territorial integrity or political independence of the coastal State, or in any other manner in violation of the principles of international law embodied in the Charter of the United Nations;

(*b*) any exercise or practice with weapons of any kind;

(*c*) any act aimed at collecting information to the prejudice of the defence or security of the coastal State;

(*d*) any act of propaganda aimed at affecting the defence or security of the coastal State;

(*e*) the launching, landing or taking on board of any aircraft;

(*f*) the launching, landing or taking on board of any military device;

(*g*) the loading or unloading of any commodity, currency or person contrary to the customs, fiscal, immigration or sanitary laws and regulations of the coastal State;

(*h*) any act of wilful and serious pollution contrary to this Convention;

(*i*) any fishing activities;

(*j*) the carrying out of research or survey activities;

(*k*) any act aimed at interfering with any systems of communication or any other facilities or installations of the coastal State;

(*l*) any other activity not having a direct bearing on passage.

Article 20. *Submarines and other underwater vehicles*

In the territorial sea, submarines and other underwater vehicles are required to navigate on the surface and to show their flag.

Article 22. *Sea lanes and traffic separation schemes in the territorial sea*

1. The coastal State may, where necessary having regard to the safety of navigation, require foreign ships exercising the right of innocent passage through its territorial sea to use such sea lanes and traffic separation schemes as it may designate or prescribe for the regulation of the passage of ships.

2. In particular, tankers, nuclear-powered ships and ships carrying nuclear or other inherently dangerous or noxious substances or materials may be required to confine their passage to such sea lanes.

3. In the designation of sea lanes and the prescription of traffic separation schemes under this article, the coastal State shall take into account:

(*a*) the recommendations of the competent international organization;

(*b*) any channels customarily used for international navigation;

(*c*) the special characteristics of particular ships and channels; and

(*d*) the density of traffic.

4. The coastal State shall clearly indicate such sea lanes and traffic separation schemes on charts to which due publicity shall be given

Article 23. *Foreign nuclear-powered ships and ships carrying nuclear or other inherently dangerous or noxious substances*

Foreign nuclear-powered ships and ships carrying nuclear or other inherently dangerous or noxious substances shall, when exercising the right of innocent passage through the territorial sea, carry documents and observe special precautionary measures established for such ships by international agreements.

Article 24. *Duties of the coastal State*

1. The coastal State shall not hamper the innocent passage of foreign ships through the territorial sea except in accordance with this Convention. In particular, in the application of this Convention or of any laws or regulations adopted in conformity with this Convention, the coastal State shall not:

(*a*) impose requirements on foreign ships which have the practical effect of denying or impairing the right of innocent passage; or

(*b*) discriminate in form or in fact against the ships of any State or against ships carrying cargoes to, from or on behalf of any State.

2. The coastal State shall give appropriate publicity to any danger to navigation, of

which it has knowledge, within its territorial sea.

Article 25. *Rights of protection of the coastal State*

1. The coastal State may take the necessary steps in its territorial sea to prevent passage which is not innocent.

2. In the case of ships proceeding to internal waters or a call at a port facility outside internal waters, the coastal State also has the right to take the necessary steps to prevent any breach of the conditions to which admission of those ships to internal waters or such a call is subject.

3. The coastal State may, without discrimination in form or in fact among foreign ships, suspend temporarily in specified areas of its territorial sea the innocent passage of foreign ships if such suspension is essential for the protection of its security, including weapons exercises. Such suspension shall take effect only after having been duly published.

Article 30. *Non-compliance by warships with the laws and regulations of the coastal State*

If any warship does not comply with the laws and regulations of the coastal State concerning passage through the territorial sea and disregards any request for compliance therewith which is made to it, the coastal State may require it to leave the territorial sea immediately.

Article 37. *Scope of this section*

This section applies to straits which are used for international navigation between one part of the high seas or an exclusive economic zone and another part of the high seas or an exclusive economic zone.

Part III, Section 2. TRANSIT PASSAGE

Article 38. *Right of transit passage*

1. In straits referred to in article 37, all ships and aircraft enjoy the right of transit passage, which shall not be impeded; except that, if the strait is formed by an island of a State bordering the strait and its mainland, transit passage shall not apply if there exists seaward of the island a route through the high seas or through an exclusive economic zone of similar convenience with respect to navigational and hydrographical characteristics.

2. Transit passage means the exercise in accordance with this Part of the freedom of navigation and overflight solely for the purpose of continuous and expeditious transit of the strait between one part of the high seas or an exclusive economic zone and another part of the high seas or an exclusive economic zone. However, the requirement of continuous and expeditious transit does not preclude passage through the strait for the purpose of entering leaving or returning from a State bordering the strait, subject to the conditions of entry to the State.

3. Any activity which is not an exercise of the right of transit passage through a strait remains subject to the other applicable provisions of this Convention.

Article 39. *Duties of ships and aircraft during transit passage*

1. Ships and aircraft, while exercising the right of transit passage, shall:

(*a*) proceed without delay through or over the strait;

(*b*) refrain from any threat or use of force against the sovereignty, territorial integrity or political independence of States bordering the strait, or in any other manner in violation of the principles of international law embodied in the Charter of the United Nations;

(*c*) refrain from any activities other than those incident to their normal modes of continuous and expeditious transit unless rendered necessary by *force majeure* or by distress;

(*d*) comply with other relevant provisions of this Part.

2. Ships in transit passage shall:

(*a*) comply with generally accepted international regulations, procedures and practices for safety at sea, including the International Regulations for Preventing Collisions at Sea;

(*b*) comply with generally accepted international regulations, procedures and practices for the prevention, reduction and control of pollution from ships.

3. Aircraft in transit passage shall:

(*a*) observe the Rules of the Air established by the International Civil Aviation Organization as they apply to civil aircraft; state aircraft will normally comply with such measures and will at all times operate with due regard for the safety of navigation;

(*b*) at all times monitor the radio frequency assigned by the competent internationally designated air traffic control authority or the appropriate international distress radio frequency.

Signatories as of 1 May 1989:[*]
Afghanistan, Algeria, Angola, *Antigua and Barbuda*, Argentina, Australia, Austria, *Bahamas, Bahrain,* Bangladesh, Barbados, Belgium, *Belize,* Benin, Bhutan, Bolivia, Botswana, *Brazil,* Brunei Darussalam, Bulgaria, Burkina Faso, Burma (Myanma), Burundi, Byelorussia, *Cameroon,* Canada, *Cape Verde,* Central African Republic, Chad, Chile, China, Colombia, Comoros, Congo, Cook Islands, Costa Rica, *Côte d'Ivoire, Cuba, Cyprus,* Czechoslovakia, Democratic People's Republic of Korea, Denmark, Djibouti, Dominica, Dominican Republic, *Egypt,* El Salvador, Equatorial Guinea, Ethiopia, *Fiji,* Finland, France, Gabon, *Gambia,* German Democratic Republic, *Ghana,* Greece, Grenada, Guatemala, *Guinea, Guinea-Bissau,* Guyana, Haiti, Honduras, Hungary, *Iceland,* India, *Indonesia,* Iran, *Iraq,* Ireland, Italy, *Jamaica,* Japan, Kampuchea (Cambodia), *Kenya, Kuwait,* Lao People's Democratic Republic, Lebanon, Lesotho, Liberia, Libya, Liechtenstein, Luxembourg, Madagascar, Malawi, Malaysia, Maldives, *Mali,* Malta, Mauritania, Mauritius, *Mexico,* Monaco, Mongolia, Morocco, Mozambique, *Namibia (United Nations Council for Namibia),* Nauru, Nepal, Netherlands, New Zealand, Nicaragua, Niger, *Nigeria,* Niue, Norway, Oman, Pakistan, Panama, Papua New Guinea, *Paraguay, Philippines,* Poland, Portugal, Qatar, Republic of Korea, Romania, Rwanda, Saint Christopher and Nevis, *Saint Lucia,* Saint Vincent and the Grenadines, Western Samoa, *Sao Tome and Principe,* Saudi Arabia, *Senegal,* Seychelles, Sierra Leone, Singapore, Solomon Islands, Somalia, South Africa, Spain, Sri Lanka, *Sudan,* Suriname, Swaziland, Sweden, Switzerland, *Tanzania,* Thailand, *Togo, Trinidad and Tobago, Tunisia,* Tuvalu, Uganda, Ukraine, United Arab Emirates, Uruguay, USSR, Vanuatu, Viet Nam, Yemen Arab Republic, *People's Democratic Republic of Yemen, Yugoslavia, Zaire, Zambia,* Zimbabwe

[*] States and other entities printed in italics in the above list have also *ratified* the UNCLOS Convention, as of 1 May 1989.

Source: *The Law of the Sea* (United Nations: New York, 1983)

THE SOUTH PACIFIC NUCLEAR FREE ZONE TREATY (RAROTONGA TREATY)

Signed in Rarotonga, Cook Islands, on 6 August 1985
Entered into force on 11 December 1986
Depositary: Director of the South Pacific Bureau for Economic Co-operation

Excerpts

The Parties to this Treaty,
Have agreed as follows:

Article 1. *Usage of terms*

For the purposes of this Treaty and its Protocols:

(*a*) 'South Pacific Nuclear Free Zone' means the areas described in Annex 1 as illustrated by the map attached to that Annex;

(*b*) 'territory' means internal waters, territorial sea and archipelagic waters, the seabed and subsoil beneath, the land territory and the airspace above them;

(*c*) 'nuclear explosive device' means any nuclear weapon or other explosive device capable of releasing nuclear energy, irrespective of the purpose for which it could be used. The term includes such a weapon or device in unassembled and partly assembled forms, but does not include the means of transport or delivery of such a weapon or device if separate from and not an indivisible part of it;

(*d*) 'stationing' means emplantation, emplacement, transportation on land or inland waters, stockpiling, storage, installation and deployment.

Article 2. *Application of the Treaty*

1. Except where otherwise specified, this Treaty and its Protocols shall apply to territory within the South Pacific Nuclear Free Zone.

2. Nothing in this Treaty shall prejudice or in any way affect the rights, or the exercise of the rights, of any State under international law with regard to freedom of the seas.

Article 5. *Prevention of stationing of nuclear explosive devices*

1. Each Party undertakes to prevent in its territory the stationing of any nuclear explosive device.

2. Each Party in the exercise of its sovereign rights remains free to decide for

itself whether to allow visits by foreign ships and aircraft to its ports and airfields, transit of its airspace by foreign aircraft, and navigation by foreign ships in its territorial sea or archipelagic waters in a manner not covered by the rights of innocent passage, archipelagic sea lane passage or transit passage of straits.

PROTOCOL 1

Excerpts

The Parties to this Protocol,
Have agreed as follows:

Article 1

Each Party undertakes to apply, in respect of the territories for which it is internationally responsible situated within the South Pacific Nuclear Free Zone, the prohibitions contained in Articles 3, 5 and 6, in so far as they relate to the manufacture, stationing and testing of any nuclear explosive device within those territories, and the safeguards specified in Article 8(2)(c) and Annex 2 of the Treaty.

Article 3

This Protocol shall be open for signature by France, the United Kingdom of Great Britain and Northern Ireland and the United States of America.

PROTOCOL 2

Excerpts

The Parties to this Protocol,
Have agreed as follows:

Article 1

Each Party undertakes not to contribute to any act which constitutes a violation of the Treaty or its Protocols by Parties to them.

Article 2

Each Party further undertakes not to use or threaten to use any nuclear explosive device against:

(*a*) Parties to the Treaty; or

(*b*) any territory within the South Pacific Nuclear Free Zone for which a State that has become a Party to Protocol 1 is internationally responsible.

Article 4

This Protocol shall be open for signature by France, the People's Republic of China, the Union of Soviet Socialist Republics, the United Kingdom of Great Britain and Northern Ireland and the United States of America.

PROTOCOL 3

Excerpts

The Parties to this Protocol,
Have agreed as follows:

Article 1

Each Party undertakes not to test any nuclear explosive device anywhere within the South Pacific Nuclear Free Zone.

Article 3

This Protocol shall be open for signature by France, the People's Republic of China, the Union of Soviet Socialist Republics, the United Kingdom of Great Britain and Northern Ireland and the United States of America.

Parties as of 1 June 1989: Australia, Cook Islands, Fiji, Kiribati, Nauru, New Zealand, Niue, Western Samoa, Tuvalu

Signatories as of 1 June 1989: Papua New Guinea

Protocol 2: China, USSR

Protocol 3: China, USSR

Source: Conference on Disarmament document CD/633, 16 Aug. 1985

AGREEMENT BETWEEN THE USA AND THE USSR ON NOTIFICATIONS OF LAUNCHES OF INTERCONTINENTAL BALLISTIC MISSILES AND SUBMARINE-LAUNCHED BALLISTIC MISSILES (BALLISTIC MISSILE LAUNCH NOTIFICATION AGREEMENT)

Signed in Moscow on 31 May 1988
Entered into force on 31 May 1988

The United States of America and the Union of Soviet Socialist Republics, hereinafter referred to as the Parties,

Affirming their desire to reduce and ultimately eliminate the outbreak of nuclear war, in particular, as a result of misinterpretation, miscalculation, or accident,

Believing that a nuclear war cannot be won and must never be fought,

Believing that agreement on measures for reducing the risk of outbreak of nuclear war serves the interests of strengthening international peace and security,

Reaffirming their obligations under the Agreement on Measures to Reduce the Risk of Outbreak of Nuclear War between the United States of America and the Union of Soviet Socialist Republics of 30 September 1971, the Agreement between the Government of the United States of America and the Government of the Union of Soviet Socialist Republics on the Prevention of Incidents on and over the High Seas of 25 May 1972, and the Agreement between the United States of America and the Union of Soviet Socialist Republics on the Establishment of Nuclear Risk Reduction Centers of 15 September 1987,

Have agreed as follows:

Article I

Each Party shall provide the other Party notification, through the Nuclear Risk Reduction Centers of the United States of America and the Union of Soviet Socialist Republics, no less than 24 hours in advance, of the planned date, launch area, and area of impact for any launch of a strategic ballistic missile: an intercontinental ballistic missile (hereinafter 'ICBM') or a submarine-launched ballistic missile (hereinafter 'SLBM').

Article II

A notification of a planned launch of an ICBM or an SLBM shall be valid for four days counting from the launch date indicated in such a notification. In case of postponement of the launch date within the indicated four days, or cancellation of the launch, no notification thereof shall be required.

Article III

1. For launches of ICBMs or SLBMs from land, the notification shall indicate the area from which the launch is planned to take place.

2. For launches of SLBMs from submarines, the notification shall indicate the general area from which the missile will be launched. Such notification shall indicate either the quadrant within the ocean (that is, the 90-degree sector encompassing approximately one fourth of the area of the ocean) or the body of water (for example, sea or bay) from which the launch is planned to take place.

3. For all launches of ICBMs or SLBMs, the notification shall indicate the geographic co-ordinates of the planned impact area or areas of the re-entry vehicles. Such an area shall be specified either by indicating the geographic co-ordinates of the boundary points of the area, or by indicating the geographic co-ordinates of the center of a circle with a radius specified in kilometers or nautical miles. The size of the impact area shall be determined by the notifying Party at its discretion.

Article IV

The Parties undertake to hold consultations, as mutually agreed, to consider questions relating to implementation of the provisions of this Agreement, as well as to discuss possible amendments thereto aimed at furthering the implementation of the objectives of this Agreement. Amendments shall enter into force in accordance with procedures to be agreed upon.

Article V

This Agreement shall not affect the obligations of either Party under other agreements.

Article VI

This agreement shall enter into force on the date of its signature.

The duration of this Agreement shall not be limited.

This Agreement may be terminated by either Party upon 12 months written notice to the other Party.

——————

Source: Conference on Disarmament document CD 847, 29 July 1988

——————

AGREEMENT BETWEEN THE USA AND THE USSR ON THE PREVENTION OF DANGEROUS MILITARY ACTIVITIES (PDMA AGREEMENT)

Signed in Moscow on 12 June 1989
Will enter into force on 1 January 1990

The Government of the United States of America and the Government of the Union of Soviet Socialist Republics, hereinafter referred to as the Parties,

Confirming their desire to improve relations and deepen mutual understanding,

Convinced of the necessity to prevent dangerous military activities, and thereby to reduce the possibility of incidents arising between their armed forces,

Committed to resolving expeditiously and peacefully any incident between their armed forces which may arise as a result of dangerous military activities,

Desiring to ensure the safety of the personnel and equipment of their armed forces when operating in proximity to one another during peacetime, and

Guided by generally recognized principles and rules of international law,

Have agreed as follows:

Article I

For the purposes of this Agreement:

1. 'Armed forces' means, for the United States of America: the armed forces of the United States, including the United States Coast Guard; for the Union of Soviet Socialist

Republics: the armed forces of the USSR, and the Border Troops of the USSR.

2. 'Personnel' means any individual, military or civilian, who is serving in or is employed by the armed forces of the Parties.

3. 'Equipment' means any ship, aircraft, or ground hardware of the armed forces of the Parties.

4. 'Ship' means any warship or auxiliary ship of the armed forces of the Parties.

5. 'Aircraft' means any military aircraft of the armed forces of the Parties, excluding spacecraft.

6. 'Ground hardware' means any materiel of the armed forces of the Parties designed for use on land.

7. 'Laser' means any source of intense, coherent, highly directional electromagnetic radiation in the visible, infrared, or ultraviolet regions that is based on the stimulated radiation of electrons, atoms, or molecules.

8. 'Special Caution Area' means a region, designated mutually by the Parties, in which personnel and equipment of their armed forces are present and, due to circumstances in the region, in which special measures shall be undertaken in accordance with this Agreement.

9. 'Interference with command and control networks' means actions that hamper, interrupt or limit the operation of the signals and information transmission means and systems providing for the control of personnel and equipment of the armed forces of a Party.

Article II

1. In accordance with the provisions of this Agreement, each Party shall take necessary measures directed toward preventing dangerous military activities, which are the following activities of personnel of its armed forces when operating in proximity to personnel and equipment of the armed forces of the other Party during peacetime:

(*a*) Entering by personnel and equipment of the armed forces of one Party into the national territory of the other Party owing to circumstances brought about by *force majeure*, or as a result of unintentional actions by such personnel;

(*b*) Using a laser in such a manner that its radiation could cause harm to personnel or damage to equipment of the armed forces of the other Party;

(*c*) Hampering the activities of the personnel and equipment of the armed forces of the other Party in a Special Caution Area in a manner which could cause harm to personnel or damage to equipment; and

(*d*) Interfering with command and control networks in a manner which could cause harm to personnel or damage to equipment of the armed forces of the other Party.

2. The Parties shall take measures to ensure expeditious termination and resolution by peaceful means, without resort to the threat or use of force, of any incident which may arise as a result of dangerous military activities.

3. Additional provisions concerning prevention of dangerous military activities and resolution of any incident which may arise as a result of those activities are contained in Articles III, IV, V and VI of this Agreement and the Annexes thereto.

Article III

1. In the interest of mutual safety, personnel of the armed forces of the Parties shall exercise great caution and prudence while operating near the national territory of the other Party.

2. If, owing to circumstances brought about by *force majeure* or as a result of unintentional actions, as set forth in Article II, subparagraph 1(a) of this Agreement, personnel and equipment of the armed forces of one Party enter into the national territory of the other Party, such personnel shall adhere to the procedures set forth in Annexes 1 and 2 to this Agreement.

Article IV

1. When personnel of the armed forces of one Party, in proximity to personnel and equipment of the armed forces of the other Party, intend to use a laser and that use could cause harm to personnel or damage to equipment of the armed forces of that other Party, the personnel of the armed forces of the Party intending such use of a laser shall attempt to notify the relevant personnel of the armed forces of the other Party. In any case, personnel of the armed forces of the Party intending use of a laser shall follow appropriate safety measures.

2. If personnel of the armed forces of one Party believe that personnel of the armed forces of the other Party are using a laser in a manner which could cause harm to them or damage to their equipment, they shall immediately attempt to establish communications to seek termination of such use.

If the personnel of the armed forces of the Party having received such notification are actually using a laser in proximity to the area indicated in the notification, they shall investigate the relevant circumstances. If their use of a laser could in fact cause harm to personnel or damage to equipment of the armed forces of the other Party, they shall terminate such use.

3. Notifications with respect to the use of a laser shall be made in the manner provided for in Annex 1 to this Agreement.

Article V

1. Each Party may propose to the other Party that the Parties agree to designate a region as a Special Caution Area. The other Party may accept or decline the proposal. Either Party also has the right to request that a meeting of the Joint Military Commission be convened, in accordance with Article IX of this Agreement, to discuss such a proposal.

2. Personnel of the armed forces of the Parties present in a designated Special Caution Area shall establish and maintain communications, in accordance with Annex 1 to this Agreement, and undertake other measures as may be later agreed upon by the Parties, in order to prevent dangerous military activities and to resolve any incident which may arise as a result of such activities.

3. Each Party has the right to terminate an arrangement with respect to a designated Special Caution Area. The Party intending to exercise this right shall provide timely notification of such intent to the other Party, including the date and time of termination of such an arrangement, through use of the communications channel set forth in paragraph 3 of Article VII of this Agreement.

Article VI

1. When personnel of the armed forces of one Party, in proximity to personnel and equipment of the armed forces of the other Party, detect interference with their command and control networks which could cause harm to them or damage to their equipment, they may inform the relevant personnel of the armed forces of the other Party if they believe that the interference is being caused by such personnel and equipment of the armed forces of that Party.

2. If the personnel of the armed forces of the Party having received such information establish that this interference with the command and control networks is being

caused by their activities, they shall take expeditious measures to terminate the interference.

Article VII

1. For the purpose of preventing dangerous military activities, and expeditiously resolving any incident which may arise as a result of such activities, the armed forces of the Parties shall establish and maintain communications as provided for in Annex 1 to this Agreement.

2. The Parties shall exchange appropriate information on instances of dangerous military activities or incidents which may arise as a result of such activities, as well as on other issues related to this Agreement.

3. The Chairman of the Joint Chiefs of Staff of the United States shall convey information referred to in paragraph 2 of this Article through the Defense Attache of the Union of Soviet Socialist Republics in Washington, D.C. The Chief of the General Staff of the Armed Forces of the Union of Soviet Socialist Republics shall convey such information through the Defense Attache of the United States in Moscow.

Article VIII

1. This Agreement shall not affect the rights and obligations of the Parties under other international agreements and arrangements in force between the Parties, and the rights of individual or collective self-defense and of navigation and overflight, in accordance with international law. Consistent with the foregoing, the Parties shall implement the provisions of this Agreement, taking into account the sovereign interests of both Parties.

2. Nothing in this Agreement shall be directed against any Third Party. Should an incident encompassed by this Agreement occur in the territory of an ally of a Party, that Party shall have the right to consult with its ally as to appropriate measures to be taken.

Article IX

1. To promote the objectives and implementation of the provisions of this Agreement, the Parties hereby establish a Joint Military Commission. Within the framework of the Commission, the Parties shall consider:

(a) Compliance with the obligations assumed in this Agreement;

(b) Possible ways to ensure a higher level of safety for the personnel and equipment of their armed forces; and

(c) Other measures as may be necessary to improve the viability and effectiveness of this Agreement.

2. Meetings of the Joint Military Commission shall be convened annually or more frequently as may be agreed upon by the Parties.

Article X

1. This Agreement, including its Annexes, which form an integral part thereof, shall enter into force on January 1, 1990.

2. This Agreement may be terminated by either Party six months after written notice thereof is given to the other Party.

3. This Agreement shall be registered in accordance with Article 102 of the Charter of the United Nations.

ANNEX 1. PROCEDURES FOR ESTABLISHING AND MAINTAINING COMMUNICATIONS

Section I. *Communications Channels*

For the purpose of implementing this Agreement, the armed forces of the Parties shall provide for establishing and maintaining, as necessary, communications at the following levels:

(a) The Task Force Commander of the armed forces of one Party present in a Special Caution Area and the Task Force Commander of the armed forces of the other Party in the same Area;

(b) Commander* of a ship, aircraft, ground vehicle or ground unit of the armed forces of one Party and the Commander* of a ship, aircraft, ground vehicle or ground unit of the armed forces of the other Party; and

(c) Commander* of an aircraft of the armed forces of one Party and an air traffic control or monitoring facility of the other Party.

---

* 'Commander' means the individual with authority to command or lead a ship, aircraft, ground vehicle or ground unit.

Section II. *Radio Frequencies*

1. To establish radio communication, as necessary, the following frequencies shall be used:

(*a*) between aircraft of the Parties or between an aircraft of one Party and an air traffic control or monitoring facility of the other Party: on VHF band frequency 121.5 MHz or 243.0 MHz, or on HF band frequency 4125.0 KHz (alternate 6215.5 KHz); after initial contact is made, the working frequency 130.0 MHz or 278.0 MHz, or 4125.0 KHz should be used;

(*b*) between ships of the Parties and ship-to-shore: on VHF band frequency 156.8 MHz, or on HF band frequency 2182.0 KHz;

(*c*) between a ship of one Party and an aircraft of the other Party: on VHF band frequency 121.5 MHz or 243.0 MHz; after initial contact is made, the working frequency 130.0 MHz or 278.0 MHz shall be used; and

(*d*) between ground vehicles or ground units of the armed forces of the Parties: on VHF band frequency 44,0 MHz (alternate 46.5 MHz), or on HF band frequency 4125.0 KHz (alternate 6215.5 KHz).

2. The Parties agree to conduct necessary testing to ensure reliability of the communications channels agreed by the Parties.

Section III. *Signals and Phrases*

1. The Parties recognize that the lack of radio communication can increase the danger to the personnel and equipment of their armed forces involved in any incident which may arise as a result of dangerous military activities. Personnel of the armed forces of the Parties involved in such incidents who are unable to establish radio communication, or who establish radio communication but cannot be understood, shall try to communicate using those signals referred to in this Section. In addition, such personnel shall attempt to establish communications with other personnel of their armed forces, who in turn shall take measures to resolve the incident through communications channels set forth in this Agreement.

2. Ship-to-ship and ship-to-shore communications shall be conducted using signals and phrases as set forth in the International Code of Signals of 1965 and the Special Signals developed in accordance with the Agreement between the Government of the United States of America and the Government of the Union of Soviet Socialist Republics on the Prevention of Incidents On and Over the High Seas of 1972. Aircraft-to-aircraft communications shall be conducted using signals and phrases for intercepting and intercepted aircraft contained in the Rules of the Air, Annex 2 to the 1944 Convention on International Civil Aviation (Chicago Convention). The additional signals and phrases contained in paragraph 4 of this Section may also be used.

3. Whenever aircraft of the Parties come into visual contact with each other, their aircrews shall monitor the frequency 121.5 MHz or 243.0 MHz. If it is necessary to exchange information, but communications in a common language are not possible, attempts shall be made to convey essential information and acknowledgement of instructions by using phrases referred to in paragraphs 2 and 4 of this Section. If radio communication is not possible, then visual signals shall be used.

4. The following table contains additional signals and phrases for communications between aircraft, ships, ground vehicles or ground units, in accordance with this Agreement:

Additional signals, phrases and appropriate responses

A. Meaning of signal/phrase	B. Visual signals for aircraft	C. Phrase	D. Pronunciation	E. Appropriate response
1. You are in close proximity to our national territory.	Day and Night—The intercepting aircraft, flying above and parallel to the intercepted aircraft, rocking wings, and flashing navigation lights at slow regular intervals, followed by a series of shallow bank 'S' turns, in the horizontal plane, approximately 10 degrees either side of line of flight.	'CLOSE TO TERRITORY'	CLOSE–TO TERR–I–TORY	Intercepted aircraft turns away from national territory.
2. You have entered into our national territory.	Day and Night—The intercepting aircraft, flying above and parallel to the intercepted aircraft, rapidly flashing navigation lights while rocking wings, followed by a shallow turn executed in the horizontal plane, with a 15–20 degree bank in the direction of the intercepted aircraft. The approach shall be accomplished with great caution and not closer than one wing span. Repeat until intercepted aircraft acknowledges or radio contact is established.	'TERRITORY ENTERED'	TERR–I–TORY EN–TERED	Intercepted aircraft shall follow the appropriate instructions of the intercepting aircraft.
3. I need to land.	Day and Night—The aircraft flashes its navigation lights repeatedly and rapidly while rocking wings, followed by a gentle porpoising of the aircraft.	'REQUEST LANDING'	RE–QUEST LAN–DING	Intercepting aircraft assists intercepted aircraft.

A. Meaning of signal/phrase	B. Visual signals for aircraft	C. Phrase	D. Pronunciation	E. Appropriate response
4. I request radio communications on 130.0 MHz or 278.0 MHz. (Initial contact is established on 121.5 MHz or 243.0 MHz.)	Day and Night—If 121.5 MHz and 243.0 MHz are inoperative, aircraft continuously alternates one long with one short flash of navigation lights while rocking wings.	'RADIO CONTACT'	RA–DI–O CON–TAC	Acknowledge requesting aircraft, ship, or air traffic control or monitoring facility with phrase 'RADIO CONTACT'. After contact is made, turn to 130.0 MHz or 278.0 MHz.
5. My aircraft requests radio contact with your ship on 121.5 MHz or 243.0 MHz.	Day and Night— Aircraft circling the ship, in a left hand turn, at a safe distance and altitude until radio contact is established.	'RADIO CONTACT'	RA–DI–O CON–TAC	The aircraft and ship establish radio contact by exchanging the phrase 'RADIO CONTACT'; then both shall switch to 130.0 MHz or 278.0 MHz, as appropriate, for further radio communication.
6. I am experiencing a dangerous level of interference with my command and control network. (Transmit PHRASE on contact frequency.)	None	'STOP INTERFER-ENCE'	STOP IN–TER–FER–ENCE	Investigate the circumstances and, as appropriate, terminate any activities which may be causing the dangerous interference.
7. My planned use of a laser may create danger in this area. (Transmit PHRASE on contact frequency.)	None	'LASER DANGER'	LAS–ER DAN–GER	Take appropriate measures to prevent harm to personnel or damage to equipment.
8. I am experiencing a dangerous level of laser radiation. (Transmit PHRASE on contact frequency.)	None	'STOP LASER'	STOP LA-SER	Investigate the circumstances and, as appropriate, terminate any use of a laser that could cause harm to personnel or damage to equipment.

ANNEX 2. PROCEDURES FOR THE
RESOLUTION OF INCIDENTS RELATED
TO ENTERING INTO NATIONAL
TERRITORY

This Annex sets forth the procedures for the
expeditious resolution, by peaceful means, of
any incident which may arise during entry
being made by personnel and equipment of
the armed forces of one Party into the national
territory of the other Party owing to
circumstances brought about by *force majeure*
or as a result of unintentional actions, as set
forth in Article II, subparagraph 1(a) of this
Agreement.

Section I. *Entering Into National Territory
Owing To Circumstances Brought About By
Force Majeure*

1. When personnel of the armed forces of
one Party are aware that, owing to
circumstances brought about by *force
majeure*, they may enter or have entered into
the national territory of the other Party, they
shall continuously attempt to establish and
maintain communications with personnel of
the armed forces of the other Party, as
provided for in Annex 1 to this Agreement.

2. Upon receiving a communication from
personnel of the armed forces of a Party who
are aware that they may enter or have entered
into the national territory of the other Party,
personnel of the armed forces of that other
Party shall provide them appropriate
instructions as to subsequent actions, and
assistance to the extent of existing
capabilities.

3. If personnel and equipment of the armed
forces of a Party enter into the national
territory of the other Party, the personnel shall
take into consideration any instructions
received from the personnel of the armed
forces of the other Party that are appropriate
to the existing circumstances and, subject to
the provisions of the Article VIII, paragraph 1
of this Agreement, shall either depart the
national territory or proceed to a designated
location.

4. Personnel of the armed forces of a Party
having entered into the national territory of
the other Party, upon arrival at the location
designated by personnel of the armed forces
of that other Party, shall be:

(*a*) Accorded an opportunity to contact
their Defense Attache or consular authorities
as soon as possible;

(*b*) Cared for properly and their equipment
protected; and

(*c*) Assisted in repairing their equipment in
order to facilitate their departure from the
national territory, and in departing at the
earliest opportunity.

Section II. *Entering Into National Territory
As A Result Of Unintentional Actions Of
Personnel*

1. When the personnel of the armed forces
of one Party establish that personnel and
equipment of the armed forces of the other
Party may enter into their national territory as
a result of unintentional actions or that such
an entry has already taken place, the
personnel who have made this determination
shall continuously attempt to establish and
maintain communications with the personnel
of the armed forces of that other Party, as
provided for in Annex 1 to this Agreement.
The purpose of such communications is: to
alert personnel of the armed forces of that
other Party of the possibility of entry or the
fact of entry into national territory; to clarify
the reasons for and circumstances of their
actions; to recommend that they take
measures to prevent such an entry, if possible;
or, to render them assistance as appropriate.

2. Personnel of the armed forces of a Party,
having been alerted that they may enter into
the national territory of the other Party, shall,
if possible, undertake measures so that their
actions do not result in such an entry.

3. If personnel and equipment of the armed
forces of a Party enter into the national
territory of the other Party, the personnel shall
take into consideration any instructions
received from the personnel of the armed
forces of the other Party that are appropriate
to the existing circumstances and, subject to
the provisions of Article VIII, paragraph 1 of
this Agreement, shall either depart the
national territory or proceed to a designated
location. With respect to personnel and
equipment which have arrived at a designated
location, the procedures provided for in
Section I, paragraph 4 of this Annex shall be
applicable.

AGREED STATEMENTS IN
CONNECTION WITH THE AGREEMENT
BETWEEN THE GOVERNMENT OF THE
UNITED STATES OF AMERICA AND
THE GOVERNMENT OF THE UNION OF
SOVIET SOCIALIST REPUBLICS ON THE
PREVENTION OF DANGEROUS
MILITARY ACTIVITIES

In connection with the Agreement Between the Government of the United States of America and the Government of the Union of Soviet Socialist Republics on the Prevention of Dangerous Military Activities, the Parties have agreed as follows:

First agreed statement. In the case of any entry by personnel and equipment of the armed forces of one Party into the national territory of the other Party owing to circumstances brought about by *force majeure* or as a result of unintentional actions by such personnel, as set forth in Article II, subparagraph 1(a) of the Agreement Between the Government of the United States of America and the Government of the Union of Soviet Socialist Republics on the Prevention of Dangerous Military Activities, the procedures set forth in Annexes 1 and 2 to this Agreement shall apply regardless of whether that other Party has been made aware of the circumstances of such entry.

Second agreed statement. As indicated in Article VIII of the Agreement Between the Government of the United States of America and the Government of the Union of Soviet Socialist Republics on the Prevention of Dangerous Military Activities, this Agreement does not affect rights of navigation under international law, including the right of warships to exercise innocent passage.

Source: Official copy of the PDMA Agreement, from the US Department of Defense, mimeo

Select bibliography

Arkin, W. M. and Handler, J., 'Limiting nuclear navies will be the next step', *International Herald Tribune*, 1 July 1988, p. 6.

Arkin, W. M., 'Provocations at sea', *Bulletin of the Atomic Scientists*, vol. 41, no. 10 (Nov. 1985), pp. 6–7.

Arkin, W. M., 'Navy autonomy thwarts arms control', *Bulletin of the Atomic Scientists*, vol. 43, no. 7 (Sep. 1987), pp. 14–18.

Armitage, R., 'Asserting US rights on the Black Sea', *Arms Control Today*, vol. 18, no. 5 (June 1988), pp. 13–14

Ausland, J., 'The silence on naval nuclear arms should be broken', *International Herald Tribune*, 12 Mar. 1986.

Banks, T., 'Caution over northern seas suggestion', *Jane's Defence Weekly*, 17 Oct. 1987, p. 877.

Barnes, H., 'Moscow seeks naval reduction in Arctic', *Financial Times*, 21 Sep. 1988, p. 22.

Best, R. A., Jr, 'Indian Ocean arms control', US Naval Institute *Proceedings*, vol. 106/2/924 (Feb. 1980), pp. 42–48.

Blair, B., 'Arms control implications of anti-submarine warfare (ASW) programs', in US House of Representatives, Committee on International Relations, *Evaluation of Fiscal Year 1979 Arms Control Impact Statements: Towards More Informed Congressional Participation in National Security Policymaking* (US Government Printing Office: Washington, DC, 1978), pp. 103–19.

Blechman, B. M., *The Control of Naval Armaments: Prospects and Possibilities* (Brookings Institution: Washington, DC, 1975).

Blechman, B., 'Soviet interest in naval arms control: prospects for naval disengagement in the Mediterranean', in *Soviet Naval Developments: Capability and Context* (Centre for Foreign Policy Studies, Dalhousie University: Nova Scotia, 1973), pp. 439–52.

Booth, K., 'Law and strategy in northern waters', *Naval War College Review*, vol. 34, no. 4 (July-Aug. 1981), pp. 3–21.

Borawski, J. and Whitlow, E., 'A Nordic zone of peace?', *Naval Forces*, vol. 8, no. 6 (1987), pp. 10–12.

Borawski, J., 'Risk reduction at sea: naval confidence-building measures', *Naval Forces*, vol. 7, no. 1 (1987), pp. 18–28.

Brooks, L., '"New" as in nuclear land attack Tomahawk', US Naval Institute *Proceedings*, vol. 3, no. 4 (Apr. 1985), pp. 127–28.

Brooks, L., 'Nuclear SLCMs add to deterrence and security', *International Security*, vol. 13, no. 3 (winter 1988/89), pp. 169–74.

Brown, E., 'The demilitarisation and denuclearisation of hydrospace', *Annales d'études internationales*, 1973, pp. 71–92.

Burns, R., 'Inspection of the mandates, 1919–1941', *Pacific Historical Review*, vol. 37, no. 4 (Nov. 1968), pp. 445–62.

Buzan, B., 'The status and future of the Montreux Convention', *Survival*, vol. 18, no. 6 (Nov./Dec. 1976), pp. 242–47.

Byers, R. B., 'Seapower and arms control: problems and prospects', *International Journal*, vol. 36, no. 3 (summer 1981), pp. 485–514.

Byers, R. B. (ed.), *The Denuclearisation of the Oceans* (Croom Helm: Beckenham, 1986).

Cable, J., 'Arms control at sea', *Navy International*, vol. 93, no. 10 (Nov. 1988), pp. 519–23.

Caldwell, H. A., Jr, 'Nuclear war at sea', US Naval Institute *Proceedings*, vol. 114, no. 2 (Feb. 1988), pp. 60–63.

Caldwell, D., 'Permissive action links for sea-based nuclear weapons?', *NATO's Sixteen Nations,* vol. 33, no. 1 (Feb.–Mar. 1988), pp. 47–51.

Cottrell, A. J. and Hahn, W. F., *Naval Race or Arms Control in the Indian Ocean (Some Problems in Neogitating Naval Limitations)* (National Strategy Information Center: New York, 1978).

Daadler, I. and Zimmerman, T., 'Banning nuclear weapons at sea: a neglected strategy', *Arms Control Today,* vol. 18 , no. 9 (Nov. 1988), pp. 17–23.

De Luca, A., 'Soviet–American politics and the Turkish Straits', *Political Science Quarterly*, vol. 92 (1977), pp. 503–24.

Dornan, J. E., 'SALT and SLCM's: the asymmetrical equation', *Seapower*, vol. 20 (Aug. 1977), pp. 11–15.

Dupuy, T. and Hammerman, G., *A Documentary History of Arms Control and Disarmament* (R. R. Bowker: New York, 1973).

Eayrs, J., 'Arms control on the Great Lakes', *Disarmament and Arms Control*, vol. 2, no. 4 (autumn 1964), pp. 372–404.

Eichelberger, C. A. (Lt. Com.), 'The law and the submarine', US Naval Institute *Proceedings*, vol. 77 (July 1951), pp. 691–99.

Erickson, S., 'Balancing the nuclear attack', US Naval Institute *Proceedings*, vol. 110/9/979 (Sep. 1984), pp. 60–65.

George, B., 'Soviets challenge Montreux', *Jane's Defence Weekly,* 12 Jan. 1985, pp. 56–57.

George, J. L., 'START & the Navy', US Naval Institute *Proceedings*, vol. 112/4/998 (Apr. 1986), pp. 31–38.

Goldblat, J., 'Law of the Sea and the security of coastal states', in *Law of the Sea: Caracas and Beyond* (Ballinger: Cambridge, Mass., 1975), pp. 301–23.

Gordon, M. R., 'Issue of sea-launched cruise missiles is revived', *New York Times,* 18 June 1986, p. 12.

Gottemoeller, R., 'Finding solutions to SLCM arms control problems', *International Security*, vol. 13, no. 3 (winter 1988/89), pp. 175–83.

Grove, E. and Hill, R., 'Naval cooperative security', in S. Windass and E. Grove (eds), *Common Security in Europe 1988* (Foundation for International Security: Adderbury, UK, 1988), pp. 1–12.

Gsponer, A., 'Technical feasibility of the detection of nuclear weapons', eds S. Lodgaard and M. Thee, SIPRI, *Nuclear Disengagement in Europe* (Taylor & Francis: London, 1983), pp. 209–19.

Gunnarsson, G., 'Naval arms control', *ADIU Report*, vol. 8, no. 4 (July–Aug. 1986).

Haass, R., 'Arms control and the Indian Ocean', ed. R. Burt, *Arms Control and Defense Postures in the 1980s* (Westview Press: Boulder, Colo., 1982), pp. 143–60.

Haass, R., 'Arms control at sea: the United States and the Soviet Union in the Indian Ocean, 1977–78', *Journal of Strategic Studies,* vol. 10, no. 2 (June 1987), pp. 231–47.

Haass, R., 'Confidence-building measures and naval arms control', in *The Future of Arms Control: Part III: Confidence-Building Measures*, Adelphi Paper no. 149 (International Institute for Strategic Studies: London, 1979), pp. 23–29.

Haass, R., 'Naval arms limitation in the Indian Ocean', *Survival*, vol. 20, no. 2 (Mar./Apr. 1978), pp. 50–57.

Heppenheimer, T., 'Signalling subs', *Popular Science*, Apr. 1987, pp. 44–47.

Hiatt, F. and Atkinson, R., 'Insertable nuclear warheads could convert arms', *Washington Post,* 15 June 1986, p. A1.

Hibbs, R. S., 'An uncontrollable Tomahawk?', US Naval Institute *Proceedings*, vol. 3, no. 1 (Jan. 1985), pp. 66–70.

Huitfeldt, T., 'Soviet SS-N-21 equipped "Yankee" in Norwegian Sea', *Jane's Defence Weekly*, vol. 9, no. 2 (16 Jan. 1988), p. 44.

Johnson, P., 'Arms control: upping the ante', US Naval Institute *Proceedings*, vol. 109/8/966 (Aug. 1983), pp. 28–34.

Kincade, W. H., Yinger, N. V. and Duffy, G. C. (eds), *Approaches to East–West Arms Control,* Part III, 'Naval Forces and Arms Control' (Arms Control Association: Washington, DC, 1979).

Knudsen, B., 'Naval limitations in the North Atlantic', in *Approaches to East–West Arms Control* (Arms Control Association and International Institute for Strategic Studies: Washington, DC, 1979), pp. 94–105.

Larson, D. and Tarpgaard, P., 'Law of the Sea and ASW', *Marine Policy*, vol. 6 (Apr. 1982), pp. 90–102.

Leggett, J., 'Could cruise missiles stop START?', *Nature*, vol. 334 (28 July 1988), pp. 307–308.

'Letter from Soviet Foreign Minister Gromyko to U.N. Secretary-General Pérez de Cuéllar: Limitation of Naval Armaments', 10 Apr. 1984, *Documents on Disarmament, 1984* (United Nations: New York, 1985), pp. 250–53.

Lind, W. and Gray, C., 'The maritime strategy—1988: bad strategy or global deterrent?', US Naval Institute *Proceedings*, vol. 114, no. 2 (Feb. 1988), pp. 52–61.

Lissitzyn, O., 'Electronic reconnaissance from the high seas and international law', *Naval War College Review*, vol. 22, no. 6 (Feb. 1970), pp. 26–34.

Lobov, V. (Colonel-General), 'Peace and Stability for World Ocean [*sic*]', translation of original *Krasnayas Zvezda* [*Red Star*] article (28 June 1987) made available by the Soviet Press Office, Stockholm, Sweden.

Lynn-Jones, S.M., 'A quiet success for arms control: preventing incidents at sea', *International Security*, vol. 9, no. 4 (spring 1985), pp. 154–84.

Mack, A., 'US should change course on SLCM limits', *International Herald Tribune*, 17 May 1988, p. 8.

McDevitt, J., 'Current international law problems of the Navy', *Naval War College Review*, vol. 22, no. 9 (May 1970), pp. 41–49.

McNaughton, D., 'Arms control measures to protect the sea-based deterrent', in *Approaches to East–West Arms Control* (Arms Control Association and International Institute for Strategic Studies: Washington, DC, 1979), pp. 109–15.

Miller, G., 'Who needs PALs?', US Naval Institute *Proceedings*, vol. 114/7/1025 (July 1988), pp. 50–56.

Miller, W. O. (Capt.), 'A new international law for the submarine?', US Naval Institute *Proceedings*, vol. 92, no. 10 (Oct. 1966), pp. 96–103.

Mustin, H., 'The sea-launched cruise missile: more than a bargaining chip', *International Security*, vol. 13, no. 3 (winter 1988/89), pp. 184–90.

Nazarenko, V., 'The Tomahawks in START's way', *New Times*, vol. 45, no. 24 (June 1988), pp. 11–12.

Neubauer, R., 'The right of innocent passage for warships in the territorial sea: a response to the Soviet Union', *Naval War College Review*, vol. 41, no. 2 (spring 1988), pp. 49–56.

(No author),'Maritime law and the Soviet Union', *Survival*, vol. 18, no. 6 (Nov./Dec. 1976), The Montreux Convention, abridged, pp. 266–71.

Pincus, W., 'Administration seeks money for new nuclear sea weapon', *Washington Post*, 5 Apr. 1986, p. A2.

Postol, T., 'Banning nuclear SLCMs', *International Security*, vol. 13, no. 3 (winter 1988/89), pp. 191–202.

Purver, R. G., *Arctic Arms Control: Constraints and Opportunities*, Occasional Paper no. 3 (Canadian Centre for Arms Control and Disarmament: Ottawa, Feb. 1988).

Quester, G. H. (ed.), *Navies and Arms Control* (Praeger: New York, 1980).

Ranger, R., 'Learning from the naval arms control experience', *Washington Quarterly*, vol. 10, no. 3 (summer 1987), pp. 47–58.

Rao, P., 'Legal regulation of maritime military uses', *Indian Journal of International Law*, vol. 13, no. 3 (July–Sep. 1973), pp. 425–54.

Rubin, J. P., 'Sea-launched cruise missiles: facing up to the arms control challenge', *Arms Control Today* (Apr. 1986), pp. 2–11.

Ruhala, K., 'Naval confidence-building measures (CSBMs) in the Baltic', in ed. W. Gutteridge, *European Security, Nuclear Weapons and Public Confidence*, (Macmillan: Hong Kong, 1982), pp. 122–24.

Sahaydachny, S. A., 'The Law of the Sea and military activities: a North Atlantic perspective', background paper presented to the third conference of the North Atlantic Network, Bergen, Norway, 22–25 Aug. 1985.

Sigal, L., 'For a ban on nuclear cruise missiles at sea', *International Herald Tribune*, 1 July 1988, p. 6.

Sitnikov, A., 'Calling a halt to the naval arms race', translation of original *Pravda* article (27 Aug. 1987) made available by the Soviet Press Office, Stockholm, Sweden.

Stefanick, T. A., 'America's maritime strategy—the arms control implications', *Arms Control Today*, vol. 16, no. 9 (Dec.1986), pp. 10–17.

Tarquini, A., 'The objectives of naval arms control', in *Approaches to East–West Arms Control* (Arms Control Association and International Institute for Strategic Studies: Washington, DC, 1979), pp. 89–93.

Towle, P., 'The Montreux Convention as a regional arms control treaty—negotiation and practice', *Military Affairs*, vol. 45, no. 3 (Oct. 1981), pp. 121–26.

Trost, C. H. (Adm.), 'Why NATO can't agree to vacate Europe's sea', *International Herald Tribune*, 5 May 1988, p. 6.

Trost, C. H. (Adm.), 'Demilitarized seas in Europe would handicap NATO', United States Information Service, Foreign Policy Document (USIS Press Section, United States Embassy: Stockholm, Sweden, 28 Apr. 1988), pp. 7–8.

United Nations, *The Naval Arms Race*, Document Number A/40/535, UN Study Series No. 16 (UN Department for Disarmament Affairs: New York, l986).

'US: Independent Naval Activities Not Notifiable at CDE', United States Information Service, Foreign Policy Document (USIS Press Section, United States Embassy: Stockholm, Sweden, 18 Dec. 1985).

US Congress, House Committee on International Relations (HCIR), *Evaluation of Fiscal Year 1979 Arms Control Impact Statements: Toward More Informed Congressional Participation in National Security Policymaking*, 3 Jan. 1979 (US Government Printing Office: Washington, DC, 1979).

Wilson, G., 'Soviets to seek Navy curb, Crowe says', *Washington Post*, 1 July 1988.

Wolf, A. F., 'Agreement at sea: the United States–USSR agreement on incidents at sea', *Korean Journal of International Studies*, vol. 9, no. 3 (1978), pp. 57–80.

Young, E., 'Law of the Sea—an arms control issue', *Bulletin of the Atomic Scientists*, vol. 34, no. 9 (Nov. 1978), pp. 53–56.

Zimm, A., 'The first salvo', US Naval Institute *Proceedings*, vol. 3, no. 2 (Feb. 1985), pp. 55–60.

About the contributors

William M. Arkin (USA) is Director of the National Security Program at the Institute for Policy Studies, Washington, DC. He is the author of numerous books on military and nuclear weapon issues and is co-editor (with Thomas B. Cochran) of the *Nuclear Weapons Databook* series. He is a contributing editor to the monthly *Bulletin of Atomic Scientists*. He is a consultant to Greenpeace and co-editor of the joint Greenpeace–IPS *Neptune Papers* monographs on naval nuclear weapon issues.

Derek Boothby (UK) served as an officer in the Royal Navy, after which he joined the United Nations in 1978 in the Department of Political and Security Council Affairs. After working with the Military Staff Committee, the Special Political Committee and the Special Committee on Peacekeeping Operations, in 1980 he moved to disarmament matters. A Senior Political Affairs Officer in the Department for Disarmament Affairs, he was the Secretary of the UN Study on Conventional Disarmament and the Study on the Naval Arms Race and has worked with the General Assembly's First Committee. He is Secretary of the Preparatory Committees for the Fourth Review Conference of the Parties to the Treaty on the Non-Proliferation of Nuclear Weapons, to be held in 1990.

Ove Bring (Sweden) is Special Legal Adviser to the Swedish Ministry of Foreign Affairs and has served with the Ministry since 1976. He is Associate Professor of Law at the University of Stockholm. He specializes in international law, arms control and neutrality issues and has published a number of works in the field. His most recent book is *Nedrustningens Folkrätt [The International Law of Disarmament]* (1987).

Rear Admiral Eugene J. Carroll, Jr (USN, Ret.) (USA) is Deputy Director of the Center for Defense Information, Washington, DC. He served in the US Navy for 37 years and was involved in planning and training for nuclear war at sea as an aviator, as Commanding Officer of the aircraft-carrier *USS Midway* and as Commander of the Carrier Battle Force of the US Sixth Fleet in the Mediterranean. Serving as Director of US Military Operations for all US forces in Europe and the Middle East, he was the primary officer responsible for the command and control, security and readiness of the 7000 US nuclear weapons then in Europe.

Hervé Coutau-Bégarie (France) is a freelance analyst in naval and strategic affairs. He is Associate Professor at the Institut d'Etudes Politiques and the Ecole Pratique des Hautes Etudes, Paris. He is a former member of the United Nations study group on the naval arms race and is the author of *La puissance maritime soviétique* (1983), *Géostratégie de l'Atlantique Sud* (1985), *Géostratégie du Pacifique* (1987) and other works.

Richard Fieldhouse (USA) is Research Fellow and Leader of the Project on Naval Forces and Arms Control at the Stockholm International Peace Research Institute. He is co-author (with William M. Arkin) of *Nuclear Battlefields: Global Links in the Arms Race* (1985) and (with Shunji Taoka) of *Superpowers at Sea: An Assessment of the Naval Arms Race* (SIPRI, 1989).

Jozef Goldblat (Sweden) was in 1969–88 Senior Researcher and Director of the Arms Control and Disarmament Programme at the Stockholm International Peace Research Institute. In 1989 he became Senior Research Fellow in the Programme for Strategic and International Security Studies at the Graduate Institute of International Studies and a consultant to the UN Institute for Disarmament Research (UNIDIR), in Geneva. He has written extensively on arms control agreements and their implementation.

Rear Admiral Richard Hill (RN, Ret.) (UK) entered the Royal Naval College in 1942. He served on surface ships from 1946 to 1962 and thereafter mainly in staff appointments in the Ministry of Defence, London. In 1972 he was a Defence Fellow at King's College, London University, studying the international law of the sea. His last appointment in the Royal Navy was a Flag Officer, Admiralty Interview Board, and he retired in 1983. He is currently Under Treasurer of the Middle Temple, London, and editor of *The Naval Review*. He has written five books and numerous articles on naval strategy and warfare, including *Arms Control at Sea* (1989).

Commander Patrick Howard (RDN, Ret.) (Denmark) was the Military Attaché at the Danish Embassy in Stockholm until his retirement in October 1988. He served as a member of the Danish Delegation to the Stockholm Conference on Confidence- and Security-Building Measures and Disarmament in Europe in 1984–86.

Herbert Lin (USA) is a Staff Member with the House Armed Services Committee of the US Congress. He was a post-doctoral Research Fellow in 1984–86 in the Defense and Arms Control Studies Program in the Center for International Studies at the Massachusetts Institute of Technology. In 1986 he received a Congressional Science Fellowship from the American Association for the Advancement of Science. He has published several articles and papers on naval nuclear arms and verification.

Sean M. Lynn-Jones (USA) is managing editor of *International Security* and a Research Fellow at the Center for Science and International Affairs in the John F. Kennedy School of Government, Harvard University. His previous articles, including several on the USA–USSR Incidents at Sea Agreement, have appeared in *Foreign Policy, International Security* and various edited volumes.

Jan Prawitz (Sweden) has been the Special Assistant for Disarmament in the Swedish Ministry of Defence since 1970 and an adviser in the Swedish Delegation to the Conference on Disarmament in Geneva since 1962. He served as a member of the Group of Experts who prepared the UN Study on the Naval Arms Race in 1985. In 1984–86 he was a member of the Swedish Delegation to the Stockholm Conference on Confidence- and Security-Building Measures and Disarmament in Europe.

Index